U.S. Immigration Policy, Ethnicity, and Religion in American History

Michael C. LeMay

 PRAEGER™

An Imprint of ABC-CLIO, LLC
Santa Barbara, California • Denver, Colorado

Library of Congress Cataloging-in-Publication Data

Names: LeMay, Michael C., 1941–, author.
Title: U.S. immigration policy, ethnicity, and religion in American history / Michael C. LeMay.
Description: Santa Barbara : Praeger, [2018] | Includes bibliographical references and index.
Identifiers: LCCN 2017061839 (print) | LCCN 2018013772 (ebook) | ISBN 9781440864384 (ebook) | ISBN 9781440864377 (alk. paper)
Subjects: LCSH: United States—Emigration and immigration—Government policy—History. | United States—Emigration and immigration—Religious aspects. | United States—Ethnic relations—History. | United States—Race relations—History. | Immigrants—United States—History. | Minorities—United States—History. | United States—History.
Classification: LCC JV6483 (ebook) | LCC JV6483 .L469 2018 (print) | DDC 325.73—dc23
LC record available at https://lccn.loc.gov/2017061839

ISBN: 978-1-4408-6437-7 (print)
       978-1-4408-6438-4 (eBook)

22 21 20 19 18   1 2 3 4 5

This book is also available as an eBook.

Praeger
An Imprint of ABC-CLIO, LLC

ABC-CLIO, LLC
130 Cremona Drive, P.O. Box 1911
Santa Barbara, California 93116-1911
www.abc-clio.com

This book is printed on acid-free paper ∞

Manufactured in the United States of America

Contents

Tables and Boxes   ix

Introduction   xi

Chapter 1   An Overview of U.S. Immigration Policy Making   1
                 Introduction: The Importance of Immigration and
                     Religion in America   1
                 The Waves of Immigration   5
                 Established Religions, Newcomers, and Religious Freedom   7
                 The Six Phases of Immigration Policy Making   13
                 Conclusion   28
                 Chronology   28
                 References   42

Chapter 2   The Open Door Era, 1820–1880   47
                 Introduction: Religious Motivation in Colonial
                     Immigration   47
                 Religious Influences on Early American Politics   48
                 Religious/Ethnic Groups in the Old Immigrant Wave   51
                 Nativist Political Reaction to Changing Immigration
                     and Their Policy Demands   69
                 Conclusion   84
                 References   86

Chapter 3   The Door Ajar Phase, 1880–1920   93
                 Introduction: The Change in Immigrant Waves   93
                 The New Immigrant Wave: Changing Flow,
                     Changing Laws   96
                 Italian Immigrants   98
                 Greek Immigrants   103

	Polish Immigrants	105
	Russian Immigrants	106
	Eastern European Jews	109
	The First Restrictionist Laws: Attempts to Close the Golden Door	111
	The Push to Further Close the Door, 1890–1920	115
	Conclusion	123
	References	124
Chapter 4	**The Pet Door Era, 1920–1950**	**129**
	Introduction: Establishing the Quota System	129
	The Quota Act of 1921	130
	The Immigration Quota Act of 1924	139
	The National Origins Quota Act of 1929	145
	The Great Depression Decade, 1930–1940	152
	The World War II Years	157
	Hasidic Jewish Migration and Immigration	161
	Conclusion	163
	References	164
Chapter 5	**The Dutch Door Era, 1950–1985**	**167**
	Introduction: Postwar Immigration Policy	167
	The Immigration and Naturalization Act of 1952	170
	The Immigration and Nationality Act of 1965	179
	Exponential Rise in Unauthorized Immigration, 1970–1985	193
	Conclusion	194
	References	196
Chapter 6	**The Revolving Door Era, 1985–2001**	**201**
	Introduction: Religious Trends and Policy— Development of IRCA	201
	The Push to Formulate a Legislative Response	203
	Policy Adoption: Passing of IRCA, 1986	212
	Split Congressional Voting Blocs	217
	Two Models of Policy Conflict	218
	Legislative Strategies and Intent	222
	Policy Implementation: Problems with IRCA	224
	Legislative Policy Making Post-IRCA	226
	Conclusion	228
	References	230

Chapter 7   The Storm Door Era, 2001–2018   233
                 Introduction: Religious Trends and the Making
                    of Fortress America   233
                 The USA Patriot Act   234
                 Dissolving the INS, Creating the DHS   240
                 Groupthink and Other Problems in the Rush
                    to Create DHS   242
                 Further Actions to Build Fortress America   247
                 Legislative Proposals Introduced and Pending
                    Since 2013   253
                 President Trump and the Attack on Muslims and
                    Sanctuary Cities   255
                 Conclusion   257
                 References   262

Bibliography   267

Index   285

Tables and Boxes

Tables

1.1 Foreign-Born Population by Region of Birth, U.S. Census, 2010 2

1.2 Religions in the United States, 2010 Census 4

1.3 World Religions by Percentage of World Population 4

2.1 Rank Order of Immigration to the United States, Top 25 Nations of Origin, 1820–2000, Claimed Ancestry 53

2.2 Presidential Election Results, 1836–1880 72

3.1 Foreign-Born Population as Percentage of Total U.S. Population, by Census Years, 1870–1920 98

3.2 Immigrants through Ellis Island Station, 1892–1931, Top 15 Nations of Origin Rank Ordered 102

3.3 Immigrants Arriving through Ellis Island, Selective Years, 1892–1914, Compared to All Immigrants, and Percentage of Total 102

4.1 Comparison of Immigration Quotas under 1890 Census and Various National Origin Quota Plans for Typical European Nations 148

4.2 Comparison of Quotas Allotted to Selected Countries under Three Different Versions of the Quota System 149

4.3 President Hoover's Proclamation Quotas 151

4.4 Quota Immigrants Admitted, 1930–1940, by Region 153

4.5   Sources of Immigration to the United States, 1910–1950,
          by Decades and by Percentages from Region   156

4.6   Annual Immigrant Arrivals and Departures,
          United States, 1924–1948   160

5.1   Private Immigration and Nationality Bills, 1949–1972   177

7.1   Trends in Removals, 2011–2013   251

7.2   Unaccompanied Alien Children Encountered, by Fiscal
          Year, Country-of-Origin, 2009–2014   252

7.3   Highlights of the 2016 Elections   256

Boxes

2.1   Act of March 2, 1819 (Re: Immigration)   51

2.2   Know-Nothing Party Leaders   81

4.1   Summary Excerpts of the Quota Act of 1921, the
          "Emergency Quota Act"   132

4.2   Summary Excerpts of the Major Provisions of the
          Johnson-Reed Immigration Act of 1924   144

5.1   Summary of Major Provisions of the Immigration
          and Naturalization Act of 1965 (79 Stat. 911,
          October 3, 1965)   180

5.2   President Lyndon Johnson's Statement at the Signing
          of the 1965 Immigration and Nationality Bill, Liberty
          Island, New York, October 3, 1965   182

5.3   Executive Summary Recommendations of the Select
          Commission on Immigration and Refugee Policy, 1981   192

6.1   Summary of the Immigration Reform and Control Act   215

7.1   Excerpts from the USA Patriot Act of 2001 (HR 3162)   235

7.2   Summary of the Immigration-Related Provisions of the
          Homeland Security Act of 2002 (HR-5005)   240

7.3   Immigration-Related Provisions of the Intelligence
          Reform Act of 2006   248

Introduction

I have been interested in the subject of immigration ever since my early childhood. No doubt that was due, in part, to the fact that I am the grandson of four immigrants—both grandparents on my father's side were Catholic, French Canadian immigrants, and both on my mother's side were German immigrants, Catholics leaving northern German states that with the unification of the country under Chancellor Otto Von Bismarck, were Catholics in predominantly Lutheran areas of Germany. I was privileged, as a young teenager, to care daily for my German-born grandmother, who lived with us for a dozen years while I was growing up. She went suddenly blind during the last two years of her long life (92 years). During many hours while I cared for her, she would talk about the old country, her youth, and her coming to America. I thought, then, what an adventure that must have been for a young girl (she immigrated, alone and not yet married, at age 19). She came in 1889, knowing little English and, as a farm girl, with few job skills suitable to life in urban America. She and my grandfather met, married, and lived the rest of their lives in Milwaukee, Wisconsin, a community with a large German American population.

Then, too, immigration history and immigration policy and policy making have been career-long subjects of interest to me. I have been reading about, studying, analyzing, and thinking deeply about them for the past 35 years. This book is a culmination of those efforts—in some respects, the synthesis of a dozen books that I have written or edited over my career and since my first published book in 1985, as well as of the hundreds of books by other scholars in the field I have been fortunate to study and ponder. They are cited in the chapters and listed in the extensive bibliography.

U.S. Immigration Policy, Ethnicity, and Religion in American History is about U.S. immigration policymaking: what forces shape it at any given point in time; how and why major changes are made to it; which actors play important roles in determining immigration policy; and where might it be heading in the future. It is also about religion in American history and how religious trends and immigration trends intertwined in complex and fascinating ways. The book is also about ethnicity and immigration, as many immigrants came as ethno-religious groups. It might also serve as a supplemental book for courses dealing with the analysis of public policy or for United States history courses using a topical approach rather than a chronological one.

Immigration is an extraordinarily complex process. Crafting immigration policy is likewise complex, always contentious, and for many observers of American politics and policy making, often obtuse and frustrating. The impact of immigration policy is enormous and filled with dramatic human interest. It has been impacted by the immigration of an astounding array of ethno-religious groups that have profoundly impacted the diversity of American culture, politics, and society. Given the fact that the U.S. Congress has been struggling with the issue of comprehensive immigration reform for more than the past decade, it is an important and timely topic, and something of a public policy conundrum.

The United States leads the world as an immigrant-receiving nation in total numbers, if not in percentage of total population (Alienkoff and Klusmeyer 2000; LeMay 1989). Other high-level immigration-receiving countries, such as Australia, Canada, and Israel to name but three, may have comparable immigration flows as a percentage of their total populations, but none has experienced immigration from so many and varied nations-of-origin nor of such a religiously diverse population as has the United States. Since 1820, when the first immigration law was enacted—a "manifest law" that simply enumerated immigrants arriving for permanent resettlement—the United States has received more than 80 million legal immigrants. The total number of immigrants who have come for permanent resettlement likely approaches 85 to 90 million persons if one includes the estimated number of unauthorized immigrants, commonly referred to as illegal immigrants. In the 2010 census, the foreign-born residing in the United States were nearly 40 million and comprised 12.9 percent of the total population (www.census.gov/acs/www/). The United States was home to a significant number of residents born in about 170 countries from around the globe. Estimates of worldwide migration suggest that approximately two-thirds of all people immigrating for permanent resettlement do so to the United States.

The impact of receiving so many individuals from so many and such varied nations-of-origin has had a profound effect on the economy, culture, and politics of American society (Barone 2013; Hayes 2012; Motomura 2014; Zolberg 2008). Immigration has quite literally transformed America (LeMay 2013, v. 1–3). It may be a cliché, but it is none the less true that the United States is "a nation of nations." A student of American history, as well as the general reader, can better understand that history by paying attention to the transformative role of the immigration process. As this volume discusses, immigration has dramatically shaped and been shaped by ethno-religious groups coming to America motivated by freedom of religion. As I have shown elsewhere, Congress is frequently, even perennially, concerned with immigration policy making, whether tinkering with minor amendments, or grappling with major overhauls.

Another reason to study immigration and immigration policy making is that it is an inherently interesting subject. How the United States absorbed so many millions of immigrants, why and how they came to America from across the globe, and how they mixed and mingled in American society, if not melted into one, is a compelling story.

Immigrant groups of different religions often bitterly conflicted in the Old World, but lived side by side in relative peace in the New World. Their experiences changed the very nature of how they perceived religious freedom and the role of religion in society and politics in what can be viewed as revolutionary in nature (Witte 2012). How immigration policy making influenced—by itself it cannot be said to determine—the composition of that mixture, and particularly how the religious composition of the immigration flow in turn has shaped immigration laws, is a story rich in human interest. It ought to be of significance to any student of the public policy process.

Immigration policy is a subject that offers a good deal of insight into the complexity of the policy-making process. Immigration policy is *intermestic* in nature (Manning 1977), involving inherent considerations of both international and domestic policy inextricably intertwined. It is also an insightful policy area to examine regulatory policy making, and why regulatory policy so often fails to achieve its intended goals (Anderson 1979: 126–128; Ingraham 1987: 610–628). Not all regulatory policies are as clear-cut as immigration policy can sometimes be in its dramatic impact on the social and political environment. Seldom can the student of the policy process see a more extensive change as a result of a change in policy as will be seen in the following chapters. Two examples are mentioned here to illustrate the point. In 1881, 11,900 Chinese immigrated to the United States, and more than 39,500 came in 1882. The number of Chinese immigrant arrivals plunged after enactment of the Chinese Exclusion Act of May 6, 1882 (22 Stat. 58; 8 U.S.C.). In no small measure, that law was enacted as a result of the political agitation of Protestant evangelicals who feared the influx of "heathens" who they felt could not or should not mingle with Christian Americans. Religious-based fears of the "Yellow Peril" contributed significantly to the push to ban them. In 1883, only 8,031 Chinese immigrants came to the United States, and by 1885, a mere 23 arrived (LeMay 2013, v. 2: 11).

A second example concerns the enactment of the national origins quota act. In the decade before it was passed, nearly 8.8 million immigrants came, the largest number in a single decade up to that point in history, and among them more than 70 percent were from Southern, Central and Eastern European countries. The Protestant majority in America feared what they saw as a "flood" of Greek and Russian Orthodox adherents, of Eastern European Jews, and of Roman Catholics from Italy and other southern Europeans. In stark contrast, in the decade following enactment of the quota system, the United States received the smallest number of immigrants in history (just more than one half million), and those coming from South, Central, and Eastern Europe fell from 70 to 37 percent of that far smaller total amount of immigration.

Of course, the intended results of a change in immigration law are not always achieved nor last for a very long time. In 1986, for example, Congress passed the Immigration Reform and Control Act (IRCA), which imposed employer sanctions provisions designed to reduce the flow of illegal immigration by "de-magnetizing" the draw of the U.S. economy through law by making it illegal to hire an illegal immigrant (aimed at undocumented immigration from Mexico) and imposing fines on employers who did so. It reduced the flow of illegal immigration, as measured by apprehensions at the southern border, but for less than two years before the flow resumed to equal and then exceed the pre-IRCA level (LeMay 1994: 112–116; Crane et al. 1990; White, Bean, and Espanshade 1989). An unanticipated consequence of IRCA was simply to be a spur to the fraudulent documents industry (GAO 1988a).

Immigration policy making is an excellent lens through which to view the interaction of the branches and levels of government in the federal system. Studying immigration policy making enables one to see in action the checks-and-balances system established by the constitution. The legislative branch—both the U.S. Congress and state legislatures—view problems, issues, and often proposed solutions to immigration as domestic policy matters; how will *my* district be affected? Legislators, representing smaller geographic areas often with fairly ethnically homogeneous populations, respond to a few vested interest groups important to their district. The majority of legislators come from "safe" districts in terms of political party competition (LeMay 2017: 105–108). They do not have to consider how their position on an immigration bill will impact their party's chances in national electoral politics. As a result, they see an immigration "problem" differently than does the executive.

Executives, especially the president, view those same matters through the prism of foreign policy; how will immigration policy making affect the relations of the United States with other countries, or impact ongoing treaty negotiations, or impact the overall economy, and so on? The president, as the only elected official of all the people residing in the United States, responds to a far wider array of interest groups. The president, as the titular head of a political party, must consider how immigration policy making will influence the electoral prospects of the party. As a result, a president views the problem through a different lens. Rather frequently presidents of both political parties have had adversarial relations with the Congress over immigration policy making, on occasion even with congressional members of their own political party. As will be seen, presidents have exercised executive powers—the veto, proclamations, executive agreements, executive actions, executive authority over administrative departments and bureaus, establishing presidential study commissions, and so on—to promote their position on immigration policy matters. The most recent and obvious example is President Trump's travel ban, opposed by many and ruled by federal district and appellate courts, as an unconstitutional Muslim ban.

The judiciary frequently acts as the arbiter in clashes between the executive and legislative branches, and federal district courts and the U.S. Supreme Court, on occasion, do so between the national and state governments, sometimes upholding the actions of the other branches, sometimes overturning such actions. As will be seen in these chapters, the Supreme Court has sometimes held laws to be constitutional or not, and those decisions have always influenced subsequent immigration policy making and implementation. What has been referred to as the "religious right" has been especially vocal in pursuing judicial policy making to further their goals.

Then too, factors other than the laws enacted often have a more profound impact on the total number of immigrants coming to the United States than do laws designed to do so. For example, there are dramatic drops in the number of immigrants arriving during the years of the American Civil War, the Spanish-American War, World War I, the Great Depression, World War II, the Korean War, and the Vietnam War. Depressions, severe recessions, and wars profoundly influence people's decisions whether or not to emigrate.

An examination of immigration policy illuminates what Anderson identifies as the six stages of policy making: (1) problem formation, (2) agenda setting, (3) policy formulation, (4) policy adoption, (5) policy implementation, and (6) policy evaluation (Anderson 1979: 23–24). Every such category of activity or stage in the policy process is evident in this study of immigration policy making as it shifts over time. This study, moreover, is policy *analysis* not *policy advocacy*. Its long-term historical perspective enables the reader to judge for themselves the pros and cons of any particular policy enacted into immigration law. Its objective approach will allow readers to be better informed when making their assessments as to the merits of each side of the current debate over immigration policy and of the piecemeal versus comprehensive approach to reform of immigration law.

Using a long-term historical analysis helps an attentive observer to identify a number of commonalities in the story of how immigration policy achieves a consensus for a time, then how and why that consensus changes in response to events in the political environment that precipitate a reassessment to the weight given four basic elements involved in all immigration policy making: (1) national security concerns (which in earlier years was called "ensuring domestic tranquility"), (2) economic needs and considerations, (3) racism, and (4) the collective sense of national identity or "people-hood," at times in American history perceived of as America being a "Christian nation."

This analysis distinguishes six periods of immigration policy making: (1) an Open Door era, from 1820 to 1880; (2) the Door Ajar era, from 1880 to 1920; (3) the Pet Door era, from 1920 to 1950; (4) the Dutch Door era, from 1950 to 1986; (5) the Revolving Door era, from the 1986 to 2001; and (6), the Storm Door era, from 2001 to the present. Each such era in which a major revision in immigration policy occurred was preceded by considerable economic turmoil (historically variously referred to as a panic, recession, or depression). Each was a period of considerable social unrest and anxiety: for example, the religious upheavals associated with the Second Great Awakening and fundamental religious revivalism; of the labor unrest and strife of the 1870s; or the "Red Scare" and foreign policy fears of communism in 1919; the social unrest of the civil rights movement of the early to mid-1960s, and the post-Korean and Vietnam War agitation; the rise of the Reagan Conservative movement in the 1980s; and the current post-9/11 terrorist attacks with the perceived need to establish a "Fortress America" to protect the nation from "radical Islamic international terrorism."

Associated with each shift to a new era of immigration policy was a dramatic change in the composition of the immigrant population. For example, a change from Protestants from Northwestern Europe to Catholics and Jews largely from Southeastern Europe led to the enactment of the quota system to limit and redress that change in the composition of the flow of immigrants. The need to deal with the refugee crisis after World War II and the coming of the Cold War in U.S. foreign policy was reflected in the Immigration Act of 1952 that compelled another substantial change—to the preference system enacted in 1965. The current and massive immigration flow shifting away from NW Europe toward Mexico, Central and South America, and Asia has led to the new demands to "control the borders" and to protect Fortress America from the danger of international terrorist cells entering the nation amidst a wave of undocumented immigrants, or a wave of displaced refugees from the Middle East.

Each shift in immigration policy examined herein came after one or more of the major political parties dominant in American politics at the time decided to advocate such change as an important plank in their party platform. Likewise, each shift followed the formation of specific ad-hoc interest groups advocating or opposing such change: from the Know-Nothing Party in the 1840s to the Asian Exclusion League of the 1880s and 1890s to the Ku Klux Klan in the 1920s to the Federation for American Immigration Reform and Zero Population growth of the 1990s to the Tea Party and the Heritage Foundation of today. These interest groups formed coalitions to advocate the need for fundamental change in immigration policy.

The long-term historical perspective highlights recurrent arguments, like variations on a theme in a symphony, from advocates for immigration policy change. Time and again concern is expressed over the impact of immigration on jobs, wages, and working conditions. Over and over, advocates for change in immigration policy voice their xenophobic attitudes toward the newcomers, whom they argue cannot, will not, or should not be allowed to assimilate into American society. These social forces fear that the newcomers will damage U.S. culture, religious freedom, social mores, and politics—in their view forever changing the face of America in a detrimental way, putting the country on what they perceive of as "the wrong track" and necessitating the need "to take back America" or to "make America great again."

There is a recurrent search for a new *method* to "fix" the immigration problem. Advocates of change suggest some new method or device to screen immigrants. These varied over time from the use of excluded categories, to a literacy test to imposition of a quota system to development of an elaborate preference system to employer sanctions to barring immigrants from social and welfare services to militarizing the border or amending the constitution to deny birthright citizenship to persons born in the United States of parents who are in the country illegally, or to ban entire groups on the basis of their religious affiliation. Calls for the implementation of "extreme vetting" are thinly disguised attempts to legally ban Muslims. What is consistent throughout the six eras is that each shift is associated with the advocacy of some new solution to a perceived immigration problem.

The long-term view of immigration history demonstrates that throughout, four main elements figure prominently in the formulation of immigration policy: (1) national security/foreign policy; (2) economics, (3) racism, and (4) a sense of populist nationalism or national identity. Sometimes two or more of these elements work in harmony, reinforcing each other. At other times they work in conflict with one another, and the contending forces seek to influence immigration policy by stressing different elements. But in all cases, these four elements are central to understanding U.S. immigration policy.

Throughout American history, immigration policy advocates form and maintain stable coalitions of interest groups generally advocating more or less unrestricted immigration versus a coalition of groups advocating the need for restrictionist policy. Time and again there is a coalition of business and ethno-religious associations favoring immigration doing battle with labor, "patriotic," or social conservative groups advocating restrictions to "take back" the country from the influence of newcomers whom they deem to be undesirable. Time and again these coalitions lobby and work with and through fairly consistently stable factions in the Congress, which sometimes establish an informal "caucus" of legislators that often may be bipartisan in membership, but whose members share a common interest important to their respective electoral districts.

U.S. Immigration Policy, Ethnicity, and Religion in American History uses historical analysis to focus on those commonalities and themes evident in the story of U.S. immigration policy making from 1820 to the present, highlighting particularly ethno-religious-related interest groups advocating or opposing change at any given time, and the coalition of congressional political party or congressional caucus forces that they marshal in seeking to implement or to oppose a policy shift.

Interest groups are treated herein as organized bodies of individuals who share some common goals and who try to influence public policy to better pursue those goals. Group theory suggests public policy is the product of the struggle among groups. It views policy as "the equilibrium reached in this [group] struggle at any given moment, and it represents a balance which the contending factions or groups constantly strive to weight in their favor" (Latham 1965: 36). While group theory may not be the answer to better understand policy making in every arena of public policy, it is the case with respect to immigration policy making. This analysis of immigration policy underscores its essential gatekeeping function (hence the door image designating each era). It clearly demonstrates that immigration policy is one which reflects the interest of dominant groups. As groups gain or lose power and influence, policy is altered in favor of those gaining influence at the expense of those whose influence is waning. As Latham puts it:

> The legislature referees the group struggle, ratifies the victories of the successful coalitions, and records the terms of the surrenders, compromises, and conquests in the form of statutes. Every statute tends to represent compromise because the process of accommodating conflicts of group interests is one of deliberation and consent. (1965: 35–36)

This review of the history of immigration policy making shows the constant struggle for control of the immigration process. It highlights the recurrent trend in American religious developments that influence, or are influenced by, the flow of immigration—where it comes from and how large and diverse is that flow. It is a story of periodic attempts to achieve a politically acceptable consensus about procedural justice in the matter of regulating the entrance for permanent residency of individuals and groups. It shows that the disparities in power among competing groups seeking to influence that balance or consensus is the key to one's understanding of immigration policy (Kritz 1983: 363). The interplay among groups is central to understanding the shifts in policy making, the periodic review and revisions in policy and procedures designed to arrive at a new consensus as to how open or closed will be the door to America at any given time.

The book is divided into seven chapters. Chapter 1 presents a brief overview of U.S. immigration policy, identifying various "waves" in the composition of immigrants. It depicts the shifting among the four basic elements of immigration policy with an oscilloscope image of changing policy during six eras of immigration policy making. Chapters 2 through 7 are each devoted to a discussion of an era in policy: the Open Door era, 1820–1880, when there are none to few restrictions on immigration; the Door Ajar era, 1880–1920, which saw the beginnings of restrictionism in policy; the Pet Door era, 1920–1952, when the highly restrictionist national-origin quotas system was policy; the Dutch Door era, 1950-1985, when immigration increased but still gave preference to certain groups who entered "at the top" over others in that they came in as special refugees from communism or possessed certain characteristics enabling them to enter under an elaborate system of preferences; the Revolving Door era, 1986–2001, when unauthorized immigration increased exponentially and the Congress struggled with how to control the borders and fix the illegal immigration problem; and the Storm Door era, 2001-present, when concern with international (read Islamic) terrorism and perceived threats from illegal immigrant smugglers and narcotics traders dominated American politics, resulting in an attempt to secure "Fortress America." The final chapter closes with a discussion of current policy proposals, including those proposed by the new Trump administration.

The 200-hundred-year-long analysis of immigration policy affords insights into the advantages and disadvantages, as well as some of the likely anticipated and unanticipated impacts, in this latest attempt at a major revision of immigration policy.

References

Alienkoff, T. Alexander, and Douglas Klusmeyer, eds. 2000. *From Migrants to Citizens: Membership in a Changing World*. Washington, DC: The Brookings Institute.

Anderson, James. 1979. *Public Policymaking*. New York: Holt, Rinehart and Winston.

Barone, Michael. 2013. *Shaping Our Nation: How Surges of Migration Transformed America and Its Politics*. New York: Crown Forum.

Crane, Keith et al. 1990. *The Effects of Employer Sanctions on the Flow of Undocumented Immigrants to the United States*. Santa Monica, CA: The Rand Corporation Press, and the Urban Institute Press.

Hayes, Patrick. 2012. *The Making of Modern Immigration: An Encyclopedia of People and Ideas*. Santa Barbara, CA: ABC-CLIO.

Ingraham, Patricia. 1987. "Toward a More Systematic Consideration of Policy Design." *Policy Studies Journal* 15(4): 610–628.

Kritz, Mary. 1983. *U.S. Immigration and Refugee Policy: Global and Domestic Issues*. Lexington: Lexington Books.

Latham, Earl. 1965. *The Group Basis of Politics*. New York: Octagon Books.

LeMay, Michael. 1987. *From Open Door to Dutch Door: An Analysis of U.S. Immigration Policy Since 1820*. New York: Praeger Press.

LeMay, Michael, ed. 1989. *The Gatekeepers: Comparative Immigration Policy*. Westport, CT: Praeger Press.

LeMay, Michael. 1994. *Anatomy of a Public Policy: The Reform of Contemporary Immigration Law*. Westport, CT: Praeger Press.

LeMay, Michael, ed. 2013. *Transforming America: Perspectives on Immigration*, 3 vols. Santa Barbara, CA: ABC-CLIO.

LeMay, Michael. 2015. *Illegal Immigration: A Reference Handbook*, 2nd edition. Santa Barbara: ABC-CLIO.

LeMay, Michael. 2017. *The American Political Party System: A Reference Handbook*. Santa Barbara, CA: ABC-CLIO.

Manning, Bayless. January 1977. "The Congress, the Executive, and Intermestic Affairs: Three Proposals." *Foreign Affairs*, available at: www.foreignaffairs. com/authors/bayless-manning.

Motomura, Hiroshi. 2014. *Immigration Outside the Law*. New York: Oxford University Press.

White, M. J., F. D. Bean and T. J. Espanshade. 1989. *The U.S. Immigration Reform Act and Undocumented Migration to the U.S.* Washington, DC: The Urban Institute.

Witte, John, Jr. 2012. *No Establishment of Religion: America's Original Contribution to Religious Liberty*. New York: Oxford University Press.

Zolberg, Aristide. 2008. *A Nation by Design: Immigration Policy in the Fashioning of America*. Cambridge, MA: Russell Sage Foundation at Harvard University Press.

CHAPTER ONE

An Overview of U.S. Immigration Policy Making

Introduction: The Importance of Immigration and Religion in America

The arrival, since 2012, of tens of thousands of unauthorized immigrants, many of whom are children from Central America who arrive unaccompanied by adults, has led to an assessment by many that the U.S. immigration policy system is simply broken and in need of an overhaul—a legislative effort to enact comprehensive immigration reform. Since 1820, when the United States formally began keeping count of immigration, more than 80 million persons have immigrated, admitted for permanent resident status (commonly referred to as legal immigrants). According to data in the American Community Survey Reports of U.S. Census bureau, as of the 2010 census, the foreign born totaled 39,956,000 or 12.9 percent of the total population of 309,350,000. Among the foreign born, 17,476,000 were naturalized citizens (5.6%), and 22,480,000 were noncitizens (7.3%). In broad categories, the region of birth of the foreign-born population spanned the entire globe as detailed in Table 1.1. The foreign-born population from Latin America was the largest region-of-birth group, comprising over half (53%) of all foreign born, and 55 percent of them were from Mexico. Of the total foreign-born population of just under 40 million, 29 percent were from Mexico.

In the U.S. population, the foreign born are widely dispersed, residing in every state, ranging in terms of their percentage of the state's population from a low of 1 percent in West Virginia to a high of 27 percent in California. Despite their wide dispersal, they are concentrated in

Table 1.1   Foreign-Born Population by Region of Birth, U.S. Census, 2010

Region of Birth	Population (in 000)	Percentage (%)
Total	39,958	100.0
Africa	1,607	4.0
Asia	11,284	28.2
Europe	4,817	12.1
Latin America/ Caribbean	21,224	53.1
Mexico	11,711	29.3
Central America	3,053	7.6
South America	2,730	6.8
Caribbean	3,731	9.3
North America	807	2.0
Oceania	217	0.5

Source: www.census.gov/acs/www/.

10 states, which collectively are home to 74 percent of all the foreign born. The top 10 states and their percentage of the total foreign born are California, 25.4 percent; New York, 10.8 percent; Texas, 10.4 percent; Florida, 9.2 percent; New Jersey, 4.6 percent; Illinois, 4.4 percent; Massachusetts, 2.5 percent; Georgia, 2.4 percent; Virginia, 2.3 percent; and Washington, 2.2 percent (U.S. Bureau of the Census 1975). The top four states in terms of the foreign born are also the top four states in terms of their total populations: California with 37.3 million, Texas with 25.3 million, New York with 19.4 million, and Florida with 18.8 million. Collectively, these four states represent 33 percent of the total U.S. population.

The foreign born are also mostly recent arrivals: nearly two-thirds (62%) entered since 1990, and 35 percent entered since 2000. Among those coming from South America, 41 percent arrived since 2000, as did 39 percent of those coming from Central America. In terms of period of entry, 19.6 percent of the foreign born came before 1980, 18.6 percent came between 1980 and 1989, 27.2 percent came between 1990 and 1999, and 34.7 percent came since 2000. Despite the rhetoric decrying "anchor babies," the census data show that they came to work. The percentage of the population aged 16 years and older who are in the labor force is 64.4 percent when counting both sexes, but among the native born, 63.8 percent are in the labor force whereas 67.7 percent of the foreign born are in the labor force. Among men, 69.8 percent of all men of working age (16+) are in the labor force; but where 68.1 of the native-born men are working, 79.9 percent of the foreign-born men are in the labor force. Among women, 59.3 percent of all are in the labor force, 59.7 percent of the native born, and 57 percent among the foreign-born women (U.S. Bureau of the Census 1975).

From its inception, immigration to the United States has been the result of the needs of the overcrowded nations of Europe, Asia, and, more recently, Mexico, and the needs of a relatively underpopulated United States. The Old World experienced massive and radical social and economic change to a great extent engendered by overpopulation. These forces required societal reorganization. Agriculture shifted from the feudal system's communal subsistence farming to individually owned farms oriented to supplying a mass market urban economy. The large mass of landless peasants from the British Isles to Russia led to the Industrial Revolution, starting first in England (around 1760) and moving gradually across the European continent, especially in Northwestern Europe. The Industrial Revolution added new strains to the social order as former age-old employment patterns disintegrated. Displaced artisans and farm workers alike joined the waves of immigrants braving the transatlantic crossing to the United States. Population pressures and economic dislocations fueled religious and political persecution. Various European and Asian governments began to encourage emigration as a means to relieve pressure. When famine was added to the list of push factors compelling people to choose to leave their countries of birth, the numbers leaving soon climbed to the millions. The 1800s witnessed a mass migration on a scale unprecedented in human history. Push factors accounted for why millions left Europe, but it was pull factors that drew them to the United States.

During its colonial and revolutionary periods, one of the most important and compelling of pull factors was that the colonies and then the United States offered religious freedom to those fleeing religious persecution (Ahlstrom 1972; Bonomi 1986; Butler 2006; Byrd 2013; Fantel 1974; Heimert 1966; Lambert 2003; and Miller 1986). A sense of how that resulted in the complexity of religious diversity in the United States is also illustrated in Table 1.2, which presents the breakdown in claimed religious affiliations by the American population in the 2010 census data.

Those data can be compared to the percentage of adherents to the major world religions as of 2010, as seen in Table 1.3. Whereas about

Table 1.2   Religions in the United States, 2010 Census

Religious Group	Number/2010	Percentage in 2010 (%)
Total U.S. Population	308,745,538	100.0
Evangelical Protestant	50,013,107	16.2
Mainline Protestant	22,568,258	7.3
Black Protestant	4,877,067	1.6
Catholic	20,800,000	23.0
Mormon	10,600,000	2.9
Jehovah's Witnesses	800,000	0.02
Eastern Orthodox	500,000	0.016
Other Christian	400,000	0.012
Jewish	6,141,325	2.0
Muslim	2,600,000	0.08
Buddhist	2,000,000	0.07
Hindu	400,000	0.01

Source: Data from 2010 Census. https://www.census.gov/2010census.

Table 1.3   World Religions by Percentage of World Population

Religious Group	Percentage of World's Population (%)
Christians	33.32
Muslims	21.01
Non-Religious	14.09
Hindus	13.26
Other Religions	12.48
Buddhists	5.84

Source: https://www.newsmax.com/thewire/most-popular-religions-sects-images.

33 percent of the world's population are Christian adherents, more than 70 percent of the population of the United States claim that affiliation.

Yet, another important pull factor was that America's politically open society drew those escaping political repression, much of which overlapped religious affiliation. The reputation of the United States as a land of nearly boundless opportunity drew those compelled to flee dire economic deprivation and sometimes starvation conditions in their homelands (e.g., the Irish fleeing famine in 1848–1852). So, too, did America's reputation as the land of opportunity draw Europe's entrepreneurs and its most adventurous individuals. It drew farmers from Europe, where the top soil was measured in centimeters, and where agricultural land was increasingly scarce, to America's abundant open frontier lands where the top soil was measured in feet and land was given away or sold "dirt cheap" to homesteaders. Until the closing of the American frontier at the dawn of the 20th century, the United States needed to augment its population to defend itself from hostile Indians and from the potential threat of European colonial powers (LeMay 2006: 33–37).

Cities in the United States were growing exponentially and needed unskilled laborers to build their infrastructure (LeMay 2013, v. 1: 47–72). Ironically, many immigrants were drawn to the United States as "the land where the streets were paved with gold" only to discover those streets were often unpaved, and they would be ones to do the paving in brick and cobblestone (LeMay 2009: 13, 123). Rapid industrialization (in the United States, from around 1850 to 1900) was made possible in no small measure by the cheap labor supplied by immigrants. This kept wages down and enabled the accumulation of the vast sums of capital necessary to industrialize the economy. Mass immigration provided a large pool of unskilled labor precisely at the time it was most needed.

The Waves of Immigration

The surging and ebbing of immigrant arrivals to the shores of the United States suggest a wave metaphor to characterize the flow. The distinctions among the waves are based on the size and the composition (numbers arriving from certain nations-of-origin) of the flow that comprised each successive wave.

The first wave, from 1820 to 1880, was comprised of over 10 million immigrants entering the United States for permanent resettlement. Among them, European nations sent from 80 to 90 percent, with those coming from Northwestern Europe predominating throughout the period, on average totaling about 80 percent of the total. From 1820 to 1860, for example, Northwestern Europeans made up 85 percent, with 3 percent coming from North America (Canada), and 2 percent from Southern and Eastern Europe. Immigrants who came during this first wave are commonly referred to as the "old" immigrants. The wave marked a sudden and dramatic increase in total immigration to the United States (LeMay 2013, v. 1: 4–10). From the end of the Revolutionary War to 1819, an estimated 125,000 immigrants entered as legal immigrants. Their numbers had to be estimated because no formal count was kept nor mandated by law. Most were Protestants from the British Isles and northern Europe. That began to change after the 1830s. Irish and German peasants came by the millions after the potato famines and the economic depressions of the 1840s and a failed attempt at revolution in 1848. This sudden influx of Catholics led to the first anti-Catholic, anti-immigrant reaction, which will be discussed in more detail in the next chapter. The main pre-Civil War restrictionist group was the American Party (better and more commonly known as the Know Nothing Party). It was not only distinctly anti-immigrant, it was also notoriously and often violently anti-Catholic (LeMay 1987: 32–33).

The second major wave, commonly referred to as the "new" immigrants, occurred from 1880 to 1920. During this wave, nearly 23.5 million immigrants arrived in the United States in what was perceived of as a "flood" of immigration. These new immigrants were predominantly from Southern, Central, and Eastern Europe (SCE). These new immigrants were more visibly different from the native stock than were those of the first wave. Moreover, they brought with them a perceived flood of migrants with different religious affiliations alarming to many Protestant Christians in the native stock: they were overwhelmingly Catholic, Greek and Eastern Orthodox, and Jewish. This religious diversity set off a xenophobic reaction that culminated in the restrictive immigration law marking the end of the second wave—the three quota laws passed in 1921, 1924, and 1929 (Lieberson 1980; each law summarized in LeMay and Barkan 1999).

The third wave lasted from 1920 to 1950. Its size was a dramatic drop from the first wave: from about 23.5 million in 40 years' time to just over 5.5 million in 30 years' time. This wave is marked by several changes in the composition of the immigrant influx. Europeans comprised roughly 60 percent of the wave, with immigrants from Northwestern Europe gradually rising from just over 30 percent at the beginning of the period to nearly 50 percent by the end of the period. Immigrants from the Western Hemisphere rose to around 30 to 35 percent of the total (Immigration and Naturalization Service 1979: 2). While the former composition of the flow tilted the religious affiliations of immigrants back toward more traditional Protestantism, the latter portion of the flow were more heavily Catholics from Mexico, Central, and South America.

The fourth wave, 1950–1985, exhibited an increase in total immigration, nearly doubling to just over 10 million in the 35-year period. Immigrants coming from the Western Hemisphere predominated during this wave, rising to half of the total. A dramatic increase in Asian immigration also distinguishes this wave, especially post-1970, and they brought with them a host of Asian religious affiliations (Lee, Matsuoka, Yee, and Nakasone 2015).

As will be described in more detail in the next section, U.S. immigration policy reflects the perceived needs of the nation as those needs shifted over time in response to changing economic conditions, and in reaction to the changing nature and composition of the immigrant waves. Various cold war, economic, ethnic, foreign policy, and religious issues played key roles in the debates over immigration policy.

Shifts in immigration policy reflect conflicting value perspectives which tug and pull at one another, resulting in a sort of oscillation in policy making among them. On the one hand is the perspective that valued immigrants as a source of industry and renewed vigor, a desirable infusion of new blood into the American body politic, enriching the national heritage and spurring new economic growth. This perspective forms the traditional base for a more open immigration policy. One leading scholar of immigration puts it thus:

> In addition to the historical inheritance of asylum as one of the founding myths, the United States, as leader of the Western Alliance of democracies against the Soviet Union, has become the champion of the human right to emigrate. Such advocacy, of course, implies the right to immigrate, too, even though it must be limited by practical necessity. In addition, there is the simple political fact of well-organized ethnic constituencies pushing for family reunification and refugee admission. (Lawrence Fuchs, quoted in Kritz 1983: 289)

The other perspective calls for varying degrees of restriction. Its proponents fear the strangers who cannot, or in their view, should not be assimilated, or in more current terminology, be incorporated. These forces fear what they deem the dilution of American culture. They fear that such vast waves of immigrants will destroy the economy or at least severely depress wages and working conditions. They advocate restricting immigration to avoid such dire effects. They fear what some in their ranks deplore as the "mongrelization" or the "browning" of America. In their view, such unbridled and uncontrolled immigration is adversely changing the very face of the American population.

Established Religions, Newcomers, and Religious Freedom

Fears of too much diversity competing with the tradition of America as asylum can usefully be viewed from the backdrop of religious diversity in colonial and early America. A series of wars of religion in Old World Europe spawned the movement to the New World of North America to espouse freedom of religion, which became closely tied to the ideals of

American freedom and independence, and the idea that church and state should be separate as being beneficial to both (Kornelly, in LeMay 2013, v. 1: 189–213). Those ideals were the result of an evolutionary movement nearly 200 years in the making (Ahlstrom 1972; Baltzell 1996; Butler 2006; Miller 1986).

The story of that evolutionary movement for the separation of church and state in America began in 1620 when Puritans fled religious persecution from the established Anglican Church of England to settle in the New World seeking their promised land and a refuge in which to express their religious beliefs. The evolutionary movement for religious freedom and the separation of church and state ended with the establishment of the new constitutional republic in 1789, with its First Amendment clauses that guaranteed freedom of religious expression and banned the establishment of religion by the national government.

The success of the Puritans encouraged other religious communities to follow their example. However, in each such colony, those fleeing persecution in their homelands tended to be less tolerant, or outright intolerant to other religious dissenters residing within their colony. The Puritans punished non-Puritans with imprisonment, whipping, exile, and even hanging. Their excesses of intolerance led to the formation of new colonies in Rhode Island and Pennsylvania. Virginia and the Carolinas were royal colonies and thus had Anglicanism as their official religion. But by the early to mid-1700s, dozens of ethnic groups, each with their own religious denominations, had settled in the North American colonies. In part, the arrival of many immigrants holding different religious beliefs and denominational affiliations compelled the founding fathers, themselves often Deists, to establish a nation built on the premise of separation of church and state and religious freedom as a foundational principle of American society (Holmes 2006; Mapp 2003; Walters 1992). European perceptions of America's religious tolerance became an important pull factor drawing millions to the New World (LeMay 1987: 2).

The division between Catholic and Protestant empires reinforced ethnic and linguistic differences leading to separate national and cultural identities in Europe. The Protestant Reformation was felt most heavily in German-speaking principalities, in Scandinavia, and in England. Several Protestant denominations which developed were united in a central Christian philosophy and a distrust of Roman Catholicism. But even slight theological distinctions among Protestant groups were intensified by cultural, linguistic, and geographical barriers, and the Protestant Reformation was prone to schism into distinct denominations. When they immigrated to America, they tended to settle in areas where they shared the ethnic and religious heritage of other members of that community. This migration pattern reinforced Old World ethnic divisions and helped develop regional cultures in the American colonies and led to the development of religious pluralism and eventually religious tolerance in North America (Kornelly, in LeMay 2013: 192–194). In Pennsylvania, for example, radical Protestant groups formed small but significant alternatives to the mainline Lutheran or Reform churches. These groups were quite diverse and rejected the formal establishment of religion. By the mid-17th century, Pietists challenged the tenets of mainstream Protestantism. Anabaptists (rebaptizers) and Quakers made the radical assertion that religious practice should be separate from civil governance.

Schwenkfelders and Mennonites comprised closely knit communities that followed the spiritual principles of a revered leader. The implicit political nature of such European radical Protestant groups made them vulnerable to persecution as they defied the authority not only of the Roman Catholic Church but also of the more established and conservative form of Protestantism. When these groups migrated to North America, they founded their communities and forged the American frontier according to their beliefs. Conformity to the church was severely enforced against so-called radical Protestants, such as the Quakers and Anabaptists, who believed that religious and political affairs should be completely separated. As more and more people immigrated to the colonies, attitudes toward the role of religion became more divergent (Ulrich 1991: 108). For example, in 1649, the Maryland proprietary colony granted to Cecelius Calvert, Lord Baltimore, enacted the Act of Toleration, outlining greater religious freedom than existed in the two Puritan colonies of Massachusetts and Connecticut (Kornelly, in LeMay 2013: 200). Exiles from the Massachusetts colony founded Rhode Island as their own refuge from religious intolerance of the Puritans. Separatist Roger Williams and Pietist Anne Hutchinson were granted the first colonial charter to explicitly grant freedom of religious conscience (Fantel 1974; Gaustad 1999).

Providence became a safe haven for those who clashed with the established churches in the other New England colonies (largely Anglicans, Congregationals, and Presbyterians). The Rhode Island colony was an idea well ahead of its time. Other colonies, such as Virginia, continued to have an established church (Anglican) that was government-run and subsidized by local taxes. In 1691, in Maryland, King William III revoked Lord Baltimore's charter, making it a royal colony, and the Anglican Church became its established church in 1703, and Maryland became one of the most vigilant colonial supporters of the Church of England. Similarly, in 1661, Virginia passed strict regulations against Baptists and

Quakers. As a result, a virtual religious revolution led to the Great Awakening, which characterized religious life in America for much of the 18th century (Kornelly, in LeMay 2013: 199). In 1681, in the Carolinas, the Anglican Church was the established church, but South Carolina had substantial numbers of Puritans and Baptists, who had migrated there from New England, as well as French Huguenots and Quakers. North Carolina had a growing number of German-speaking Pietist communities who migrated there following the American Revolution.

Georgia received its charter in 1732. King George II tasked them with creating a buffer between the established English colonies to the north and the territories claimed by the Catholic French and Spanish to the south. Georgia's proprietors invited persecuted Protestant religious communities to settle in the colony, attracting a group of Moravian Brethren there in 1735, soon followed by Salzburg Lutherans and other Pietist communities. Although the Anglican Church was the established church, the colony was loosely governed with respect to religion. John Wesley, who went on to develop the Methodists, and George Whitefield, were among the early Anglican priests there and they were arguably among the most significant evangelists of the Great Awakening in America.

Before the American revolutionary war, Virginia had many converted Baptists who were successful in evangelizing many of its frontier settlers. Thomas Jefferson, then a young lawyer, witnessed the plight of such nonconformists and advocated for their rights. That experience shaped Jefferson's thoughts on church and state relations, resulting in his writing the Virginia Statute of Religious Freedom (Hening 1823: 84–85; see also Ahlstrom 1972; Butler 2006; Heimert 1966; Holmes 2006; Mapp 2003; Peterson and Vaughn 1988; and Walters 1992). In later life, Thomas Jefferson claimed to be more proud of his authorship of that statute than he was of having been elected president of the United States (Jefferson 1977; see also Holmes 2006; Levy 1994; Miller 1986; and Peterson and Vaughn 1988).

The mid-Atlantic region was first settled in 1609 by the Dutch in the north, and, in 1638, by Sweden to the south, where they established the Dutch Reformed church and Swedish Lutheran churches respectively. In 1664, the English took over from the Dutch, but the royal governors realized the economic benefits of socially liberal rule, especially when it came to religious practices. Upstate New York became home to the Shakers in 1774. The Shakers, founded in 1770, by Quaker Ann Lee, were informally called the "Shaking Quakers" for their shaking as they danced and spoke in tongues during their religious services. Mother Ann Lee was viewed by her followers as the female component of Christ's spirit and represented the second appearance of Christ on earth—hence their official name was the United Society of Believers in Christ's Second Appearance. In 1774, they settled in western New York, eventually founding 18 settlements stretching from Kentucky to Maine (Portman and Bauer 2004; see also Bilhartz 1986; Butler 2006; Heimert 1966, and Holmes 2006).

New Jersey became home to many Scotch-Irish Presbyterians who left famine and unrest in Northern Ireland during the latter half of the 18th century. New Sweden's colony was founded by William Penn and a small group of fellow Quakers who founded West New Jersey in 1674. Further persecution in England led to more Quakers settling in the Delaware valley, until Penn chartered the Commonwealth of Pennsylvania in 1681. Their religious tolerance attracted other persecuted groups, like the Pietist community of Moravians in 1702. The colonial charter ensured freedom of religious conscience to all but Roman Catholics (Fantel 1974; Ahlstrom 1972; Baltzell 1996; Butler 2006, and Miller 1986). Penn's sons converted to Anglicanism, and the decline in Pennsylvania's Quakerism was followed by an increase in immigrants to the colony, including the Scotch-Irish Presbyterians, who entered through the port of Philadelphia at a rate of 12,000 in 1740, and by an estimated 120,000 German-speaking immigrants who landed between 1683 and 1820, which made them the largest non-English-speaking population in North America by 1820 (LeMay 1987: 21–22). By the dawn of the 19th century, one-third of Pennsylvania's population were German immigrants or of German ancestry. Most belonged to the German Lutheran or German Reformed churches, as well as small communities of German Pietists, who viewed Penn's "Holy Experiment" as an opportunity to establish a home there. They were soon joined by entire groups of hundreds of Mennonites, Dunkers, Lutherans, Calvanists, and even a few Jews, arriving from such German states as Palantine, Salzburg, Wurttemberg, and Hanover (LeMay 1987: 23; and LeMay 2009: 192–200; see also Boyton 1986, Driedger and Kraybill 1994; and Nolt 1992).

The Mennonites are an Anabaptist sect named after Menno Simons, their prominent leader who united them with a Dutch group in 1536. The Amish split off into another sect in 1693, in Alsace, France, following the Anabaptist leader, Jakob Ammann. He stressed the practice of shunning of persons excommunicated from the faith. They migrated to the United States in the 18th century. Old Order Mennonites and the Old Order Amish set up small communities of 500 or so centered in Berks County and Lancaster County, Pennsylvania. They maintained their cultural separateness by use of the *Ordnung*, or understandings, which prescribed expectations for Amish and Mennonite life and practice. They became the mother settlements of both the Amish and Mennonite communities that were soon founded throughout Pennsylvania, Virginia, and the Carolinas (LeMay 2009: 193–200; Nolt 1992; Kraybill and Nolt 1995). They spoke a German dialect that came to be called "Pennsylvania Dutch," which is not the Dutch language, but derived from their pronunciation of "Deutsch."

Conflict between majority society and both the Old Order Amish and Old Order Mennonites centered on aspects of their faith and culture, which the majority society deemed dangerous. Their pacifism brought persecution on them during the U.S. Civil War, and even greater discrimination during World War I, when many Amish and Mennonite conscientious objectors refused to fight and received verbal abuse, beatings, were forced to shave their beards (prescribed by their faith), and were occasionally even "baptized" (urinated on) in camp latrines, purposely mocking their Anabaptist beliefs (Nolt 1992; Wenger 1961).

The Church of the Brethren, more commonly called the Dunkers, were a small community of radical Pietist Anabaptists from the German Palatinate who emphasized celibacy, shared property, and the practice of ancient Christian rites, such as a triple, full-body immersion for baptism, from which their common name derived. This practice distinguished them from the sprinkling Lutherans and Methodists, or the pouring Mennonites, or the single dunking Baptists (Holmes 2006: 3–5). They immigrated between 1719 and 1733 to Pennsylvania's German-speaking communities. They originally called themselves New Baptists. They founded settlements in Pennsylvania, New Jersey, Maryland, Virginia, and the Carolinas, always alongside a river wherein they could use their triple-immersion baptismal rite.

Mennonites emerged out of the Dutch Reform movement in America in 1750. Closely tied to them, the Amish pressed for more stringent observance of Mennonite practices. They left their Swiss homeland in 1727, eventually settling in Central Pennsylvania and then moving their settlements westward.

The Schwenckfelders were another insular Pietist group who followed the teachings of Kaspar Schwenckfeld von Ossig, who emphasized inner spirituality and building the true, invisible church. The founder of the Moravians, Count Nicholas Von Zenzendorf, protected a group of Schwenckfelders from persecution in Germany and sent the first group to settle in Central Pennsylvania in 1734. They were later joined by immigrants from Scandinavia. The Moravian Brethren were arguably the most vocal and prominent of the German-speaking Pietist communities to immigrate to North America. They first settled in Georgia in 1735, but under the guidance of the evangelical preacher George Whitefield, established a central community in Bethlehem, Pennsylvania (Kornelly, in LeMay 2013: 207; LeMay 2009: 192–200).

European Unitarianism flowered in Poland and Transylvania in the 16th century. Faustus Socinus was a leading theologian in a group of non-Trinitarian liberal congregations in Poland. They promoted religious liberty, reason, and tolerance, for which they were persecuted. In 1568, in Transylvania, King John Sigismund declared the first edict of religious toleration. In England, a Unitarian minister, Joseph Priestley, espoused a number of liberal and unpopular causes. His home, laboratory (he is noted as the discoverer of oxygen), library, and Unitarian chapel were attacked and burned. He fled to America, in 1794, at the invitation of Thomas Jefferson, and brought Unitarianism with him. Another English Universalist, John Murray, was released from debtor's prison and allowed to emigrate. His ship was grounded off the coast of New Jersey, and he went ashore, landing at a farm owned by Thomas Potter, who had built a chapel and was waiting for a preacher to appear. Murray preached in Potter's chapel, soon bringing Universalism to the colonies. Unitarianism and Universalism took root, offering relief from the Calvanist notion of damnation. Hosea Ballou became the movement's greatest leader and religious liberals formed their own theologies of human free will, dignity, and rationality. By the early 19th century, many Puritan Congregational churches began to call themselves Unitarian (First Unitarian Church).

At given points in time, then, when immigration policy making shifts markedly from a previous era, one can see analytically that immigration policy seems to oscillate between four elements, trying to achieve a balance among them: national security concerns, racism, the needs of the economy, and the sense of national identity or "people-hood." Immigration policy making shifts between the four elements as it progresses, shifts, and changes during six eras or phases of immigration policy making.

The Six Phases of Immigration Policy Making

Immigration policy performs a gate-keeping function: who is or is not allowed entrance into the United States for legal, permanent resettlement (LeMay 1989). The policy shifts both reflect and result in dramatic changes in the size and composition of the waves of immigration. The gate-keeping function suggests the use of a door image to characterize immigration policy at a given point in U.S. history. Phase one, from 1820 to 1880, can be viewed as the Open Door era. During this phase, policy making entailed virtually no, or at most only a few, restrictions on immigration. Practically all who sought entrance were allowed to do so. Indeed, government policy was to reach out and seek immigrants. Many state governments and a number of industries just beginning in the United States sent agents to Europe to recruit immigrants, particularly farmers. The second phase, the Door Ajar era, lasted from 1880 to 1920. This phase witnessed the beginnings of restrictions, even while the door was still open to most who sought to enter. During this phase, legislators experimented with a number of provisions—called excluded categories—enacted into law as measures to control the immigration process. The third phase, the Pet Door era, lasted from 1920 to the early 1950s. In this period, the national origin system formed the basis of immigration policy. A highly restrictive and racially biased policy, it allowed in only a favored few and by design, it tilted the flow of a much reduced level of immigration of immigrants coming from South/Central/Eastern Europe back to Northwestern Europe. A fourth phase followed—the Dutch Door era, basically from 1952 to 1986. It established a somewhat more open policy but still had a decided bias favoring those who entered "at the top." It was based on an elaborate seven point preference system. A fifth phase, the Revolving Door era, began in 1986 with enactment of the Immigration Reform and Control Act (IRCA) and was marked by exponential increases in unauthorized immigration with many illegal immigrants coming in and out of the country, especially across the southwestern border. It may have lasted longer than 2001, had not the terrorist attacks of 9/11 occurred. Those attacks, and subsequent legislation resulting from reaction to them, mark the beginning of the sixth and current phase, the Storm Door era (fifth and sixth phases and door images, LeMay 2009: 27–28).

Each of the six phases will be examined in greater detail in subsequent chapters but are briefly summarized here.

The Open Door Era

The asylum perspective on immigration, articulated by President George Washington, determined the policy making of the first phase (LeMay 2009: 18; LeMay and Barkan 1999: 10). With the successful establishment of an independent nation and then its newly revised constitution, from the 1790s the official policy was to keep its doors open to all. Little opposition to this policy was even voiced in the first decade of the new government. When the nation took its first census, in 1790, it recorded a population of 3,227,000, mostly descendants of 17th- and

18th-century arrivals, or recent immigrants themselves. The British Isles were the nation of origin for more than 75 percent of the population, with about 8 percent of German origin, and the remainder of Dutch, French, or Spanish origin. In addition to those officially counted, roughly one-half million were black slaves, and about the same number were Native Americans. This relatively tiny population occupied a land that was vast, sparsely settled, but obviously rich in natural resources just waiting to be exploited. The population density in 1790 was 4.5 persons per square mile (Select Commission on Immigration and Refugee Policy 1981: 165). The need for labor was obvious as well—to build the cities, clear the frontier lands, and push ever westward the Native American population. Additional population, and faster growth than could happen through the natural birth rate, was highly desired to strengthen the new nation's defenses against Indians (at the time, national security was referred to as "to secure domestic tranquility") and to avoid coming under control of European colonial powers still expanding their empires across the globe. The U.S. Constitution enshrined the prevailing sentiment of the majority of the population at the time—that their nation was a brave and noble experiment in freedom. They felt this freedom should be broadly shared with any and all who desired to be free, regardless of their former nationality, and to a lesser degree, regardless of their religious affiliation (LeMay 2006: 17–18).

The nation's new president, George Washington, summed up this prevailing view and the nation's first policy with respect to immigration, when he stated:

> The bosom of America is open to receive not only the opulent and respectable stranger, but the oppressed and persecuted of all Nations and Religions; whom we shall welcome to a participation of all our rights and privileges, if by decency and propriety of conduct they appear to merit the enjoyment. (Letter of George Washington on America as Asylum, in LeMay and Barkan 1999: Document 6, 10)

It is notable and perhaps surprising that the U.S. Constitution said nothing about immigration policy. Article 1 prohibited the national government, through Congress, from limiting the states from importing slaves until 1808 (Section 9) but allowed a tax on the importation of slaves for up to $10 per person. It granted Congress the power to set a uniform rule regarding naturalization (Section 8) and to make such laws as were "necessary and proper" to execute that power (also Section 8). Its commerce clause gave Congress the power to regulate commerce with foreign nations and among the states (Section 8). Supreme Court cases soon interpreted that language in an expansive way that impacted subsequent immigration policy.

In the 1790s, Congress passed laws regulating naturalization. The first act was, for its time and in comparison with virtually any other country in the world, very liberal, requiring only a two-year residency and the renunciation of former allegiances (Act of March 26, 1790, 1 Stat. 103; summarized in LeMay and Barkan 1999: 11). However, turmoil in Europe increased fears about foreign influence, and Congress passed, on January 29, 1795, a more stringent naturalization act that required five-year residency and a renunciation of titles of nobility as well as allegiance (this after many of the French nobility came to the United States fleeing the French Revolution) (1 Stat. 414; LeMay and Barkan 1999: 12). Then, in 1798, when Congress was under the control of the Federalist Party, it raised the residency requirement to 14 years. Federalists pushed through the Alien Acts, which allowed the president to deport summarily any alien considered to be a threat to the nation (Act of June 25, 1798, 1 Stat. 570; LeMay and Barkan 1999: 15–16). The Federalist Party acquired an anti-immigrant reputation that contributed to its decline. The substantial influx of newcomers who quickly became citizens joined the ranks of voters who rejected the party in large numbers. In 1810, the Federalists made an effort (which proved to be too little, too late) to attract naturalized immigrants with the ditty: "Come Dutch and Yankee, Irish Scot, With intermixed relation, From whence we came, it matters not; We all make now, one nation" (Roucek and Eisenberg 1982: 5).

The Alien and Sedition Acts were allowed to expire when the Jeffersonian Democratic Republicans replaced the Federalists in power. In 1802, a new act reestablished the five-year provision of the 1795 Act (Act of April 14, 1802, 54 Stat. 1172; LeMay and Barkan 1999: 17–18). That five-year standard has remained in the law ever since. Then, in 1819, Congress passed a law requiring a listing of all entering ship passengers, which indicated their sex, occupation, age, and the "country to which they belonged" (known as the Manifest of Immigrants Act of March 2, 1819, 3 Stat. 489; LeMay and Barkan 1999: 20; Select Commission on Immigration and Refugee Policy 1981: 169).

The surge of Irish Catholics coming during the late 1830s to mid-1840s set off a dramatic anti-foreign reaction. They were easy scapegoats on which to lay the blame for the problems facing a rapidly changing society as it began to urbanize and industrialize. Irish immigrants in particular (there were by then also a goodly number of German Catholics immigrating) were alleged to be importing crime, poverty, and drunkenness.

Social reformers, who desired to preserve the nation's institutions, and Protestant evangelicals who formed part of the Great Awakening social/religious revivalism, sought to "save the nation's purity," joined forces to form such anti-immigrant associations as the Secret Order of the Star Spangled Banner, which, when it morphed into a budding political party movement, became better known as the Know Nothing Party (Byrd 2013; Heimert 1966; Jones 1960: 147–276; Lambert 2003; Document 20, LeMay and Barkan 1999: 26–27).

These groups advocated restrictive immigration policy and more stringent naturalization laws. A xenophobic, nativist hysteria led to violent anti-Catholicism. Inflamed by a spate of virulent anti-Catholic literature, violent attacks took place during riots in a number of cities: Baltimore, Boston, Cincinnati, Hartford, Louisville, Philadelphia, Providence, New Orleans, New York, San Francisco, and St. Louis (Barone 2013, Beals 1960; Billington 1974; Higham 1955; Perea 1997; Schrug 2010; Zolberg 2008; Document 21, Letter of Abraham Lincoln regarding the Know Nothing Party, LeMay and Barkan 1999: 27).

Nativism, however, did not prevail over public policy. The more economically and political powerful portion of the native stock continued their support for open and unlimited immigration. The need for cheap labor to supply manpower to expanding cities and an ever-growing number of factories was the determining factor in public policy. Basic economic needs, coupled with the philosophical idealism regarding America as a land of opportunity and freedom (the prevailing sense of national identity) triumphed over the narrow views of the anti-Catholic, anti-foreigner movement.

In 1848, the discovery of gold in California drew a vast population to the West Coast. The post-Civil War period created an insatiable need for immigrants. The transcontinental railroad-building boom opened up vast lands to further settlement. Massive numbers of unskilled laborers were needed to build the railroads—the Irish building from East to West, and Chinese "coolie" labor building from West to East. Massive numbers of immigrant laborers were needed to mine the coal and ore, to work the mills, and to man the factories spurred by industrialization during and after the Civil War (Barone 2013; LeMay 2013, v. 1: 215–236; Zolberg 2008).

When these economic developments drew an immigration wave from China to the West Coast, and when the composition of European immigrant waves began to change, with South, Central, and Eastern Europeans beginning to outnumber the Northwestern European immigrants, sentiment regarding immigration policy began to shift. Economic recessions and a depression (then called Panics) generated renewed political pressure to enact restrictions. The ban on the immigration of convicts and prostitutes passed in 1875, and the 1880s ushered in a new phase in immigration policy.

The Door Ajar Era

Ironically, at the very time when the Statue of Liberty was being erected, symbolizing as nothing else did, that the nation was open to all the "poor and oppressed" of the world, the new immigrant wave was engendering fear and dislike among many of the native stock in the population. The new immigrants looked more alien—strange coloring, physiques, customs, languages, and, especially, religions—arousing fear that these strangers would be unable to assimilate. A spate of pseudo-scientific studies by historians, sociologists, and biologists attacked the newcomers from South, Central, and Eastern Europe as biologically and racially inferior. Such racist fervor led to the first blatantly restrictionist immigration law, the Chinese Exclusion Act of 1882 (Act of May 6, 1882, 22 Stat. 58, 8 U.S.C.; LeMay and Barkan 1999: 51–54).

Nativist arguments that the new immigrants were racially inferior and more inherently likely to become criminals or diseased were given popular credence. Such arguments undercut the earlier tradition of welcome to "all the poor and the oppressed." Restrictive immigration policies responded to four historical trends culminating in the 1880s and 1890s: (1) the mushrooming of cities and rapid industrialization (LeMay 2013, v. 1: 47–71); (2) the official closing of the frontier; (3) the persistence among the new immigrants to maintain their culture and traditions far longer and more visibly than did the old immigrants (Lieberson 1980); and (4) the greater religious divergence from Protestantism among the new immigrants, who were overwhelmingly Catholic, Jewish, or Greek and Russian Orthodox (LeMay 2013, v. 2: 10–15).

Immigrants who were adherents to a number of non-Christian, or non-traditional "Christian sects," entered the country in fairly significant numbers from the 1880s to the early 1900s: Buddhism from China and Japan, Daoism from China, Shintoism from Japan; Old Order Amish and Mennonite Anabaptists, Pietists like the Old German Baptist Brethren, and Moravian Brethren, Yiddish-speaking Jews such as the Chabad/Hasidic sect, Sandemanarians, Shaker Quakers, and Unitarians (LeMay 2017).

The Immigration Act of August 3, 1882 (22 Stat. 214, 8 U.S.C.), barred the immigration of "lunatics, idiots, convicts, and those liable to become public charges." It added new categories of exclusion that reflected the hysteria of the nativist movement: those suffering from "loathsome or contagious diseases" and persons convicted of crimes of "moral turpitude" were denied entry. The law also provided for the medical inspection of new arrivals (LeMay and Barkan 1999: 55–56; LeMay 2015: 32).

Still, enactment of these laws did not satisfy the restrictionist forces. The continued and even increased immigration during the 1880s led them to renew their efforts to change immigration law even more drastically. They began to focus on a proposed new device for restrictive regulation—that of a literacy test.

The first literacy bill was introduced into Congress in 1895, where it quickly passed both houses but was vetoed by President Grover Cleveland (Document 48, LeMay and Barkan 1999: 80–82). In 1906, another comprehensive immigration act was proposed that included both a literacy test for admission and an English-language test for naturalization. Labor unions joined the restrictionist coalition to advocate this new approach to policy. The unions were increasingly wary of the economic threat to their wage scales and working conditions implicit in unrestricted immigration. They had backed successfully the enactment of an 1887 law to prohibit contract labor (Act of February 23, 1887, 24 Stat. 414, 8 U.S.C.; LeMay and Barkan 1999: 59–60).

The groups advocating restriction succeeded in all but passage of the literacy requirement for entry or naturalization. English-language proficiency was accepted for citizenship. In 1907, Congress passed a law creating a joint congressional/presidential commission to study the impact of immigration. Begun in 1909, the Dillingham Commission, as it was known after its chairman, espoused the pseudo-scientific, racist theories so prevalent in the United States at the time. The commission's recommendations, published in 1911, called for a literacy test and other restrictive legislation (Document 61, LeMay and Barkan 1999: 103–107).

Despite these efforts, they were striving against an immigration tide. War in Europe was generating economic growth and labor demands in the United States, both of which ran counter to restrictive policy. The growing political influence of the new immigrant groups, coupled with the demand of business enterprises for new labor, preserved the more "free-entry" policy. In 1912, Congress again passed a literacy test bill, only to have it vetoed by President Taft (LeMay and Barkan 1999: 106–107). In 1915, when yet another literacy bill was passed by Congress again, it was vetoed, this time by President Woodrow Wilson.

The United States entered World War I in 1917. Congress passed another literacy bill, and this time finally overrode yet another veto by President Wilson. The 1917 law made literacy an entrance requirement. It codified a list of aliens to be excluded, and effectively banned all immigration from Asia (Act of February 5, 1917, 39 Stat. 874, 8 U.S.C.; LeMay and Barkan 1999: 109–112). The xenophobic reaction during the war years contributed significantly to the success of the restrictionist forces in Congress. A frenzy of anti-German activity culminated in an "Americanization" movement to "educate" the foreign born into U.S. language and customs. Between 1919 and 1921, 27 states passed laws creating Americanization programs (Barone 2013; Higham 1955; LeMay 2013, v. 2: 107–111 and 188–193; Zolberg 2008). For the first time ever, even industry joined the movement. This resulted in a new phase of immigration policy, the national origin quota system.

The Pet Door Era

When industry, exemplified by such groups as the National Association of Manufacturers, and industrial giants like the International Harvester Company, and such prominent business leaders and notorious anti-Semites as Henry Ford, joined with labor unions and nativist and "patriotic" pressure groups, like the Ku Klux Klan and the 100 Percenters, all calling for restrictive immigration policy, change became inevitable (LeMay 1987: 73–102).

Two restrictionist groups, organized labor and a group known as the "100 Percenters," called for the suspension of all immigration. Labor feared the competition for jobs that occurred with the entry of aliens enhanced by the labor market realignments occurring in the post-World War I economy. The 100 Percenters were nativists who simply feared that European ideas, most notably the "red menace" of Bolshevism, would contaminate U.S. institutions, customs, and society generally. Xenophobic reaction to World War I led to an anti-foreign hysteria in which sauerkraut became liberty cabbage, hamburgers became Salisbury steaks, and streets and towns with foreign-sounding names were given "American" names (LeMay 1987: 74).

The U.S. Senate led the way with a law designed to reduce total immigration and to change the composition of those far-fewer numbers entering the United States after World War I. A bill, the Quota Act of 1921 (Act of May 19, 1921, 42 Stat. 5, 8 U.S.C. 229; LeMay and Barkan 1999: 133–135), was similar to one originally sponsored by Senator Dillingham of the earlier immigration commission. It was crafted to ensure access for immigrants from Northwestern Europe while restricting those from Southern, Central and Eastern Europe. Congress passed the bill and President Harding signed it into law, introducing the concept of national origin quotas. This approach was expanded in 1924 with enactment of the Johnson-Reed Act, known as the National Origin Act (May 26, 1924, 43 Stat. 153, 8 U.S.C. 201; LeMay and Barkan 1999: 148–151). It provided for an annual limit of 150,000 Europeans, a total ban on Japanese, the issuance of visas against set quotas in U.S. consular offices abroad rather than upon arrival at America's shores, and the creation of quotas based on the contribution of each nationality to the overall U.S. population, rather than on the foreign-born population, with admission of immigrants until 1927, by annual quotas of 2 percent of the nationality's proportion of the U.S. population as registered in the 1890 census. It was amended in 1929, when the national origin quotas were permanently set by proclamation by President Herbert Hoover (Act of March 2, 1929, 45 Stat. 1512, 8 U.S.C. 106a; and Proclamation 1872, March 22, 1929; LeMay and Barkan 1999: 162–165).

The Immigration Act of 1924 remained in force until 1952. It rejected the open-door tradition of U.S. immigration policy. The new policy, plus the decline in emigration from Europe during the Great Depression, reduced overall immigration dramatically for three decades. In 1925, Congress created the Border Patrol as an effort to halt illegal immigrants, an estimated half-million of which entered during the 1920s (Act of February 27, 1925, 43 Stat. 1049–1050, 8 U.S.C. 110; Chiswick 1982: 13; LeMay and Barkan 1999: 152).

The National Origin policy remained unchallenged and in force throughout most of the 1940s before any pressure for change in restrictionist immigration policy began to be felt and voiced. A slight relaxation was induced by World War II. The need for the labor of aliens after the United States entered the war in 1941 led to the establishment of the "Bracero" program (meaning strong arm). This was a temporary guest-worker program to import workers from Mexico to fill war-time needs (Calavita 1992; Craig 1971; LeMay 2007: 318; LeMay 2013, v. 2: 144–146). Despite poor housing conditions in the camps and very exploitive wages and working conditions, the program seemed desired by Mexican and Central American farm laborers fleeing even worse conditions at home (Cohen et al. 2001; Massey et al. 1987; Meier and Gutierrez 2000; Navarro 2005; Snodgrass 2011). Its greatest significance for subsequent immigration flows is that it forged the chain-migration links that last even to the present (LeMay 2007:186).

In response to the foreign policy concerns and the war-time alliance with China, Congress repealed the 60-year ban on Chinese immigration (Act of December 17, 1943, 57 Stat. 600, 8 U.S.C. 212(a); LeMay and Barkan 1999: 196–197). As news of the Nazi atrocities became widespread at the end of the war, President Harry Truman issued a directive admitting 120,000 alien wives, husbands, and children of members of the armed forces to immigrate to the United States separate from the quota system and admitting certain displaced persons and refugees in Europe (December 22, 1945; Document 111, LeMay and Barkan 1999: 204–205). Congress joined President Truman's initiative two years later when it passed the Act of December 28, 1945, commonly known as the War Brides Act (59 Stat. 659, 8 U.S.C. 232–236; LeMay and Barkan 1999: 206–207). A number of nongovernment agencies and actors, such as the American Jewish Committee, the Citizens Committee on Displaced Persons, and the American Federation of Labor, pushed the administration and Congress to enact the first refugee law, the Displaced Persons Act (Act of June 25, 1948, 62 Stat. 1009; LeMay and Barkan 1999: 210–213). Its most outspoken opponent was the American Legion. The Displaced Persons Act ultimately allowed for the admission of more than 400,000 displaced persons through the end of 1951 by "mortgaging" their entry against future immigration quotas. It served as the precursor to the fourth phase, the Dutch Door era, when special provisions allowed for the easier entry of various favored groups.

The Dutch Door Era

In 1952, Congress passed the Immigration and Nationality Act, better known as the McCarran-Walter Act (66 Stat. 163; LeMay and Barkan 1999: 220–223). While it did not fully abolish the national origin quota approach (and received a veto from President Truman as a result, June 25, 1952), it added some "preferences" for certain skilled labor and for relatives of U.S. citizens and permanent resident aliens, increased the numerical limits for the Eastern Hemisphere (from 120,000 to 150,000) and retained the unlimited number for the Western Hemisphere, and added a small quota for overall Asian immigration. Congress overrode President Truman's veto. This law, since it first broached the idea of preference categories, can be viewed as the beginning of the Dutch Door era that is characterized by the preferences approach to immigration policy making.

President Truman established a Presidential Commission on Immigration in January 1953. Among other things, it recommended abolishing the quota system (LeMay and Barkan 1999: 233–236).

Further erosion of the quota system policy came in 1953, 1956, and 1957 when Congress enacted additional "refugee" measures outside of the quota system. The Refugee Relief Act of August 7, 1953 (67 Stat. 400;

LeMay and Barkan: 237–239), provided for entrance of refugees still in camps in Europe after World War II. President Dwight D. Eisenhower favored more generous immigration policy and sent Congress a message calling on it to enact such policy in February 1953. Congress debated immigration for some time, then passed two laws: the Act of September 11, 1957, which amended the 1952 act to allow more refugee admissions (71 Stat. 639; LeMay and Barkan 1999: 244–245) and the Act of July 25, 1958, to allow admission for permanent residence for Hungarian refugees, known as the Hungarian Freedom Fighters, fleeing communism after their failed revolution attempt in 1956 (72 Stat. 419; LeMay and Barkan 1999: 245–246). A host of religious affiliated groups, all opposed to "godless communism," supported the shift in refugee policy to allow the entry of "anti-communists." It established a category for refugees from communist-dominated countries in Europe or from the Middle East. It expanded entrance for certain relatives of U.S. citizens and lawfully resident aliens by the Act of September 22, 1959 (73 Stat. 644), and for further resettlement of World War II refugees still in camps in Europe in 1960 (74 Stat. 504; LeMay and Barkan 1999: 246–249). These various acts indicated that Congress was approaching the policy position of scrapping the quota system itself as it was no longer a workable policy position to govern immigration, where the need so far exceeded the limits allowable under the quota acts.

The election of President John F. Kennedy and the development of the civil rights movement and its campaign against overt racism in U.S. law (e.g., the "de jure" segregation of the southern states) further signaled the willingness of Congress to consider changing the immigration system in a major overhaul way. It did so when it honored the then "martyred" President Kennedy by enacting the Immigration and Nationality Act of 1965 (commonly known as the Kennedy immigration act, which officially amended the 1952 Act)—the Act of October 3, 1965 (79 Stat. 911; LeMay and Barkan 1999: 257–261). This act reflected the civil rights era and domestic policy concerns regarding de jure segregation and racism entrenched in U.S. law just as the McCarran-Walter Act had earlier reflected the Cold War period of U.S. foreign policy concerns. The 1965 Act abolished the quota system and replaced it with a seven-category preference system that was more liberal and generous with respect to immigration levels. It raised total legal immigration to 160,000, to be distributed on the basis of 20,000 persons per country for all nations outside the Western Hemisphere, placed an overall limit of 120,000 on Western Hemisphere nations but without individual national limits. The first several of the seven preferences opened up immigration for family

reunification, and the act had a couple of other high-preference categories for certain desired occupational skills.

President Lyndon Johnson pushed Congress to enact the law in honor
of the slain president. In order to secure its passage, the open door policy
for Western Hemisphere nations was ended. It ended the Bracero program.
That action soon resulted in increasing backlogs for applicants from Latin
America, and especially from Mexico. It essentially fueled undocumented
(illegal) immigration. Congress amended it in 1978, to increase slightly a
worldwide limit of 290,000 but kept the basic seven-category preference system. Special "parole" programs were established to handle refugee waves
from Cuba, Vietnam, and Soviet country refugees. Finally, on March 17,
1980, Congress passed the Refugee Act, aimed at correcting deficiencies in
existing policy by providing an ongoing mechanism for admission and aid
of refugees. It changed the legal definition of refugee to remove previous
geographic and ideological restriction (i.e., refugees from communist
countries) and set a new ceiling for refugees (entering over and above the
numbers allowed through the preference system) of 50,000 annually
through 1982. It was quickly outmoded by worldwide events that increased
the pool of refugees desiring to enter into the millions and for which the
50,000 limit was soon totally outmoded. These events set up political
pressures resulting in the next phase: the Revolving Door era.

The Revolving Door Era

Beginning in 1980 with the refugee act, and continuing especially
through to 2000, immigration policy can be described as a Revolving Door
era in which ever increasingly large numbers of unauthorized immigrants,
mostly although not exclusively undocumented immigrants crossing the
southwestern border, came and went to the United States, adding to the
influx of legal immigrants, which we have seen, also increased as a result
of the Immigration and Nationality Act of 1965. Indeed, the most significant unintended consequence of the 1965 Act was the resulting exponential growth of undocumented immigrants, a major portion of whom had
been Bracero program workers or compatriots influenced by them and following chain-migration patterns forged during the years of the Bracero
program. When the Bracero program ended, many of the Bracero workers
continued to come as illegal immigrants. During the final few years of the
Bracero program, upwards of 350,000 guest workers a year came to the
United States to work (Calavita 1992). Although every bit motivated by
racism as it was by anti-Catholicism, the movement opposing the change
was certainly fueled by the fact that Hispanics from Mexico and Central

America were overwhelmingly Roman Catholic. When Mexico received a quota of 20,000 legal immigrants, that quota simply could not satisfy the demand, and so the chain migration continued unabated but illegally. Until 1986, moreover, many came illegally, worked for a season or two, then returned to Mexico for a while, before recrossing again. When Congress enacted the Immigration Reform and Control Act of 1986 (104 Stat. 4981; LeMay 1994; LeMay and Barkan 1999: 282–295), which significantly imposed a new tool designed to stop the illegal flow by imposing employer sanctions on those who knowingly hired undocumented immigrants, it resulted in but a temporary decline in illegal border crossings, and also resulted in those in the United States in unauthorized status (whether undocumented or visa-overstayers) to remain rather than returning to their nations of origin expecting to easily recross some time later. More than 3 million undocumented immigrants, moreover, who satisfied the requirements of the amnesty program of Immigration Reform and Control Act (IRCA) had their status changed to legal resident aliens. Those members could now acquire a legal work permit card (commonly called a green card, although it was by then actually a white card). Many nuclear families were separated by this process—husbands from wives, fathers or both parents from their children. To be reunited legally, family members in Mexico or Central America who wished to join their family members residing in the United States faced ever-increasingly long backlogs, typically stretching to seven years or longer before a legal visa would be available (LeMay 2004: 100–105). Rather than face years apart, they too crossed illegally as undocumented entrants to reunite with their family members. The estimated number of unauthorized immigrants climbed each year after 1986, numbering 7.9 million by 2000 (Pew Research Center).

Seeing that the employer sanctions provision of IRCA was failing to halt the exponential rise of undocumented immigrants, Congress tried other legislative actions.

The vast majority of undocumented immigrants came seeking work and participated in the labor force at a percentage rate exceeding that of U.S. citizens. Nonetheless, Congress subscribed to the notion that welfare services were drawing them to the United States, and as a result, Congress passed two laws in 1996 designed to "demagnetize" the draw of welfare benefits. The first law was the Personal Responsibility and Work Opportunity Act of August 22, 1996 (HR 3734—PL 104–193, Document 148, LeMay and Barkan 1999: 301–304; LeMay 2004: 170–172). It enacted as national legislation and policy many of the provisions of California's Proposition 187 that had been overturned by a federal district court as unconstitutional in *LUCLAC et al. v. Wilson et al.* (November 20, 1995, 908

F. Supp. 755 [C.D. Cal. 1995]), which denied welfare services to immigrants, both legal and illegal. Congress also folded several provisions into the omnibus fiscal 1997 spending bill (The Illegal Immigration Reform and Immigrant Responsibility Act of September 30, 1996, HR 3619—PL 104–209) (LeMay and Barkan 1999: 304–310; LeMay 2004: 172–174).

As economic conditions improved and the anti-immigrant fervor eased, several adjustments to the restrictions of the 1996 laws were passed, in December 2000, aimed at restoring some benefits to legal immigrants: the Legal Immigration and Family Equity Act (LIFE) of 2000 (LeMay 2004: 174–175).

The Revolving Door era came to a fiery end with the terrorist attacks of 9/11, which ushered in the current phase of immigration policy making, the Storm Door era.

The Storm Door Era

Several legislative enactments demarcate the beginning of immigration policy making that may be viewed as the Storm Door era, an attempt to establish legislatively "Fortress America." Various laws were passed between 2000 and 2006 that were designed to "harden" and to "take control" of the U.S. borders, particularly the southwestern border, by asserting a border management approach to immigration policy making.

The first such action was the USA Patriot Act of 2001 (HR 3162, signed into law by President Bush on October 26, 2001; LeMay 2013, v. 3: 66–67). Its name is an acronym for United and Strengthening America by Providing Appropriate Tools Required to Intercept and Obstruct Terrorism Act (Platt and O'Leary 2003: 5). It grants to the Justice Department broad powers to refuse admission, to monitor students and resident aliens, and to detain and expedite the removal of noncitizens suspected of links to terrorist organizations merely upon certification of the attorney general as to their being threats to national security on whatever grounds. The law received much criticism for being too sweeping and too dangerous to constitutional checks and balances (Torr 2004: 16; it is discussed in LeMay 2013, v. 3: 66).

A year later, Congress enacted, on November 19, 2002, the Homeland Security Act (HR 5005). It is a law of around 400 pages in the U.S. Code, merging 22 federal agencies and reorganizing 170,000 federal employees (the Department of Homeland Security, DHS). It is the most sweeping reorganization of the federal bureaucracy since the creation of the Department of Defense in 1947. With respect to immigration policy making, it establishes within the new department two bureaus, each headed by an undersecretary: the Bureau of Border Transportation Security and the Bureau of Citizenship and Immigration Services (LeMay 2004: 178–179; LeMay 2013, v. 3: 67–68).

Congress passed the Intelligence Reform and Terrorism Prevention Act of 2004 (PL 108–458, signed into law by President Bush on December 17, 2004). Among its various sections, it established a Director of National Intelligence (DNI) to oversee the work of 15 intelligence agencies, and a National Counterterrorism Center, and authorized annually the addition of 2,000 agents to the Border Patrol (Immigration and Customs Enforcement, or ICE) for five years, set new standards for information that must be contained in driver's licenses, and made it easier to track suspected terrorists referred to as lone wolves (LeMay 2013, v. 3: 67–68).

In May 2005, Congress passed the Real ID Act (PL 109–12; 119 Stat. 302). It modified national law by elaborating on the ways to authenticate and on issuance procedures used by state and local governments for state's driver's licenses and state-issued photographic identification cards (for persons not able to have a driver's license). It also waived several environmental restrictions that could potentially interfere with construction of a border fence (LeMay 2013, v. 3: 68).

In 2006, Congress enacted and President Bush signed into law the Secure Fence Act (PL 109–367; LeMay 2013, v. 3: 68). It approved $1.2 billion to construct a steel fence along the 2,000 mile southern border with Mexico. To date just over 600 miles have been constructed, and in 2010–2014 bills have been introduced to authorize an additional 350 miles. The most significant impact of the border fence has been to induce immigrants to cross elsewhere—through Arizona, Texas, and New Mexico—where the fence has not been built and where the terrain has proven to be more dangerous and has resulted in a number of deaths of undocumented immigrants attempting the crossing.

In March 2006, Congress passed a renewed USA Patriot Act (referred to in the media as Patriot Act II). This law made it easier for the DHS to remove aliens (called expedited removal), and the numbers of those deported soared, as did the number of those who voluntarily departed (LeMay 2006: 263). Finally, in January 2017, Republican president Donald Trump signed his "Travel Ban" executive order barring entry of persons from seven predominantly Muslim countries and advocated the building of a wall along the southern border with Mexico for which he said Mexico would have to pay, then ordered the immediate cessation of President Obama's DACA and DAPA executive actions, increased staffing of the Border Patrol, and other policies designed to "harden border control." These policy shifts or attempted shifts will be discussed more fully in Chapter 7.

Conclusion

This brief overview of immigration policy making demonstrates the complexity of immigration policy, the frequency of unanticipated consequences, and the impact of push factors beyond the scope of influence of U.S. policy to effectively control the immigration process. Finally, Chronology 1.1 presents a synopsis of events and policy making about U.S. immigration from 1790 to 2015.

Chronology

Precursor Legislation: Setting the Stage for Things to Come

1790	In one of its first official actions, the U.S. Congress establishes a uniform rule of naturalization that imposes a two-year residency requirement for aliens who are "free white persons of good moral character."
1802	Congress revises the 1790 act to require a five-year residency requirement and that naturalizing citizens renounce allegiance and fidelity to foreign powers.
1819	Congress enacts law requiring shipmasters to deliver a manifest enumerating all aliens transported for immigration and requiring the secretary of state to inform Congress annually of the number of immigrants admitted. This act, for the first time, keeps count of the number of immigrants who enter "legally" for the purpose of permanent immigration. In short, it is the first official "immigration act."
1848	Treaty of Guadalupe Hidalgo guarantees citizenship to Mexicans remaining in the territory ceded by Mexico to the United States. This action sets the first base for the flow of Mexicans to the United States and provides for a citizen base from Mexico into which future immigrants, both legal and undocumented, can assimilate. It forges the first link into what develops as "chain migration" from Mexico and even Central America to the United States.
1855	Castle Garden becomes New York's principal port of entry for legal immigration. Its volume of immigrants sets the stage for later development of "visa overstayers" who are able to remain because such extensive numbers overwhelm the ability of immigration authorities to keep accurate track of them.
1862	Congress enacts the Homestead Act, granting acres of free land to settlers who develop the land in frontier regions and remain on it for five years, spurring heavy levels of immigration.

1868	The Fourteenth Amendment is ratified. It guarantees that all persons born or naturalized in the United States and subject to its jurisdiction are citizens and states that no state may abridge their rights without due process or deny them equal protection under the law. The amendment ensures citizenship rights of the former slaves and thereby changes the "free white persons" phrase of citizenship to include blacks. It further establishes the supremacy of federal law over actions by state governments in matters pertaining to citizenship, naturalization, and immigration.
1870	Congress enacts a law granting citizenship to persons of African descent.
1882	Congress passes the Chinese Exclusion Act, barring the immigration of Chinese laborers for 10 years and denying Chinese eligibility for naturalization. The act is reenacted and extended in 1888, 1892, and 1904. Its harsh provisions induce many Chinese immigrants to get around the law by using falsified documents—such as "paper sons and daughters." This sets a precedent for using phony documents by illegal aliens that persists to the present day.
1885	Congress passes an act making it unlawful for laborers to immigrate to the United States under contract with a U.S. employer who in any manner prepays passage to bring the laborer to the country. In some ways, it serves as the precursor to employers who hire illegal aliens using fake documents: the employer simply does not verify the accuracy of the documents, in some cases knowing or suspecting that they are illegal.
1886	*Yick Wo v. Hopkins* overturns a San Francisco municipal ordinance against Chinese laundry workers as discriminatory and unconstitutional on the grounds that the Fourteenth Amendment prohibits state and local governments from depriving any person (even a noncitizen) of life, liberty, or property without due process.
1888	Congress expands the Chinese Exclusion Act by rescinding reentry permits for Chinese laborers and thus prohibiting their return (also known as the Scott Act).
1889	In the case of *Chae Chan Ping v. United States*, the Supreme Court upholds the right of Congress to repeal the certificate of reentry as contained in the 1888 act, thereby excluding ex post facto certain Chinese immigrants who had previously entered legally.
1891	Congress expands the classes of individuals excluded from admission, forbids the soliciting of immigrants, and creates the position of superintendent of immigration.

1892	Ellis Island is opened as the nation's leading port of entry. It becomes the source of many visa overstayers from European countries.
1894	Congress extends the Chinese Exclusion Act and establishes the Bureau of Immigration within the Treasury Department, the first of several such home departments to immigration services.
1897	A federal district court decides the case *In re Rodriquez*. This west Texas case affirms the citizenship rights of Mexicans based on the 1848 Treaty of Guadalupe Hidalgo and notwithstanding that such persons may not be considered "white."
1898	In the case of *Wong Kim Ark v. United States*, the Supreme Court rules that a native-born son of Asian descent is indeed a citizen of the United States despite the fact that his parents may have been resident aliens ineligible for citizenship.
1903	Congress enacts a law making immigration the responsibility of the Department of Commerce and Labor.
1906	The Basic Naturalization Law codifies a uniform law for naturalization. With some amendments and supplements, it forms the basic naturalization law thereafter.
1907	Congress adds important regulations about issuing passports and the expatriation and marriage of U.S. women to foreigners. It continues to stir controversy until Section 3 of the act is repealed in 1922. President Theodore Roosevelt issues an executive order, known as the Gentleman's Agreement, by which Japan agrees to restrict emigration of laborers from Japan and Korea (which was then under Japanese jurisdiction). Picture brides, however, are permitted to emigrate. Congress passes the White-Slave Traffic Act forbidding importation of any woman or girl for the purpose of prostitution or similar immoral purposes.
1911	The Dillingham Commission issues its report, whose recommendations form the basis for the quota acts of the 1920s.
1915	The Americanization/100 Percentism campaign begins and is supported by both government and private enterprise. These social movements represent the first attempt at "forced assimilation" encouraging the adoption of the English language and social customs. After World War I, its perceived failure will contribute to the disillusionment that set the stage for the quota acts of the 1920s.

1917	The United States enters World War I in April. Congress enacts an immigration act that includes a literacy test and bars all immigration from a specified area known thereafter as the Asian barred zone. The Departments of State and of Labor issue a joint order requiring passports of all aliens seeking to enter the United States and requiring that the would-be entrants be issued visas by U.S. consular officers in their country of origin rather than seeking permission to enter the United States only when arriving at the port of entry. Puerto Ricans are granted U.S. citizenship.
1918	Congress gives the president sweeping powers to disallow the entrance or the departure of aliens during time of war. Similar presidential declarations are used in virtually all periods of war thereafter.
1919	Congress enacts a law granting honorably discharged Native Americans citizenship for their service during World War I. In the summer, the Red Scare following the Bolshevik revolution in Russia leads to the summary deportation of certain specified "radical" aliens deemed thereby to be a threat to U.S. security. It serves as a precursor to the USA Patriot Act in that respect.
1921	Congress passes the first Quota Act, in which immigration from a particular country is set at 3 percent of the foreign-born population from that country based on the 1910 census.
1922	Congress passes the Cable Act, stating that the right of any woman to become a naturalized citizen shall not be abridged because of her sex or because she is a married woman unless she is wed to an alien ineligible for citizenship. This latter provision is later repealed.
1923	The U.S. Supreme Court rules in *United States v. Bhagat Singh Thind* that "white person" means those persons who appear and would commonly be viewed as white. Thus, East Asian Indians, although Caucasians, are not "white" and are therefore ineligible for citizenship through naturalization.
1924	Congress enacts the Immigration Act, known as the Johnson-Reed Act, setting the national-origin quota for a particular country at 2 percent of the foreign-born population from that country as of the census of 1890. This new system drastically shifts the sources of immigration from South, Central, and Eastern Europe to Northwestern Europe. The act bars the admission of most Asians, who are thereby classified as "aliens ineligible for citizenship." Congress passes an act granting citizenship to those Native Americans who had not previously received it by allotments under the 1887 Dawes Act or by military service during World War I.

1925   Congress establishes the Border Patrol, charged with policing
              the U.S. borders against illegal or undocumented entrants. It
              is also charged with finding and deporting illegal aliens from
              the interior who had managed to elude apprehension at the
              border.

1929   President Herbert Hoover proclaims new and permanent
              quotas in which national-origin quotas for European
              immigrants are based on the proportion of those nationalities
              in the total population as determined by the 1920 census. The
              total number of such to be admitted is fixed at just over
              150,000.

1929–1939   U.S. immigration levels slow dramatically in response to the
              worldwide Great Depression.

1940   Congress passes the Registration Law, which requires
              noncitizens to register their addresses every year. The
              process remains in effect until 1980. Millions of such forms
              are backlogged and "lost" in INS warehouses. The failure of
              this program contributes to the calls during the 1980s to
              crack down on illegal immigration and visa overstayers
              through enhanced capability of the INS, which is never
              achieved.

1941   President Franklin D. Roosevelt issues a proclamation to
              control persons entering or leaving the United States based on
              the first War Powers Act.

1942   Agreement with Mexico to allow migrant farmworkers to enter
              as temporary labor to satisfy wartime labor shortages in
              agriculture.

              President issues Executive Order 9066, leading to the
              evacuation, relocation, and internment of Japanese and
              Japanese Americans into relocation camps.

1943   The Supreme Court rules, in *Hirabayashi v. United States*, that
              the executive orders for curfews and evacuation programs were
              constitutional based upon "military necessity."

1944   The Supreme Court decides *Korematsu v. United States*, again
              affirming the constitutionality of the executive orders
              excluding Japanese Americans from remaining in certain
              "excluded zones."

              The court also rules, in *Ex Parte Mitsuye Endo*, that the
              internment program was an unconstitutional violation of the
              habeas corpus rights of U.S. citizens—namely, the Nisei.

1949   Congress passes the Agricultural Act with provision to recruit
              temporary farmworkers from Mexico—the Bracero Program.

1956	President Eisenhower establishes a "parole" system for Hungarian freedom fighters. Two years later, Congress endorses the procedures to an act to admit Hungarian refugees.
1959	Congress amends the Immigration and Nationality Act of 1952 to provide for unmarried sons and daughters of U.S. citizens to enter as "nonquota" immigrants.
1960	Congress enacts a program to assist resettlement of refugees from communist countries who have been paroled by the attorney general (mostly Cubans).
	President John F. Kennedy is elected.
1963	President Kennedy is assassinated.
1964	Bracero Program ends.

The Revolving Door Era, 1965–2000

1965	Congress passes the Immigration and Nationality Act. It amends the 1954 act by ending the quota system and establishing a preference system emphasizing family reunification and meeting certain skill goals, standardizing admission procedures, and setting per-country limits of 20,000 for Eastern Hemisphere nations, with a total of 170,000. The first ceiling on Western Hemisphere immigration is set at 120,000.
1966	Congress amends the 1965 act to adjust Cuban Refugee status. This sets up the distinction between refugees based on anticommunist U.S. foreign policy goals and those based on economic refugee status.
1967	UN Convention and Protocol on Refugees; 130 nations sign the protocol accords. Refugees entering under its provisions (such as Cuban refugees) get resettlement assistance, whereas those entering based on economic grounds (Haitian refugees) are excluded.
1968	Bilingual Education Act is passed.
	President Johnson issues a proclamation on the UN Protocols on the Status of Refugees, essentially endorsing the U.S. commitment to the multinational protocols.
1972	The House passes, but the Senate kills, a bill that would have made it illegal to knowingly hire an illegal alien. It becomes the first of many attempts prior to 1986 to impose what becomes known as "employer sanctions" for hiring illegal aliens.

	Haitian boat influx of illegal aliens begins arriving on the East Coast, mostly in Florida. Haitian detention camps are set up in Miami. France implements its *regularisation* program.
1975	The fall of Saigon, then Vietnam along with Cambodia and Laos, precipitates a massive flight of refugees to the United States from the Indochina region. Vietnamese, Cambodians, and Laotians are classified as refugees from communist countries and are thereby assisted in resettlement and aided by "assimilation assistance" programs, many conducted by church-based organizations that assist immigrants.
	President Carter establishes and Congress funds the Indochinese Refugee Resettlement Program.
	Soviet Jews begin fleeing in large numbers. Civil war in El Salvador leads to beginning of their refugee movement. Haitians continue arriving in large numbers.
1976	Congress amends the 1965 act by extending the per-country limits of visa applicants on a first-come, first-served basis to Western Hemisphere nations as regulated by the preference system.
	The U.S. Supreme Court rules, in *Matthews v. Diaz*, that an alien has no right to Social Security or Medicare benefits.
	The Ford administration establishes a cabinet-level committee to study immigration options.
1978	President Carter and the Congress set up the Select Commission on Immigration and Refugee Policy (SCIRP).
1979	SCRIP begins its work.
	Vietnamese and Southeast Asian Boat People influx.
1980	Congress passes the Refugee Act to systematize refugee policy. It incorporates the UN definition of refugee, accepting 50,000 persons annually who have a "well-founded fear" of persecution based on race, religion, nationality, or membership in a social or political movement. Provides for admission of 5,000 "asylum seekers."
1981	Economic recession begins.
	March 1: The SCIRP issues its Final Report, recommending many changes in policy that form the basis of IRCA and other subsequent reform acts, several of which underlie proposed reforms even after 2001.
	President Reagan creates Task Force on Immigration and Refugee Policy, which reports in July.

	France implements its second *regularisation* (amnesty) program.
1982	Federal district judge rules the lockup of Haitians unconstitutional, ordering release of 1,900 detainees.
	Major bill to amend the Immigration and Nationality Act is introduced into House.
1983	Immigration reform bill is reintroduced into Congress.
	The Supreme Court rules, in *INS v. Chadha et al.*, that the use of the legislative veto to overturn certain INS deportation proceedings, rules, and regulations by the House of Representatives was unconstitutional.
	France implements its third "legalization" program.
1984	Immigration reform bill passes in different versions in both chambers, dies in conference.
1985	Senator Alan Simpson (R-WY) reintroduces what becomes known as the Simpson/Mazzoli/Rodino bill.
1986	The Supreme Court rules in *Jean v. Nelson* on INS denial of parole to undocumented aliens. Congress enacts IRCA's employer sanctions/legalization approach granting amnesty to about 1.5 million illegal aliens and more than 1 million special agricultural workers.
1987	In *INS v. Cardoza-Fonseca*, by a vote of 6 to 3, the Supreme Court rules that the government must relax its standards for deciding whether aliens who insist that they would be persecuted if they returned to their homelands are eligible for asylum.
1988	The Senate passes, but the House kills, the Kennedy-Simpson bill in what becomes the 1990 act.
	U.S.-Canada Free Trade Implementation Act is signed.
	Congress amends the 1965 Immigration Act regarding H-1 category used by nurses.
1989	Conference for Central American Refugee is held.
1990	Congress passes a major reform of the laws concerning legal immigration, setting new ceilings for worldwide immigration, redefining the preference system for family reunification and employment, and setting up a new category of preference called "the diversity immigrants." It enacts special provisions regarding Central American refugees, Filipino veterans, and persons seeking to leave Hong Kong. Significant changes were included with respect to naturalization procedures.

1993	Congress ratifies the North American Free Trade Agreement (NAFTA).
	Donald Huddle issues his report, "The Cost of Immigration," setting off the decades-long debate over the relative costs and benefits of immigration and illegal immigration.
1994	California passes Proposition 187, the "Save Our State" initiative.
	Congress enacts the Violent Crime Control and Law Enforcement Act, the "Smith Act," giving the attorney general more authority to issue visas, the "S Visas." Congress passes the Violence against Women Act with provision to grant special status through cancellation of removal and self-petitioning provisions.
1995	Federal district court for California rules, in *LULAC et al. v. Wilson et al.*, that many of Proposition 187's provisions are unconstitutional.
	The General Accounting Office issues its first major and comprehensive report on the costs of illegal aliens to governments and to the overall economy.
	A Human Rights Watch report is highly critical of the INS and alleged abuses.
1996	June: The Board of Immigration Appeals (in re: Fauziya Kasinga, A73479695) grants the first woman asylum on the basis of gender persecution (female genital mutilation).
	Congress enacts Personal Responsibility and Work Opportunity Act (welfare reform), with numerous immigration-related provisions. Congress essentially enacts aspects of Proposition 187 regarding welfare and other public benefits that had been overturned.
	Congress passes the Illegal Immigration Reform and Immigrant Responsibility Act (IIRIRA), the 60-plus immigration-related provisions of the Omnibus Spending Bill. It removes other welfare and economic benefits to illegal aliens and to some legal resident aliens.
	The Anti-Terrorism and Effective Death Penalty Act of 1996 is passed. Among its provisions, it gives INS inspectors the power to make "on-the-spot credible fear" determinations involving asylum. It takes effect on April 1, 1997, as part of IIRIRA reforms beginning then.
	The Central American Regional Conference on Migration is held in Puebla, Mexico.

Border Patrol makes a record 1.6 million apprehensions at the borders nationwide. Congress authorizes the addition of 1,000 new Border Patrol agents annually.

1997   The Jordan Commission on Immigration Reform, set up by the 1996 law, recommends restructuring of the INS in its final report.

The "Expedited Enforcement Rules" of the IIRIRA of 1996 take effect at U.S. land borders, international airports, and seaports to issue and enforce expulsion orders. Some 4,500 INS officers are added at 300 ports of entry.

The General Accounting Office issues its Report on the Fiscal Impact of Newest Americans.

1998   President Clinton sends another immigration bill to Congress seeking, in part, a restructuring of the INS. It dies in committee when the Judiciary Committee begins hearings on impeachment.

The Agriculture Job Opportunity Benefits and Security Act establishes a pilot program for 20,000 to 25,000 farmworkers.

The Social Security Board of Trustees Report is issued, documenting positive effects of immigration on the status of the Social Security fund but also on the dire, long-term crisis in the Social Security account as the U.S. population ages and fewer active workers support ever- growing numbers of retirees.

Congress passes the American Competitiveness and Workforce Improvement Act, which expands the H-1B category to the computer industry.

California voters approve its Proposition 227, which ends bilingual education programs in state schools. The Children of Immigrants Longitudinal Study is issued.

France implements its latest *regularisation* program.

1999   The Carnegie Endowment for International Peace presents its International Migration Policy Program. Twenty-one nongovernmental organizations concerned with immigration call for INS restructuring, separation of enforcement from visa and naturalization functions, and the sending of some functions to the DOL and HHS. INS provides Border Patrol/ adjudication.

In *INS v. Aguirre-Augirre* (67 U.S.L.W. 4270), a unanimous Supreme Court rules that aliens who have committed serious nonpolitical crimes in their home countries are ineligible to seek asylum in the United States regardless of the risk of persecution when returned to their countries.

Representative Christopher Smith (R-NJ) introduces the Trafficking Victims Protection Act of 1999.

With a restored economy, President Clinton's administration restores some of the benefits stripped away from legal aliens by the 1996 acts.

November 22, 1999: Elian Gonzalez is rescued off the Florida coast.

UNHCR issues guidelines related to Detention of Asylum Seekers in Geneva, Italy.

Trafficking Victims Protection Act is passed.

2000   Negotiations regarding the Elian Gonzalez case begin.

April: Attorney General Reno approves a Justice Department "raid" on the Miami home to "return Elian Gonzalez" to his father in Cuba.

May: Senator Sam Brownback (R-KS) introduces a bill to establish "T-Visa."

June 1: In *Gonzales v. Reno*, the Eleventh Circuit Court rules that only the father of Elian Gonzalez can speak for the boy.

The Storm Door Era: 2001–?

2001   September 11: Terrorists attack the World Trade Center's Towers in New York and the Pentagon in Washington, D.C. Immediate calls for a crackdown on terrorists begin.

October 24: Congress passes the USA Patriot Act, granting sweeping new powers to the attorney general, the FBI, and the Department of Justice regarding immigrants and the authority to detain "enemy combatants" involved in or suspected of terrorism.

American Competitiveness in 21st Century Act is approved. "DREAM ACT" bill introduced for the first time. Reintroduced annually thereafter.

2002   The INS issues notice to several of the (now dead) hijackers that they are given permission to enroll in U.S. flight training programs. Immediate calls for restructuring of INS to remove Border Patrol functions result.

November: Congress establishes a cabinet-level Department of Homeland Security. The attorney general is granted sweeping new powers for expedited removal. INS is extensively restructured into the new department. As of March 2003, the INS is abolished; the undersecretary for Border and Transportation Security begins oversight of Immigration Enforcement and Citizenship and Immigration Services.

The United Nations issues its Protocols on Human Trafficking and Immigrant Smuggling in Palermo, Italy. The protocols are signed by 141 countries.

2003   January: The Terrorist Threat Integration Center is created.

2004   The 9/11 Commission issues its report detailing the intelligence failures contributing to the success of the terrorist cells and their attacks. Congress passes the Intelligence Reform and Terrorism Prevention Act. It establishes the director of National Intelligence position. President Bush appoints John Negroponte, ambassador to Iraq, as the first DNI.

National Counterterrorism Center is created, largely housed and staffed in the CIA.

Unauthorized immigrants within the United States reach an estimated record of 11 million. The ICE reports 1.1 million apprehensions at the nation's borders.

2005   The House passes the Border Protection, Anti-Terrorism and Illegal Immigration Control Act, also known as the REAL ID Act.

The State of Virginia passes a law prohibiting unauthorized immigrants from receiving state or local public benefits.

New Mexico passes a law extending state tuition to unauthorized immigrants.

Arizona enacts a measure preventing cities from constructing day labor centers if such centers serve unauthorized immigrants.

Nine states pass anti–human trafficking laws.

Nine states pass laws banning the issuing of driver's licenses (identification) to unauthorized immigrants.

Three states pass laws mandating state and local law enforcement agencies to enforce federal immigration laws against unauthorized immigrants.

The governors of Arizona and New Mexico issue "state of emergency" declarations because of the extreme adverse impacts of illegal immigration on their respective states.

The AIC launches a state-by-state campaign aimed at enacting state laws against illegal immigration.

The European Union Ministers approve the use of biometric cards for immigration to EU countries.

The Netherlands enacts stricter anti–illegal immigration measures.

Hong Kong imposes the temperature screening of all incoming travelers.

England's High Court approves several measures announced by the government designed to "crack down" on illegal immigrants and ease procedures to deport them.

Japan begins fingerprinting all incoming immigrants.

France expels thousands of illegal immigrants.

Russia imposes fines for hiring illegal immigrants.

2006   Poland increases its border patrol by 50 percent.

Congress extends the USA Patriot Act. In March, it renews the Uniting and Strengthening America by Providing Appropriate Tools Required to Intercept and Obstruct Terrorism Act of 2001 (the USA Patriot Act).

Congress passes Secure Fence Act and President Bush signs it into law, Act authorizes construction of a 700-mile bollard-type fence along southwestern border.

Advocacy group, Border Action Network, established.

State of Colorado holds special session to pass measure imposing fines on businesses that employ unauthorized immigrants.

2008   President Obama's administration begins a surge in use of expedited removals to deport unauthorized immigrants under the Trafficking Victims Protection Reauthorization Act (TVPRA).

2009   President Obama uses executive action to mitigate certain aspects of IIRIRA.

2010   State of Arizona enacts law mandating state and local police to demand anyone suspected of being illegal to show documents to prove their legal status.

In *Arizona v. U.S.* (132 S.Ct.2492) Supreme Court rules Arizona law unconstitutional. In Congress, Democrats introduce "earned legalization" measures. Republicans block the measure.

2012   President Obama issues executive action order, DACA, granting temporary, conditional legal status to "Dreamer" children.

2013   Senate passes S.744, a Comprehensive Immigration Reform measure in bi-partisan vote. Measure is blocked in the House of Representatives and dies.

Senator David Vitter (R-LA) and Representative Steve King (R-IA) introduce bill to end birthright citizenship to persons born in United States of parents who are in illegal status.

2014   President Obama issues executive order, DAPA, granting temporary, conditional legal residency to unauthorized immigrant parents of U.S. citizens and legal permanent resident aliens.

Surge of arrivals of children unaccompanied by adults from El Salvador, Guatemala, and Honduras arrives. President Obama grants "Temporary Protected Status" to about 5,000 such children for whom it is deemed too unsafe to return to country of origin.

Senator John Cornyn (R-TX) and Representative Henry Cuellar (D-TX) introduce the Humane Act to amend the 2008 TVPRA's section 235.

Representative Matt Salmon (R-AZ) introduces the Expedited Family Reunification Act of 2014, allowing all UAC to be treated equally under the TVPRA, removing any distinction between contiguous and noncontiguous nations, allowing for all UAC to be processed as Mexican children are now and be subject to immediate voluntary return.

Senators Jeff Flake (R-AZ) and John McCain (R-AZ) introduce the CREST Act, which requires mandatory detention, use of asylum judges (adds 100 temporary immigration judges), and increases number of refugee visas to 5,000 each for El Salvador, Honduras, and Guatemala.

Representative John Carter (R-TX) introduces Protection of Children Act—treats all UAC equally under TVPRA.

Representative Bob Goodlatte (R-VA) and Jason Chaffetz (R-UT) introduce the Asylum Reform and Border Protection Act placing all UAC under expanded expedited removal.

Senator Mike Johanns (R-NE) introduces the UAC State Notification Act; and Senator Steve King (R-IA) a resolution calling on southern border states to deploy National Guard troops to secure the border.

Senator Ted Cruz (R-TX) introduces bill to stop the Deferred Action for Childhood Arrivals (DACA) program.

2015   House Republicans, Homeland Security Committee, introduce the Secure Our Borders First Act of 2015.

February 17, Andrew Hanen, U.S. District Judge, South Texas, places injunction on Obama administration's implementation of executive actions of DAPA.

March 3, 2015: House passes "clean" bill to fund DHS, of Senate-passed version, 257–167, with all Democrats and some Republicans, with no provision to defund Obama's executive actions on immigration.

President Obama issues the DAPA executive action granting temporary and conditional legal residency to unauthorized immigrant parents of U.S. citizens and legal permanent aliens. A surge in arrivals of children who are unaccompanied by adults, largely from El Salvador, Guatemala, and Honduras, prompts President Obama to grant "Temporary Protected Status" to approximately 5,000 such children whom the Department of Justice deems too unsafe to return to their country of origin. Annual legal immigration to the United States is 1,051,031.

2016   On February 17, U.S. District Judge, Texas, Andrew Hanen, places an injunction on the Obama administration's implementation of the DAPA order. In the November election, Donald Trump is elected president of the United States, winning the necessary majority of the Electoral College votes despite losing the popular vote by nearly 3 million.

2017   In January, President Trump appoints John Kelly as secretary of the Department of Homeland Security. On January 25, President Trump issues an executive order to start a pilot program to build a wall on the U.S.-Mexico border. That same day, he issues an executive order against "sanctuary cities" known as "Enhancing the Public Safety in the Interior of the United States." On January 27, he issues his (first) Muslim travel ban. On January 31, he fires Acting Attorney General Sally Yates for refusing to defend the travel ban order in federal court. On February 3, Federal District Judge James Robart, in Seattle, Washington, rules that the travel ban is unconstitutional. On February 9, Jefferson Sessions, the former U.S. senator from Alabama, is sworn in by Vice President Mike Pence, as attorney general of the United States. He directs the DOJ to crack down on sanctuary cities and moves to defend the travel ban before the U.S. Supreme Court. On March 6, Trump issues his second travel ban order. Judge Watson, a federal district judge in Hawaii, and Judge Chuang of the Maryland Federal District Court, also rule the order is unconstitutional. In May, President Trump orders the DHS to establish the Victims of Immigration Crime Enforcement (VOICE) program. On June 21, 2017, the U.S. Supreme Court partially upholds the second travel ban order and schedules oral arguments on the order for fall, 2017.

References

Ahlstrom, Sydney. 1972. *A Religious History of the American People.* New Haven, CT: Yale University Press.

Baltzell, E. Digby. 1996. *Puritan Boston and Quaker Philadelphia.* New Brunswick, NJ: Transaction Books.

Barone, Michael. 2013. *Shaping Our Nation: How Surges of Migration Transformed America and Its Politics.* New York: Crown Forum.

Beals, Carleton. 1960. *Brass Knuckle Crusade.* New York: Hasting House.

Bilhartz, Richard. 1986. *Fragile Glory: A Portrait of France and the French.* New York: Knopf.

Billington, Ray. 1974. *The Origins of Nativism in the United States, 1800–1844.* New York: Arno Press.

Bonomi, Patricia U. 1986. *Under the Cope of Heaven: Religion, Society, and Politics in Colonial America.* New York: Oxford University Press.

Boyton, Linda L. 1986. *The Plain People: An Ethnography of the Holdeman Mennonites.* Salem, WI: Sheffield.

Butler, Jon. 2006. *Religion in Colonial America.* New York: Oxford University Press.

Byrd, James P. 2013. *Sacred Scriptures, Sacred War: The Bible and the American Revolution.* New York: Oxford University Press.

Calavita, Kitty. 1992. *Inside the State: The Bracero Program, Immigration and the INS.* New York: Routledge.

Chiswick, Barry R., ed. 1982. *The Gateway: U.S. Immigration Issues and Policies.* Washington, DC: American Enterprise Institute.

Cohen, Steve, Beth Humphries, and Ed Mynott, eds. 2001. *From Immigration Controls to Welfare Controls.* New York: Routledge.

Craig, Richard. 1971. *The Bracero Program: Interest Groups and Foreign Policy.* Austin: University of Texas Press.

Driedger, Leo, and Donald B. Kraybill. 1994. *Mennonite Peacemaking.* Scottsdale, PA: Herald Press.

Fantel, Hans. 1974. *William Penn: Apostle of Dissent.* New York: William Morrow.

Gaustad, Edwin S. 1999. *Liberty of Conscience: Roger Williams in America.* Valley Forge, PA: Judson Press.

Heimert, Alan. 1966. *Religion and the American Mind: From the Great Awakening to the Revolution.* Cambridge, MA: Cambridge University Press.

Hening, William Walton, ed. 1823. *Statutes at Large of Virginia,* vol. 12, 84–86. VaGenWeb, www.vagenweb.org/hening/vol01-00.htm.

Higham, John. 1955. *Strangers in the Land: Patterns of American Nativism, 1866–1925.* New Brunswick, NJ: Rutgers University Press.

Holmes, David R. 2006. *The Faith of the Founding Fathers.* New York: Oxford University Press.

Immigration and Naturalization Service. 1979. *Population Trends and Public Policy.* Washington, DC: U.S. Government Printing Office.

Jefferson, Thomas. 1977. *The Portable Thomas Jefferson.* Edited by Merrill Petersen. New York: Penguin Books.

Jones, Maldwyn. 1960. *American Immigration.* Chicago: University of Chicago Press.

Kornelly, Sharon. 2013. "A Holy Experiment: Religion and Immigration to the New World." In *Transforming America: Perspectives on U.S. Immigration,* vol. 1. Edited by Michael LeMay, 189–214. Westport, CT: Praeger Press.

Kraybill, Donald B., and Steven M. Holt. 1995. *Amish Enterprises: From Plows to Profits.* Baltimore: The Johns Hopkins University Press.

Kritz, Mary M. 1983. *U.S. Immigration and Refugee Policy: Global and Domestic Issues.* Lexington, KY: Lexington Books.

Lambert, Frank. 2003. *The Founding Fathers and the Place of Religion in America.* Princeton, NJ: Princeton University Press.

Lee, Jonathan, Fumitake Matsuoka, Edmond Yee, and Ronald Nakasone, eds. 2015. *Asian American Religious Cultures*, 2 vols. Santa Barbara, CA: ABC-CLIO.

LeMay, Michael. 1987. *From Open Door to Dutch Door.* Westport, CT: Praeger Press.

LeMay, Michael, ed. 1989. *The Gatekeepers: Comparative Immigration Policy.* Westport, CT: Praeger Press.

LeMay, Michael. 1994. *Anatomy of a Public Policy: The Reform of Contemporary Immigration Law.* Westport, CT: Praeger Press.

LeMay, Michael. 2004. *U.S. Immigration: A Reference Handbook.* Santa Barbara, CA: ABC-CLIO.

LeMay, Michael. 2006. *Guarding the Gates: Immigration and National Security.* New York: Praeger Security International.

LeMay, Michael. 2007. *Illegal Immigration: A Reference Handbook.* Santa Barbara, CA: ABC-CLIO.

LeMay, Michael. 2009. *The Perennial Struggle*, 3rd edition. Upper Saddle River, NJ: Prentice Hall.

LeMay, Michael, ed. 2013. *Transforming America: Perspectives on Immigration*, vols. 1–3. Santa Barbara, CA: ABC-CLIO.

LeMay, Michael. 2015. *Doctors at the Borders: Immigration and the Rise of Public Health.* Westport, CT: Praeger Press.

LeMay, Michael. 2017. *Religious Freedom in America: A Reference Handbook.* Santa Barbara, CA: ABC-CLIO.

LeMay, Michael, and Elliott Barkan, eds. 1999. *U.S. Immigration and Naturalization Laws and Issues: A Documentary History.* Westport, CT: Greenwood Press.

Levy, Leonard W. 1994. *The Establishment Clause and the First Amendment.* Chapel Hill: University of North Carolina Press.

Lieberson, Stanley. 1980. *A Piece of the Pie: Black and White Immigrants Since 1880.* Berkeley: University of California Press.

Mapp, Alf. 2003. *The Faith of Our Fathers: What America's Founders Really Believed.* Lanham, MD: Rowman and Littlefield.

Massey, Douglas, Rafael Alarcon, Jorge Durand, and Humberto Gonzalez. 1987. *Return to Aztlan: The Social Process of Immigration from Western Mexico.* Berkeley: University of California Press.

Meier, Matt S., and Margo Gutierrez. 2000. *Encyclopedia of Mexican-American Civil Rights Movement.* Westport, CT: Greenwood Press.

Miller, William Lee. 1986. *The First Liberty: Religion and the American Republic.* Washington, DC: Georgetown University Press.

Navarro, Joseph. 2005. *Mexican Political Experience in Occupied Aztlan.* Lanham, MD: Altamira Press.

Nolt, Steven M. 1992. *A History of the Amish.* Intercourse, PA: Good Books.

Perea, Juan. 1997. *Immigrants Out! The New Nativism and the Anti-Immigrant Impulse in the United States.* New York: New York University Press.

Peterson, Merrill D., and Robert C. Vaughn, eds. 1988. *The Virginia Statute for Religious Freedom: Its Evolution and Consequences in American History.* Cambridge, MA: Cambridge University Press.

Pew Research Center. http://www.pewhispanic.org/2014/11/18/unauthorized-immigrant-totals-rise-in-7-states-fall-in-14/. Accessed February 27, 2015.

Platt, Tony, and Cecelia O'Leary. 2003. "Patriot Acts." *Social Justice,* Spring, 30(1): 5–22.

Portman, Rob, and Cheryl Bauer. 2004. *Wisdom's Paradise: The Forgotten Shakers of Union Village.* Wilmington, OH: Orange Frazer Press.

Roucek, Jospeh S., and Bernard Eisenber, eds. 1982. *America's Ethnic Politics.* Westport, CT: Greenwood Press.

Schrug, Peter. 2010. *Not Fit for Our Society: Nativism and Immigration.* Berkeley: University of California Press.

Select Commission on Immigration and Refugee Policy (SCRIP). 1981. *Staff Report.* Washington, DC: U.S. Government Printing Office.

Snodgrass, Michael. 2011. "The Bracero Program, 1942–1964." In *Beyond the Border: The History of Mexican-U.S. Migration.* Edited by Mark Overmyer-Valisquez, 79–102. New York: Oxford University Press.

Torr, James D., ed. 2004. *Homeland Security.* San Diego: Greenhaven Press.

Ulrich, Laurel Thatcher. 1991. *A Midwife's Tale.* New York: Vintage Books.

U.S. Census. www.census.gov/acs/www/.

Walters, Kerry S. 1992. *The American Diests: Voices of Reason and Dissent in the Early Republic.* Lawrence: University Press of Kansas.

Wenger, John. 1961. *The Mennonites in Indiana and Michigan.* Scottsdale, PA: Herald Press.

Zolberg, Aristide. 2008. *A Nation by Design: Immigration Policy in the Fashioning of America.* Cambridge, MA: Russell Sage Foundation at Harvard University Press.

CHAPTER TWO

The Open Door Era, 1820–1880

Introduction: Religious Motivation in Colonial Immigration

As stated in Chapter 1, the United States is almost unique as a nation in terms of the degree to which it has absorbed immigrants from other nations. No other nation has experienced as many and as varied an immigration of various religious/ethnic groups as has the United States. The country's initial policy was to keep open its doors to immigrants, welcoming all. A number of state governments on the frontier of settlement, as well as many businesses in the early stages of industrialization, reached out to recruit immigrants from Northwestern Europe. During the open door phase, a total of 10,189,420 immigrants were admitted for permanent resident alien status. Among them, 80 percent came from Europe, 6.1 percent from the Americas, and 13.9 percent from all other sources (LeMay 2006: 14).

The U.S. Constitution says little about immigration. It grants to Congress the power to establish a policy for *naturalization*, which implied its having the authority to set immigration policy. The key phrase in Article 1 was that Congress could "make such laws as were necessary and proper to execute that power." Section 8 of Article 1 gives Congress the power to regulate commerce, which was later interpreted by the Supreme Court to include immigration. The Court has been expansive in interpreting the powers of Congress to regulate immigration, and has been restrictive when it comes to state government laws or actions with respect to immigration and the rights of aliens (Byrne-Hessick and Chin 2014; Suro 2015). After passage of the Fourteenth Amendment, the Supreme Court gradually (mostly after 1940) began to apply the religious free exercise and establishment clauses of the First Amendment to state and local governments as well.

The Constitution's nonexistent or vague language on citizenship, naturalization, and immigration followed the tradition of the Articles of Confederation, which left to the states the right to determine citizenship. It took the development of further laws and Supreme Court decisions to elaborate upon the meaning of the vague language of Article 1. Congress acted quickly on its constitutional authorization. In 1790, Congress passed its first law regulating naturalization by requiring only a two-year period of residency and the renunciation of former allegiances. In 1795, it revised that law, increasing to five years the period for naturalization, but maintained a very liberal approach to immigration and naturalization (Act of January 29, 1795, 1 Stat. 414).

In June 1798, the federalists feared that French radicals, who had immigrated to the United States, might stir turmoil akin to the excesses of the French Revolution. That concern led Congress to pass the first law concerning aliens (Act of June 18, 1798, 1 Stat. 566; LeMay and Barkan 1999: 13–14). It granted then president John Adams, a Federalist, the authority to deport any alien found guilty of seditious activities. President Adams never invoked those powers, but its passage set a precedent for later presidential action, invoked on several occasions during wartimes. It was perhaps the first example of xenophobic-inspired public policy making, and its enactment foreshadowed subsequent legislation that was more effectively restrictive. The 1798 law stated:

> That it shall be lawful for the President of the United States at any time during the continuance of this act, to order all such aliens as he shall judge dangerous to the peace and safety of the United States, or shall have reasonable grounds to suspect are concerned in any treasonable secret machinations against the government thereof, to depart out of the territory of the United States. (1 Stat. 570; excerpted in Document 10: LeMay and Barkan 1999: 15–16)

The law expired in 1800 and had little impact on the actual immigration flow during the open door phase, mostly because soon after they came to power, the Jeffersonian Democrat-Republicans passed a law reinstating the five-year provision (Act of April 14, 1802, 54 Stat. 1172; LeMay and Barkan 1999: 16–18).

Religious Influences on Early American Politics

Religious communities in the United States diverged from their European counterparts. The Methodists and Baptist denominations were part of the widespread movement of evangelism as small religious communities spread into the American frontier. The frontier settlements became havens for freedom of religious belief and practice separate from official, established religion. Baptists and Shakers believed that members did not need a church to cultivate spirituality. Nonconformist churches centralized their institutions in Philadelphia. In 1790, when the United States took its first census, Philadelphia was the second largest city in the country, with a population of 28,511 (LeMay 2013, vol. 1: 56). The city became home to the central assemblies for the Quaker, Baptist, and Presbyterian Churches and played a significant role in the development of the Protestant Episcopal Church and American Lutheranism as well (Baltzell 1996; Miller 1986).

Even as the nonconformist denominations began to centralize, the state-sponsored churches began to disestablish. Freedom of religious choice became rallying points for uniting the American identity, and the Bill of Rights provided for the separation of church and state in the federal government. As noted in Chapter 1, Virginia led the way to end state-sponsored churches. Its statute, written by Thomas Jefferson and secured in its adoption by James Madison, the Virginia law became the model for other states to include freedom of religion clauses in their state constitutions. By 1833, all the states followed this model (Hening 1823; Levy 1994; Mapp 2003; Miller 1986; Peterson, Vaughan, and Lovin 1988; Vile 2015). The Virginia statute stated: ". . . that no man shall be compelled to frequent or support any religious worship, place, or ministry whatsoever, nor shall be enforced, restrained, molested, or burthened in his body or goods, nor shall otherwise suffer on account of his religious opinions or belief, but that all men shall be free to profess, and by argument to maintain, their opinion in matters of religion, and that the same shall in no wise diminish, enlarge, or affect their civil capacities" (cited in Hening 1823: 86; see also Kornelly, in LeMay 2013: 211).

In the late colonial and early years of the American republic, Deism played a significant role. It would seem that some of the Founders were Non-Christian Deists: Thomas Paine, Ethan Allen, and James Monroe. Christian Deists included George Washington, John Adams, and Thomas Jefferson. Samuel Adams, John Jay, Elias Boudinot, and Patrick Henry were Orthodox Christians (Butler 2006; Holmes 2006; Miller 1985; Nuovo 2002, Peterson, Vaughan, and Lovin, 1988, and Walters 1992).

Benjamin Franklin noted: "When a religion is good, I conceive it will support itself, and when it does not support itself, and God does not take care to support it so that its professors are obligated to call for help of the civil power, 'tis a sign, I apprehend, of its being a bad one" (Americans for Religious Liberty).

No matter their personal faith beliefs, without doubt Deism influenced a majority of the Founding Fathers in that the movement opposed barriers to moral improvement and to social justice, stood for rational inquiry, skepticism about dogma and mystery, and for religious tolerance. Its adherents favored universal education, freedom of the press, and the separation of church and state. The Founding Fathers notably embraced political ideas that were remarkably liberal for their time and informed their insistence on enacting the First Amendment in the Bill or Rights.

Early American treaties also impacted religion in America. The Pinckney Treaty of 1795 resolved tensions between Spain and the United States. It granted to the United States the right to navigate the Mississippi River and for Americans to transfer their goods from river-going vessels to ocean-going vessels at New Orleans. However, that situation changed when France acquired Louisiana from Spain in 1800 and took possession in 1802. Napoleon Bonaparte was anxious to revive the French empire and intended to use the territory as a base to put down a slave rebellion (on today's Haiti), and as a source of grain for his empire. The United States, and its population in the then western region, were especially worried and President Jefferson sent James Monroe to France to seek to purchase New Orleans and West Florida for $10 million. A yellow fever plague decimated half of Napoleon's army on Haiti, and he decided to sell the entire territory to the United States for $15 million. Jefferson approved the deal, and the Congress concurred, based on the principle of "implied powers" of the federal government. The purchase by treaty meant that the residents of the territory (many from Spain, and a lesser but significant number from France) who were overwhelmingly Roman Catholics, became United States citizens by treaty. There were suddenly many more Catholics in the population (Office of the Historian).

In matters regarding immigration, in 1819, Congress enacted the law that required the enumeration of all immigrant passengers according to the country from which they came (by which was meant, their nation of birth or origin). Passage of this "Manifest of Immigration" Act of March 2, 1819 (3 Stat. 489) marked the first time that the United States began keeping track of the immigration flow, and marks the formal beginning of the Open Door phase of immigration policy making. The law was quite simple in its intent, and left to the various state governments the primary responsibility for the actual processing of immigrants done quite casually on the docks and wharfs at the ports of debarkation.

Box 2.1 presents a summary of the two key sections of the "Manifest Act" exemplifying the public policy approach of the Open Door period—that of allowing nearly unfettered entrance to the United States. The enumeration and description of the immigrant flow also reflects a sense of the impact immigration has on national security (then known as "domestic

---

Box 2.1: Act of March 2, 1819 (Re: Immigration)

Sec. 4. And be it further enacted, That the captain or master of any ship or vessel arriving in the United States or any of the territories thereof, from any foreign place whatever, at the same time that he delivers a manifest of all cargo, and, if there is no cargo, then at the time of making a report of entry of the ship or vessel, pursuant to the existing laws of the United States, shall deliver and report, to the collector of the district in which the ship or vessel shall arrive, a list or manifest of all passengers taken on board of the said ship or vessel at any foreign port or place; in which list or manifest it shall be the duty of said master to designate, particularly, the age, sex, and occupation of the said passengers, respectively, the country to which they severally belong, and that of which it is their intention to become inhabitants; and shall further set forth whether any, and what number, have died on the voyage; which report and manifest shall be sworn to by the said master, in the same manner as is directed by the existing laws of the United States, in relation to the manifest of the cargo, and that the refusal or neglect of the master aforesaid, to comply with the provisions of this section, shall incur the same penalties, disabilities, and forfeitures, as are at present provided for a refusal or neglect to report and deliver a manifest of the cargo aforesaid.

Sec. 5. And be it further enacted, That each and every collector of the customs, to whom such manifest or list of passengers as aforesaid shall be delivered, shall, quarter yearly, return copies thereof to the Secretary of State of the United States, by whom statements of the same shall be laid before Congress each and every season.

Source: Manifest of Immigrants Act of March 2, 1819 (3 Stat. 489).

---

tranquility") and on the national identity. There was as yet no attempt to ban or bar immigrants but merely to record where and how many were arriving, and some sense of their identity as reflected in their age and occupation backgrounds, as well as their nation of birth (origin).

The next section describes the groups who comprised the "old" immigrant wave, their religious diversity, and how public policy influenced their immigration and subsequent incorporation into American society.

Religious/Ethnic Groups in the Old Immigrant Wave

Those whom scholars label the old immigrants came overwhelmingly from Northern and Western Europe and include the Germans, Irish, and

Scandinavians. They arrived in two major surges, from 1845 to 1860, when the German and Irish immigrants predominated, and from 1865 to 1880, when the British and Scandinavians also figured heavily in addition to the continued arrival of the Germans and Irish.

German Immigrants

Throughout American immigration history since 1820, Germany was the nation of origin for the largest number of immigrants, totaling 7 million. Indeed, in the 2000 U.S. census, Americans were asked to specify their ancestry, and those claiming German heritage totaled more than 46 million people and comprised 17 percent of the total U.S. population. Table 2.1 puts that claimed ancestry in context, presenting the top 25 nations of origin in rank order, as cited by respondents in the 2000 census (the last census to ask that question). One can readily see that the nations of origin associated with the "old" immigrant wave, which predominated in the immigration flow of the Open Door phase, comprise 13 of the top 25 ranks.

People from the German states immigrated steadily and in significant numbers throughout American history. However, they can be grouped usefully into three surges: (1) the colonial period, when they immigrated mostly for religious and economic reasons; (2) from 1848 to the Civil War, when they came for political and economic reasons; and (3) the post-Civil War period, when they came for economic opportunity, often having been recruited by one of several major industries and by various state governments, the railroads, or friends and relatives already living in the United States (i.e., chain migration). Although the native-stock (i.e., those from the British Isle at this time) treated them as one group based on their language, German immigrants were a diverse group splintered in their homelands by regional strife and especially along religious lines. Germany did not become a unified nation-state until 1871. Prior to 1871, it was a loose federation or simply a collection of German-speaking states or kingdoms (such as Prussia).

Colonial era German immigration can be distinguished by the movement of entire communities bound together by religious creeds not accepted in the region of their homelands. They came in groups as Mennonites, Dunkers, Lutherans, Calvinists, and Jews. Geographically, the majority came from southern regions of present-day Germany, which at the time was predominately Roman Catholic and whose rulers therefore encouraged the emigration of adherents of minority religions—Lutherans

Table 2.1   Rank Order of Immigration to the United States, Top 25
Nations of Origin, 1820–2000, Claimed Ancestry

Rank-Order Ancestry Claimed	2000 Population
1. German	46,428,321
2. Irish	33,048,744
3. English	28,222,890
4. Italian	15,916,396
5. French	9,794,218
6. Polish	9,029,440
7. Scottish	5,406,421
8. Scotch-Irish	5,205,335
9. Dutch	5,203,974
10. Norwegian	4,524,953
11. Swedish	4,342,160
12. Russian	2,975,628
13. French Canadian	2,211,688
14. West Indian	1,914,410
15. Welsh	1,895,726
16. Sub-Saharan African	1,530,987
17. Hungarian	1,510,878
18. Danish	1,505,450
19. Czech	1,407,495
20. Portuguese	1,315,574
21. Arab	1,237,947
22. Greek	1,175,591
23. Swiss	993,552
24. Ukrainian	857,460
25. Slovak	817,302

Source: Table by author; data from U.S. Bureau of the Census, *2000 Profile of Social Characteristics*. Washington, DC. http://www.census.gov. Accessed April 3, 2015.

and various Anabaptist and Pietist sects. They self-identified as immigrants from Palatine, Baden, Wurttemberg, and Bavaria. They settled to cultivate some of the richest farmlands in colonial America; their granaries served as the breadbasket of the Revolution. They were scattered thinly among the native-stock Anglo population, united only by their language. They exercised little political influence, and showed interest only in their local and private affairs (LeMay 1985: 34–38).

The Revolutionary War changed all that. Although widely scattered, they still comprised the single largest nationality/language group after the British. German immigrants felt no special loyalty to the crown and were often unfriendly toward the Tories who favored continued union with England. While at first reluctant to become involved, they were easy converts to the cause of independence, and several German regiments were raised and fought prominently and well in the Revolutionary War. This wartime service became a major step towards their political incorporation. As their general social and economic conditions improved, they began taking a more active part in public affairs. Politically, after 1828, they tended to affiliate with the Jacksonian-Democrats, reflecting their small-farmer backgrounds. They were less at home with the "eastern seaboard establishment" represented by the Federalists (LeMay 1985: 34–38). Wherever the Federalists predominated, moreover, they tended to establish the Anglican Church. As noted in Chapter 1, this did not sit well with the religious minorities from the German states, particularly the Anabaptist and Pietists, like the Dunkers—the Old German Baptist Brethren, and the Moravian Brethren, and the cultural separatists like the Old Order Amish and Old Order Mennonites.

The wave arriving during the 1830s and 1840s emigrated for more varied reasons. By then the agricultural revolution hit central Europe, especially in the southeastern area of present-day Germany. Changes in inheritance laws forced the division of agricultural lands among all the children, and coupled with a population explosion, these economic changes led many farmers occupying farms too small for even subsistence farming to leave agriculture and migrate to cities where they turned to manufacturing of clocks, tools, and related crafts. They were still vulnerable to economic change, and when the potato famine that plagued much of Europe in the late 1840s struck, their choice was often reduced to emigration or starvation.

Fortunately for them and for the United States, these events coincided with the opening of the American Midwest which served as pull factors drawing the émigrés to the United States (although many also went to Canada). State governments, railroads, shipping lines, and manufacturers sent agents to Germany to entice immigration. The development of steamship lines made the transatlantic journey less arduous and less hazardous (Fox 2003). Texas, the Great Lakes region, and the

Ohio River valley became home to the new German immigrant settlers. Midwestern cities mushroomed in population (LeMay 2013, v. 1: 47–72). Cities like Chicago, Detroit, Milwaukee, Cincinnati, and St. Louis anchored a 200-mile wide region of land stretching from New York to Maryland to the Mississippi River that become known as "the German belt" (LeMay 1985: 36).

Another surge followed the political turmoil and the 1848 failed attempt at a revolution. Many German intellectuals fled to the United States. Collectively known as the "Forty-Eighters," they made major contributions to the liberal movement in the states where they settled and where their influence far exceeded their numbers, as they became leaders of the German American community. They started German-language newspapers (among some 265 such newspapers was the *Illinois Staatsanzeiger*, which was an important supporter of Lincoln's candidacy), reading and choral societies, theatres, and related cultural activities. They became influential in the public education movement, exemplified by the kindergarten innovation (McLaughlin 2013: 97–119). The full extent of their influence in the founding of the Republican Party and in national-level politics is debated (see Barone 2013; Fuchs 1968; Higham 1978; O'Connor 1968; Rippley 1973; Schafer 1968; Wittke 1967; Zolberg 2008), but they undoubtedly provided leadership to the labor movement, the Union Army, and the nation's conservation movement (Hoeder 1982; LeMay 2006: 42–44; Rosenblum 1973). They were mostly anti-slavery, and their religious convictions on the matter influenced their political association with the Republican Party.

A Forty-Eighter, Carl Schurz, for example, after serving as a major general in the Civil War, became an important education leader in New York, then led the drive to save virgin forest land and went on to become the first Secretary of the Interior in 1877. Franz Sigel was another German-born, Forty-Eighter, and major general in the Union Army. There were several brigadier generals: August Willich, Louis Bleckner, Max Weber, Alexander Schimmelfennig. An estimated 200,000 German-born served in the Union Army in 10 divisions from New York, Ohio, Pennsylvania, Missouri, Indiana, and Wisconsin. Eleven German-born who served in the Union Army during the Civil War won the Congressional Medal of Honor, among the first to whom it was awarded. The Medal of Honor was created in 1861, and nearly half of its 3,493 recipients were awarded in that conflict (Congressional Medal of Honor). New York alone provided 36,000 German-born Union troops; Missouri some 30,000; and Ohio 20,000. Prominent units were the 9th Ohio, the 74th Pennsylvania, the 9th Wisconsin, and the 32nd Indiana. They fought in a host of key battles: Chancellorsville, Gettysburg, Chattanooga and Nashville (with Sherman), Shiloh, Missionary Ridge, Chickamauga Creek, and Vicksburg. The patriotism they displayed during the Civil War did much to secure their acceptance and assimilation (Rosengarten 1980; Sarnito 2009; Wily 1979; Civil War–German). Indeed, the war-related policy of granting speedy naturalization to honorably discharged soldiers set a precedent used in every American war since then (Act of July 17, 1862, 40 Stat. 546; Kettner 1978; LeMay and Barkan 1999: 30). Arguably, it had a far greater impact on subsequent immigration and on the incorporation of immigrants into American society than did any overt immigration policy designed to do so.

The members of a number of German pacifist sects struggled what position to take on the Civil War, much as did the pacifist Quakers. Those who came as religious communities maintained their pacifism opposed service or support for the Civil War. Those whose moral stance on slavery was the stronger religious-based motivation, enabled them to serve or at least support the Civil War.

German immigrants were prominent in the anti-slavery movement and claimed some credit in the founding of the Republican Party (in Ripon, Wisconsin), and for the election of Lincoln, who shrewdly had invested in the German-language newspaper, *Illinois Staatsanzeiger* (Adamic 1945: 181; Parrillo 1980: 133; but disputed by Rippley 1973; and Schafer 1968). Carl Schurz served on the Republican Party Platform Committee in 1860 and led a unit of German soldiers during the war, a unit which served as a presidential guard and as an honor guard after his assassination (Civil War-German).

German immigrant labor during and after the Civil War filled desperately needed openings in the northern industrial labor force opened up by the war (Hoeder 1982; Rosenblum 1973). A postwar booming economy drew labor to areas in high demand. This became a major factor in their rapid incorporation into the mainstream of American life. Arguably the strongest influence drawing German immigrants to the United States immediately after the Civil War was the free land provided through the Homestead Act of 1862 (Act of May 20, 1862: 392–393; LeMay and Barkan 1999: 29–30); and land granted to Civil War veterans; and the Act of July 17, 1862, granting citizenship to honorably discharged soldiers who served in the Union Army (40 Stat. 546) (Kettner 1978; Thernstrom 1980).

German immigrants did face some opposition, most notably, from the Know-Nothing Party of the 1850s (the Order of the Star-Spangled Banner); and the American Party, whose main platform was the rejection of the foreigner (Nevins 1947; O'Connor 1968: 122; Smith 1969). The anti-immigrant platform and the narrow focus of the parties contributed to their short duration as minor or "third" parties. The Republican Party and the Democratic Party, by contrast, welcomed immigrants and went on to become or retain their status as the two major parties of the Open Door phase.

Irish Immigrants

Irish Americans are second only to the German Americans in the number of claimed ancestry (see Table 2.1). Like the Germans, they trace their immigration back to colonial years when they settled mostly in Pennsylvania and Maryland. In the 1790 census, the Irish comprised about 2 percent of the nation's population of about 3.5 million. In the 1840s, their arrival in massive numbers in but a half-decade, however, and their Catholicism precipitated the first strong and overt discrimination. After 1830, when the Irish began fleeing political and religious persecution under British rule, Irish immigration swelled to flood levels. An estimated 4.5 million Irish immigrated to the United States between 1820 and 2000. As of the 2000 census, more than 33 million Americans claim Irish ancestry, just over 12 percent of the U.S. population. They are still heavily concentrated in the east, in New York, Massachusetts, Pennsylvania, and New Jersey (Brown 1966; Miller 1985; O'Grady 1973; Sarnito 2009; Thernstrom 1980; Wily 1979).

The potato famine of the late 1840s precipitated a massive emigration, when their choice was to emigrate or to starve. Between 1847 and 1854, roughly 1.2 million Irish arrived in the United States (many others went to Canada, some staying there but a short few years before migrating down to the United States). Their wave peaked in 1851, when nearly a quarter-million arrived. The famine-induced emigration was critical in that it created a sudden and perceived deluge of immigrants all settling into the urban areas along the East Coast, and activating existing prejudice. Their sheer numbers, their extreme poverty, their Catholicism, and their openly anti-British feelings all contributed to the antagonism against them. Many came weakened by the famine and succumbed to (and were also blamed for bringing with them) disease epidemics like cholera, yellow fever, influenza, and small pox (Table 3.1, LeMay 2013, v. 2: 51–52). Due to their poverty, more than one million coming from largely rural backgrounds were trapped in the nation's seaboard cities, not a prescription for rapid incorporation (or assimilation as it was then called).

They were derided as "papists" by Protestant Americans. They experienced religious discrimination in the pre-Civil War era and set off a dramatic xenophobic reaction. They were easy scapegoats on which to place the blame for the social and economic problems generated by a rapidly urbanizing and industrializing country and economy (LeMay 2009: 353). They were accused of importing crime and drunkenness. Protestant evangelizers seeking to preserve the nation's "purity" joined forces with radical nativists like the Secret Order of the Star-Spangled Banner, which soon morphed into the American Party, better known as the Know-Nothing Party. A wave of xenophobia led to violent attacks on churches and convents, and inflammatory anti-Catholic literature, often led by a splinter group called the "Plug Uglies." They rose up "to burn Catholic convents, churches, and homes, assault nuns, and murder Irishmen, Germans, and Negroes" (Beals 1960; LeMay 1987: 32–34; see also Bailey 1976 and Billington 1974). The Know-Nothing movement died out by the time of the Civil War, but conflicts with Roman Catholicism over parochial schools, prayers in public schools, and which version of the Bible to be read in schools, arose again in the 1870s and 1880s, when large waves of immigrants from Italy brought a new infusion of Catholics and the Ku Klux Klan espoused radical and often violent anti-Catholicism and anti-Semitism (LeMay 1987: 44).

Coming with high rates of illiteracy and few job skills, they were forced into unskilled labor. This resulted in their acquiring lower class status precisely when the United States was developing class consciousness (Dinnerstein and Reimers 1975; Handlin 1959, 1979; Parrillo 1980: 137). They were viewed as a special threat, a great flood of "indigent foreigners" who were lower class and who formed the first huge pool of manual labor (O'Grady 1973: 65; Rosenblum 1973).

Irish immigrants became the first group to face overt job discrimination when advertisements in Boston, New York, Baltimore, and Philadelphia for some time included the line, "No Irish Need Apply" (Beals 1960; Billington 1974; O'Grady 1973). They accepted whatever work was open to them—unskilled jobs like stevedores, teamsters, ditch diggers, and hod carriers. They formed construction gangs that razed or erected buildings in the mushrooming cities. They built the roads, canals, and railroads connecting the east with the Midwest and beyond. Those jobs were often seasonal, always low-paying, mostly back breaking, and subject to a constant threat of job competition, a factor leading to problems of race relations where the Irish regarded blacks and Chinese as special menaces to their own very precarious position (Hoeder 1982).

Their wartime service in the American Civil War, like that of German immigrants, was instrumental in speeding up their acceptance and incorporation. Their service in the Civil War was truly exemplary. The term "Fighting Irish," used by the football team of Notre Dame University, refers to the Irish Brigade—the Fighting 69th. The brigade suffered heavy casualties—more than 4,800 killed or wounded. The brigade alone had 961 killed in action. Irish-born immigrants fought with the 63rd N.Y. Infantry, the 69th New York Infantry, the 88th New York Infantry, the 28th Massachusetts Infantry, and the 116th Pennsylvania Infantry. Irish-born immigrants were the single-largest group of foreign-born recipients of the Congressional Medal of Honor (258, followed by German-born at 128). Notable Irish-born MOH awardees include Pvt. Peter Rafferty of the 69th, Lt. John Tobin of the 9th, Coxswain John Cooper, of the USS Brooklyn, Army-surgeon William Blackwood of the 48th Pennsylvania Infantry, and Pvt. George Platt, 6th U.S. Cavalry (Congressional Medal of Honor; Civil War-Ireland; Sarnito 2009; Miller 1985).

The Irish Brigade distinguished itself at a number of battles: Fair Oaks, Pennsylvania; Seven Days Battles; Bull Run, First Manassas; Second Manassas; Antietam (where the Brigade suffered 60 percent casualties); Fredericksburg; Chancellorsville; Gettysburg; Siege of Petersburg; and the Battle of Appomattox Courthouse. Among the more notable Irish-born officers in the Civil War were Brigadier General Thomas Francis Meagher, Brigadier General Thomas Reade Cobb; General Thomas A. Smyth (killed in action); General Robert Nugent; and Colonels Michael Corcoran, Patrick Daniel Kelly (killed in action); Richard Byrnes (killed in action), and Richard Earight (Miller 1985; Sarnito 2009; Wily 1979; Civil War-Ireland).

To break out of their minority status and move up even a few rungs on the socioeconomic ladder, they became involved in the American labor movement and used politics to advance their position. They seldom had experience with labor union affairs, but their unstable working condition led them to join the budding labor associations. They were early leaders in the formation of unions from New York to San Francisco. These unions ran the gamut of skilled craftsmen from tailors to bricklayers, shoemakers, carpenters, and longshoremen. In the 1850s, unions operated solely at the local level, but by the 1860s, they began to appear at the national level. In 1861, Irish immigrant Martin Burke helped form and led the American Miners Association. By the 1870s, a second-generation Irish American, Terrance Powderly, controlled the first truly effective national-level labor union, the Knights of Labor. Peter McGuire, who became known as the "Father of Labor Day," formed the American Federation of

Labor in 1886 (Glazer and Moynihan 1963; Hoeder 1982; O'Grady 1973: 163; Rosenblum 1973;).

Coming in annually by the tens of thousands, the Irish contributed to the burgeoning cities where urbanization required an increasing number of local government work forces: police departments, public works departments, fire departments and, so on. By 1863, Irish-immigrant John A. Kennedy, led the New York City police force. In the 1870s, a city detective of Irish descent, Michael Kerwin, became police commissioner.

They joined and then soon led a growing number of urban political machines, like the most famous one, New York's Tammany Hall (Glazer and Moynihan 1963; LeMay 2013, v. 1: 53–70; Levine 2006). Politics became their principal means of climbing the ladder up American society, and the primary avenue of political incorporation (Fuchs, 1968; Greenstein 1970; Litt 1970).

Notable Irish-American politicians number in the hundreds, including 22 U.S. presidents of Irish heritage; 7 signatures to the Declaration of Independence; 6 Tammany Hall leaders; 6 mayors of Boston; 10 mayors of New York City; 6 mayors of Chicago; 4 governors of New York; 5 governors of Massachusetts, and 8 U.S. Supreme Court justices. (Archdeacon 1983; Brown 1966; Fuchs 1968; Glazer and Moynihan 1975; Handlin 1959; Levy and Kramer 1972; Levine 2006; Litt 1970; Maguire 1969; O'Grady 1973; Thernstrom 1980).

One of the most contentious issues that the Irish immigrants struggled with in relation to public policy implemented and enforced by the majority society centered on public schools and their effort to protect the right to maintain parochial schools which they increasingly organized. They did so when they felt that the public schools were threatening to establish a Protestant value system in the public schools by readings from the King James Bible, saying mandatory prayers in schools that were written by school administrators and which they felt reflected Protestantism (Ravitch 1974).

Scandinavian Immigrants

Scandinavians were among the first European people to explore America, with Viking explorations and minute settlements dating back to around 1,000 CE. In the mid-1600s, several settlements of immigrants from the Scandinavian region (Norway, Sweden, Denmark) were established in what is now the state of Delaware. A few of them came during colonial times, but their numbers were not significant until after the Civil War. From then on, motivated by religious dissension, disenfranchisement, crop failures, and related economic factors, Scandinavians emigrated in large numbers, most of them to the United States. Their total immigration exceeded 3 million, and all three nations of origin of the region rank among the top 25 in numbers claiming their ancestry in the 2000 census—in total more than 10.3 million Americans (see Table 2.1). The Swedes hit their peak in 1910, the Norwegians and Danes in the 1920s. Although these three national origin groups came from countries with diverse governments, traditions and spoken languages, their physical similarities, and the tendency to settle together in midwestern states led to the use of the term "Scandinavian" to refer to immigrants from all three nations. As Babcock describes it:

> The common use of the term Scandinavian to describe Swedes, Norwegians, and Danes in a broad and general way is one of the products of commingling of these three peoples on the American side of the Atlantic. The word usually fits them even more loosely than does the word British to indicate the English, Welsh, and Scotch. It was applied early in the history of the settlements in Wisconsin and Illinois, to groups which comprised both the Norwegians and Danes on the one hand, or Norwegians and Swedes on the other hand, when no one of the three nationalities were strong enough to maintain itself separately, and when the members of one were inclined to resent being called by the other names . . . The Scandinavian Synod of the Evangelical Lutheran Church, organized in 1860, included both Norwegians and Danes . . . The use and acceptability of the word grew steadily; the great daily paper in Chicago took the name *Scandinaven* in 1889 . . . the term has become a household word universally understood in the sense in which we here use it to designate the three nationalities. (1914: 15–16)

Beginning by the 1890s, they were increasingly attracted to the industrial opportunities in the Northeast and Middle-Atlantic states, and to the lumber industry in Minnesota, northern Wisconsin, and the Pacific Northwest. By 1920, Chicago had the largest number of Swedes of any city but Stockholm, and more Norwegians than any city but Oslo—their respective capital cities (LeMay 1985: 44).

On the whole they were a very successful group of immigrants. Several factors worked to their advantage for incorporation into American society. They worked hard, and arrived in better financial shape than many other European nation groups, and were thus able to escape the dire poverty and the slums of the East Coast cities. They were Protestant, and so avoided anti-Catholic prejudice. Not being trapped in the tenement slums, they escaped that stigma as well. By 1880, the average Scandinavian immigrant brought about $50 to $70 with him, enabling them to reach the Midwest, where they could take advantage of the cheap land and put their farming and lumbering skills to use. They went into business, commerce, manufacturing, finance, and the professions. In their then frontier settlements, they soon established their own stores, shops, factories, and banks. During the Open Door era, they settled in midwestern states whose soil and climate reminded them of their homelands. Successful settlers drew others. Minnesota, Wisconsin, Iowa, Illinois, and the Dakotas all saw dramatic increases in their populations from immigration and notably Scandinavian immigration (Babcock 1914; Barone 2013; Friis 1976; Fuchs 1968; Jones 1960; Kettner 1978; Miller and Marzik 1977; Stephenson 1969; Zolberg 2008).

Their entrance in smaller numbers, and their settlement in the interior, accounts for their slower involvement in politics. At first they struggled with simply establishing viable settlements on the then frontier. Strongly desiring to assimilate, they insisted on mastering English as quickly as possible. Public schools were established and they insisted on school being conducted only in English. Political involvement came after they had achieved a degree of economic and social success. Their standard of living was soon comparable to that of the native stock in frontier settlements. Describing Norwegian settlers in 1889, one writer said of them: "Most of them came with just enough money to buy government land and build a shack. Now they loan money to their neighbors . . . Every county has a Norwegian worth $25,000 to $50,000, all made since settling in the Dakotas" (cited in Dinnerstein and Reimers 1975: 97–98).

By 1880, they had acquired a good understanding of American politics. They were openly patriotic, and learned the political ropes by organizing new townships, working the town machinery, carrying out local elections, levying and collecting taxes, and laying new roads. Since they often created whole new towns, more than one-fifth of the men participated in local affairs, including many who were not yet naturalized citizens but were allowed to vote in local elections (Friis 1976). By the time of the Civil War, they were mostly affiliated with the Republican Party (Zolberg 2008).

As was the case with other immigrant groups, Scandinavian political activity was initially centered on local offices. The first Scandinavian-born politician to succeed at state-level politics was a Norwegian, James Reymert, who represented Racine County in the second constitutional convention in Wisconsin in 1847. After the Civil War, however, Scandinavians became visibly involved in state-level politics, at least as can be measured by their electoral success. Norwegian-born Knute Nelson was the first governor of a state with many Scandinavian immigrants. He was elected in succession to the legislatures of Wisconsin and Minnesota, and to the governorship of Minnesota on the Republican Party ticket in 1892. By the 1890s, many Scandinavians served in the Wisconsin, Minnesota, and Dakota state legislatures (LeMay 1985: 46).

When they first came in significant numbers to the United States, just prior to the Civil War, the slavery question aroused them, and they quickly indoctrinated other newcomers to their communities (again, often by chain migration patterns) to the anti-slavery issue, then the most burning political issue in American politics, and the most hotly contested public policy concern. With that as the base issue for them as a voting bloc, they stuck together on other policy questions as well. Using their religious ideas (staunchly Protestant) to help them decide on many political issues, they allied themselves as a significant voting bloc with the Republican Party. They considered the GOP as the party of "moral ideas" and seldom defected from it. On the Greenback vote in Wisconsin, for example, only 3 percent of Scandinavians voted Democratic, and only 2 percent went so in Minnesota. That was the first time the Scandinavians "broke" with the Republican Party, small though that break was seen. They broke several more times in other issues, such as agricultural education, and on election reforms. Each break resulted in fewer returning to the flock, but for the most part, Scandinavians to this day are strongly Republican (LeMay 1985: 46).

The tradition churches in the Scandinavian region were the Danish National Church, the Church of Sweden (both the national branches of Lutheranism), and the Norwegian Lutheran Church. Norwegian immigration began in 1825, and in the 1830s a group known as "sloopers" (since they sailed in smaller groups of 50–100 on board sloop ships) settled in Illinois, then spread out to Iowa, Wisconsin, and Minnesota in the 1850s, and to the Dakotas in the 1870s, drawn by the Homestead Act land. They were among the most rural of the major nineteenth century immigrant groups. Among the sloopers were many Lutheran Pietists and Quakers, who chose to emigrate as a result of persecution by Lutheran clergy in their homeland. Their exodus rose in the 1840s, and by 1865 nearly 80,000 Norwegians had settled in the United States, and during the 1870 to 1880 decade, about 110,000 arrived.

In the then frontier region of the upper Midwest, their Lutheran churches became the focal point in rural settlements, and a conservative force in their political life. Scandinavian congregations became all-encompassing institutions for their members, providing tight social networks that touched all aspects of immigrant life and helped with their rapid incorporation into American society. Traditional religious practice also made the Norwegian and Swedish churches important institutions in the urban environment as well, especially in the Chicago area. The freedom of religion atmosphere that characterized American life before and after the Civil War shaped their development. Norwegian Lutherans exhibited a tradition of disharmony and denominational schisms. The Church of Norway essentially abandoned the immigrants to America, and as a result some 14 Lutheran synods were founded by Norwegian immigrants between 1846 and 1900. There were also substantial numbers of Methodists among the Norwegian Americans, especially in the Chicago area. They established a Norwegian Methodist seminary in Evanston, Illinois. Others converted to the Baptist faith. As noted, there were Quakers and Pietists among the "sloopers." And some joined the Mormons and were among those who made the Great Trek west to Salt Lake City.

Their assimilation was comparatively rapid. By the 1930s, Scandinavians had ceased to be thought of as a foreign ethnic group that was appreciably different, and therefore subject to discrimination. By the 1950s, third-generation Scandinavian Americans were fully a part of the WASP (White Anglo-Saxon Protestant) majority in the United States. "By appearance, by democratic attitude, by ambition, and by religion, the Scandinavians took root quickly in America" (Babcock 1914: 27).

Other Old Immigrant Groups

Several other national origin groups arrived in sufficient numbers during the 1820–1880 era to be grouped with the old immigrant wave: the Dutch, French, Scots, Scotch-Irish, and Welsh. They exhibit patterns similar to those discussed earlier and will be but briefly touched upon here (LeMay 1985: 47–50).

The Dutch

Total immigration from the Netherlands is under one-half million. In the 2000 U.S. census, which is the last one that asked respondents to self-identify their ancestry, just over 5.2 million claimed Dutch ancestry, and immigrants from the Netherlands ranked 9th of the top 25 in claimed ancestry nation of origin. Although more than half of those who came from the Netherlands did so in the 1880–1920 era, and thus among the new immigrants, they are grouped with the old immigrants because they came in significant numbers during the earlier era, and their greatest impact on American society was during the Colonial and pre-Civil War periods (Brinks 1995; Goodfriend 1992; Van Hinte 1985). Dutch influence is especially strong in New Jersey and New York. Indeed, European settlement in what is now New York State began as the Dutch Colony of New Amsterdam. The director-general of the New Amsterdam colony, equivalent to the state's governor, was Peter Stuyvesant, who served as such from 1647 until the British captured it in 1664. Brooklyn, the Bowery, and the Bronx, for example, all take their names as derivatives of Dutch words. By 1790, there were about 100,000 Dutch settled in the United States. The Dutch language remained a major one in the area for some time, still being spoken as late as 1950 among older people in Ramapo valley, New Jersey (DeJong 1975; Goodfriend 1992; LeMay 1985: 47; Swierenga 1985).

The most prominent American-born politician of Dutch ancestry was Martin Van Buren (1782–1862). Van Buren is generally credited with forming the Albany Regency in New York State politics, and with being the "founding organizer" of the Jacksonian Democratic Party. He and his wife, Hannah, spoke Dutch at home. He went on to serve as the eighth president of the United States (1837–1841) and had also served as vice president and as the tenth secretary of state (both under Andrew Jackson).

The Dutch exemplify another nationality group among whom religious dissenters from the Old World founded colonies in the United States. In the case of those from the Netherlands, these religious dissenters settled in Michigan and Iowa in 1846 (Brinks 1995; Swierenga 1985). Their emigration coincided with the potato famine and the ensuing economic depression which hit their Dutch homeland, as it did much of northern Europe, in the mid-to late 1840s (Van Hinte 1985). These religious separatists established a settlement which became Holland, Michigan, and it served as the prototype for a new wave of immigrants settling in Wisconsin, Illinois, as well as Michigan and Iowa. The soil and climate were favorable to them as evocative of their homeland.

The uniting force among these settlements was religion rather than national identity. Subsequent religious schisms resulted in the formation of the Dutch Reformed Church, the Christian Reformed Church, and the Netherlands Reformed Church. The Holland, Michigan, settlement was especially successful. They achieved high social status, in part reflected by their establishment of Hope College. The Christian Reformed Church, a more conservative group, emulated their example by founding Calvin

College in Grand Rapids, Michigan (Van Hinte 1985; LeMay 2013, v. 1: 38). Dutch settlers, whether rural or urban, generally were middle-class in income and occupational status. As one scholar puts it:

> Although most of the Dutch immigrants have come to the United States during the same period as the southern, central, and eastern Europeans, they have not encountered ethnic antagonism and they have assimilated more easily. Their physical features, their religion, and their comparatively small numbers, and their more urbanized backgrounds have enabled them to both adapt and to gain approval from the dominant society more easily than other groups. (Parrillo 1980: 127)

As was the case with the German immigrants, Dutch immigrants achieved economic success and status before entering American politics, except in New York and New Jersey, where they were active in politics from the colonial period onward.

The French

France has been the source of a significant and rather lengthy flow of immigrants to the United States. Their immigration pattern can be usefully categorized into three distinct subgroups: (1) immigrants coming from France itself and especially in the early days of the American republic (roughly 40 percent of the total); (2) French Louisianans, for the "Cajun," who were expelled from Acadia French Canada when the British took over Canada in 1755; and (3) French Canadians who migrated south and settled primarily in New England, and in Upper Peninsula Michigan, the Midwest, and later to California. The total number of French immigrants was under one million, but in the 2000 census, Americans claiming French descant numbered just under 10 million and France ranked 5th among the top 25 claimed nations of origin (Table 2.1) (Brasseaux 1990; Duroselle 1976; Ekberg 1998; Houde 1994; Robbins 1981).

Many colonial era immigrants from France were Huguenots, Protestants who were fleeing religious persecution (Bernstein 1990; Robbins 1981). Many of them readily changed to the Anglican Church in America, and that religious denominational conversion, plus their rapid adoption of English, eased their assimilation. They experienced some hostility, however, as a result of their anti-British animosity. They often anglicized their names and customs, however, which resulted in the animosity towards them being relatively short-lived. When France became a major ally during the American Revolutionary War, their assimilation was greatly facilitated. It was the French diplomat, De Crevecoeur, who first used the concept of the United States as the asylum for the poor of Europe and who popularized the image of America as being a great melting pot (Parrillo 1980: 128; Rischin 1976: 24).

In stark contrast, a wave of French immigrants came to the United States (and some fled to Quebec province, Canada) immediately after the French Revolution. That surge included many French aristocrats, who unlike their earlier compatriots, kept to themselves and interacted less with the American native-stock whom they held to be socially inferior. They rejected citizenship and many returned to France after the fall of Napoleon (LeMay 1985: 48–49).

The French Revolution briefly aroused anti-French sentiment—in some respects to the point of hysteria—registered as fear of the extremism and violence associated with the bloody "Reign of Terror," 1793–1794. Maximilien Robespierre, who led the Committee on Public Safety, ruled as a virtual dictator for about a year. More than 16,000 persons were executed by guillotine, and some estimates on the number who died in the revolution's bloodiest year may have been as many as 40,000 (Bernstein 1990). The excesses of the French Revolution raised fear among the population in the American eastern-seaboard states. Anti-French xenophobia led the Federalist Party to enact the Alien and Sedition acts that directly resulted in changes in naturalization policy (although not yet any immigration policy per se). The Federalist Party controlled Congress in 1795, and turmoil in Europe influenced the foreign policy making of President John Adams's Administration (1797–1801), its domestic policy on naturalization, and on presidential power to deport aliens. President Adams was one of the Founding Fathers and the second president, and a prominent Federalist, the only one to serve under that party label. While under control of the Federalist Party, Congress amended the Naturalization Act of 1795 (1 Stat. 414), which had set the period of required residency from two to five years, and the renunciation of former allegiances. The Naturalization Act of June 18, 1798 (1 Stat. 566), further and dramatically increased the residency period to 14 years and required the renunciation of former titles of nobility (although not stipulated as such, only the French aristocrats would be affected by it). Those same fears inspired the Federalists to enact the Alien Act of 1798 (Act of June 25, 1798, 1 Stat. 570). This Act, too, did not specify that it was directed at French immigrants, although events in France clearly inspired the law. It required the oath of allegiance, and granted the president sweeping power to remove aliens deemed suspected of sedition. The law had a two-year sunset clause and was not renewed in 1801 when the Jeffersonian Democrats took power and controlled both the White House and the Congress. Although President Adams did not use the power granted to him by the Alien Act to summarily deport any French immigrants, it's passage set the precedent whereby Congress would later enact restrictive laws of immigration and granted the president, through the secretary of state, sweeping enforcement powers concerning immigration used in subsequent war periods (in particular during the War of 1812, the Spanish-American War, World War I, and World War II) (LeMay and Barkan 1999: 13–16).

The Louisiana French became part of the United States by absorption in the Louisiana Purchase in 1803 (negotiated by President Jefferson with Napoleon, who was anxious to sell the land when he was desperate for an infusion of money to help finance his wars of imperialism and colonization) (Brasseaux 1990). The Cajuns exhibited a pattern of slower assimilation reflecting their strong and persistent subculture that absorbed people of other ethnic cultures who moved into their territory, often through intermarriage with Cajon people, especially Cajun women, and its strongly matriarchal socialization. Their subculture emphasized the role of their French-speaking clergy, the appeal of the French way of life, and the continued use of French language (or its Cajun dialect) that persisted for years.

French Canadians migrated after American independence into New England states and northern Michigan, Illinois, and Wisconsin (Ekberg 1998). They left when overpopulation in French-speaking Quebec and the diminishing size of agricultural land that had been subdivided to the point even subsistence farming was tenuous. Their peak period was between 1860 and 1900 when an estimated 300,000 emigrated, drawn to the mill and factory towns of New England and to Michigan, Illinois, and Wisconsin. Parrillo estimates the total French-Canadian influx at a half-million. Like their Cajun cousins, the family and church structures account for their persistent subculture and slow rate of assimilation (Bugelski 1961: 148–153; Dinnerstein and Jaher 1977; Ekberg 1998; Fitzpatrick 1966; Greely 1974; LeMay 1985: 48–49; Parrillo 1980: 131; Thernstrom 1980).

The Scots, Scotch-Irish, and the Welsh

The Scots, Scotch-Irish, and Welsh immigrants exhibit similar patterns of immigration, assimilation and incorporation. They all began their immigration to the United States during colonial times, and have all assimilated comparatively easily.

In the 2000 census, respondents claiming Scot heritage ranked 7th among the top 25 countries of origin, and numbered just under 5.5 million. The Scotch-Irish ranked 8th, and numbered just over 5 million. The Welsh ranked 15th, and numbered just under 1.9 million (Table 2.1). The Scotch-Irish came from Ireland, but from the northern and Protestant portion of Ireland. Many were descendants of Scots who had migrated to Ireland under English rule and policy to move Protestants to settle in Ireland. They used the term "Scotch-Irish" to identify themselves in America to avoid animosity and discrimination as being distinct from the Irish immigrants from the south who were Roman Catholic.

They settled especially in the Mid-Atlantic region. In religious preferences, they were Presbyterians, Episcopalians, and Anglicans, which helped promote their reputations for following a strict moral code, the Protestant work ethic, and a common image for frugality and honesty, which helped their assimilation among Calvinist New Englanders. They were farmers or miners. In the latter occupation, they were sought for as skilled workers and often served as superintendents and foremen. That did inspire some degree of animosity among the native-stock workers who saw them as economic threats (Hansen 1961: 49; McClemore 1980: 36).

Nativist Political Reaction to Changing Immigration and Their Policy Demands

The successive surges of the old immigrants did not go unnoticed by the native stock, White-Anglo-Saxon Protestant (WASP) majority population (Barone 2013; LeMay 2013, v. 1: 215–236). What began as a social movement that came to be known as the Know-Nothing Party was unquestionably the most significant anti-immigrant movement prior to the Civil War. It had roots in other political party developments, such as the Whig and the Free Soil parties. Like the Tea Party movement of today's American politics, it developed as a true grassroots social movement, a loose collection of secret social organizations that quickly coalesced into a third political party in the 1850s, with meteoric political successes and an equally stunning and rapid political demise.

It can be argued reasonably that the Know-Nothing movement was the first truly effective xenophobic movement in the United States. Like an intricate tapestry, it wove together strands of cultural identity, economic ideology, nativism, a political ideology, racism, religion and religious fundamentalism and evangelism, and xenophobia. Its various wings, factions, and organizational parts were stridently anti-Catholic, anti-foreign, and anti-Semitic; and a portion of its membership, primarily its southern wing, was proslavery and anti-black as well (Alexander 1961; Anbinder 1992; Beals 1960; Bennet 1988; Billington 1974; Higham 1955; Holt 1992; Howe 1973; Mulkern 1997; Nevins 1947; Overdyke 1968; Silbey 1991; Wilentz 2005).

In some of its tactics, the Know-Nothing Party, and in particular its violent Plug-Ugly faction, was what would be described in today's parlance a terrorist organization that foreshadowed the post-Civil War development of the Ku Klux Klan (Melton 2005).

As both a social movement and a political movement, it was the very embodiment of nativism, and arguably the purest political manifestation of the WASP in American politics and society, and in their pressure to amend immigration policy (Billington 1938).

As we have seen, in the decades between the Founding and 1830, about 350,000 immigrants came to the United States, and between 1830 and 1850, nearly two million arrived. The dramatic increase in the rate of immigrant arrivals coupled with the all-too-apparent Democratic Political Party involvement with Roman Catholic immigrants in places like New York City, where they were so heavily concentrated, aroused the first manifestations of nativism. Historian John Higham defines and describes the xenophobic characteristic of nativism so evident within the social movement:

"The grand work of the American Party," proclaimed one of the Know-Nothing journals in 1855, "is the principle of nationality . . . we must do something to protect and vindicate it. If we do not, it will be destroyed." Here is the ideological core of nativism in every form. Whether the nativist is a workingman or a Protestant evangelist, a southern conservative or a northern reformer, he stood for a certain kind of nationalism. He believed—whether he was trembling at a Catholic menace to American liberty, fearing the invasion of pauper labor, or simply rioting against the great English actor William Macready—that some *influence originating abroad* threatened the very life of the nation from within. Nativism, therefore, should be defined as intense opposition to an internal minority on the ground of its foreign (i.e. "un-American") connections. (Higham 1955: 4, my italics)

Membership in the movement was limited to Protestants of British ancestry over the age of 21. They were mostly middle class. The movement began in 1843 in New York under the name of the American Republican Party, then spread and became a regional party in 1845 with the name of Native American Party. It renamed itself yet again in 1855 as simply the American Party, but has always been better known as the Know-Nothing Party (Billington 1938: 337; Wilentz 2005).

The rapid increase in immigration, especially of Catholics from Germany and Ireland, was viewed with alarm by the Whig Party, integral to the Second Party System, that formed during the early to mid-1830s largely in opposition to the policies of President Andrew Jackson and his Democratic Party (Anbinder 1992; Howe 1973; Silbey 1991).

The Whigs favored modernization and protectionism, and congressional rather than presidential dominance in the national government's policy-making apparatus. The party emerged from the remnants of the Federalist Party, the National Republican Party, and the Anti-Masonic Party. It adopted its name to evoke the image of the patriots of 1776, who in the style of the day donned powdered wigs. The members of the Whig Party thus indicated they envisioned themselves, like the Founding Fathers, as opposing tyranny (Holt 1992: 27–30), which characteristic they attributed to Andrew Jackson.

The Whig Party's most notable leadership included Senator Daniel Webster, President William Henry Harrison, and Senator Henry Clay. The former Federalist president, John Quincy Adams, joined the party after he was elected back into the House of Representatives in 1831. For the presidential elections between 1836 and 1860, the party splintered and nominated war heroes of the War of 1812: Zachary Taylor and Winfield Scott (in an obvious effort to counter the appeal of war-hero Andrew Jackson). It nominated but lost the election of 1836 when the party factionalized and nominated several candidates with regional appeal. Table 2.2 lists the presidential tickets, electoral-college votes, and percent popular votes for the elections between 1836 and 1880.

Abraham Lincoln began his political life as a Whig Party leader in Illinois. They held their first nominating convention in 1839. The party succeeded in having two of its nominees elected president only to die in office—William Harrison and Zachary Taylor. Harrison won, in part, by promising only to run for one term, and partly because of the unpopularity of President Van Buren over the Panic of 1837. John Tyler, Harrison's vice president, and a Virginian and states' rights absolutist, succeeded him after Harrison's mere 31 days in office. Tyler was expelled from the party after his veto of the Whig economic program in 1841. In the 1844 election, the Whigs nominated then former senator Henry Clay, who lost. The Whigs won with General Zachary Taylor in 1848, with his vice presidential running mate, Millard Fillmore, a New York State Comptroller. Fillmore became president upon the death of Taylor. He was the last Whig to

Table 2.2 Presidential Election Results, 1836–1880

Year: Party	Ticket	ECV	% PV
1836	Democrat	Martin Van Buren, VP. Richard Johnson	170	50.8
	Whig	William Harrison, VP Francis George	73	36.6
	Whig	Hugh White, VP John Tyler	76	9.7
	Whig	Daniel Webster, VP Francis George	14	2.7
1840	Whig	William Harrison, VP. John Tyler	234	52.9
	Democrat	Martin Van Buren, VP Richard Johnson	60	46.8
1844	Democrat	James Polk, VP. George Dallas	170	49.5
	Whig	Henry Clay, VP. Theodore Frelinghuysen	105	48.1
1848	Whig	Zachary Taylor, VP Millard Filmore	163	47.3
	Democrat	Lewis Cass, VP. William Butler	127	42.5
	Free Soil	Martin Van Buren, VP Charles Adams	0	10.1
1852	Democrat	Franklin Pierce, VP. William King	254	50.8
	Whig	Winfield Scott, VP. William Graham	42	43.9
	Free Soil	John Hale, VP George W. Julian	0	4.9
1856	Democrat	James Buchanan, VP John Breckinridge	174	45.3
	Republican	John Fremont, VP. William Dayton	114	31.3
	Whig-American	Millard Fillmore, VP Andrew J. Donelson	8	21.6
1860	Republican	Abraham Lincoln, VP. Hannibal Hamlin	180	31.9

Year: Party	Ticket	ECV		% PV
	S. Democrat	John Breckinridge, VP. Joseph Lane	72	18.1
	Const. Union	John Bell, VP. Edward Everett	39	12.6
	Democrat	Stephen Douglas, VP. Herschel Johnson	12	29.5
1864	Republican	Abraham Lincoln, VP. Andrew Johnson	212	55.1
	Democrat	George McClellan, VP. George Pendleton	26	44.9
1868	Republican	Ulysses Grant, VP. Schuyler Colfax	214	52.7
	Democrat	Horatio Seymour, VP. Francis Blair	80	47.3
1872	Republican	Ulysses Grant, VP. Henry Wilson	286	55.6
	Democrat	Horace Greeley, VP. Benjamin Brown	0	43.8
1876	Republican	Rutherford Hayes, VP. William Wheeler	185	48
	Democrat	Samuel Tilden, VP. Thomas Hendricks	184	51.0
1880	Republican	James Garfield, VP. Chester Arthur	214	48.3
	Democrat	Winfield Hancock, VP. William English	155	48.2

Source: Table by author; data from www.presidency.ucsb.edu/showelection.php?Year.

be president, serving from 1850 to 1853. In 1856, the Whigs nominated Fillmore again, along with a former U.S. ambassador, Andrew Jackson Donelson, a nephew of President Jackson. They were the ticket, as well, of the American Party, better known as the Know-Nothing Party. It was founded in 1845, was forthrightly anti-immigrant, and advocated the total rejection of foreigners (LeMay and Barkan 1999, Document 23: 28–29).

In the 1860 election, the last in which the Whigs fielded a ticket, they nominated former senator John Bell, who was also on the Constitutional Union ticket with former senator Edward Everett. It lost the election. It

ceased to exist after the 1860 election, with most of its adherents supporting the Republican Party of Abraham Lincoln thereafter, and with its
southern wing joining the Democrats (Alexander 1961; Silbey 1991; Holt
1992; Howe 1973).

To a degree, the Whig Party was organized in opposition to Andrew
Jackson, who they viewed as dangerously reactionary. They were formed
under the leadership of Federalist John Quincy Adams and Kentucky
senator Henry Clay. They controlled the Senate in the mid-1830s and
passed the Compromise of 1833 (on tariff policy) as well as a censure
motion denouncing President Jackson as usurping executive power in the
face of the true will of the people as represented by Congress. Clay had
opposed Jackson in 1832, but had lost the popular vote by a wide margin,
and the vote in the Electoral College vote by Jackson's 219 to his 49.

The Whig Party suffered from factionalism throughout its time on the
national scene. Its strength depended on a network of newspapers, such
as the powerful *New York Tribune*, edited by Horace Greeley. It had a successful showing in the 1840s in the Northeast, with its strong manufacturing base, and the region in which the party won nearly half of the
governorships. The Know-Nothing movement was strong in the same
regional base. It was a power in Ohio, where several newspapers, in
Youngstown and Cleveland, espoused the movement's beliefs. WASPs in
Ohio disliked the Catholic Church for opposing taxation to finance public schools. Ohio's American Party allied with the Fusion Party, a precursor to the Republican Party. The Know-Nothing Party appealed to the
professional and business classes: to doctors, lawyers, merchants, ministers, bankers, shop owners, and factory owners (who today would be
referred to as small businessmen), commercially oriented farmers (as
opposed to the small farmer, or yeoman in Jefferson's terminology), and
large-scale plantation owners.

Protestant religious revivals, common in the 1840s and early 1850s
and referred to as the Second Great Awakening, injected a moralistic fervor to the Whigs and the American Party (Anbinder 1992; Bilhartz 1986;
Green 2010; Howe 1973; Voss-Hubbard 2002). They opposed the Democrats who were strongest in the West and the South, and whose coalition
reached out to the Irish and German Catholic immigrants who voted
heavily Democratic. In no small measure, the Whig's demise can be
attributed to their failure to reach out positively to the ever-growing number of naturalized immigrant citizens.

In 1850, the Kansas-Nebraska Act opened new territories to slavery.
Southern Whigs supported it, Northern Whigs opposed it. The latter
increasingly joined the newly established Republican Party, reacting

strongly to the repeal of the Missouri Compromise. Many former Whigs shifted to the Know-Nothing Party (i.e., the American Party), attracted by its nativist crusade against the "corrupt" Irish and German immigrants (Anbinder 1992; Billington 1974; Howe 2007; McGreevey 2003; Mulkern 1997).

The increasing number of immigrants and especially Catholic immigrants and their influence in Eastern cities where both Irish and German Catholic immigrants concentrated, led to the reaction whereby nativist societies formed to combat what they viewed to be the undue foreign influence and to uphold the "American view." Largely local, often secret, societies and associations spawned a grassroots social movement that quickly took on political party aspirations. The American Party formed in 1843 in New York State, spread to neighboring states, under the moniker of the Native American Party, which went national with its Philadelphia Convention on July 4, 1845. In its declaration of party principles, the party stated that the danger of foreign influence threatened the very destruction of national institutions, and threatened to poison American policy with the influence of a "European policy," one, in their view, at war with the fundamental principles of the Constitution (Holt 1992; LeMay and Barkan 1999: 26–29).

German and Irish Catholics loudly proclaimed their independence from the clergy when it came to politics and public policy, but the Protestants comprising the Know-Nothing movement did not believe them. The movement feared that the pope (Pius IX, at the time) would adversely affect American politics as they asserted he had done to European politics over the failed liberal revolutions in 1848. They saw the pope and the American hierarchy of the church (especially the bishops in Boston, New York City, and Philadelphia, who were selected by the pope), as an ally of tyranny. The social movement that came to be called the Know-Nothing Party began as the Order of the Star-Spangled Banner in 1848–1849, in New York City. The order was created by Charles Allen. This secret society formed the nucleus of much of the American Party (McGreevey 2003: 22–25; *Encyclopedia Britannica*).

The grassroots social movement soon morphed into a political one. The Know-Nothing movement spread rapidly, stalled but briefly by the Mexican War in 1848. It revived and formed chapters in Massachusetts and Pennsylvania, then spread to Rhode Island, New Hampshire, Connecticut, Delaware, Maryland, Kentucky, and Texas. By the 1854 elections, it exhibited strong influence in Virginia, Georgia, Alabama, Mississippi, and Louisiana (Nevins 1947: 329; Smith 1969: 141). In 1854, it won the governorship of New York as well as 40 seats in the New York

State legislature. In 1855, they elected a host of local government officials as well as eight state governors. They elected 43 of their members to the U.S. House of Representatives and 5 to the U.S. Senate. The Party's membership increased in 1854–1855 from an estimated 50,000 to an estimated 1 million members (Anbinder 1992: 75–102).

> The key to Know Nothing success in 1854 was the collapse of the second party system brought about primarily by the demise of the Whig party. The Whig party, weakened for years by internal dissent and chronic factionism, was nearly destroyed by the Kansas-Nebraska Act. Growing anti-party sentiment, fueled by anti-slavery as well as temperance and nativism, also contributed to the disintegration of the party system. The collapsing second party system gave the Know Nothings a much larger pool of potential converts than was available to previous nativist organizations, allowing the Order to succeed where other nativist groups had failed. (Anbinder 1992: 95)

Despite their electoral success, the party's elected members were unable to pass significant bills in Congress that called for the prohibition of foreign-born paupers. They failed to enact literacy tests for voters in several states where they attempted to do so.

By then, moreover, the debates over slavery dominated the national scene. When the issue appeared, briefly, to be laid to rest by the Compromise of 1850, the nativist social movement reemerged and the number of secret orders grew. The most important and notable among them were the Order of United Americans and the Order of the Star-Spangled Banner. At first but loosely knit secret societies, their members battled political managers of the established political parties (Democrats and Whigs). Attempts to subsume them were stifled by their members meeting all inquiries of the parties with the statement that they, in effect, knew nothing of the movement—which gave rise to their becoming known as the Know Nothings, although there was never an organization with that as its official name (Bailey 1976: 135; Billington 1938: 337).

The social movement was, at first, simply anti-immigrant and advocated highly restrictive immigration policy but became increasingly political when the loose coalition of social movement groups began to insist that its followers elect only native-born Americans to office, and agitating for a 20- to 25-year residency qualification for naturalization. In 1850, the party sold lithographs that depicted an idealized, white American, known as Uncle Sam's Youngest Son, Citizen Know-Nothing. The Library of Congress notes that the portrait represents the nativist ideal of the Know-Nothing Party. The social movement spread rapidly in the 1850s and its members and leaders began to associate with the group of Whigs who followed Millard Fillmore into the American Party. The party came under the leadership of a New York City merchant and political leader, James W. Barker. They nearly captured New York State in the 1854 election and had great success in Massachusetts and Delaware, where they swept the polls. In the 1856 presidential election, Fillmore carried only the state of Maryland, and by then the American Party took a stance that was too blatantly anti-Catholic to succeed nationally, and in the election was purposively silent on the slavery question. Millard Fillmore received only 874,534 votes and played the spoiler, with the presidency going to Democrat James Buchanan who defeated Republican John Fremont as well as Fillmore (Table 2.2; Mulkern 1997). By this time all the party's candidates had to be native-born. The party was clearly trying to disenfranchise Irish Catholics, by then arriving in great numbers, who would be unable thereby to vote for many years.

In other states they had considerable success at the local office level. In California, where the population swelled as a result of the 1848 Gold Rush, they elected city officials in the then boom city of San Francisco, as well as several statewide officials. The San Francisco chapter of the party, begun by Sam Roberts, was formed in opposition to Chinese and Irish immigrants (Anbinder 1992). Following their success in 1849, a Know-Nothing judge on California's Supreme Court ruled that the Chinese were forbidden to testify against white men in court (LeMay 2013, v. 1: 222). As the movement spread to the South, by 1854, and aided by the disintegration of the Whig Party, the Know-Nothing Party made great strides as a national social movement. In 1855, they assumed the name American Party and cast aside their character as a secret society. In 1855, Know-Nothing candidate Levi Boone was elected mayor of Chicago, where he barred all immigrants from city jobs. The American Party, however, was less effective state-wide. In 1855, the party also gained strength in Ohio, even winning over German American Lutherans (who were native-born, second generation), Scotch-Irish Presbyterians, and Dutch Reformed Church adherents, to whom the party's anti-Catholicism appealed (Anbinder 1992: 34–43). In Alabama, the party congealed with a mix of former Whigs, unhappy Democrats, and other political outsiders who ran on a slate to build more railroads. They failed to carry the state as concern grew that the American Party could not protect the institution of slavery from the influence of the party's northern and staunchly abolitionist wing (Bennet 1988: 15). One historian of the movement notes: "Know Nothingism originated in the South for the same reason it spread in the North—nativism, anti-Catholicism, and animosity toward unresponsive politicos—not because of conservative unionism" (Holt 1992: 856).

The Party's peak year was 1854. It scored impressive victories in Massachusetts, taking control of the state legislature, and polled 40 percent of the vote in Pennsylvania. In the South, as noted, it attracted former Whigs. It was the last election before the newly formed Republican Party emerged as the second major party in the United States.

The peak year for the social movement was 1855. Its name gained wide, if brief, popularity. Nativism became something of a rage, with such items as Know-Nothing candy, Know-Nothing tea, and Know-Nothing toothpicks. Stagecoaches were dubbed the Know Nothings, and a shipmaster from Maine even called his freighter, Know Nothing (Bennet 1988: 15).

Precisely at its peak as a social movement, however, in June 1855, at a meeting of the political party's national council held in Philadelphia, the southerners in the social movement and the recently coalesced national political party, took control of the political side of the movement and adopted a resolution calling for the maintenance of slavery. The contentious slavery issue emerged front and center in American politics after the Kansas-Nebraska Act in 1850. Between 1850 and the 1856 national elections, the slavery issue loosened ties so that many voters who were not yet ready to cast their votes with either the pro-slavery Democrats or the anti-slavery Republican Party, found a temporary home in the Know-Nothing Party. Deep-rooted feelings among many in the native stock, stirred by the massive immigration that followed the potato famine in Ireland and Northern Europe, aroused fear and hostility that led to the party's rapid rise and local and state electoral successes. By 1855, however, as the party took a position on the all-important slavery question, the movement was essentially broken over the issue. Even the party leader, James Barker of New York City, left the party and supported Abraham Lincoln in the 1860 election (Beals 1960; Billington 1974; Nevins 1947; Smith 1969).

The American Party declined in the north as rapidly as it had arisen. It was divided over the slavery issue in the 1856 election. Its northern faction supported former Whig president Millard Fillmore, and Andrew Jackson Donelson. The ticket was designed to appeal to loyalists from both the Whigs and the Democrats. Despite its balanced slate, it received only 23 percent of the popular vote. The Supreme Court's decision in the 1857 Dred Scott case proved to be the party's death knell. The anti-slavery wing joined the Republicans en masse, and the proslavery wing remained active only at the state and local levels in the South. By 1860, the party was no longer a serious national party and its few remaining members supported the Constitutional-Union Party in that election (Anbinder 1992: 103).

As a loose-knit social movement, Know Nothings attracted the working class who feared their jobs were or would be overtaken by foreigners who would also undermine institutions at the very core of society. They feared the increasing political clout of the urban machines, like Tammany Hall. Such fears were not unfounded. The new immigrants were flocking into the cities (LeMay 2013, v. 1: 47–71). In the eyes of the Know-Nothing movement's adherents, immigrants caused unbelievable overcrowding. They constituted a massive pool of cheap labor which employers were quick to exploit. New immigrants were willing to do almost any job for very low pay and the business elite continued to advocate for a totally open door approach to immigration policy. Know-Nothing supporters felt large-scale immigration led to overall low pay and absolutely deplorable working conditions. This position attracted some support among the by then largely local but growing labor unions, and among a variety of urban social reformers.

Still others were attracted to the social movement out of a deep-seated fear of Catholicism, the denominational affiliation evident among ever larger portions of the immigrants surging into the country after 1840 (Barone 2013). Immigration from Germany was increasingly Catholic. Immigrants from Ireland were, by 1850, mostly from Southern Ireland, also overwhelmingly Catholic rather than the previous Presbyterian, Scotch-Irish from northern counties. Persons attracted to the Know-Nothing movement, whether its social or its political side, feared that if the Catholic immigrants gained too much political power, they would bring the nation under the control of and take order from the pope in Rome. As early as 1834, groups who called themselves "Nativists" chased a group of students and Ursuline nuns from their school and burned the building. By 1835, New Yorkers organized a state political party, the Native American Party, which ran on a platform of opposing Catholics and immigrants. By 1840 such groups appeared in Baltimore, Philadelphia, and Providence (LeMay 1985: 50–53). The groups seemingly appeared and disappeared over time, but eventually the overarching theme of hostility toward immigrant foreigners began to unite such social groups into opposition to the perceived costs of trying to support and educate the indigent foreigner.

In response to the growing anti-immigrant rhetoric of the movement, ethnic associations among immigrant groups formed to counter the hostility expressed against them. Reacting to the prejudice, they formed protective associations, like the Irish Catholic Benevolent Union, founded by

Dennis Dwyer, which by 1870 was playing a significant role in electoral politics (LeMay 2009: 126).

Plug Ugly groups associated with the Know-Nothing movement rose up to burn Catholic convents, churches and homes, assault nuns, and murder Irishmen, Germans, and Negroes (Beals 1960: 9). A violent hate campaign was unleashed and a number of cities where immigrants were concentrated experienced violent anti-immigrant rioting. Philadelphia saw a series of riots in 1844, from May 6 to 8, and again from July 6 to 7. These were referred to as the "prayer riots." They began with clashes between nativist Protestants and Roman Catholics over Bible reading in public schools, specifically over which version (English translation) of the Bible would be used: the Protestant King James version or the Roman Catholic Douai Rheims version. Bishop Francis Kenrich wrote a letter requesting that Catholic students be allowed to read from the Douai version. Nativists in the Southwark neighborhood of Philadelphia attacked St. Philip Nen's Catholic Church. In the May 6–8 riot, 14 were killed and 50 injured and about 200 fled their homes. The military was called in to quell the riot. Tensions broke out again in July when nativists attacked the seminary of the Sisters of Charity. They burned down St. Michael's Catholic Church and rectory. Two of the attacking nativists were killed, and before the riot ended on July 7, an estimated 20 people were killed, 50 injured, and some 5,000 militia were needed to quell the riot (Bennet 1988).

In New York City, mobs of Irish immigrants and Know-Nothing members clashed, leaving two dead, and many wounded (depicted fictionally in the 2002 Martin Scorsese movie *The Gangs of New York*). Nativists objected to the undue influence of New York City's Irish Roman Catholic Bishop, John Hughes. Tensions were so high that, in 1849, the Order of United Americans, the social movement group related to the Know-Nothing Party, organized a distinctively American regiment, legally formed in October 1850, as the 71st Infantry Regiment of New York, and called the American Rifles. Its founders were Know-Nothing leaders J. M. Parker, Hamilton Fish Jr., and William Kellock. The regiment was comprised of eight companies. In 1852, it was enrolled in the New York State Militia, and was used for riot control in 1857, as well as serving in the Civil War.

In Newark, a mob of an estimated 2,000 Protestant and Catholics squared off, leaving one dead, dozens wounded, and a Catholic church burned to the ground. In 1855, Know-Nothing members and German immigrants clashed in Louisville in an intense riot during which 20 died, and hundreds were wounded in the mayhem. In Baltimore, where the party was especially strong, numerous clashes took place, and a riot in 1854 left eight dead (Hofstadter and Wallace 1971: 313). The Plug Uglies, a splinter group of the Know-Nothing movement, was often responsible (LeMay 2009: 97; Melton 2005).

Immigrants became easy scapegoats on which to lay blame for all the problems associated with a rapidly urbanizing and industrializing society. As ghetto-like ethnic enclaves formed in the tenement slums of big cities like New York and Boston, social reformers desiring to preserve the nation's institutions and Protestant evangelicals anxious to save the nation's purity joined associations like the secret Order of the Star-Spangled Banner. As the Irish and German naturalized citizens began to become politically active, the Know-Nothing movement's leadership adopted increasingly overt political action as well (LeMay 2009: 353). They supported stringent immigration restrictions, the exclusion of the foreign-born from holding public elective office, and residency requirements of 20 to 25 years. Reformers and evangelicals sought to limit the sale of alcohol and insisted on Bible readings in public schools and tried to ensure that only Protestants would be hired to teach in public schools.

This intricate weaving in and out of the Know-Nothing Party as a social movement and as a political party is well exemplified by the brief career highlights of several notable Know-Nothing Party leaders, presented in Box 2.2.

Box 2.2:   Know-Nothing Party Leaders

Anna Ella Carroll, political pamphleteer, from Maryland. She first joined the Whig Party as a pamphleteer. She joined the American Party in 1854, after planters on the Eastern Shore formed the Maryland chapter in 1853. Along with other reformers, she campaigned against the urban machine in Baltimore and the threat of the power of the Catholic Church there. She campaigned for Fillmore in 1856, wrote two influential anti-clerical, anti-Catholic books, and several pamphlets. In 1857, she became the chief publicist for Maryland governor Thomas Hicks. With Lincoln's election in 1860, she freed her own slaves and became an abolitionist, and as a Republican, an advisor to President Lincoln.

Anson Burlingame, American diplomat and ambassador to China. Born in New York but a practicing lawyer in Boston, he was first an active leader in the Free Soil Party, serving in the state senate for them in 1853–1854. In 1855, he was elected to the House of Representatives as a Know-Nothing candidate. By 1861, he was a Republican in the Lincoln administration, as ambassador first to Austrian Empire, then to China where he served with distinction.

Henry Winter Davis, member of the House of Representatives from Annapolis, Maryland. He was at first a Whig, then switched to the American Party, and ended as a Republican and radical Reconstructionist who opposed President Lincoln's plans for Reconstruction during the Civil War.

John Crittenden, from Kentucky, served in both the House of Representatives and the U.S. Senate. He was a Whig who joined the Know-Nothing Party in 1854, and went on to serve as U.S. attorney general for Presidents Harrison and Fillmore, and then as the 17th governor of Kentucky.

William Allison, from Ohio, joined the Whig Party in 1834, then the Know-Nothing Party, and represented Iowa's Dubuque area from 1863 to 1871 as a Republican and as the Republican senator of Iowa from 1873 to 1908.

Zebulon Vance, of North Carolina, was the Know-Nothing governor of the state, then was elected to the House of Representatives as the American Party candidate in 1858. After one term, he was elected to the U.S. Senate, but during the Civil War, sided with the Confederacy and became a Democrat.

Horace Greeley, journalist, was the son of a New England farmer and day laborer in New Hampshire and began his journalism career as an apprentice to a Vermont newspaper editor. In 1831, he went to New York City. He started a new journal, *Log Cabin*, in 1834. He was a Whig Party supporter who worked in the Harrison campaign in 1840. He launched his most successful newspaper venture, *The New York Tribune*, and he became involved with the Transcendentalist movement. He was staunchly anti-slavery and opposed the Kansas-Nebraska Act in 1850. He was a Know-Nothing supporter in 1850 but by 1856 had switched to the Republican Party and attended its national convention in Pittsburgh in 1856. In Chicago, in 1860, at the Republican Convention, he supported Lincoln. During the Civil War he broke with Lincoln over reconstruction policy, and Greeley opposed Andrew Johnson's reconstruction plans as well, and advocated for Johnson's impeachment.

Schuyler Colfax is yet another Whig to Know Nothing to Republican politician, who went on to serve as vice president. Born in New

York City, Colfax moved to Indiana in 1836. He befriended Horace Greeley and wrote articles on Indiana for the *New York Tribune*, and became editor of the South Bend *Free Press* in 1845. In 1848, he joined the Whig Party and went to its national convention that year, when he also went to the Indiana Constitutional Convention. He affiliated with the American Party when the Whig Party collapsed in 1856. His anti-slavery views led him to join the Republican Party when it fused with northern Whigs. He was elected to the House of Representatives as a Republican, in 1858, was elected Speaker of the House in 1862. As Speaker, he announced passage of the 13th Amendment, in 1865. In 1868, he was elected as the 17th vice president of the United States on the ticket with President Ulysses S. Grant.

Henry Wilson, the 18th vice president, was born in New Hampshire, moved to Massachusetts in 1833, and served in the state legislature from 1841 to 1852. He was a newspaper editor of the *Boston Republic*, from 1848 to 1851. He served on the state's Constitution Convention in 1853, then ran for but lost a race to be governor in 1854. In 1855, he was elected to the U.S. Senate as a Free Soil/American Party candidate. He was reelected to the Senate in 1859 as a Republican and again in 1865 and 1871. He resigned from the Senate in 1873 to serve as vice president to Ulysses S. Grant.

Source: Adapted from LeMay 2013, v. 1: 228–231.

On the West Coast, the movement was similarly anti-immigrant but with a focus on anti-Chinese sentiment. Chinese laborers were drawn to California by the gold rush (the Chinese name for the United States was Land of the Golden Hills). Chinese immigrants were well-organized into work gangs led by a single contractor (who spoke some English) and were willing to take on virtually any job. They served as ranch hands, farm laborers, domestic servants, and most notably, worked for the Central Pacific Railroad building from the West Coast eastward. The Central Pacific employed some 9,000 immigrants (Bailey 1976; Kenefick 1985). By 1860, they comprised about 10 percent of California's population and roughly 25 percent of its labor force (LeMay 2009: 75; Thompson 1996). This explosive growth rate spurred xenophobic fear of the Yellow Peril.

By 1850, anti-Chinese sentiment was rampant in the mining regions where they were often beaten and robbed, and occasionally murdered. The Chinese could not seek redress in the courts given a Know-Nothing judge's ruling, in 1854, that they could not testify in courts against white men (*People v. Hall*, in McClain 1994: 21). Crimes against them went unpunished. Miscegenation laws (forbidding men of the Asian race from marrying white women) were but one manifestation of the legal constraints against Chinese immigrants.

By 1850, the Know-Nothing Party was a power at the state level. California essentially expelled Chinese laborers from the mining camps in 1855 with enactment of the Foreign Miners' Tax. Since the Chinese were excluded from citizenship (then open only to whites), they were forced to pay ever-higher taxes. That act, coupled with violence against them, drove them out of the mine fields.

Conclusion

Although the Know-Nothing Party ended in 1860, its anti-immigrant legacy lived on in other groups and associations after the Civil War, both as social movements and as minor political party organizations. The tapestry that was the Know-Nothing social movement and the then political party organization may have unwound by 1860, but the legacy left by the threads that had intertwined to make up the movement were still within the fabric of American political and social life. The ideas and concerns voiced by the Know-Nothing Movement and by the American Party continued through the decades after the Civil War, and can be seen up to today (LeMay 2013). Numerous parallels between the Movement and subsequent American politics are evident in succeeding decades.

Anti-immigrant minor parties carried on the tradition of the American Party's opposition to the Open Door immigration policy. Their tradition was reflected in the Prohibition Party in the 1890s, the Workingmen's Party in California in the 1880s and 1890s, in the People's Populist Party in 1890, and to a degree in the Progressive Party of the 1920s. There was another American Party formed in the 1920s that pushed for the Quota Acts to restrict immigration (Bennet 1988; Divine 1957). Likewise, in the 1960s, the George Wallace wing split from the Democratic Party when he ran for president on the American Independent Party ticket (LeMay 2009: 246; Safire 2008: 375–376). The preamble to the party platform is worth citing for its parallels to the Know-Nothing Party's principles:

> As this great nation searched vainly for leadership while beset by riots, minority-group rebellions, domestic disorders, student protests, spiraling living costs, soaring interest rates, a frightening increase in the crime rate, war abroad and the loss of liberty at home, while our national political parties and their leaders pay homage to the legions of dissent and

disorder and worship at the shrine of political expediency, only this Party, the American Independent Party, and its candidates, George C. Wallace and Curtis E. LeMay, possessed the courage and fortitude to openly propose and advocate to the nation those actions which are necessary to return the country to its accustomed and deserved position among the community of nations and to offer hope to our people of some relief from the continued turmoil, frustration, and confusion brought about through the fearful and inept leadership of our national political parties. (4president.org)

Like the Know-Nothing Party, these minor parties were all short-lived, rising and declining quickly, and espousing a narrow anti-immigration policy too limited to engender a national following large enough to achieve major party status. They, too, soon unraveled.

Various groups exemplify the continuity to the social movement of Know-Nothing nativism. After the Civil War, in 1870–1890, and again as revived in 1910–1920, the Ku Klux Klan spread not only as an anti-black organization but also as an anti-Catholic, anti-Jewish, and anti-immigrant movement and the Know Nothing-like political movement of its day, using secrecy and violence to achieve its ends (LeMay 2009: 234, 361; Reimers 1990; Safire 2008: 375–376). Klan members lynched a Jewish manager of a pencil factor, Leo Frank, in 1915. Between 1882 and 1959, Klan members lynched 2,595 blacks in nine southern states. The Klan's use of violence reflected the violent behavior of the Plug Uglies.

On the West Coast, the Workingmen's Party used electoral politics, legislative policy, and riots and violence to pursue its anti-Chinese and anti-Asian goals. In an echo of the Know Nothings, the Workingmen's Party reached a fever-pitch in the mid-1870s. In 1871, 21 Chinese were killed in a Los Angeles riot. In June 1876, the Truckee Raid occurred in which whites burned two Chinese-occupied cabins and shot and wounded the residents as they fled the flames, one of whom died of his wounds. In 1890, Denver was rocked by an anti-Chinese riot. The Order of Caucasians advocated elimination of the Chinese through the use of violence (today it would be labeled "ethnic cleansing"). They raided and burned various Chinatowns, driving hundreds from their homes. In 1885, in Rock Springs, Wyoming, a mob killed 28 Chinese. In Tacoma, Seattle, and Oregon City, mobs expelled hundreds of Chinese from those cities (LeMay 2009: 76).

The Know-Nothing social and political movement was the first embodiment of anti-immigrant attitudes of nativism in American life. It grew out of reactions to economic and social strife associated with the transformation of America from an agricultural to an industrial society, from a WASP nation to a nation-of-nations, from a rural to an urban nation, as immigrants surged in unprecedented numbers. The American Party never achieved major party status precisely because its programs and policy prescriptions were too narrow and its party platform too stridently anti-Catholic and anti-immigrant. As immigration swelled and as immigrants were naturalized in ever-larger numbers, only those parties that reached out to them with naturalization and immigration policy survived since the Civil War. Minor parties like the American Party, who were ideologically and culturally opposed to wide-scale immigration, simply withered and died (LeMay 2013, v. 1: 208–212).

The political and social groups pushing for more restrictive immigration policy were able to reach the problem formulation and the agenda-setting stages of the public policy-making process but failed to get their proposals enacted. Business groups favored open immigration and dominated the policy enactment and implementation stages of immigration policy making. There were, as always, unanticipated consequences of the current policy which led the way to the next era.

The attitudes that the social movement and the political party embodied, however, continued on in American politics and paved the way for the next era of immigration policy making, the Door Ajar era from 1880 to 1920, which will be described and analyzed in Chapter 3.

References

Adamic, Louis. 1945. *Nation of Nations.* New York: Harper Brothers.

Alexander, Thomas. 1961. "Persistent Whiggery in the Confederate South, 1860–1877." *Journal of Southern History* 27(3): 305–329.

The American Presidency Project. www.presidency.ucsb/showelections.php?Year.

Americans for Religious Liberty. https://www.arlinc.org/about/history.html. Accessed February 11, 2017.

Anbinder, Tyler. 1992. *Nation and Slavery: The Northern Know-Nothings and the Politics of the 1850s.* New York: Oxford University Press.

Archdeacon, Thomas. 1983. *Becoming American: An Ethnic History.* New York: Free Press.

Babcock, Kendrick. 1914. *The Scandinavian Element in the United States.* Urbana: University of Illinois Press.

Bailey, Thomas. 1976. *Voices of America.* New York: Free Press.

Baltzell, E. Digby. 1996. *Puritan Boston and Quaker Philadelphia.* New Brunswick: Transaction Publishers.

Barone, Michael. 2013. *Shaping Our Nation: How Surges of Migration Transformed America and Its Politics.* New York: Crown Forum.

Beals, Carleton. 1960. *Brass Knuckle Crusade.* New York: Hasting House.

Bennet, David. 1988. *The Party of Fear: From Nativist Movements to the New Right in American History.* New York: Random House.

Bernstein, Richard. 1990. *Fragile Glory: A Portrait of France and the French.* New York: Knopf.

Bilhartz, Terry D. 1986. *Urban Religion and the Second Great Awakening.* Madison, NJ: Fairleigh Dickenson University Press.

Billington, Ray. 1938. *The Protestant Crusade, 1800–1860.* New York: Macmillan.

Billington, Ray. 1974. *The Origins of Nativism in the United States, 1800–1844.* New York: Arno Press.

Brasseaux, Carl. 1990. *The "Foreign-French": Nineteenth Century French Immigration to Louisiana.* Lafayette Center for Louisiana Studies, University of Southwestern Louisiana Press.

Brinks, Herbert. 1995. *Dutch Immigrant Voices, 1850–1930.* Ithaca: Cornell University Press.

Brown, Thomas. 1966. *Irish-American Nationalism.* New York: J. P. Lippincott.

Bugelski, B. R. 1961. "Assimilation through Intermarriage." *Social Forces* 40: 148–153.

Bureau of the Census. *2000 Profile of Social Characteristics.* Washington, DC. http://www.census.gov./ Accessed April 3, 2015.

Butler, Jon. 1990. *Awash in a Sea of Faith: Christianizing the American People.* Cambridge, MA: Harvard University Press.

Byrne-Hessick, Carissa, and Gabriel J. Chin, eds. 2014. *Strange Neighbors: The Role of States in Immigration Policy.* New York: New York University Press.

Civil War. German. http://www.civilwarhome.com/german.htm. Accessed April 6, 2015.

Civil War. Irish. http://www.civilwarhome.com/irishbri.htm. Accessed April 6, 2015.

Congressional Medal of Honor Society. http://www.cmohs.org/recipients-archive .php. Accessed April 6, 2015.

DeJong, Gerald. 1975. *The Dutch in America, 1609–1974.* Boston: Twayne.

Dinnerstein, Leonard, and David Reimers. 1975. *Ethnic Americans.* New York: Harper and Row.

Dinnerstein, Leonard, and Frederick Jaher. 1977. *Uncertain Americans.* New York: Oxford University Press.

Divine, Robert A. 1957. *American Immigration Policy, 1924–1952.* New Haven, CT: Yale University Press.

Duroselle, Jean-Baptiste. 1976. *France and the United States: From Beginnings to Present.* Chicago: University of Chicago Press.

Ekberg, Carl. 1998. *French Roots in the Illinois County: The Mississippi Frontier in Colonial Time.* Urbana: University of Illinois Press.

Encyclopedia Britannica. https://www.britannica.com/topic/Know-Nothing-party.

Fitzpatrick, Joseph. 1966. "The Importance of Community in the Process of Immigration Assimilation." *International Migration Review*, 1 (January): 6–16.

4president.org. www.4president.org/brochures/1968/wallace1968brochure.htm.

Fox, Stephen. 2003. *Transatlantic*. New York: Perennial/Harper Collins.

Friis, Erick, ed. 1976. *The Scandinavian Presence in North America*. New York: Harper and Row.

Fuchs, Lawrence. 1968. *American Ethnic Politics*. New York: Harper.

Glazer, Nathan, and Daniel Moynihan. 1963. *Beyond the Melting Pot*. Cambridge, MA: Harvard University Press.

Glazer, Nathan, and Daniel Moynihan. 1975. *Ethnicity: Theory and Experience*. Cambridge, MA: Harvard University Press.

Goodfriend, Joyce. 1992. *Before the Melting Pot: Society and Culture in Colonial New York City, 1664–1730*. Princeton, NJ: Princeton University Press.

Greely, Andrew M. 1974. *Ethnicity in the United States*. New York: John Wiley.

Green, Steven K. 2010. *The Second Disestablishment: Church and State in Nineteenth Century America*. New York: Oxford University Press.

Greenstein, Fred. 1970. *The American Party System and the American People*. Upper Saddle River, NJ: Prentice Hall.

Handlin, Oscar. 1959. *Immigration as a Factor in American History*. Upper Saddle River, NJ: Prentice Hall.

Handlin, Oscar. 1979. *Boston's Immigrants*. Cambridge, MA: Harvard University Press.

Hansen, Marcus. 1961. *The Atlantic Migration, 1607–1860*. New York: Harper Torch.

Hening, William Walter, ed. 1823. *Statutes at Large of Virginia*, vol. 12: 84–86. www.vagenweb.org/hening/vol01-00.htm.

Higham, John. 1955. *Strangers in the Land: Patterns of American Nativism, 1860–1923*. New Brunswick, NJ: Rutgers University Press.

Higham, John., ed. 1978. *Ethnic Leadership in America*. Baltimore: The Johns Hopkins University Press.

Hoeder, Dirk, ed. 1982. *American Labor and Immigration History, 1877–1920*. Urbana: University of Illinois Press.

Hofstadter, Richard, and Michael Wallace. 1971. *American Violence*. New York: Knopf.

Holmes, David R. 2006. *The Faith of the Founding Fathers*. New York: Oxford University Press.

Holt, Michael. 1992. *Political Parties and American Political Development: From the Age of Jackson to the Age of Lincoln*. New York: Barnes and Noble.

Houde, Jean Louis (translated by Hubert Houle). 1994. *French Migration to North America, 1600–1900*. Chicago: Editions Houde.

Howe, Daniel. 1973. *The American Whigs: An Anthology*. New York: John Wiley.

Immigration to the United States. www.immigrationtounitedstates.org/immigrant-groups. Accessed May 11, 2015.

Jones, Maldwyn. 1960. *American Immigration*. Chicago: University of Chicago Press.

Kenefick, John C. 1985. *Union Pacific and the Building of the West*. New York: Newcomen Society.

Kettner, James H. 1978. *The Development of American Citizenship, 1608–1970.* Chapel Hill: University of North Carolina Press.

Kornelly, Sharon. 2013. "A Holy Experiment: Religion and Immigration in the New World." In *Transforming America: Perspectives on Immigration*, vol. 1. Edited by Michael LeMay, 189–213. Westport, CT: Praeger Press.

LeMay, Michael. 1985. *The Struggle for Influence.* Lanham, MD: University Press of America.

LeMay, Michael. 1987. *From Open Door to Dutch Door: An Analysis of U.S. Immigration Policy Since 1820.* Westport, CT: Praeger Press.

LeMay, Michael. 2001. "Assessing Assimilation: Cultural and Political Integration of Immigrants and Their Descendants." In *In Defense of the Alien.* Edited by Lydio Tomasi, 163–176. New York: Center for Migration Studies.

LeMay, Michael. 2006. *Guarding the Gates: Immigration and National Security.* Westport, CT: Praeger Security International.

LeMay, Michael. 2009. *The Perennial Struggle*, 3rd edition. Upper Saddle River, NJ: Prentice Hall.

LeMay, Michael, ed. 2013. *Transforming America: Perspectives on Immigration*, vol. 2. Santa Barbara, CA: ABC-CLIO.

LeMay, Michael, and Elliott Barkan. 1999. *U.S. Immigration and Naturalization Laws and Issues: A Documentary History.* Westport, CT: Greenwood Press.

Levine, Edward. 2006. *The Irish and the Irish Politician.* Notre Dame: University of Notre Dame Press.

Levy, Leonard W. 1994. *The Establishment Clause and the First Amendment.* Chapel Hill: University of North Carolina Press.

Levy, Mark, and Michael Kramer. 1972. *The Ethnic Factor.* New York: Simon and Schuster.

Litt, Edgar. 1970. *Ethnic Politics in America.* Glenview, IL: Scott-Foresman.

Maguire, John F. 1969. *The Irish in America.* New York: Arno Press.

Mapp, Alf. 2003. *The Faith of Our Fathers: What America's Founders Really Believed.* Lanham, MD: Rowman and Littlefield.

McClain, Charles. 1994. *In Search of Equity: The Chinese Struggle against Discrimination in Nineteenth Century America.* Berkeley: University of California Press.

McClemore, Dale. 1980. *Racial and Ethnic Relations in America.* Boston: Allyn and Bacon.

McGreevey, John T. 2003. *Catholicism and American Freedom: A History.* New York: W. W. Norton.

McLaughlin, James. 2013. "The Common and Uncommon Schooling of Immigrants to the United States, 1787–1865." In *Transforming America: Perspectives on Immigration*, v. 1. Edited by LeMay, 97–119. Santa Barbara, CA: ABC-CLIO.

Melton, Tracy. 2005. *Hanging Henry Gambrill: The Violent Career of Baltimore's Plug Uglies, 1851–1860.* Baltimore: Maryland Historical Society.

Miller, Kerby. 1985. *Emigrants in Exile: Irish and the Irish Exodus to North America.* New York: Oxford University Press.

Miller, R. M., and T. D. Marzik, eds. 1977. *Immigrants and Religion in Urban America.* Philadelphia: Temple University Press.

Miller, William Lee. 1986. *The First Liberty: Religion and the American Republic.* Washington, DC: Georgetown University Press.

Mulkern, John. 1997. *The Know-Nothing Party in Massachusetts.* Boston: University of Massachusetts Press.

Nevins, Allan. 1947. *Ordeal in the Union: A House Dividing.* New York: Charles Scribner and Sons.

Nuovo, Victor. 2002. *John Locke: Writings on Religion.* New York: Oxford University Press.

O'Connor, Thomas. 1968. *The German Americans.* Boston: Little, Brown.

Office of the Historian. http://www.history.state.gov/milestones/1801-1829/louisiana-purchase. Accessed February 11, 2017.

O'Grady, Joseph. 1973. *How the Irish Became Americans.* New York: Twayne.

Overdyke, W. Darrell. 1968. *The Know Nothing Party in the South.* Gloucester, MA: Peter Smith.

Parrillo, Vincent. 1980. *Strangers to These Shores.* Boston: Houghton Mifflin.

Peterson, Merrill D., Robert C. Vaughan, and Robin Lovin, eds. 1988. *The Virginia Statute for Religious Freedom: Its Evolution and Consequences in American History.* Cambridge, England: Cambridge University Press.

Ravitch, Diane. 1974. *The Great School Wars: New York City, 1805–1973.* New York: Basic Books.

Reimers, David. 1990. *Natives and Strangers*, 2nd edition. New York: Oxford University Press.

Rippley, LeVern T. 1973. *The German Americans.* Chicago: Claretian Press.

Rischin, Moses, ed. 1976. *Immigration and the American Tradition.* Indianapolis: Bobbs-Merrill.

Robbins, Albert. 1981. *Coming to America: Immigrants from Northern Europe.* New York: Delacorte Press.

Rosenblum, Gerard. 1973. *Immigrant Workers: Their Impact on American Labor Radicalism.* New York: Basic Books.

Rosengarten, Joseph. 1980. *The German Soldier in the Wars of the United States.* Philadelphia: J. B. Lippincott.

Safire, William. 2008. *Safire's Political Dictionary.* New York: Oxford University Press.

Sarnito, Christian. 2009. *Becoming American under Fire.* Ithaca, NY: Cornell University Press.

Schafer, Joseph. 1968. "Who Elected Lincoln?" In *American Ethnic Politics.* Edited by Lawrence Fuchs. New York: Harper.

Silbey, Joel H. 1991. *The American Political Nation, 1838–1893.* Stanford, CA: Stanford University Press.

Smith, Theodore. 1969. *Parties and Slavery.* New York: Negro University Press.

Stephenson, George M. 1969. *The Religious Aspect of Swedish Immigration.* New York: Arno Press.

Suro, Roberto. 2015. "California Dreaming: The New Dynamism in Immigration Federalism and Opportunities for Inclusion on a Variegated Landscape." *Journal on Migration and Human Society* 3(1): 1–25.

Swierenga, Robert. 1985. *The Dutch in America: Immigration Settlement and Cultural Change.* New Brunswick, NJ: Rutgers University Press.

Thernstrom, Stephen. 1980. *Harvard Encyclopedia of American Ethnic Groups.* Cambridge, MA: Harvard University Press.

Thompson, William. 1996. *Native American Issues.* Santa Barbara, CA: ABC-CLIO.

VaGenWeb. www.vagenweb.org/hening/vol01-00.htm. Accessed May 2, 2017.

Van Hinte, Jacob. 1985. *Netherlanders in America: A Study of Emigration and Settlement in the Nineteenth and Twentieth Centuries of the United States of America.* Grand Rapids, MI: Baker Book House.

Vile, John R. 2015. *Encyclopedia of Constitutional Amendments, Proposed Amendments, and Amending Issues, 1789–2015,* 4th edition, 2 vols. Santa Barbara, CA: ABC-CLIO.

Voss-Hubbard, Mark. 2002. *Beyond Party: Cultures of Antipartisanship in Northern Politics before the Civil War.* Baltimore: The Johns Hopkins University Press.

Walters, Kerry S. 1992. *The American Deists: Voices of Reason and Dissent in the Early Republic.* Lawrence: University Press of Kansas.

Wilentz, Sean. 2005. *The Rise of American Democracy: Jefferson to Lincoln.* New York: W. W. Norton.

Wily, Irwin. 1979. *Billy Yank: The Common Soldier of the Union.* Baton Rouge: Louisiana State University Press.

Wittke, Carl. 1967. *We Who Built America.* Akron, OH: Case Western Reserve University Press.

Zolberg, Aristide. 2008. *A Nation by Design: Immigration Policy in the Fashioning of America.* Cambridge, MA: Russell Sage Foundation, Harvard University.

CHAPTER THREE

The Door Ajar Phase, 1880–1920

Introduction: The Change in Immigrant Waves

Until the current surge of legal and illegal immigration, the era of 1880–1920 was the period with the greatest number of immigrants coming to the United States. The new immigrants arriving between 1880 and 1920 totaled just slightly less than 23.5 million. Although immigrants from Southern, Central, Eastern European nations (SCE) had arrived during colonial times and during the first phase, the Open Door phase, their numbers and influence were comparatively small until after 1880. The turning-point year in which the numbers of immigrants from South, Central, and Eastern Europe exceeded for the first time those arriving from Northwestern Europe was 1896. It is not hyperbole to say that the new immigrant wave of the Door Ajar phase literally transformed America (LeMay 2013, v. 2: 1). Prior to the Civil War, the United States was overwhelmingly a rural and agricultural society of relatively small farmers. By the end of the Door Ajar period, the majority of Americans lived in cities, and the United States was emerging on the world scene as a major industrial power. The huge swell in immigration helped bring about that transformation, perhaps more so than any other single factor. From 1865 to 1880, the average annual number of immigrants arriving was just over 286,000. That number swells, nearly doubling, to 525,000 a year, in the decade 1881–1890. It subsides somewhat, to just over 368,000 a year in the 1891–1900 decade, then swells again and peaks at nearly 880,000 per year in the 1901–1910 decade, then ebbs to 573,000 per year for the decade 1911–1920.

Not only do the numbers swell, subside, swell, and ebb yet again, but the composition of the waves changes in the primary nations of origin, from Northwestern Europe to Southern, Central and Eastern Europe. As shall be seen in detail in this chapter, changes in the composition of immigrant waves led to changes in immigration policy, which results in corresponding changes in the composition yet again. Forces not directly the result of immigration policy and law, such as war and economic recessions and depressions, are more significant influences on the size and composition of the immigration flow than are any laws passed by the U.S. government, or by any state government, as incentives or disincentives (that is to say, push factors tend to be more determinative of the flow than are pull factors) (Bernard 1950; LeMay 2013, v. 2: 1–3; Taylor 1971).

For several Eastern European immigrant groups, moreover, religious persecution in their homelands—for example, pogroms against Jews—contributed as powerful push factors, compelling many to flee such persecution.

The fact that the newcomers, referred to by scholars of immigration history as the new immigrants, were different in their appearance, in their physical and cultural features, in their religious affiliations, and in the suitability of their economic backgrounds than were those of the old immigrants, and from that of the native-stock of WASPs, of course, was significant for the reception they received upon arrival to the United States. Also significant is the fact they arrived in sizable enough surges to preserve their cultural and ethnic identities within the various ethnic enclaves of the burgeoning cities of the United States into which they settled. These factors worked to increase the prejudice they faced and the discrimination they experienced. As one scholar puts it:

> What accounted for the exceptionally unfavorable response to the newcomers from those more distant parts of Europe? Several new forces were operating: religious issues, concentration in urban centers; implicit and often explicit racial notions; anxiety about assimilation; and the threats to existing institutions posed by the enormous numbers arriving. These concerns, later exaggerated by domestic issues during World War I as well as the social and political tumult that followed, eventually led to the end of an unrestricted migration policy in the 1920s. (Lieberson 1980: 21)

In addition to the millions of Catholics arriving, many of the newcomers were Greek or Russian Orthodox, or Jews. More than two million Jews fled Europe during this period, and nearly 90 percent of them came to the United States. Jewish population rose from around 250,000 in 1877 to over 4 million in 1927 (Dinnerstein and Reimers 1988: 37–38; Janikowsky 1964).

As was the case during the Open Door phase, several push and pull factors were at work in this vast migration which saw some 27 million immigrants leave Europe, most of whom came to the United States or Canada. One push factor was the urbanization and industrialization spreading across Europe, which caused severe political, economic and social disruptions. The new immigrants were often fleeing horrendous conditions in their homelands: high birth rates, overpopulation, cholera and small pox epidemics, dense crowding into unhealthy slums to name but a few. In turn, these conditions led to political unrest and often repressive governments coping with revolutionary pressures brought on by the overpopulation. These European governments found that emigration was an expedient policy and openly encouraged the waves of immigrants bound for the United States.

Unrest in Czarist Russia, for example, prompted the government to blame Jews for all the country's ills. Jews became scapegoats subjected to government-sponsored pogroms that began in 1881 with the assassination of Czar Alexander II and continued for some 30 years thereafter, forcing many Jews to flee. The brutal campaigns of beatings, killings, and lootings are exemplified by the 1903 pogrom in Kishineff, Russia, were some 2,750 families were affected: 47 persons were killed, 424 wounded, and scores of homes burned down and their shops pillaged (Dinnerstein and Reimers 1988: 38).

Another push factor was the periodic epidemics of highly contagious and deadly maladies that became pandemic outbreaks (LeMay 2013, v. 2: 51–52). Small pox, cholera, tuberculosis, bubonic plague, influenza, and typhus, scarlet, and yellow fever epidemics pushed many to emigrate. On arrival, however, they often found themselves trapped in the teeming urban centers of East Coast and West Coast cities where slum-bred cholera epidemics killed many. The mortality rate of New York City rose dramatically, especially in the city's East Side which then comprised the world's most densely populated district. It had some 290,000 persons per square mile; far greater than the 175,000 persons per square mile of Old London. In response, the U.S. government opened new immigration receiving and quarantine stations—such as Angel Island in San Francisco and Ellis Island in New York—to process the massive immigration flow. Doctors of the U.S. Marine Hospital Service, the precursor to the U.S. Public Health Service, acted as health barriers against pandemic disease, while allowing millions of immigrants to enter the United States (LeMay 2006: 39; LeMay 2015; LeMay and Barkan 1999: 66–70).

Pull factors were at work as well. As the United States fought several wars—the Plains Indian Wars, the Spanish-American War, and World War I—the needs for and the contributions made by the foreign born and their children serving as volunteers in the armed forces impacted national defense policy (LeMay 2006; 2013, v. 2: 25–37). Speedy naturalization in return for military service induced immigration.

Another pull factor was changes in transportation technology. Steam liners were developed to transport the millions of immigrants across the Atlantic and Pacific Oceans in crossings that were safer and faster than ever before (Lynch 2013: 73–89). Letters home from friends and relatives in the United States induced many to come. The promise of the "land of golden opportunity" was a magnet that drew many (Taylor 1971; Hoerder 1982).

The great influx of new immigrants were drawn to, as well as made possible, the vast urbanization and industrialization of the United States. Whereas the number and size of cities in the United States mushroomed during the Open Door phase, they virtually exploded during the Door Ajar era when many cities grew exponentially (LeMay 2013, v. 2: 122–123). Chicago, for example, grew from less than 10,000 in population in 1848 to more than 1,690,000 in 1900. Immigrants contributed significantly to that explosive rate of growth. By 1920, new immigrants comprised 44 percent of New York City's population, 41 percent of Cleveland's, 39 percent of Newark's, and 24 percent of Boston's, Buffalo's, Detroit's, Philadelphia's and Pittsburgh's (LeMay, 2013, v. 2: 123–146). Such explosive rate of urbanization required a massive workforce of cheap labor to literally erect the cities and to serve in their ever-expanding bureaucracies who provided the services necessary for a dense population to survive and thrive.

The millions arriving annually after 1900 had unprecedented impact—on health and education policy, and on citizenship itself. These facts compelled a response in American politics. Groups for and against open immigration versus restrictive immigration policy agitated to redefine immigration law to influence the size, scope, rate, and composition of the migration. Policy skirmishes changed the nature of American federalism as immigration policy became more exclusively the policy domain of the national level of government in both enactment and implementation (LeMay and Barkan 1999: 55–125).

The following section of this chapter highlights the immigration patterns of the major ethnic groups comprising the new immigrant wave and notes the impact of their far greater religious diversity than was characteristic of the Open Door phase.

The New Immigrant Wave: Changing Flow, Changing Laws

After 1880, instead of coming from Germany, Ireland, and Scandinavia, the majority of immigrants began coming from Italy, Greece, Poland,

and Eastern Europeans Jews from Hungary, Russia, Poland, and the Baltic nations. South/Central/Eastern European immigrants predominated between 1880 and 1920. Their numbers and diversity transformed America to a true nation of nations (Adamic 1945; LeMay 2013, v. 2). Their arrival in such massive numbers alarmed many in the United States. Whereas prior to the Civil War, as we have seen, 80 percent of immigrants came from Northwestern Europe, by 1920 European total percentage dropped to 60 percent, and shifted within Europe from Northwestern to Southern, Central and Eastern Europe.

To WASP America, the shift seemed sudden. By the 1880–1890 decade, millions of Catholics were arriving, adding to the many Greek and Russian Orthodox or Jews. A host of scholars have noted that their different religious denominational affiliation was a major factor in the anti-immigrant attitudes that arose after 1870 (Barone 2013; Dinnerstein and Reimers 1988; Grant 1916; Handlin 1963; Higham 1955; Lieberson 1980; Litt 1970; Ringer 1983, Sowell 1981; Zolberg 2008). In 1887, the American Protective Association was founded. It led the anti-Catholic movement of the 1890s and was manifested clearly in the Temperance Movement. The Anti-Saloon League, formed in 1896, directed a campaign in which "Rum, Romanism and Rebellion" were pitted against "Prohibition, Protestantism, and Patriotism" (LeMay 1985: 109). They failed, however, to get the highly restrictive immigration policy adopted into law before the arrival of millions of immigrants from South, Central, and Eastern Europe in the 1890s to 1920s.

Religious groups have often played supporting roles in public policy debates, particularly those involving military and foreign policy. In wars, God is always invoked as being on the side of the given nation-state government. Formal religious affiliation has been associated with prejudice in complex ways. Gordon Allport has shown that a person who is most devout, most personally absorbed in his or her religion is less likely to be prejudiced against others, whereas persons of religious affiliation who evidence an institutional type of attachment, more external and political in nature, turn out to be more highly associated with prejudice. "The chief reason why religion becomes the focus of prejudice is that it usually stands for more than faith—it is the pivot of the cultural tradition of a group" (Allport 1958: 445).

And likewise, their religious-based organizational life was especially important as a coping mechanism for all Southern, Central, Eastern European groups (Adamic 1945; Davis 1976; Dinnerstein and Reimers 1988; Nelli 1970; Ringer 1983; Sowell 1978, 1981; Ward 1971). More than 2 million Jews fled Eastern Europe during the period (Janikowsky 1964).

Table 3.1 Foreign-Born Population as Percentage of Total U.S. Population, by Census Years, 1870–1920

Census Year	Total U.S. Population	Total Foreign-Born	Percentage of Foreign-Born
1870	29,095,665	5,567,229	19.8
1880	36,843,291	6,679,943	14.5
1890	45,979,391	9,249,547	20.1
1900	56,595,379	10,341,276	18.2
1910	68,386,412	13,579,886	19.7
1920	81,108,161	13,920,693	17.1

Source: Table by author; data from the U.S. Department of Commerce, 2003, *Statistical Abstract of the United States, 2002*. Washington, DC: Bureau of the Census, U.S. Government Printing Office.

Table 3.1 presents the U.S. foreign-born population and their percentage of the total population for the census years 1870 to 1920.

Italian Immigrants

The new immigrant wave swelled every bit as dramatically as had the flood of famine-induced Irish in the decade prior to the Civil War. Italian immigrants, for example, rose from a few hundred thousand to more than 5 million in a few decades. They are second only to Germany as the nation of origin of immigrants, and the largest number arriving during the Door Ajar era. In the 2000 census, respondents claiming Italian ancestry number nearly 16 million (Table 2.1), and Italy ranked fourth among the top 25 nations of origin by persons who did so. Pre-1880 Italian immigrants were mostly from northern Italy and were often skilled artisans recruited to the United States. By 1848, two Italian immigrants had been elected to the Texas legislature (a significant number arriving through the port at Galveston, Texas). In 1849, Secchi de Casali began publishing *L'Echo d' Italia*, a prominent Italian-language newspaper in New York City that supported the Whig Party and later the Republicans (Iorizzo and Mondello 1971: 26). By the early 1850s, there was an Italian settlement in Chicago where they served as saloon operators, restaurant operators, fruit venders, and confectioners; but also as common ditch-diggers and commissioned artists (Nelli 1970). They were lured to California in the gold rush, but instead of mining they became wine growers, vegetable farmers, and merchants, giving rise to the "Italio-American folklore that 'the miners mined the mines, and the Italians mined the miners'" (Iorizzo and Mondello

1971: 13). The fact that Italian immigrants came as skilled craftsmen from northern Italy changed dramatically after 1870.

Repression in Europe in the 1870s forced Italian intellectuals and revolutionaries to emigrate. The Risorgimento, resulting in the unification of Italy, sparked an exodus of nearly 9 million Italians who crossed the Atlantic to both North and South America seeking better economic conditions. Extreme poverty was prevalent in southern Italy and Sicily. The region was wracked with periodic epidemics in the 1870s and 1880s (Kohn 1995: 360–372). From 1881 to 1910, about 3 million Italians came to the United States, settling in the cities of the industrial Northeast, usually in ethnic enclaves called Little Italy by the native-stock. They were perceived as flooding into U.S. cities. New York City's Italian American population, by 1930, numbered more than one million and comprised 15.5 percent of the total population (Federal Writers Project 1969: viii).

In the 1910 census, Italian immigrants accounted for 77 percent of the foreign-born population of Chicago, 78 percent of New York's, 74 percent of Boston's, Cleveland's and Detroit's (Andrews 1995; LeMay 2013 v. 2: 8; Nelli 1970: xi; Steen 2006). Nor were they a static bloc. Many Italian immigrants had a sojourners attitude, intending to stay only a while, working to earn enough to buy land back in Italy or Sicily (LeMay 2009: 129). They often used a "padroni" system for finding work and for social services. Between 1910 and 1914, nearly half of those who arrived in the United States returned to Italy to winter there, working the remainder of the year in America (Nelli 1970: 48). But many Italian immigrants showed their U.S. patriotism, and the draw of military service for speedy naturalization, by serving in the armed forces: some 300,000 served in the U.S. military during World War I (LeMay 2009: 128–129). There was an Italian regiment in the Civil War—the Garibaldi Guard. Some 100 Italian-born soldiers served in the Union Army, three of whom achieved the rank of general (Iorrizo and Mondello 1971: 30).

The contrast in wages between Italy and America was stark: miners in Italy earned 30 to 56 cents per day; general laborers earned $3.50 for a six day, 60-hour work week in Italy. In the United States, they earned $9.90 for a 56-hour week. Carpenters in Italy were paid 30 cents to $1.40 per day, or $1.80 to $8.40 for a six-day week. That same carpenter in America took home an average of $18.00 for a 50-hour work week (Federal Writers Project 1969: 36–49; Iorrizo and Mondello 1971: 43–44).

Other push factors were floods, volcanic eruption, and earthquakes that plagued Italy and contributed to its bleak agricultural outlook. Southern Italy was hit by phylloxera, a disease that killed off agricultural plants on a scale similar to the Irish potato blight of the 1840s. Still others fled frequent outbreaks of malaria, cholera, and small pox (Kraut 1994). Others fled to avoid conscription into military service during the wars of unification.

Pull factors for Italian immigrants included the development of steamship lines that made the transatlantic journey cheaper, faster, and safer. Glowing reports by the returning "Americani," who sometimes made the trip back and forth or who returned to Italy seeking brides, about the opportunities afforded in America created a strong chain-migration effect. State governments, like California, Illinois, Louisiana, New York, and Pennsylvania hired agents to contract for laborers to come. So massive was the flow between 1890 and 1914 that:

> One author told the humorous and probably apocryphal tale of a mayor who greeted the Prime Minister of Italy then touring the provinces: "I welcome you in the name of five thousand inhabitants of this town, three thousand of whom are in America, and the other two thousand preparing to go." (Iorizzo and Mondello 1971: 48)

Their huge surge in arrivals spurred anti-Catholic, anti-Italian, and anti-immigrant sentiment. In the 1880s and 1890s, depression-induced violence broke out directed at Italian immigrants. A few were lynched, some murdered, and more attacked in mob violence in the years 1870–1920, which will be described more fully next.

To assist them in adjusting to life in America, a variety of self-help associations were founded. In San Francisco, an Italian Mutual Aid Society was begun in 1857. The Society of Italian Union and Fraternity started in New York City in 1857 as well. By 1912, New York City had 258 societies, including the most influential, the Society for Italian Immigrants, founded in 1901 (Iorrizo and Mondello 1971: 95). By 1919, Chicago had 80 associations, including the influential Union Sicilian, the Columbian Federation, and the Order of the Sons of Italy in America. In virtually every city with large Italian enclaves, local Catholic parishes became foci for social as well as their religious life (Nelli 1970: 172).

Mob violence against them contributed to their development of crime associations as, in part, self-protective associations (labeled La Cosa Nostra by Sicilians or the Mafia by Anglos). Careers in crime became "a curious ladder of social mobility" (Vecoli and Lintelman 1984: 205). When the urban machines and crime organizations linked in 1910–1920, crime was associated with political party activity and became a source of political leadership in places like Chicago where Colosimo, Torrio, and Al Capone emerged (Nelli 1970: 113–114). It also became a source of negative stereotyping of Italians as a criminal element. That, and a depression in 1913, revived anti-Italian fervor by groups like the Ku Klux Klan, and led to the use of pejorative terms like "wop" and "dago."

Wop was prevalent in New York and the New England area. It derived from the fact that so many Italians arriving through Ellis Island were pinned with signs W.O.P., designating their arrival without papers, that the term became applied to all Italians. Dago was more common in the South. It was derived originally from the Spanish term, Diego, applied to Spanish, Portuguese or Italian sailors (Italian American One Voice Coalition).

The major ports of embarkation of Italian immigrants bound for the United States were Rome, Naples, Genoa, Florence, and in Sicily, Messina and Palermo. Their principle ports of debarkation in the United States were Baltimore, Boston, Galveston, New York, New Orleans, and Philadelphia. By far, most came through Ellis Island, once it was opened in 1892. Italian immigrants were the most numerous of all immigrants who were processed through the Ellis Island station (Moreno and LeMay 2013, v. 2: 199).

Italian Americans came to political activity more slowly than did the Irish, and the two ethnic groups sometimes clashed. Italian American politicians emerged from political clubs and ran as Democrats, Republicans, Socialist, Independents, and Progressives. Prior to 1920, most were active solely at the local level. The first Italian American state-level politico was Charles Cois, a Chicago politician elected to the Illinois legislature in 1918. Nationally, they tended to support Democrats, but in Chicago they had a running battle against a ward boss, Irish-American John Powers, whom they called Jonny DePow or Gianni Pauli (Nelli 1970: 99). In 1912, anti-Wilson sentiment swung many Italians away from the Democratic ticket. In New York City, Republican Fiorello LaGuardia emerged as the leader of the Italian-American community and he was elected to the U.S. House of Representatives in 1915, and after a distinguished war service, again in 1918. In 1920, he won the seat vacated by Al Smith (Iorizzo and Mondello 1971).

Table 3.2 lists the immigrants entering the United States through the Ellis Island station between 1892 and 1931. It shows the rank order of the top 15 nations of origin passing through the station and shows clearly the shift from Northwestern European countries to Southern, Central and Eastern European countries of origin. The New York City immigration station on Ellis Island was the major receiving station during its years of operation (1892–1954), accounting for 70 to 80 percent of all arriving immigrants (Moreno and LeMay 2013, v. 2: 198). Table 3.3 presents the data for immigrants entering through Ellis Island for selective

Table 3.2   Immigrants through Ellis Island Station, 1892–1931, Top 15 Nations of Origin Rank Ordered

Nations of Origin	Total Number of Arrivals
Italy	2,503,310
Russia	1,893,542
Hungary	854,557
Austria-Hungary	768,557
Germany	633,148
England	551,969
Ireland	520,904
Sweden	348,036
Greece	245,058
Norway	226,778
Scotland	191,023
Poland	153,444
Portugal	120,725
France	109,687
Denmark	99,414

Source: Table by author; data from Moreno and LeMay, 2013, v. 2: 199.

Table 3.3   Immigrants Arriving through Ellis Island, Selective Years, 1892–1914, Compared to All Immigrants, and Percentage of Total

Year	Total Immigrants	Total, Ellis Island	%EI
1892	579,661	445,759	76.9
1894	285,631	219,046	76.6
1896	343,267	263,705	76.8
1898	229,299	178,748	77.9
1900	448,572	341,712	76.2
1902	648,743	493,262	76.0
1904	812,870	606,019	74.5
1906	1,100,713	880,036	79.9
1907	1,285,349	1,004,756	78.1
1910	1,041,570	786,094	75.5
1914	1,216,489	878,052	72.0

Source: Table by author; data from Moreno and LeMay, 2013, v. 2: 198.

years between 1892 and 1914 and compares them with the total immigration to the United States in those years, and the percentage of the total of immigrants arriving who entered through Ellis Island.

Greek Immigrants

Greeks, like the Italians, came in large numbers after 1880. Their peak period was 1901–1910 (LeMay 1985: 33). Some 350,000 arrived in the two decades, 1900–1920. In the 2000 census, just over 1 million persons claimed Greek ancestry—ranking 22 out of the top 25 nations of origin (Table 2.1). There was an ill-fated Greek settlement of New Smyrna in Florida as early as 1768 (LeMay 1987: 45; Moskos 1980: 3–5). Greek immigrants were mostly young men, unskilled workers from the villages in the Peloponnesus province of Greece. As with other Southern, Central and Eastern European groups, several push and pull factors led to their migration. Political persecution played a role, although economic conditions were the primary push factor. A rapid increase in population produced an excess that the land could no longer support. Even after heavy migration, in 1930, there were still 870 persons per square acre of cultivated land in Greece (Thernstrom 1980: 431). The Balkan War of 1912–1913 between Greece and Turkey was another major push factor. Many Greek young men fled the compulsory military service in what they considered to be a Turkish tyranny. These young men came as sojourners, hoping to earn enough money to provide for dowries for the prospective brides in their families. The fact that before 1920, 95 percent of Greek immigrants were young males meant that many returned home for brides (LeMay 1985: 45).

As with so many immigrant groups, the major pull factor to the United States was jobs. Greek immigrants who arrived during the era followed three major routes: (1) Westward to work on railroad construction gangs or in the mines; (2) to New England to work in the textile and shoe factories; and (3) to New York City, Chicago, and other large industrial cities to work in the factories or as busboys, dishwashers, bootblacks, and peddlers. They often used a "padrone" system, akin to that of the Italians. Though highly exploitive, the padrone system found them jobs, helped with language problems, and settled disputes. Often the padrone's clients were young boys sent to them directly. The padrone made an average of $100 to $200 per boy per year, and in some cases as much as $500. The boys themselves would earn $100 to $180 per year in wages. The parents back in Greece did not know about the exploitive conditions under which their sons would live (Moskos 1980: 16).

A sizable number managed to start their own businesses, concentrating on confectionaries, candy stores, and restaurants. After World War I, for example, an estimated 564 Greek restaurants were to be found in San Francisco (Moskos 1980: 17–20; Parrillo 1980: 207).

Their back-and-forth migration slowed their acculturation and led to mutual misunderstanding and at times severe conflict with WASP Americans. In 1904, for example, in Chicago, inexperienced Greeks, unaware of the conditions of a strike, served as strike-breakers. A wave of anti-Greek hysteria and anti-Greek press ensued, and out west, a virulent nativist movement directed a campaign against them (LeMay 1987: 46). In McGill, Nevada, three Greek immigrants were killed during a riot in 1908. In Utah, Mormons were especially anti-Greek. In 1917, a Greek accused of killing Jack Dempsey's brother was nearly lynched in Salt Lake City, and in 1923, in Price, Utah, local Ku Klux Klansmen led riots, attacked Greek stores, and forced the American-born girls working in them to return home (Moskos 1980: 17). In Omaha, Greek immigrant seasonal workers became involved in a strike-breaking situation and a false arrest of a Greek immigrant led to a scuffle in which a policeman died. The next day, an ugly riot caused thousands of dollars of damages to Omaha's Little Athens (Burgess 1913: 162–163).

Incidents such as those contributed to a growing anti-Greek sentiment. Even supposedly scholarly work, such as that by sociologist Henry Pratt Fairchild, reflected this negative image. His work stereotyped Greeks, as it did Italians, as being disproportionately of the criminal type, and he doubted that they would ever be able to assimilate (Fairchild 1911).

Greek assimilation was slow, compared to that of Northwestern European groups at least, and they tended to live in small enclaves (often referred to as "Little Athens") where they could socialize in Greek coffeehouses, and practice their religion. The Greek Orthodox Church, the Greek-language press, such as the *Atlantis*, and the more than 100 Greek societies, the most notable of which was the American Hellenic Educational Progressive Association (AHEPA), which was founded in 1922, helped preserve their Greek heritage and to better understand and cope with the American way of life (LeMay 2009: 133–138; Moskos 1980; Parrillo 1980; Rippley 1973; Soloutos 1964).

Greek immigrants who were religious attended the Orthodox Church, which in this period in North America was somewhat dominated by the Russian Orthodox Diocese. In 1864, the first Greek Orthodox parish established on American soil was opened in New Orleans, Louisiana.

The Orthodox Church served any Orthodox Christian coming from Serbia, Russia, and Greece. From the late 19th to the early 20th century, it was formally organized under the Russian Orthodox Church's American Diocese. That arrangement lasted until 1917, when it was dissolved after the Bolshevik Revolution. In 1921, the Greek Archdiocese was formally organized (Orthodox Church of America).

Polish Immigrants

As with the Greek immigrants, Polish immigrants (representative here for the various Slavic groups of Eastern and Central Europe) came to America in any significant numbers mostly post-1880. Total numbers for Polish immigrants is not as clear-cut as for other groups as sometimes they were counted among German immigrants, sometimes among Russian immigrants, sometimes among Austrian-Hungarian immigrants. In the 2000 census, however, Poles ranked 6th of the top 25 in claimed ancestry—at just over 9 million persons so self-identifying (Table 2.1). The area that is present-day Poland changed, at times being part of Germany, Austria-Hungary, or Russia. One of the more conservative estimates, by Thomas and Znanicki, put the number of legal immigrants from Poland at 825,000, while others put it in excess of one million (Thomas and Znanicki 1977; Dinnerstein and Reimers 1988, and Parrillo 1996 put them at over 1 million, while Lopata 1976 estimates their number at 1,670,000).

About three-fourths of Polish immigrants were farm laborers, unskilled domestic workers, and domestic servants (LeMay, 2009: 139; Lopata 1976: 3). According to immigration records, less than 12 percent were classified as skilled, and 25 percent were illiterate. Nearly all arrived with less than $50 in their possession. Like the Greeks, Polish immigrants before 1920 tended to be young male sojourners. Their attachment to their homeland was enhanced by the fact that the ills of life in Poland could be blamed on foreign occupations. Resentment of the Polish upper class seemed less than was typical among Slavic groups (Ibid: 140).

Cities with large Polish settlements include Buffalo, Chicago, Milwaukee, Pittsburgh, Detroit, and New York City. By 1920, Chicago's Polish population of more than 360,000 meant that more Poles lived in Chicago than any other city in the world except Warsaw and Ludz, Poland. Without question, the most important social institution of Polonia (the term used for the Polish American community) was the church—the Polish Roman Catholic Union, founded in 1873; and the Polish National Catholic Church, 1897. They were organized, in part, as a reaction to cope with the Irish-dominated Catholic Church. They organized parish-based mutual-aid societies, joining the Polish Roman Catholic Union, founded in 1873, the Polish National Alliance, founded in 1880, and the Polish National Catholic Church (PBCC) begun in 1897. The PNCC organized 50 independent Polish parishes. They organized and operated Catholic parochial schools—as of the late 1950s there were an estimated 250,000 elementary students being taught by Polish American Catholic nuns and more than 100,000 additional students in catechism classes, and into the 1970s, they still operated more than 600 Polish parochial schools (LeMay 1985: 82; Lopata 1976: 51–53). They lobbied on foreign policy for aid to Poland. Along with Polish American ethnic groups, they lobbied for less restrictive immigration policy, opposed the literacy test, and advocated for allowing greater numbers of Poles to immigrate.

Two other important social institutions in Polonia before 1920 were two ethnic association. The Polish National Alliance, began in 1880, and had some 300,000 members at its height. The Polish National Department was organized just before World War I and invested over $20 million into the Polish cause. Between the outbreak of World War I in Europe and 1918, when the United States entered the war, Polish Americans invested more than 18 million dollars in Polish government bonds to aid their homeland. They showed their patriotism to America as well in that 28,000 Polish-born volunteers served in World War I and Polonia purchased an estimated $67 million of American Liberty Bonds during the war (LeMay 1985: 82–83; 2006: 86–87). Polonia exerted considerable pressure on President Woodrow Wilson's administration during World War I to press the European powers to return Poland to the status of an independent nation-state, succeeding in that endeavor when Wilson included it as his thirteenth of the famous Fourteen Points.

Polonia established many self-help societies, often begun as burial societies organized at Polish Catholic churches. Soon, mutual aid societies began to organize balls, picnics, lectures, and periodicals out of which emerged a strong Polish-language press. This gave them an organizational base on which to build political coalitions when they finally became active in American politics beyond trying to influence U.S. foreign policy vis-à-vis the homeland. Polish Americans voted heavily Democratic. It is curious that a higher percentage—80 to 85 percent—of Polish Americans voted for John F. Kennedy when he ran for president in 1960 than did Irish Americans (LeMay 1985: 83)

Russian Immigrants

The earliest Russian immigration to what is now the United States was in the mid-1700s, in Alaska and California. In 1792, the first Russian

Orthodox Church was built in the United States. As early as 1812, a sizable enclave was located in Sonoma, California, which lasted some 30 years before several hundred returned to the homeland at the request of the czar (LeMay 1987: 50).

Post-1870, the first sizable surge of Russian immigration began when some 40,000 Mennonites arrived. During the period 1899 to 1913, 51,000 arrived, among whom an estimated 40 percent were Russian Jews fleeing pogroms. Their peak years of Russian migration were 1881–1914. In 1917, the Russian Revolution stopped all emigration. By the 1910 census, 60,000 Russian-born immigrants were counted, more than half of which were in New York and Pennsylvania. In the 2000 census, nearly 3 million persons claimed Russian ancestry, and Russia ranked 12th of the top 25 nations of origin (Table 2.1). The 1910 census counted 58,000 Russian-born immigrants, more than half of whom lived in New York and Pennsylvania (LeMay 1985: 86).

Russian immigrants worked in the mines and the mills in New York and Pennsylvania, and in the slaughterhouses of Chicago. In New York City, they worked in the garment industry and in cigar and tobacco manufacturing. They also held unskilled worker jobs in construction and on the railroads. They were active in unions like the United Mine Workers (formed in 1890) and the Industrial Workers of the World (1905). Their wages were typically low-scale: in 1909, on average, they earned $2 a day for a 12-hour work day. As late as 1919, Russian immigrants in Chicago earned $12 to $30 per week (Davis 1976: 17–37). Other unions in which they were active included the clockmaker's, men and women's garment workers, the Society of Russian Bookmakers, and the Society of Russian Mechanics.

As did the Greeks and the Poles, Russian immigrants sought refuge from the discrimination they faced in church and mutual-aid associations. By 1916, the Russian Orthodox Church in America had nearly 100,000 members in 169 parishes; and some 7,000 students enrolled in their 126 church-based schools. They split-off as independent churches, largely in order to be free from the strong control of the Patriarch (like an archbishop in Catholicism) who resided in Moscow, Russia. Their congregations were located in Chicago, Detroit, New York City, Boston, Philadelphia, Baltimore, Bayonne City, New Jersey, and Lawrence, Massachusetts. The Russian Orthodox Society of Mutual Aid, begun in 1895, grew to 188 chapters with more than 7,000 members. The Russian Brotherhood Society, begun in 1900, had more than 3,000 members by 1917. These groups provided health insurance, death benefits, and helped secure jobs. After the 1917 Russian Revolution, the avowedly political association, the

Society to Help Free Russia, was formed as an anti-Bolshevik political advocacy group primarily lobbying to influence American foreign policy vis-à-vis Russia (LeMay 1985: 87). By 1917, there were some 200 Russian immigrant clubs started in the United States: socialist, anarchist, and the radical Bolsheviks, the largest of which was the Union of Russian Workers. The activity of these more ideologically radical political clubs inflamed anti-Russian and anti-Bolshevik sentiment among their compatriots, and a wave of prejudice, discrimination and sometimes violence against them among WASP Americans (LeMay 2006: 88).

The American Communist Party was formed in 1919, and its membership was mostly comprised of new immigrants, as was a splinter group, the American Communist Labor Party. These political parties worked with foreign-language groups active in the Socialist movement and in the industrial union movement. Their formation set off a hysterical xenophobic reaction against "Godless Bolshevism" that culminated in the infamous Palmer Raids (named after then U.S. attorney general A. Mitchell Palmer), in the summer of 1919. The raids were in part a response to a public opinion campaign led by the 100 Percenters that spread fear of Bolshevism arising in the United States. About 10,000 persons were arrested in raids that took place in 70 cities all around the country, and eventually led to the arrest of thousands who were sent to Ellis Island while awaiting summary deportation to Russia. This policy inadvertently spread an outbreak of the Great Influenza to the island in which hundreds died of the pandemic and perhaps contributed to an outbreak in New York City as well in which several thousand died (LeMay 2016: 43). Eventually, some 500 Russian immigrants were deported. Aboard one ship, the *Buford*, dubbed "the Soviet Ark" 249 were forcibly repatriated, departing Ellis Island on December 22, 1919 (LeMay 2006: 88; LeMay 2009: 257–258).

The Socialist congressman elected from Milwaukee, Wisconsin, Victor Berger, was refused his elected seat, as were five Socialist assemblymen in the New York state legislature (Davis 1976; Draper 1957: 164–175; Draper 1960).

A related political reaction was the suppression of the Russian language press. From 1900 to 1920, a total of 52 Russian language papers were published. By 1921, only five remained, the oldest begun in 1902, and the fifth daily, the radical *Novi Mir* (The New World) was suppressed by the national government in 1921 (LeMay 1987: 51).

This suppression induced many Russian immigrants to voluntarily repatriate and it cut-off future immigration and slowed the acculturation of those immigrants who remained (LeMay 2013, v. 2: 7–8).

Eastern European Jews

Data on the immigration of the various Eastern European Jews is sketchy, as the immigration service asked the place of origin and did not count them in terms of their religious affiliation, but they are variously estimated at 40 to 50 percent of all Southern, Central and Eastern European immigrants entering between 1870 and 1930. One source puts their numbers arriving between 1899 and 1973 at 2.5 million, who comprised 8.5 percent of the total legal immigration during those years (Dinnerstein and Reimers 1988: 172–174).

The same push/pull factors that influenced SCE national origin groups were at work with respect to Jewish immigration during the era, although for them religious persecution weighed in more heavily and was for many Jewish immigrants of the period the single-most compelling cause of their migration. Jewish immigrants, more so than any of the Slavic groups, came in family groups intending to stay (they were decidedly not sojourners). By law, in Russia, Jews were forbidden to own land. This forced them to become merchants, tailors, and other commerce-related businesses. They were more urbanized than most other Eastern European immigrants, and this combination of merchant/commercial and skilled labor occupations, plus their longer experience with urban living, helped them to adjust to American society and economy (LeMay 1985: 91).

They settled in their ports of entry: New York City, Philadelphia, Baltimore, and in those cities lived in low-rent sections near the cities' business districts into enclaves that developed into ghetto-like areas (Dinnestein and Reimers 1975: 37–38; Howe 1976: 5). Ironically, their persecution in European countries made them better-suited to the environment they found themselves in within America than were the other Eastern European immigrant groups: they had a more urban background and better job-skills, which eased their assimilation into American life. Sixty percent of Jewish males were classified upon immigration as skilled workers compared to an average of 20 percent for all other groups (Dinnerstein and Reimers 1988: 44).

Jewish immigrants were quickly active in the union movement, notably in the garment industry. The Amalgamated Clothing Workers (formally the International Ladies Garment Workers Union, or ILGWU) were predominately Jewish and Italian. For example, the Dressmakers Local 22 of New York City was 75 percent Jewish, and an estimated half of the city's Jewish labor force worked in the garment trade. They also filled jobs in the cigar manufacturing, bookmaking, distilling, printing, and skilled carpentry trades. In the unskilled labor category, they were active in peddling and sales. A 1900 census found Jewish immigrants in the professions to be the highest of all non-English-speaking immigrants (Bayor 1978: 14–15; Leventman 1969: 40).

By religious affiliation, American Jews can be divided into three subgroups: Orthodox, Reformed, and Conservative. Orthodox Jews have distinct sects, such as the Hasidim (also spelled Chasidim from the Hebrew word for pious), who are highly visible for their distinctive dress, hairstyle, the character of their worship, a strong sense of "people-hood," and a dogma that operates as a self-segregating force and a conflicting factor between gentile and Jew. That sense of people-hood figures into both the discrimination they have experienced and in their manner of coping with such discrimination. Since a majority of them immigrated after this period, they will be discussed in more detail in the next chapter.

Anti-Semitism in America was experienced by them, but it was nothing like the virulent and often violent form found in Russia, Poland, Hungary, and Germany. In colonial America, Jews were commonly disenfranchised. Voting restrictions lasted until 1877 when New Hampshire became the last state ending them. Anti-Semitism attitudes were reflected in the popular culture, which commonly stereotyped Jews as avaricious scoundrels. German Jews, who had arrived before 1880, were generally able to cope easily with anti-Semitism because their numbers were relatively small, and they were mostly middle class in status. Initially, they feared the immigration of Eastern European Jews, believing their vast numbers would be the cause of new and more virulent outbreaks of anti-Semitism. They were correct in that assessment. As prejudice escalated, however, they closed ranks with the newcomers and assisted them in their adjustment to life in America.

In the 1870s, latent anti-Semitism broke out into the open. In New York State, in 1877, Jews were blackballed from the state's bar association, and in 1878, college fraternities followed suit. The Saratoga Springs resort in upstate New York began to bar them as did a host of private clubs, resorts, and private schools. The Ku Klux Klan, which revived in the early 1900s, soon became the leading anti-Semitic force (Howe 1976).

Pogroms broke out in Russia in 1903 and 1906 inspiring the American Jewish community to organize to aid them. The American Jewish Committee began to raise money for those still suffering in Europe. In 1913, the B'nai B'rith's Anti-Defamation League (ADL) was formed. By 1909, more than 2000 synagogue-based Jewish charities in America spent more than $10 million organizing orphanages, educational institutions, homes for unwed mothers and delinquent children in that year alone (LeMay 1985: 93). They set up Jewish hospitals, recreational facilities, and supported the Jewish Theological Seminary training rabbis. They formed a host of Yiddish-language newspapers. Between 1885 and 1915, 150 newspapers were begun, including the highly influential *Daily Forward* (Howe 1976: 518–551).

Jewish immigrants, in both their religious and family lives, stressed formal education. Advanced learning was especially emphasized for males. Professional occupations were held up as the ideal, being highly valued for the income and social prestige not only within the Jewish community, but within the broader American culture as well. Education became the tool by which they secured their future. Jewish immigrants used education and advanced learning to pursue their occupational and economic route to achieve security in middle-class status and as a means of acculturation into American society. "By 1915, Jews comprised 85 percent of the student body of New York's free but renowned City College, and one-fifth of those attending New York University and one-sixth of the students at Columbia" (Dinnerstein and Reimers 1988: 53).

They did not become politically active in electoral politics until the next era. The urban political machines openly operating in the cities in which Jewish immigrants were concentrated were slow to welcome them, and Jewish immigrants were uncomfortable with the style of American politics stressing what for them were strange skills, codes, vulgarities, and resultant political corruption (Howe 1976: 360; LeMay 2006: 142–145).

The First Restrictionist Laws: Attempts to Close the Golden Door

The effects of the new and massive wave of immigration and of its changing composition were significantly and quickly felt. A strong movement to restrict immigration formed in the 1870s and achieved a degree of success in the 1880s, stressing the use of a device referred to as excluded categories. Pro-restriction forces were able to influence most of the stages of the policy-making process: problem formation, policy formulation, and policy adoption or enactment. The devices they used, however, failed to achieve their desired results in implementation, and immigrants continued to arrive, as we have seen, in unprecedented numbers throughout the period despite the efforts of pro-restriction groups to close the door to immigration, such as the Page Law of 1875 and the Burlingame Treaty of 1881 (LeMay and Barkan 1999: 48–50). Push factors determining the migration flow far outweighed the impact of pull factors and their policy efforts to "de-magnetize" the draw. Bennett notes and summarizes the policy shift during this era:

> The developments of the era 1880–1920 . . . turned national policy from attempts to adjust immigration problems by treaty and executive agreements back to legislation, from attempts to restrict immigration by qualitative restrictions alone to restriction of numbers as well, and continued the established policy to discriminate among potential immigrants on the basis of other considerations if it appeared to Congress that a particular race or class of immigrants offered less chance of readily assimilating into the dominant pattern of American life. (Bennett 1963: 39)

The first targets of the movement to restrict immigration, and their first national legislative success, concerned the Chinese. Anti-Chinese sentiment began building in California by the mid-1850s, as we have seen in Chapter 2 (the discussion of the Know-Nothing Party and the Workingmen's Party). The Gold Rush had drawn more than 48,000 Chinese immigrants to California in 1848–1849. When forced out of the mines, some 10,000 went to work for the Central Pacific Railroad, building the transcontinental railroad from the West Coast eastward (Central Pacific Railroad Photographic History Museum; American Experience). Anti-Chinese sentiment quickly coalesced into a political campaign against them and against unrestricted immigration.

The California legislature imposed various legal barriers on Chinese immigrants. The Foreign Miners Tax imposed a $4 per month tax, which increased each year the foreign miner did not become a citizen. Since the Chinese were barred from naturalization, it effectively expelled them from the mining camps. They were forbidden entry into public schools, denied the right to testify in court against whites, and forbidden from marrying whites. By 1865 calls for national restrictions began. In 1867, the Democratic Party swept the state offices on an anti-Chinese platform. The Panic of 1873 inspired fears of the "Yellow Peril." In 1867, the Workingmen's Party won control of San Francisco. The party called for an end to all Chinese immigration. By 1880, anti-Chinese sentiment was so strong on the West Coast that it was virtual political suicide to take their side (LeMay 1987: 53).

Violence was employed against them. In 1871, a riot in Los Angeles killed 21 Chinese immigrants. The Truckee Raid in 1874 burned down a residence of Chinese immigrants whose inhabitants were shot as they fled the flames, killing one and wounding several. The whites tried for the crime were acquitted (Truckee-Donner Historical Society). The Order of Caucasians formed advocating the elimination of Chinese through any means, including violence. They led mobs killing Chinese, driving them from their homes and terrorizing them in such cities as Denver, Tacoma, Seattle, and Oregon City (LeMay 1985: 186).

Organized labor, such as the Teamsters, became a major force behind the anti-Chinese movement. The Workingmen's Convention, the People's Protective Alliance, and Denis Kearney's Workingmen's Party of California joined labor in leading the campaign for legal restriction on Chinese immigration. Sinophobia was so strong in California that, in 1878, its constitution was amended to place a host of legal restrictions upon them. West Coast politicians pushed for federal legislation to do likewise.

The use of state and local taxes directed explicitly at them as a means to restrict their influx was declared unconstitutional by the U.S. Supreme Court in *Henderson v. Mayor of New York* in 1875. Ire over that ruling set off a six-year campaign agitating for a federal tax law. A bill to do so, however, was opposed by the steamship lines, various business and manufacturing associations, and representatives in Congress from other western and midwestern states still wanting and needing open immigration to attract the population increases they desired. In the early 1880s, the state of New York threatened to close down Castle Garden, then the major reception station, if Congress did not act (Jones 1960: 250–251; Moreno and LeMay 2013, v. 2: 206–207).

The movement to pass legislation in Congress met opposition from the executive branch. The imperial designs of foreign policy determined United States-China relations. The administration opposed California's desires to restrict immigration. When the Congress passed a Chinese Exclusion Act in 1879, it was vetoed by President Rutherford B. Hayes (March 1, 1879; Document 30, LeMay and Barkan 1999: 35–40). President Hayes did so on the grounds that the law violated the Burlingame Treaty of 1868 (Bennett 1963: 16).

Pressure to restrict Chinese immigration continued to build. Senator Sargent of California introduced a resolution to renegotiate the Burlingame treaty. The new treaty was ratified in the Senate in 1881 and proclaimed by President Chester A. Arthur in October 1881 (Document 31, LeMay and Barkan 1999: 49–50). Congress suspended all Chinese immigration for 20 years, but President Arthur vetoed that bill as well on the grounds that it still violated the treaty (veto message, April 4, 1882: Ibid: 50–51). Congress then passed yet another bill, known as the Chinese Exclusion Act (although that term was not used in the law itself; rather it used the term "suspension"), on May 6, 1882 (22 Stat. 58; 8 U.S.C.; excerpted in LeMay and Barkan 1999: 51–54). It suspended immigration of Chinese laborers for a period of 10 years. It was the first explicit immigration law excluding a category of immigrants solely on the basis of their race. Its effect was dramatic and quick. In 1881, nearly 12,000 Chinese entered the United States, and another 40,000 came in 1882, before the law took effect. Their numbers dropped to 8,000 in 1883 and to a mere 23 by 1885 (LeMay 1985: 185–186). It also explicitly prohibited their naturalization (Bennett 1963: 17).

The forces advocating restriction were still not satisfied with what they held was a limited ban on one aspect of immigration. They passed the first general immigration law with an avowed goal to restrict immigration. The Immigration Act of August 3, 1882 (22 Stat. 214; 8 U.S.C.; LeMay and Barkan 1999: 55–56), levied a 50 cent per head tax on all immigrants, charged the Secretary of the Treasury to establish contracts with each state's commissioner of immigration designated by the Secretary of the Treasury to implement immigration processing, and banned the immigration of "any convict, lunatic, idiot or any person unable to take care of himself or herself without becoming 'a public charge,'" as yet other excluded categories (Jones 1960: 251).

Congress was still not done. In 1885, it passed the Alien Contract Labor Law (Act of February 26, 1885; 23 Stat. 332, 8 U.S.C.; LeMay and Barkan 1999: 56–57). It was commonly known as the Foran Act. The Knights of Labor and other organized labor groups, which had supported the Chinese Exclusion Act, had worked hard to enact a national law prohibiting contract labor (thus another excluded category). The Order of American Mechanics, along with patriotic, veteran, and fraternal associations pushed a strident anti-immigration campaign (Divine 1957: 3). The American Protective Association, formed in Iowa in 1887, was the largest and most powerful of the Protestant secret anti-Catholic societies. It had adopted a strong position favoring restriction. Several social scientists questioned the economic value or need for immigration and advocated the use of the immigrant groups' "ability to assimilate into society" as a criterion for assessing the desirability (or lack thereof) of immigrant groups. Their writings presaged the even more blatantly restrictionist racial arguments of the early 1900s (Jones 1960: 257–258).

Ironically, the Statue of Liberty was dedicated in October 1886, just as the anti-immigration mood was escalating and when organized nativism was reviving (Vecoli and Lintelman 1984: 99).

The mid-1880s were a period of increased labor strife, racial agitation, and renewed nativism. A radical Irish-Catholic labor group known as the Molly McGuires used a violent campaign against mine owners in Pennsylvania, whom they held were egregiously exploiting Irish immigrant labor. The Haymarket Riot in Chicago, in May 1886, preceded by but a few months the formation of a new nativist political party in California—the American Party. The passing of the American frontier, officially declared at an end with the census of 1890, further stimulated xenophobia. Congress amended, in 1884, the Chinese Exclusion Act by tightening up its restrictions regarding the importing of brides of resident aliens and requiring all permanent resident aliens to acquire a "reentry certificate," essentially that period's version of the green card, before traveling to China if they planned on reentering the United States. This was a common practice among Chinese resident aliens who returned to China to get brides, particularly since miscegenation laws forbade their marrying white women (LeMay 2009: 75–76).

In 1888, Congress amended yet again the Chinese Exclusion Act, known as the Scott Act (Act of September 13, 1888, 25 Stat. 476; 8 U.S.C., 261–99; LeMay and Barkan 1999: 60–63). In October 1888, Congress barred Chinese laborers further by rescinding, ex post facto, the validity of any certificates of reentry previously granted (25 Stat. 540; 8 U.S.C. 270). That law was challenged, but despite its ex post facto nature, was upheld by the Supreme Court in *Chae Chan Ping v. U.S.*, May 13, 1889. The Court based its decision on a concept of sovereignty but revealed its racial attitudes by referencing the "vast hordes" of a "different race who will not assimilate with us" (130 U.S. 581–611—at page 606; LeMay and Barkan 1999: 65–66). According to the Supreme Court, aliens lacked the rights of citizens and thus were not governed by nor protected by the due process clause. "In the final analysis, then, the Chinese immigrant—no matter how long he was in the United States—had no vested right to return once he left the country, and could be barred from re-entry by an Act of Congress as could any first arrival" (Ringer 1983: 673).

The Push to Further Close the Door, 1890–1920

Castle Garden was officially closed on April 18, 1890 (Moreno and LeMay 2013, v. 2: 207). A depression in 1893 led to a falling off in immigration. From 1891 to 1900, only 3,687,564 immigrants enter compared to 5,246,613 in the previous decade. The depression (called the Panic of 1893) strengthened the spectrum of support for and the arguments of the restrictionist movement.

In 1891, Congress enacted an immigration law that expanded the classes of individuals excluded from admission, forbade the advertisement for and soliciting of immigrants, increased the penalties for landing an illegal alien, created the position of superintendent of immigration, and strengthened the enforcement process. It established the decisive role of the federal government in immigration affairs (Act of March 3, 1891, 26 Stat. 1084; U.S.C. 101; summarized in LeMay and Barkan 1999: 66–70; Jones 1960: 263). The sweeping powers of Congress to enact immigration law was affirmed by the U.S. Supreme Court in *Nishimura Ekiu v. United States*, January 18, 1892 (142 U.S. 651; summarized in LeMay and Barkan 1999: 70–71). The 1891 law extended the categories of excluded persons to "paupers, polygamists, and those with contagious diseases" (Mullan 1989).

Congress established a station for immigration reception on Ellis Island, signed into law by President Harrison on April 11, 1890, and opened in January 1892 (Moreno and LeMay 2013: 207; Pitkin 1975: 13–19). At other ports—Boston, Baltimore, Galveston, Key West, Philadelphia, Portland, New Orleans, and San Francisco, the federal government took over the administration from state authorities, placed immigration services of the Office of Superintendent of Immigration in the Department of the Treasury, and established the Bureau of Immigration within the department on July 12, 1891 (Moreno and LeMay, Op. Cit.; Pitkin 1975: 15).

The depression in 1893 led to renewed restrictionist fervor. The Geary Act of May 5, 1892 (27 Stat. 25; 8 U.S.C.; LeMay and Barkan 1999: 72–73) extended the exclusion of Chinese laborers by another 10 years. It has been described as the "most repressive legislation ever experienced by the Chinese in America . . . {An Act] which violated every single one of the articles of the Treaty of 1880" (Jones 1960: 263; Ringer 1983: 658–659). Yet, Congress was not done; it amended the act again on November 3, 1893 (28 Stat. 7), and on August 18, 1894 (28 Stat. 390; 8 U.S.C. 174).

The movement to restrict immigration was also benefited by a number of "scholarly" studies supporting the need for restriction and developing the concept of racism. In 1890, General Francis Walker, president of M.I.T. and incoming president of the American Economic Association, called for a sharp reduction of immigration on economic grounds. In 1894, John Fiske, Nathaniel Shaler, and Senator Henry Cabot Lodge organized the Immigration Restriction League (Divine 1957: 3). The League led the movement for the next quarter century. It advocated for the use of a literacy test and emphasized the differences between the old and the new immigrants in their capabilities to assimilate.

That year, the American Protective Association peaked in its membership before declining a few years later due to internal factional splits (Jones 1960: 256). The Knights of Labor added their strength to the movement, although it did not advocate a literacy test until 1897. One scholar summarized the trend as follows:

> From the 1890s to the First World War, and in the succeeding decade, a large number of American scholars, journalists, and politicians devoted their talents to elaborating the doctrine of "racism" as the basis for immigration and population policy. In this country, the varied and considerable literature which they produced had a profound effect in preparing the public for the National Origins Law before it passed. We might add that these writings not only molded American attitudes but proved extremely useful in the propaganda of the leaders of Nazi Germany in later years. (Bernard 1950: 16)

The establishment of a federal immigration bureaucracy was important in the implementation of immigration policy as those immigration officers could and did operate with fairly wide latitude and their actions reflected the growing racism of the period (Document 50, LeMay and Barkan 1999: 84–86).

The movement to restrict immigration was further spurred by the arrival of a surge in Japanese immigration. Japan passed its first emigration law in 1855 (ironically, in response to American pressure to open-up Japan to trade from the West), allowing for their first influx to the United States. They came to Hawaii in 1868 as contract laborers to replace Chinese "coolie" labor there (LeMay 1985: 191; Peterson 1971: 10; Ringer 1983: 685). After an initial three-year period (the length of their contract), they began to immigrate to the mainland. In 1870, there were only 56 Japanese immigrants in California. By 1890 they exceeded 24,000; and just over 72,000 in the 1910 census. In the 1920 census, they exceeded 111,000, at which level they stabilized because they were barred by the Quota Act of 1924 (LeMay 2009: 80).

In terms of their religious affiliation, they were predominately Buddhists or Shintoists. Both those religions seemed exceedingly "foreign" and "strange" to the majority of American WASPs.

Japanese immigrants adapted well to conditions on the mainland. The ratio of male to females was about 4 to 1, and they were farmers in Japan (giving them middle-class status there), and were highly literate— 98.7 percent were able to read—distinguishing them from their Western and Eastern European counterparts. Those who immigrated to the mainland established a more diversified occupational pattern. They worked on the railroads, in the mines, as domestic servants, cooks and waiters, and in groceries and dry goods. In agriculture, they concentrated in truck farming. Prior to World War I, they farmed less than 1 percent of the agricultural land in California, and that was often marginal land, yet they produced 10 percent of the state's crops (LeMay 1987: 63). As noted by one scholar, their very success earned them a negative reaction.

No matter what their first jobs, most Japanese wanted to acquire a piece of land, and many accomplished that goal piecemeal through a succession of different types of tenure. By 1909, according to the Immigration Commission's estimate, throughout the West some 6,000 Japanese were farming a total area of more than 210,000 acres. The success of these farms derived in part from an unusual degree of specialization, but more fundamentally from the hard work and extraordinary efficiency of their owners or tenants. To block this advance, California enacted the first anti-Japanese land law in 1913. Even though President Wilson sent the Secretary of State to Sacramento to argue against it, the bill passed by 35 to 2 in the Senate, and 72 to 3 in the House. Under its terms, persons ineligible for citizenship could not own agricultural land or lease it for more than three years. (Sowell 1978: 77–78)

Japanese immigrants suffered from the legal backlash against Chinese immigrants. Increasingly restrictive laws by Congress to admit, ban, or allow individuals to remain and under whatever administrative conditions, were upheld by the Supreme Court, whose majority opinion reflected the prevailing racism of the time:

No limits can be put by the Court upon the power of Congress to protect, by summary methods, the country from the advent of aliens whose race or habits render them undesirable as citizens, or to expel such if they have already found their way into our land and unlawfully remain therein. (*Wong Wing v. U.S.* 163 U.S. 228, 237, 1896)

The immigration bureaucracy became increasingly important for the process of admission or denial in the implementation of immigration policy. Boards of Special Inquiry, established in 1893, began hearing tens of thousands of cases annually. In 1910 alone, for example, they heard 70,829 cases (Pitkin 1975: 45–46). Critics assailed the boards as arbitrary, inefficient, and often politically corrupt. Following the depression of 1896, the bureau often used special inquiries to detain hundreds of Italian immigrants by invoking the "pauper" clause. Conditions on Ellis Island were so bad that immigrants rioted. Dr. Senner, then commissioner on Ellis Island, worked openly with Prescott Hall, Robert DeCourcey Ward, and Senator Henry Cabot Lodge of the Immigration Restriction League. Inspectors were hired on the basis of the party spoils system, and throughout the 1890s were badly administered and politically corrupt. The money-exchange service, baggage handling, and food concessions were a source of wealth and an inducement for corruption for businessmen who were politically connected. The sheer volume of immigrants taxed the system, as well, when Ellis Island began to process some 6,500 immigrants daily (LeMay 1987: 65).

In 1896, Terrance Powderly became the new head—then entitled Commissioner-General of Immigration—of the Bureau of Immigration in Washington, D.C., factions in the Treasury Department developed between Washington and New York, which further negatively impacted the implementation of immigration policy (Pitkin 1975: 28).

During the early 1900s, the restrictionist movement pushed for several approaches. It called for the exclusion of all Japanese as well as Chinese, advocated the extension of excluded groups, and pushed hard to enact a literacy test. A coalition under the umbrella of the Immigration Restriction League included many officials of charitable and law enforcement agencies, Protestant evangelicals, leading sociologists and biologists, organized labor, and a variety of patriotic societies.

Opposing them against any further restrictions were an assortment of ethnic societies, such as the German-American Alliance, the Ancient Order of Hibernians, the B'nai B'rith, the Hebrew Immigrant Aid Society, and the Council of the Union of American Hebrew Congregations, who joined forces with the steamship and railroad lines, and manufacturers to form the National Liberal Immigration League, in 1906, to counterbalance the Immigration Restriction League (Pitkin 1975: 36).

The Executive and Legislative branches were at odds over immigration policy. In 1896, Senator Lodge sponsored a literacy bill that passed the House and the Senate, but was vetoed by President Cleveland during his last days in office, on March 2, 1897 (Document 48, LeMay and Barkan 1999: 80–82). During the decade 1901–1910, the United States experienced the largest-ever single decade arrival of immigrants—8,795,386. Concern over Japanese immigration, coupled with the Panic of 1907 and its subsequent economic depression, fueled the fires for a renewed effort at restriction.

Fears of the "Yellow Peril" grew markedly after Japan's defeat of Russia in the Russo-Japanese War of 1905. In May 1905, the Japanese and Korean Exclusion League formed with a claimed membership of 100,000 in California alone. It was renamed the Asiatic Exclusion League in 1907 and was comprised of 231 affiliated groups, 84 percent of which were labor organizations (Ringer 1983: 688). In 1906, despite rigorous opposition from President Theodore Roosevelt, the state of California ordered

Japanese students into segregated schools (Jones 1960: 264). In 1913, California passed the Webb-Henry bill, the California Land Act, which the U.S. Supreme Court upheld as constitutional. The bill's author, California Attorney General Webb, was frank when describing the law:

> The fundamental basis of all legislation . . . has been and is, race undesirability. It seeks to limit their presence by curtailing the privileges which they may enjoy here, for they will not come in large numbers and long abide with us if they may not acquire land . . . it seeks to limit the numbers . . . by limiting the opportunities for their activities here when they arrive. (cited in Kitano 1976: 17)

President Theodore Roosevelt, after 1902, issued reforms to clean up the worst of the political corruption of the bureau, and the administration of Ellis Island. Additional attempts at a literacy bill were passed by the Congress in 1898, 1902, and 1906, all of which were vetoed. President Theodore Roosevelt used his Executive Agreement authority to negotiate with Japan what came to be called "the Gentlemen's Agreement." Using economic pressure on Japan (and by extension, Korea), and the desire of Japan's government to save face by not having the U.S. Congress pass a specific Japanese Exclusion Act like that used against the Chinese, the Roosevelt administration got Japan to limit emigration of Japanese and Korean laborers into the United States, a ban which lasted until 1948 (Executive Order No. 589, March 14, 1907; LeMay and Barkan 1999: 100–101).

Opposition to Japanese immigration and calls for restriction came from the full spectrum of political opinion. In 1907, the American Socialist Party unanimously agreed to oppose the immigration of what it called Asiatics. The Immigration Act of February 20, 1907 (34 Stat. 898; 8 U.S.C.; LeMay and Barkan 1999: 97–98) raised the head tax on immigrants from 50 cents to $4, banned persons with tuberculosis, imbeciles, and "persons of moral turpitude." It added more stringent enforcement machinery. In 1905, Ellis Island alone processed 821,169 aliens. Each inspector had to examine 400–500 immigrants per day (LeMay 1987: 67).

The Gentlemen's Agreement had its intended impact. By 1909, after the first full year of its implementation, immigrants from Japan dropped from 16,418 for the fiscal year 1908 to 3,275. It had been 30,284 in 1907. In 1910, it was less than 3,000, many of whom were "picture brides." Between 1911 and 1920, 87,000 Japanese immigrants were admitted, but 70,000 returned to Japan, for a net gain of 17,000 for the entire decade (McLeMore 1983: 161–164; Parrillo 1980: 285; Peterson 1971: 36).

In 1909, the American Federation of Labor endorsed calls for a literacy test. Congress passed a bill in 1909, but it, too, was vetoed by President Taft. His Secretary of Labor argued there was still a need for immigrant labor (Bernard 1950: 13–14; Handlin 1959: 186).

In 1910, the Congress amended the 1907 law to remove all limitations on the deportation of alien prostitutes, an act known as the White-Slave Traffic Act (June 25, 1910, 36 Stat. 825; U.S.C. 397–404; LeMay and Barkan 1999: 101–102). Agitation for still more restriction continued, and a special commission on immigration, the Dillingham Commission, met and studied immigration policy. It was composed of nine members; three senators, three representatives, and three presidential appointees, and stacked heavily in favor of restrictionism. It issued its massive report (42 volumes) in 1911. Although described as an objective and scientific study, it was racially biased, as was evident in its findings. Not surprising, given its membership, it recommended a literacy test that it held was "demanded by economic, moral, and social considerations" (Document 61: LeMay and Barkan 1999: 103–107). It openly stated that the purpose of the literacy test was to decrease immigration by 25 percent (which it failed to do). The Commission accepted the Darwinian theories espoused by the Immigration Restriction League taken from the writings of John Commons, Edward Ross, William Ripley's *The Races of Europe* (1899), and augmented by Madison Grant's influential work, *The Passing of the Great Race in America* (1916).

The commission's recommendations did not go unchallenged. Scholars and social workers disputed the report's findings—especially by Jane Addams and the Hull House movement in Chicago, and by Grace Abbott of the Immigrants Protective League.

The pro-immigration forces had their own literature. Journalist Jacob Riis' *The Making of America*, Mary Antin's *The Promised Land*, Carl Schurz's *Reminiscences*, Edward Steiner's *On the Trail of the Immigrant*, and Louis Adamic's *Two-Way Passages* counterbalanced that of the Immigration Restriction League (Bernard 1950: 17).

Congress passed a literacy bill in 1913, which was vetoed by President Taft. It then moved the immigration service to the newly created Department of Labor (37 Stat. 737), which divided the service into two bureaus, the Bureau of Immigration headed by a commissioner general, and the Bureau of Naturalization. They were placed under the immediate direction of the Secretary of Labor, who promptly reduced the immigration service staff.

World War I saw an interlude in immigration. Where more than 1,200,000 entered in 1914, that number had dropped off by 75 percent, to just over 300,000 in 1915. In 1918, less than 30,000 were processed through Ellis Island. The reduction in immigration eased political pressure to restrict immigration by law, but in 1915 the Congress did pass another literacy bill, promptly vetoed by President Woodrow Wilson, and his veto was sustained. Wilson labeled it a test of opportunity, not of intelligence (LeMay and Barkan 1999: 107–108).

The Bolshevik Revolution in Russia, however, aroused fears of radicalism and renewed calls for restriction. They were more effective in the postwar years. The American Legion, the National Grange, and the American Federation of Labor all strongly supported a literacy bill. This time the new law was enacted over President Wilson's veto (39 Stat. 874; 8 U.S.C.; LeMay and Barkan 1999: 109–112; Daniels 1990: 278–279). The new law doubled the head tax from $4 to $8, added chronic alcoholics, vagrants, and those suffering from "psychopathic inferiority" to the list of excluded classes; barred advocates of polygamy, anarchists, or persons who advocate the overthrow by violence of the government of the United States or those who "advocate the assassination of public officials and teach the unlawful destruction of property"; as well as providing for the literacy test. In 1917, Congress also passed the Asiatic Barred-Zone, which virtually excluded all Chinese, Japanese, and Korean immigration.

In 1917, a joint order of the Department of State and the Department of Labor was issued requiring passports and certain other information from all aliens seeking to enter the United States during World War I, and the issuance of visas from American consular offices in the country of origin rather than allowing persons to enter the United States and seek permission having already arrived at the port of entry (Document 65, LeMay and Barkan 1999: 113–115). The war also led Congress to amend the naturalization laws to reward certain persons with special naturalization provisions, for example, Filipinos, seamen serving in U.S. merchant marine or on U.S. fishing vessels, or other persons serving in U.S. armed forces (40 Stat. 542: 8 U.S.C. 388).

In 1918, President Wilson issued an executive order specifying rules and regulations to implement a proclamation concerning the exclusion, entrance, and departure of aliens during the war (Executive Order 2932, August 8, 1918; LeMay and Barkan 1999: 119–120). In October 1918, Congress expanded the provisions of the 1903 Act adding membership in or espousal of communism to the list of excluded classes or those subject to expulsion which previously had stipulated anarchists, and provided the legal justification for the infamous Palmer Raids in the Red-Scare summer of 1919 (40 Stat. 1012; 8 U.S.C. 137; LeMay and Barkan 1999: 120–121).

Conclusion

Although the "golden door" to America remained open during the period 1880–1920, allowing for the entrance of an unprecedented number of immigrants, the period can be characterized as one in which forces advocating restriction became increasingly vocal in articulating what they saw as the "problem" of immigration, more effective in getting their proposed solutions on the agenda of government at the state and national levels, and increasingly successful in getting their proposals enacted into law. The door to America was still open, but it was ajar and swinging in the direction of closure.

The period also saw changes in the nature of American federalism with respect to immigration policy making, with a movement in the direction of centralization at the national level. Likewise, the interaction between the branches of government with respect to immigration policy making shifted notably. The judicial branch at both state and federal levels ruled in favor of expanding the powers of the legislative branch to enact and to implement immigration policy that was moving steadily in the direction of restriction.

At the national level, throughout the period, the various presidential administrations acted to challenge the legislative branch with respect to immigration policy making. Presidents issued proclamations and executive orders expanding on the executive's powers to negotiate agreements and to specify administrative rules and procedures in implementing immigration policy. Every president in office during the era vetoed bills passed by the Congress which were restrictive on immigration policy, most often because the administration saw such legislation as being detrimental to American foreign policy considerations.

The Door Ajar era was characterized, as well, by the formation of extensive coalitions of political pressure groups advocating or opposing enactment of restrictive policy. The forces in favor of increasing restriction found a growing number of congressional members willing to act on their behalf in passing bills that sought to close the door to open immigration, and generally succeeded in doing so. They advocated an approach to restriction that relied upon specifying more excluded categories or classes of individuals, and based those exclusions on characteristics of the excluded classes which they believed made them undesirable or unable to assimilate into American society. The bases for exclusion ranged from espousing radical political ideology to physical characteristics that might limit the immigrant's ability to work and support themselves rather than becoming public charges, to exclusion based on a growing number of diseases or to WASPs' perceptions of moral turpitude.

The political faction advocating restriction grew to become quite successful in articulating what they saw as the nature of the immigration policy (policy problem formation), and proposing and getting their solutions on the agenda of government at the local, state, and federal levels (policy formulation). They succeeded in getting quite a number of their proposals enacted into law (policy adoption). Their proposed solutions to the immigration problem, however, failed to achieve their anticipated results upon policy implementation. Despite their best efforts, immigrants arrived in ever-increasing numbers and surged or ebbed in response to push factors more than to the legislative actions to "de-magnetize" the pull factors. Depressions and wars had more impact than any law enacted to decrease the draw of America.

It was precisely those failures to reduce immigration numbers at the close of the Door Ajar era set the stage for a new approach and method to reduce immigration—the quota system—that characterized the next era of immigration policy making, the Pet Door phase, the subject of Chapter 4.

References

Adamic, Louis. 1945. *A Nation of Nations*. New York: Harper Brothers.

Allport, Gordon. 1958. *The Nature of Prejudice*. New York: Doubleday.

American Experience. www.pbs.org/wgbh/americanexperience/features/timeline/ tcrr-timeline.

Andrews, Anthony. 1995. *First Cities*. Washington, DC: Smithsonian Books.

Barone, Michael. 2013. *Shaping Our Nation: How Surges of Migration Transformed America and Its Politics*. New York: Crown Forum.

Bayor, Ronald. 1978. *Neighbors in Conflict*. Baltimore: Johns Hopkins University Press.

Bennett, Marion. 1963. *American Immigration Policy: A History*. Washington, DC: Public Affairs Press.

Bernard, William, ed. 1950. *American Immigration Policy: A Reappraisal*. Washington, DC: Public Affairs Press.

Burgess, Thomas. 1913. *Greeks in America*. Boston: Sherman, French & Company.

Central Pacific Railroad Photographic History Museum. http://www.cprr.org/ Museum/. Accessed April 11, 2015.

Daniels, Roger. 1990. *Coming to America: A History of Immigration and Ethnicity in American Life*. New York: Harper.

Davis, Jerome. 1976. *The Russian Immigrant*. New York: Arno Press.

Dinnerstein, Leonard, and David Reimers. 1988. *Ethnic Americans*. New York: Harper and Row.

Divine, Robert A. 1957. *American Immigration Policy, 1924–1952*. New Haven, CT: Yale University Press.

Draper, Theodore. 1957. *The Roots of American Communism*. New York: Viking Press.
Draper, Theodore. 1960. *American Communism and Soviet Russia*. New York: Viking Press.
Fairchild, Henry. 1911. *Greek Immigration*. New Haven, CT: Yale University Press.
Federal Writers Project. 1969. *The Italians of New York*. New York: Arno Press.
Grant, Madison. 1916. *The Passing of the Great Race*. New York: Arno Press.
Handlin, Oscar. 1959. *Immigration as a Factor in American History*. Englewood Cliffs, NJ: Prentice-Hall.
Handlin, Oscar. 1963. *The Americans*. Boston: Little, Brown.
Higham, John. 1955. *Strangers in the Land: Patterns of American Nativism, 1860–1925*. New Brunswick, NJ: Rutgers University Press.
Hoerder, Dirk, ed. 1982. *American Labor and Immigration History, 1877–1920*. Urbana: University of Illinois Press.
Howe, Irving. 1976. *World of Our Fathers*. New York: Simon and Schuster.
Industrial Workers of the World. http://www.iww.org/. Accessed April 12, 2015.
Iorizzo, Luciano, and Salvatore Mondello. 1971. *The Italian Americans*. New York: Twayne.
Italian American One Voice Coalition. http://www.iaovc.org/. Accessed April 11, 2015).
Janikowsky, Oscar. 1964. *The American Jews: A Reappraisal*. Philadelphia: Jewish Publications Society of America.
Jones, Maldwyn Allen. 1960. *American Immigration*. Chicago: University of Chicago.
Kitano, Harry. 1976. *Japanese Americans: The Evolution of a Subculture*. Englewood Cliffs, NJ: Prentice-Hall.
Kohn, George C., ed. 1995. *Encyclopedia of Plague and Pestilence*. New York: Facts on File.
Kraut, Alan. 1994. *Silent Travelers: Germs, Genes, and the "Immigration Menace."* Baltimore: The Johns Hopkins University Press.
LeMay, Michael. 1985. *The Struggle for Influence*. Lanham, MD: University Press of America.
LeMay, Michael. 1987. *From Open Door to Dutch Door*. Westport, CT: Praeger Press.
LeMay, Michael. 2006. *Guarding the Gates: Immigration and National Security*. Westport, CT: Praeger Security International.
LeMay, Michael. 2009. *The Perennial Struggle*, 3rd edition. Upper Saddle-River, NJ: Prentice Hall.
LeMay, Michael, ed. 2013. *Transforming America: Perspectives on U.S. Immigration, the Transformation of a Nation of Nations, 1865–1945*, vol. 2. Santa Barbara, CA: ABC-CLIO.
LeMay, Michael. 2015. *Doctors at the Borders: Immigration and the Rise of Public Health*. Westport, CT: Praeger Press.
LeMay, Michael. 2016. *Global Pandemic Threats*. Santa Barbara, CA: ABC-CLIO.
LeMay, Michael, and Elliott Barkan. 1999. *U.S. Immigration Laws and Issues: A Documentary History*. Westport, CT: Greenwood Press.

Leventman, Seymour. 1969. *The Ghetto and Beyond*. New York: Random House.

Lieberson, Stanley. 1980. *A Piece of the Pie*. Berkeley: University of California Press.

Litt, Edgar. 1970. *Ethnic Politics in America*. Glenview, IL: Scott, Foresman.

Lopata, Helena. 1976. *Polish Americans*. Englewood Cliffs, NJ: Prentice Hall.

Lynch, Timothy. 2013. "Immigration and Shipping Lines, 1865–1945." In *Transforming America: Perspectives on U.S. Immigration*, vol. 2. Edited by LeMay, 73–89. Santa Barbara, CA: ABC-CLIO.

McLemore, Dale. 1983. *Racial and Ethnic Relations in America*, 2nd edition. Boston: Allyn and Bacon.

Moreno, Barry, and Michael LeMay. 2013. "The Ellis Island Station." In *Transforming America: Perspectives on Immigration*. Edited by LeMay, 197–223. Santa Barbara, CA: ABC-CLIO.

Moskos, Charles. 1980. *Greek Americans: Struggle and Success*. Englewood Cliffs, NJ: Prentice Hall.

Mullan, Fitzhugh. 1989. *Plagues and Politics: The Story of the United States Public Health Service*. New York: Basic Books.

Nelli, Humbert. 1970. *Italians in Chicago: 1830–1930*. New York: Oxford University Press.

Orthodox Church in America. http://www.oca.org. Accessed May 2, 2017.

Parrillo, Vincent. 1980. *Strangers to These Shores*. New York: Houghton Mifflin.

Parrillo, Vincent. 1996. *Diversity in America*. Thousand Oaks, CA: Pine Forge Press.

Peterson, William. 1971. *Japanese Americans: Oppression and Success*. New York: Random House.

Pitkin, Thomas. 1975. *Keepers of the Gate*. New York: New York University Press.

Ringer, Benjamin. 1983. *We the People and Others*. New York: Tavistock.

Ripley, William. 1899. *The Races of Europe*. New York: Lowell Institute, Columbia University Press.

Rippley, Levern. 1973. *The German Americans*. Chicago: Claretian Press.

Soloutos, Theodore. 1964. *The Greeks in the United States*. Cambridge, MA: Harvard University Press.

Sowell, Thomas, ed. 1978. *Essays and Data on American Ethnic Groups*. Washington, DC: The Urban Institute Press.

Sowell, Thomas. 1981. *Ethnic America: A History*. New York: Basic Books.

Steen, Ivan. 2006. *Urbanizing America: The Development of Cities in the United States from the First European Settlements to 1920*. Malabar, FL: Krieger.

Taylor, Philip. 1971. *The Distant Magnet: European Emigration to America*. New York: Harper and Row.

Thernstrom, Stephen. 1980. *Harvard Encyclopedia of American Ethnic Groups*. Cambridge, MA: Harvard University Press.

Thomas, William, and Florian Znanicki. 1977. "The Polish American Community." In *Uncertain Americans*. Edited by Dinnerstein, Leonard, and Frederick Jaher. New York: Oxford University Press.

Truckee-Donner Historical Society. www.truckeehistory.org/history-and-research .html. Accessed April 11, 2015.

United Mine Workers of America. http://www.umwa.org/. Accessed April 12, 2015.

United States, Department of Commerce. 2003. *Statistical Abstract of the United States, 2002.* Washington, DC: U.S. Government Printing Office.

Vecoli, Rudolph, and Joy Lintelman. 1984. *A Century of American Immigration, 1884–1984.* Minneapolis: University of Minnesota Continuing Education and Extension.

Ward, David. 1971. *Cities and Immigrants: A Geography of Change in 19th Century America.* New York: Oxford University Press.

Wong Wing v. United States, 163 U.S. 228, 1896.

Zolberg, Aristide. 2008. *A Nation by Design: Immigration Policy in the Fashioning of America.* Cambridge, MA: Russell Sage Foundation at Harvard University Press.

CHAPTER FOUR

The Pet Door Era, 1920–1950

Introduction: Establishing the Quota System

By the 1920s, the mood of the country and support for a more restrictive approach to immigration policy making had clearly set in, as was signaled by the ability of Congress to override President Wilson's veto of the literacy act of 1917. However, the failure of the literacy test approach to achieve its desired and anticipated effect of dramatically reducing immigration upon its implementation led restrictionist forces to consider another option. In passing the literacy test bill, they had achieved their desired policy output but not their desired policy outcome. The Red Scare in the summer of 1919, reflecting a xenophobic fear of "Godless Bolshevism" coming to America with immigrants from Russia, set the stage for a new era of immigration policy making and a new approach—the use of national origin quotas (Draper 1957; Zolberg 2008). The new approach was to enact effective restrictionism, one which would close the door to all but a favored few—hence the image of the Pet Door to characterize this phase.

When it became clear that the literacy test was not enough to stem large-scale immigration, proponents of restriction were forced to advocate a more stringent measure—the imposition of absolute numbers and as a percentage of the total population.

Many in the restrictionist movement called for the total suspension of immigration anywhere from 2 to as long as 50 years. They were alarmed that during the decade 1901 to 1910, immigration to the United States reached its highest-ever levels in absolute numbers (8,795,386), and in the annual immigration as a percentage of the population (Select Commission on Immigration and Refugee Policy, 1981, *Staff Report*: 28).

Restrictionists realized a more drastic step was needed than any previous measure passed if they were to stem what they viewed as the flood of immigration. They shifted their strategy from advocating a literacy test to the imposition of quotas based on national origin, and did so with dramatic results, both in numbers and in source of origin.

The pronounced movement away from Southern, Central, and Eastern European countries toward those from Northwestern Europe is evident, as is the shift toward greater numbers from the Western Hemisphere (i.e., Canada, North and South America). The numbers arriving per decade were slashed by more than half in the first decade of the national origins system (from 8,795,386 to 4,107,209). Those numbers plunged during the next two decades (to 528,431, then to 1,035,039). The dramatic drop in the number of immigrants arriving within a decade, however, was not solely or even chiefly the result of the quota system. The numbers were far less than what was legally allowed. Immigration plunged mostly as a result of the worldwide depression of the 1930s and World War II in the 1940s.

This chapter discusses how and why those dramatic changes occurred. It begins that discussion by focusing on the 1921 emergency immigration act which introduced the quota system. It was heavily weighted in favor of immigrants from Northwestern Europe. The 1924 National Origins Act modified the quotas given to nations by the 1921 Act with an even greater bias against immigration from Southern, Central, and Eastern European nations, unquestionably due in part to aversion to their religious affiliations of Catholicism, Orthodoxy, and Judaism. The 1924 act firmly set the principle of the national origin system, which lasted more than 30 years. The immigration act of 1929 fixed the numbers permanently, although as we shall see, the quota system began to break down in the 1950s and was totally replaced in 1965.

The Quota Act of 1921

The fervor for restrictions in immigration policy making reached its zenith between 1917 and 1921. An "Americanization" movement swept the nation in the aftermath of World War I. Such was the hysteria of the war period that people had called sauerkraut "liberty cabbage," and hamburgers became "Salisbury steaks" (LeMay 1987: 74). A host of cities and towns changed street names from foreign-sounding ones to American-sounding ones. Oregon passed a law requiring all school children to attend public schools (clearly aimed directly against Catholic parochial schools), and California enacted legislation requiring every adult male alien to register and to pay a special annual poll tax of $10. Both these state laws were subsequently declared unconstitutional, but their passage demonstrated the zeal and the WASP orientation of the Americanization movement (Higham 1955: 260). Henry Ford's notorious newspaper, the *Dearborn Independent*, launched a massive anti-Jewish campaign and stressed the need to restrict immigration. The revived Ku Klux Klan (KKK) grew in membership and political influence. The Klan, which was avowedly anti-Catholic, anti-Semitic, and anti-black, advocated strict restrictions on immigration. The Klan was reborn in 1915, when the film *The Birth of a Nation* exalted the old Klansmen of the pre-Civil War era. It exploited xenophobia and spread far beyond the South. Race riots wracked 26 cities in 1919. By 1922, the Ku Klux Klan had established chapters in all states. It claimed a membership (likely exaggerated) of five million. Its zenith of power and influence was reached in 1928, when its membership was estimated at eight million. It pushed for restrictive legislation at the national level and used social discrimination and outright terrorism at the local level. The Klan's use of violence, including riots and lynchings of Catholics as well as blacks, ultimately led to its decline (LeMay 1985: 109).

The American Federation of Labor (AFL) continued its campaign, begun in 1880, to limit the immigration of "cheap labor." Both the Democratic and Republican Party platforms called for effective limits on immigration (LeMay 1987: 74; LeMay and Barkan 1999: 128, 145–148).

The fear that the economic chaos that had gripped Europe during the immediate postwar years would lead to another flood of immigrants to the United States helped increase the ranks and the appeal of the restrictionist movement. When the United States suffered a depression in 1920, the enactment of some sort of restrictionist immigration law seemed inevitable. Indeed, in 1920, the House of Representatives passed a bill to end all immigration, but the Senate refused to go that far and the bill died in Congress. Nonetheless, a number of leading senators advocated a strict restrictionist policy: Senators Warren Harding (R-OH), Hiram W. Johnson (R-CA), Henry Cabot Lodge, Senate Majority Leader (R-MA), James E. Watson (R-IN), Harry S. New (R-ID), and William Dillingham (R-VT) (Office of the Senate). There were few defenders of open immigration in the Senate.

Restrictionist were gaining not only in numbers in the U.S. Congress but also in the importance and influence of their positions: Henry Cabot Lodge (R-MA) served as the Senate Majority Leader, Senator William Dillingham (R-VT) as chair of the Senate Immigration Committee; Albert Johnson (R-WA) as chair of the House Immigration Committee—all of whom were arch restrictionist (LeMay 1987: 77; Taylor 1971: 244).

A postwar isolationism infused public sentiment and was easily tapped by those forces advocating limits on immigration. The new nationalism was committed to isolationism and disdainful of all foreigners. It figured prominently in the debates over joining the League of Nations and in large measure accounted for the rejection of the treaty. It swayed the position taken by the American Legion. It rumbled in the "konklaves" of the Ku Klux Klan. It unleashed a torrent of state laws excluding aliens from many occupations, and licensing acts barred them from practicing architecture, engineering, chiropractic, pharmacy, medicine, surgery, and executing wills. Such laws even went so far as to ban their operating motor buses (Higham 1955: 271, 301; LeMay and Barkan 1999: 128).

Responding to the resurgence of immigration in 1921 (almost doubling, up from 430,000 in 1920 to 805,000 in 1921), Congress passed the first immigration quota act, summarized in Box 4.1. It reflected the racist theories of the restrictionist movement. That racism was evident, too, in the U.S. Supreme Court decision, in November 1922, *Ozawa v. United States* (260 U.S. 195), which upheld the constitutionality of a blatantly racist law that made Japanese aliens ineligible for citizenship (LeMay and Barkan 1999: 133–138).

BOX 4.1: SUMMARY EXCERPTS OF THE QUOTA ACT OF 1921, THE "EMERGENCY QUOTA ACT"

Sec. 2. (a) That the number of aliens of any nationality who may be admitted under the immigration laws to the United States in any fiscal year shall be limited to 3 per centum of the number of foreign-born persons of such nationality resident in the United States as determined by the United States census of 1910. This provision shall not apply to the following, and they shall not be counted in reckoning any of the percentage limits provided in this Act: (1) Governmental officials, their families, attendants, servants, and employees; (2) aliens in continuous transit through the United States; (3) aliens lawfully admitted to the United States who later go in transit . . . to another foreign contiguous territory; (4) aliens visiting the United States as tourists or temporarily for business or pleasure; (5) aliens from countries from which is regulated in accordance with treaties or agreements relating solely to immigration; (6) aliens from the so-called Asiatic barred zone . . . (7) aliens who have resided continuously for at least five years immediately preceding the time of their application for admission . . . in the Dominion of Canada, Newfoundland, the Republic of Cuba, the Republic of Mexico, countries of Central and South America, or adjacent islands; or (8) aliens under the age of eighteen who are children of citizens of the United States.

(b) For the purposes of this Act nationality shall be determined by country of birth, treating as separate countries the colonies or dependencies for which separate enumeration was made in the United States census of 1910;

(c) That the Secretary of State, the Secretary of Commerce, and the Attorney General, jointly, shall as soon as feasible after enactment of this Act, prepare a statement showing the number of persons of the various nationalities resident in the United States as determined by the census of 1910, which statement shall be the population basis for the purposes of this Act;

(d) When the maximum number of aliens from any nationality who may be admitted in any fiscal year under this Act shall have been admitted all other aliens of such nationality, except as otherwise provided for by this Act . . . shall be excluded . . .

Sec. 3. That the Commissioner of Immigration and Naturalization, with the approval of the Attorney General, shall as soon as feasible after the enactment of this Act, and from time to time hereafter, prescribe rules and regulations necessary to carry the provisions of this Act into effect. He shall, as soon as feasible . . . publish a statement showing the number of aliens of the various nationalities who may be admitted to the United States . . . Thereafter he shall publish monthly statements during the time this Act remains in force showing the number of aliens of each nationality already admitted under the provisions of this Act . . . and the number who may be admitted . . . during the then current fiscal year . . . but when 75 per centum of the maximum number of any nationality . . . shall have been admitted such statements shall be issued weekly thereafter . . .

Sec. 6. That it shall be unlawful for any person, including any transportation company other than railway lines entering the United States from a foreign contiguous territory, or the owner, master, agent, or consignee of any vessel, to bring to the United States either from a foreign country or any insular possession of the United States any alien not admissible under the terms of this Act or regulations made there under. 42. Stat. 5:8 U.S.C. 229; LeMay and Barkan 1999, Document 73: 133–135.

The Red Scare in the summer of 1919, coupled with a depression, resulted in forces one might otherwise expect to have been in favor of more open policy to switch and cast their support for the Quota Act. The Progressive Party voiced concern about the nation's ability to absorb and assimilate so many aliens. *The New Republic* mused that unrestricted immigration was an element of 19th-century liberalism fated to end and that a progressive society could not allow excessive immigration to aggravate social ills (Higham 1955: 302).

Business interests that previously favored an open door policy were either silent or changed to a restrictionist position. The 1920 depression meant that there was no labor shortage. Many business leaders accepted the arguments of the "100 Percenters," the American Legion, and similar nationalist groups within the Americanization movement. Kenneth Roberts published a series of articles in the *Saturday Evening Post*. His article and the *Post* became leading proponents of the restrictionist crusade from 1920 to 1924. His article popularized an arsenal of arguments that comprised an "ethnic theory" (Divine 1957: 10). The halls of Congress echoed with calls to end the "alien flood," "barbarian horde," and "foreign tide." In the words of a representative from Arkansas:

> We have admitted the dregs of Europe until America has been orientalized, Europeanized, Africanized and mongrelized to that insidious degree that our genius, stability, greatness, and promise of advancement and achievement are actually menaced. Accordingly, I should like to exclude all foreigners for years to come, at least until we can ascertain whether or not the foreign and discordant element now in what many are pleased to term "our great melting pot" will melt into real American citizens. (cited in Ringer 1983: 801)

Such sentiments were a far cry from those words inscribed but a few decades earlier at the base of the Statue of Liberty.

When business forces were either silent or switched to a pro-restriction position, enactment of a bill limiting immigration became inevitable. Adoption of the 1921 Act was almost unopposed in Congress. As one historian of immigration policy notes:

> Fundamentally, it was the transformation in American economic and political development that set the stage for restriction. The growth of the American economy and particularly the technological changes brought about by the industrial revolution had greatly reduced the need for the raw labor furnished by immigrants. A mature industrial system required a moderate number of trained workers, not great masses of manual labor. (Divine 1957: 9)

When the United States emerged from World War I as a true world power, it developed an intense nationalism in which U.S. citizens increasingly demanded amalgamation, unity, conformity. Isolationism was the favored approach to foreign policy. The new position of the United States on the international scene became a base for restrictionist policy.

The thrust of advocating the quota approach came from several sources. The return to economic prosperity in 1921 meant economic issues became a secondary element in the debates over passage of immigration law. When the National Association of Manufacturers led the pro-immigration forces, the AFL attacked them as being interested only in cheap labor. The AFL argued strenuously that there was already an adequate supply of labor for the workforce. A leading sociologist, Henry Pratt Fairchild (1911), advocated the position taken by organized labor. Economic arguments became deadlocked between the two groups. "Ethnic theories" took on increased importance in the debate over immigration policy making. Such theories weighted more heavily the elements of racism and alien religiosity in their perception of national identity or sense of people-hood. Protestant Christian evangelists insisted that America was founded as a "Christian nation." Carl Brigham, a Princeton psychologist famous for developing the I.Q. test, William MacDougall of Harvard University, who proposed a Nordic Race superiority theory, and Dr. Harry Laughlin, the prominent "eugenist" and "biological expert" for the House Immigration Committee and who went so far as to advocate the sterilization of all inmates institutionalized, were leading proponents of the restrictionist approach (Bernard 1950: 29). Gino Speranza, a native-born citizen of Italian descent, wrote a series of articles in *World's Work* that popularized the idea of the need for national unity and conformity by defending racial and cultural homogeneity. They articulated an amalgamation model of assimilation. These sources helped forge a new concept of "racial nationality" as the sense of people-hood. Madison Grant popularized such racial theory. In *The Passing of the Great Race*, Grant opined that the United States was becoming inundated by:

> . . . a large and increasing number of the weak and broken and mentally crippled of all races drawn from the lower stratum of the Mediterranean and the Balkans, together with the hordes of the wretched submerged populations of the Polish ghettos. Our jails, insane asylums, and almshouses are filled with this human flotsam and the whole of American life, social, moral and political, has been lowered and vulgarized by them. (Grant 1916: 89–90)

Grant's book, first published in 1916, was released in new editions in 1921 and 1923, and sold nearly 16,000 copies. He also published a series of editorials in the *New York Times* and the *Saturday Evening Post.* Grant inspired a number of popular writers and even influenced some scholarly ones. He was the leading proponent of a theory that recognized within the "white race" a three-tiered hierarchy of Mediterranean, Alpine, and Nordic races. According to Grant, white Americans were Nordics, the highest race, and should regard any mixture with the other two as a destructive process to pure racial homogeneity (cited in Higham 1955: 272).

By 1921 such views were reflected in Congress. Congressmen from both major parties argued that the melting pot had failed and that immigration was causing the nation to suffer from "alien indigestion." They feared aloud that the nation was becoming an "intermingled and mongrelized people," and began substituting the idea of racial purity for the melting pot. A Maryland senator called for a racially pure country so that the United States might achieve the greatness of England, France, or Germany. A congressman from Maine invoked God and Christianity to his side of the argument over the direction of immigration policy when he opined:

> God intended, I believe, that the United States be the home of a great people. English speaking—a white race with great ideals, the Christian religion, one race, one country, and one destiny . . . It [the United States] was a mighty land, settled by northern Europeans from the United Kingdom, the Norsemen, and the Saxons. The Africans, the orientals, the Mongolians, and all the yellow races of Europe, Asia, and Africa should never have been allowed to people this great land. (cited in Ringer 1983: 801–802)

By 1921, the House Committee on Immigration was the most prominent voice of these racial theories and was stressing racial theory as the *fundamental* justification for restriction.

As mentioned, the Supreme Court held racist ideas evident in *Ozawa v. U.S.* (260 U.S., 1922; LeMay and Barkan 1999: 136–138), which used blatantly racist ideas to uphold the constitutionality of a law that made the Japanese "aliens ineligible for citizenship" (see also Ringer 1983: 790–791). In 1927, the Court upheld an ordinance of Cincinnati that barred noncitizens from operating pool halls. It acknowledged the Fourteenth Amendment's prohibition against irrational discrimination, but held that the Cincinnati ordinance was not irrational. The Court agreed with the lawyer for Cincinnati that pools halls were vile places in need of strong police powers to curb them, and since "noncitizens" were a class less familiar with the laws and customs of the nation (and in this case, the municipality), than were native-born or naturalized citizens, it was a reasonable exercise of local police power to exclude them. The Court agreed that "alien race and allegiance" may be a legitimate object of legislation so as to be made the basis of a permanent classification. The same judicial reasoning had earlier allowed for state licensing laws that limited aliens in practicing various professions (*Clarke v. Deckenbeck*, 274 U.S. 392, 1917).

The principle of allocating quotas on the basis of those already represented by the various nationalities among the foreign-born population was first introduced, in 1914, by Dr. Sidney Gulick. He intended it as a liberal alternative to positions being advocated by the strict restrictionist who had begun advocating a total suspension of immigration. Dr. Gulick was a former missionary in Asia. In 1918, he formed the National Committee on Constructive Immigration Legislation. Dr. Gulick suggested that each nationality be assigned a quota proportionate to the number of naturalized citizens and their American-born children already drawn from that nationality. His idea was that annually an immigration commission would fix a certain percentage—he suggested 10 percent—of those first and second generation citizens. As he put it: "The proved capacity for genuine Americanization on the part of those already here from any land should be the measure for the further immigration of that people" (cited in Higham 1955: 302). The former missionary must have been appalled by the way his suggested principle was applied.

The "percentage quota principle," as it became known as, was soon the central piece of all immigration passed in the 1920s. What differed among its advocates was the notion of precisely how the quotas should be established. After enactment of the 1921 law, however, the basic principle that there should be quotas was fairly well accepted. The pivotal and basic function of the quota system was to limit immigration from Europe. The congressional battles were largely over how to distribute such quotas among the various nations of Europe (there was by then a consensus that Asian immigration should be totally excluded) (LeMay 1987: 81).

In the final congressional debate over the bill, and in later skirmishes in 1923 and 1924, the primary organizational support for the national origins bill included: the American Federation of Labor, the American Legion, the Immigration Restriction League, the National Grange, the Ku Klux Klan, the Junior Order of the United American Mechanics, as well as patriotic associations such as the Sons of the American Revolution, the Patriotic Order of the Sons of America, and the Daughters of the American Revolution. The primary organizations in opposition to the national origins bill included: the Anti-National Origins Clause League, a New York taxpayers association, several industrial and employer organizations, chiefly the National Association of Manufacturers, the American Mining Congress, the Associated General Contractors, the National Industrial Conference Board, and the U.S. Chamber of Commerce, as well as some farm organizations concerned that agriculture would be denied sufficient manpower; and spokespersons for various Jewish, foreign-language and other "ethnic" groups that would be adversely affected by the use of 1890 as a base year, such as the Vasa Order of America (Swedish Lutherans), the Steuben Society, the Danish Brotherhood of America, the Sons of Norway, and the German American Citizens League (Bennett 1963: 52–53; Divine 1957: 33–37; LeMay 1987: 81).

The Senate passed a bill, sponsored by Senator Dillingham, which limited European immigration to 5 percent of the total number of foreign born of that nationality based on the 1910 census. Dillingham's bill exempted Canada and Latin America from the quota system. The Senate version would have limited total annual immigration to 250,000. It passed easily in the Senate, opposed only by several southern and western senators favoring a total suspension of immigration. The House abandoned its various suspension plans in favor of the Senate quota system, but reduced the limits from 5 to 3 percent of the 1910 census (Higham 1955: 310–11). It limited total immigration to 350,000, assigning most of that to Northwestern Europe. Congress adopted a version in a conference committee and sent the bill to President Woodrow Wilson, who killed the bill with a pocket veto during his last days in office—a veto soon to be in vain.

The incoming president, Warren Harding, called a special session of Congress. In the House, Albert Johnson supported the quota bill rather than his own total suspension bill. It passed the House without a recorded vote. In the Senate, it passed 78 to 1, and was signed into law by President Harding in May 1921. It became commonly known as the Johnson Act, the Emergency Immigration Restriction Act of 1921. It first established the principle of the quota system, heavily favoring Northwestern Europe. In setting annual immigration at 357,803, it drastically cut total immigration and shifted the composition of immigration by limiting Asia, Africa, and Oceania to less than 1,000 immigrants, Northwestern Europe to 200,000 immigrants, and Southeastern Europe to 155,000 immigrants. The act reaffirmed all previous restrictions on "excluded groups" by barring the mentally, physically, and morally undesirable classes, including those persons likely to become public charges as established in the 1917 Act. The central basis for determining each nation's quota under the 1921 law was 3 percent of the foreign-born population present in the United

States according to the 1910 census data (42 Stat.5: 8 U.S.C. 229, summarized in LeMay and Barkan: 133–135). The law was the first numerical limitation on immigration, although not the first racially or ethnically biased immigration law.

The Immigration Quota Act of 1924

Enactment of the 1921 law hardly settled the matter. Restrictionists were not fully satisfied that the law limited sufficiently the flow of immigration. The hastily set up quotas and the procedures to enforce the quotas imposed harsh injustices as ships arriving during the first months after passage of the law often carried more than the monthly quota from that country would allow for entry. Polish, Rumanian, and Italian immigrants soon jammed Ellis Island and steamships at anchor in the harbors of Boston and New York. Administrative "exemptions" to the monthly quotas necessitated by these dire conditions angered the congressional restrictionist forces.

For two years, Congress was deadlocked over attempts to set up a more permanent quota system. Albert Johnson's immigration committee in the House, with strong and vocal backing of the AFL and the American Legion, continued to advocate total suspension. Preston Hall, of the Immigration Restriction League, Madison Grant, Lothrop Stoddard, Kenneth Roberts (a novelist and journalist, who supported total restriction), and Harry Laughlin all voiced support for the Johnson Committee and stirred public debate on the issue (LeMay 1987: 82).

John Trevor, a prominent New York attorney, began to work closely with the House Immigration Committee to draft a new law. By fall of 1922, they were advocating a change in the base year on which to calculate the quotas from the census of 1910 to that of 1890, and a reduction in the percentage of foreign-born population from 3 percent to 2 percent. Calculating the quotas based on the 1890 census data, of course, meant that the total annual immigration would be less, and the continued immigration from Southeastern Europe would be reduced from a flood to a trickle. The restrictionist movement did not go unchallenged.

By 1922, the effects of the 1920 Depression were dissipating markedly, and as unemployment shrank, businesses began experiencing a labor shortage. Manufacturers began to advocate easing restriction. The National Association of Manufacturers (NAM) lobbied for easing limits and the U.S. Chamber of Commerce lobbied for adding 2 percent to the quotas. The president of U.S. Steel Corporation labeled the 1921 law "one of the worst things this country has ever done for itself economically" (cited in Higham 1955: 315). Big farming corporations were losing hired hands to the lure of better paying jobs in the factories of American cities and joined business in protesting the 1921 law.

In 1923, the Senate Immigration Committee, at the urging of NAM, considered a bill that retained the quota system but allowed for additional immigrants in times of labor shortage. Senator David Reed (R-PA) sponsored a compromise bill that increased total immigration but reduced the share of Southeastern European nations. A period of stalemate ensued as the Republican leadership in both the Senate and the House decided to defer action until 1924.

From late 1923 to early 1924, sentiment began to shift. Increased mechanization in the economy was easing labor shortages and requiring more skilled workers rather than unskilled ones. The National Industrial Conference Board, a research and public relations agency for 31 leading industrial associations, held a conference in New York City in December 1923. Business resolve for easing restrictions waned. NAM and the Chamber of Commerce by early 1924 recommended that the 1921 quotas be retained rather than being reduced, but neither organization was willing to strongly lobby Congress on the matter.

The stance of big business resulted in a shift to various ethnic organizations pushing for or opposing quotas as they assessed how the quotas would affect the immigration status from those countries. A "Nordic theory" gained ground. Newly elected president Calvin Coolidge aided the restrictionist cause when he gave his first presidential address by calling for congressional action to ensure that "America might be kept American" (cited in Higham 1955: 318). James Davis, newly appointed secretary of labor, toured Europe and submitted an administrative proposal to the House Committee. Johnson's House Immigration Committee rejected the Davis-sponsored bill, relying on his unofficial advisor, John Trevor, who supplied what eventually became the compromise solution to the deadlock.

Advocates pushed for greater restriction and for quotas that would shift further the composition of immigration toward Northwestern European nations of origin. The Klan was especially vocal in calling for stricter quotas and called for the outright suspension of immigration (LeMay and Barkan 1999, Document 77: 141–144).

The debate in Congress, begun with the "emergency" quota act of 1921, raged on and reached its peak between 1921 and 1924. Congressman William Vaile (R-CO), a leading proponent of drastic immigration restriction based on both racial and nationalistic grounds, articulated the views of restrictionists in the *Congressional Record*, "We Prefer to Base Quotas on Established Groups" (cited in full in LeMay and Barkan 1999: 145; *Congressional Record*, 68th Congress, 1st Sess., April 1–14, 1924, 65, pt. 6, pp. 5643–5645).

John Trevor designed an attack on the quota scheme of the 1921 law. Trevor argued that basing quotas on the 1910 census did not reflect the "racial status quo" of the nation. Use of 1910 census as the data base, Trevor maintained, overly favored Southeastern Europeans. He used a racial breakdown of the U.S. population published earlier by Clinton Stoddard Burr in his book, *America's Race Heritage* (1922). Trevor's analysis "proved" that, as of 1920, about 12 percent of the U.S. population derived from Southeastern European nations, but on the basis of the 1921 law, they were allocated 44 percent of the total immigration quota. If, however, the 1890 census were used, they would have only 15 percent. Chairman Johnson, relying on the Trevor brief, introduced a new bill reflecting his recommendations.

Representative Carl Vinson (D-GA) stated the House Immigration Committee's majority perspective on Johnson's bill when he said:

> Those favoring unrestricted immigration are wont to harken back to the days of the discovery, colonization and settlement of our country. In respect to this argument, I want to be thoroughly understood. Were the immigrants now flooding our shores possessed of the same traits, characteristics and blood of our forefathers, I would have no concern upon this problem confronting us, because, in the main, they belonged to the same branch of the Aryan race.
>
> Americans and their forebears, the English, Scotch and Welsh, are the same people.
>
> These ancestors of the real American people were related to one to the other and possessed, to a large degree, similar tastes, traits and characteristics.
>
> And in the amalgamation of these people and their transition into American life we find the persons who created and now maintain the greatest Nation on the globe.
>
> But it is the "new" immigrant who is restricted in emigrating to this country.
>
> The emigrants affected by this bill are those from Italy, Greece, Russia, Poland, Bulgaria, Armenia, Czechoslovakia, Yugoslavia and Turkey. I respectfully submit, with all the power within me, that the people from these countries do not yield their national characteristics, but retain them practically unimpaired by contact with others. (cited in Bennett 1963: 48)

In its report on the bill to the full House, the majority of the Committee stated:

> Since it is the axiom of political science that a government not imposed by external force is the visible expression of the ideals, standards and social viewpoint of the people over which it rules, it is obvious that a change in the character or composition of the population must inevitably result in the evolution of a form of government consonant with the base upon which it rests. If, therefore, the principles of individual liberty, guarded by constitutional government created on this continent nearly a century and a half ago are to endure, the basic strain of our population must be maintained and our economic standards preserved. (Bennett 1963: 49)

During debate on the House floor, representatives from the West Coast, particularly those from California, and those from the south, emphasized similar racial sentiments in their concerted efforts at restrictionism. California's contingent emphasized the inadequacy of the Gentlemen's Agreement and questioned the legal validity of its vagueness and ineffectiveness. They played on the "Yellow Peril" theme, warning that Japan's overpopulation and thirst for land might lead to a future "race war."

A congressman from Maine railed against past immigration policies maintaining that such policies:

> Have thrown open wide our gates and through them have come . . . alien races, of alien blood, from Asia and southern Europe, the Malay, the Mongolian, the oriental with their strange and pagan rites, their babble of tongues—a people we cannot digest, that bear no similarity to our people, that never can become true Americans, that add nothing to civilization, but are a menace to our form of government. . . . The hour has come. It may even now be too late for the white race in America, the English-speaking people, the laborer of high ideals, to assert his superiority in the work of civilization and to save America from the menace of further immigration of undesirable aliens. [Applause] . . . [to accomplish this] I wish it were possible to close our gates against any quota from southern Europe or from the orientals, the Mongolian countries and the yellow races of men. (cited in Ringer 1983: 802; see also LeMay 1987: 84–85; and Schrug 2010).

The anti-Japanese provision in the Johnson-Reed bill was to exclude "those persons who could not become citizens and who must continue to owe allegiance to a foreign country" (LeMay 2009: 82; LeMay and Barkan 1999: 148–151). The congressional debate centered on the theme of unassimilability and linked Japanese exclusion and minimal quotas for those from Southeastern European nations.

The only voice arguing for giving Japan a quota was Representative Theodore Burton (R-OH), and his views were considered to reflect the position of the administration and that of Secretary of State Charles Even Hughes. In the Senate, David Reed (R-PA), the bill's coauthor, originally fought against the provision to totally exclude the Japanese. Senators Samuel Shortridge (R-CA) and Lodge of Massachusetts fought vigorously to include the restriction of the Japanese. When opposition to the ban against the Japanese collapsed (despite the Gentlemen's Agreement which had pledged that the United States would not enact an exclusion law), even Senator Reed switched his position, supporting an amendment to the bill that precluded them. The anti-Japanese quota provision amendment passed 71 to 4 (with two opposed and two abstained) (Ringer 1983: 822). Passage of the amendment demonstrated the racist and "anti-pagan" ideas behind the restriction law.

Senator LeBaron Colt (R-RI), chairman of the Senate's Immigration Committee, adamantly opposed changing the census base year. Although he was a supporter of restriction and a leading voice for enactment of the 1921 Act, he argued changing the base year was discriminatory, which of course it clearly was. Its very intent was to discriminate, that is to reduce, the numbers coming from certain undesirable nations of origin as being people who could not nor should not be allowed to assimilate and thus dilute the purity of the American population. Secretary of State Hughes quietly supported Senator Colt's position. The Senate committee reported out a bill keeping the census year at 1910, but lowering the percentage from 3 percent to 2 percent. Senator Reed led the measure through the committee and through Senate deliberations. Senator Colt was in poor health (he died shortly thereafter), and not enthusiastic about the bill (Divine 1957: 35; "Immigration Act of 1921 Imposes Quota System, 1921–1924." *Historic U.S. Events.* Detroit: Gale. *Gale U.S. History in Context.* Web February 5, 2013).

Senator Reed then pushed a proposal through the Senate Committee that used the quota based on the 1890 census data, receiving valuable support from Senator Henry Cabot Lodge (R-MA). The full senate adopted the version using the 1910 census base and stipulated that the quota system would not go into effect until 1927 in order to give the immigration service time to formulate the quotas and procedural rules, and for the interim, the Senate accepted the House version of 2 percent, based on the 1890 census. The compromise version won by 62 to 6 in the Senate and 323 to 71 in the House, and President Coolidge signed the bill on May 26,

1924 (summarized in LeMay and Barkan 1999: 148–151; the Act of May 26, 1924, known informally as the Johnson-Reed Act, 43 Stat. 153; 8 U.S.C. 201).

The only opponents were representatives who advocated for Southeastern European groups so adversely affected by the quotas. Jewish leaders, for example, secured the vocal support of Senator Adolph Sabath (D-IL) and Senator Colt of Rhode Island, who labeled its proponents as un-American and under the influence of the Ku Klux Klan. Senator Underwood (D-AL), however, responded that his opposition to immigration was economic, not racial.

The law had bipartisan support. In the House, only 35 Republicans and 36 Democrats voted against the bill. The bill was popular in public opinion and reflected the triumph of the "Nordic majority" in the country over the southeastern minority. Its key provisions are summarized in Box 4.2. Perhaps as important as the quota system was the provision that required obtaining an *overseas visa* intended to serve as an effective regulating procedure. And, indeed, the visa process became the most effective means devised to control the use of quotas and to allow for the administrative screening of immigrants prior to their entry into the United States. The 1917 provision prohibiting persons "who might become public charges" was another effective administrative tool to enforce immigration policy, used to dramatically cut total immigration during times of depression by setting strict standards for the economic tests to demonstrate the applicant's admissibility (LeMay 1987: 86).

BOX 4.2: SUMMARY EXCERPTS OF THE MAJOR PROVISIONS OF THE JOHNSON-REED IMMIGRATION ACT OF 1924

1) It preserved all of the qualitative restrictions contained in the 1917 Immigration Act. This allowed administrative actions based on strict interpretation of the "public charge" clause.

2) It maintained the principle of numerical limitation of the 1921 Act, but reduced Total immigration numbers suing a new formula that limited total European Immigration from the 350,000 allowed in the 1921 Act to 165,000.

3) It shifted the base year of census data from 1910 to 1890, substantially reducing the proportion of immigrants coming from southeastern Europe. This provision stipulated an interim period with a permanent national origins formula to take effect in 1927 (although it was actually 1929 before such formula was enacted).

4) It reduced the annual quota admissible from three percent to two percent, based on the 1890 census data, to be used until the permanent quota formula was enacted.

5) It set up a system requiring applicants to obtain a visa from an American consulate abroad, replacing the system wherein immigrants landed on American shores perhaps to then be turned away as inadmissible, which system had caused great hardship on the immigrants and costs to the shipping lines who transported them. This provision not only avoided the problems experienced after the 1921 Act, but it further increased administrative powers of the bureaucracy overseeing the visa system.

6) It reduced the classes of aliens exempted from exclusion. It did, however, allow for a number of family exemptions to the quotas which permitted wives and minor children of naturalized American citizens.

7) It placed the burden of proof to show admissibility on the immigrant rather than on the United States, which again strengthened the administrative powers of the immigration service.

8) It excluded admission to aliens not eligible for naturalization except for certain specified classes of nonquota immigrants, called nonimmigrants. It was aimed at excluding the Japanese and touched off a diplomatic crisis with Japan which felt insulted by the Act and which was incensed with its passage in direct contradiction to provisions of the Gentlemen's Agreement of March 14, 1907.

9) The law defined more specifically "immigrants," "quota," and "nonquota immigrant."

10) It specified that "nationality" was to be determined by the country of birth, with few exceptions.

11) When the national origins formula went into effect (July 1, 1929), it reduced the annual quota still further, to 153,714. The national origins formula was then to be apportioned to the total quota (a ceiling of legal immigration) on the basis of their contributions to the population of the United States as enumerated in the 1920 census.

Summary by author. LeMay 1987: 87.

The National Origins Quota Act of 1929

Enactment of the 1924 Johnson-Reed Act did not end the battles, although it settled the major policy position firmly in favor of restriction, and of using racial considerations in setting quotas, and on use of numerical limits (quotas) as the enforcement mechanism (rather than the prior use of excluded categories or the literacy test). The national origins principle was accepted as the basis of the nation's immigration policy. Future battles (perhaps better described as skirmishes) concerned only the mechanics of how the quotas themselves would be fixed.

In an editorial in March 1924, the *New York Times* summed up the fundamental perspective of the national origins quota system, advocating what it held to be the basic needs of a permanent quota system:

> In formulating a permanent policy two considerations are of prime importance.
>
> The first is that the country has a right to say who shall and who shall not come in. It is not for any foreign country to determine our immigration policy. The second is that the basis of restriction must be chosen with a view not to the interest of any group or groups in the country, whether racial or religious, but rather with a view to the country's best interest as a whole. The great test is admissibility. Will the newcomers fit into the American life readily? Is their culture sufficiently akin to our own to make it possible for them easily to take their place among us? There is no question of "superior" or "inferior" races or of "Nordics" or of prejudice, or of racial egotism. Certain groups not only do not fuse easily, but consistently endeavor to keep alive their racial distinctions when they settle among us. They perpetuate the "hyphen," which is but another way of saying that they seek to create foreign blocs in our midst. (cited in Bennett 1963: 53)

In the years immediately following passage of the 1924 Act, Congress continued to debate the method for determining a permanent quota system. In the Senate, David Reed of Pennsylvania and Senator J. Thomas Heflin (D-AL) were leading proponents of restriction. In the House, Albert Johnson of Washington, and coauthor of the 1924 Act, continued as the leading restrictionist voice even while he pressed for total suspension. Southern support was led by Representative John Calvin Box (D-TX), who advocated extending the quota system to Mexico and Latin America (LeMay 1987: 88; and Texas Historical Association).

Representative Box did not get the extension of the quota system to Mexico as he advocated, but in 1925 the Congress did pass a law designed to enforce the immigration laws and to regulate more effectively the control of illegal aliens entering the United States, mostly through the southern border with Mexico. The 1926 Act established the Border Patrol (43 Stat. 1049–1050; 8 U.S.C. 110; summarized in LeMay and Barkan 1999: 152). Other leading voices supporting restriction in the House included William Vaile (R-CO) and Thomas A. Jenkins (R-OH). The House Immigration Committee received testimony in favor of the national origins system from 35 college biology professors, mainly from such Ivy League schools as Harvard, Princeton, and Yale (Divine 1957: 35).

By 1928, John Trevor had formed another group, the American Coalition, which was comprised of a coalition of earlier patriotic groups, which proved to be very successful. It helped popularize "racial nationalism" theories, such as Charles Goethe's articles in *Eugenics* (1929), and historian Albert Bushnell Hart's in *Current History* (1929). As with all the proponents of restrictionism at the time, their advocacy emphasized race and nationalism as opposed to economics or national defense elements of immigration policy making (Divine 1957: 61–63).

Of course, groups such as the AFL and the Junior Order of United American Mechanics and the American Legion continued their staunch support for versions of the permanent quota system that favored increased Northwestern European quotas at the expense of Southeastern quotas. By 1928, the United States Chamber of Commerce came out in support for that approach to the permanent quota formula.

The Anti-National Origins Clause League emerged as the leading group critical of the plan. It worked with a coalition of various ethnic groups opposed to the plan altogether, or favoring revisions to the quota system that would at least lessen the adverse impact on their particular nationality—and often related religious-based—groups. In the House of Representatives, Representative Ole Kvale (Farm-Labor, MN) became a leading opponent. In the Senate, Royal Copeland (D-NY) became the leading anti-restrictionist during the post-1924 law debates.

Those opposing restriction generally emphasized economic arguments, stressing the need for labor, and the fact that immigrants were willing to do the unpleasant jobs that had to be done and which native-born workers were generally unwilling to do.

The debates, of course, were more than just about racial theories versus an economic supply of cheap labor. The various formulae being debated arrived at significantly different quota limits for the various nationality groups. Table 4.1 presents a comparison of the variations in immigration quotas for selected—but typical—European nations under the 1890 census and various national origin plans. It shows dramatic differences, with some country's limits increasing or decreasing by two or three times.

Even before the permanent quota formula was fixed, the impact of the 1924 Johnson-Reed Act was dramatic. European immigration slumped from over 800,000 in 1921 to less than 150,000 by 1929. The restrictionist movement advocates were still not satisfied. The 1924 Act exempted countries in the Western Hemisphere and soon they were advocating placing limits on Latin American, and particularly on Mexico.

Table 4.1   Comparison of Immigration Quotas under 1890 Census and Various National Origin Quota Plans for Typical European Nations

European Nation	1890 Census Plan	1927 Quota Board Report	1928 Quota Board Report	1929 Quota Board Report
Germany	51,227	23,428	24,908	25,957
Great Britain	34,007	73,039	65,894	65,721
Irish Free State	28,567	13,862	17,429	17,853
Italy	3,845	6,091	5,989	5,802
Norway	6,453	2,267	2,403	2,377
Poland	5,982	4,978	6,090	6,524
Russia	2,248	4,781	3,540	2,784
Sweden	9,561	3,259	3,399	3,314

Source: Table by author; data from Divine 1957: 30; and LeMay 1987: 90.

The movement to restrict Mexican immigration began in earnest in 1926, led by Representative John Box (R-TX), an ardent restrictionist and influential member of the House Immigration Committee. His efforts were supported by Hiram Johnson (R-TX) and Thomas Heflin (D-AL). In the Senate, supporters included William Harris (D-GA), Frank B. Willis (R-OH), and David Reed (R- PA). They came up with a short and convenient slogan for their proposals for a quota for Mexican immigration, "close the back door" (Divine 1957: 53).

They depicted Mexican immigrants as peons who taxed the school systems beyond their capacities and lowered educational standards. They portrayed Mexicans as social lepers who would contaminate the American way of life. Harry Laughlin, the eugenics expert of the House Immigration Committee, testified immigration from the entire Western Hemisphere should be limited to "whites." Representative Box described Mexicans as "illiterate, unclean, peonized masses . . . a mixture of Mediterranean-blooded Spanish peasants with low-grade Indians, who did not fight extinction but submitted and multiplied as serfs. [The influx of Mexicans] creates the most insidious and general mixture of white, Indian, and negro blood strains ever produced in America" (in Divine 1957: 57).

The Box proposal ran into strong and well-organized opposition from the southwest where an economic coalition of farmers, cattlemen, sugar manufacturers, and railroad interests favored continued and unlimited Mexican immigration. Mexican workers were valued as a source of common labor preferred for being docile, unaggressive people who would do what they were told and would accept jobs that white workers refused to do.

In addition to such economic perspectives, opposition to limits on Mexican immigration was founded on "Pan-Americanism." Secretary of State Frank B. Kellogg ardently sought to foster better relations with Latin America. Senator Hiram Bingham (R-CT) and Carl Hayden (D-AZ) fought against Latin American quotas. When Senator William J. Harris (D-GA) introduced a bill in 1929 that would impose a limit on Mexican immigration, President Herbert Hoover stated that if the bill passed, he would veto it (Divine 1957: 67).

The National Origins Act of 1929 was finally settled on the quota system that became fully, and permanently, operational. President Herbert Hoover issued a presidential proclamation that stipulated the permanent quotas for each fiscal year thereafter, based on the proportion of each nationality in the population as determined by the 1920 census. The overall ceiling for non-Western Hemisphere immigration was lowered to somewhat more than 150,000. Table 4.2 compares the quotas

Table 4.2   Comparison of Quotas Allotted to Selected Countries under Three Different Versions of the Quota System

Country/Area	1921 Act	1924 Act	1929 National
	3%-1910	2%-1890	Origins Plan
Total	357,803	164,667	151,714
Asia	482	1,424	1,423
Africa/Oceania	359	1,821	1,800
Northwestern Europe			
Belgium	1,563	512	1,304
Denmark	5,619	2,789	1,181
France	5,729	2,789	3,086
Germany	67,607	51,227	25,957

(*Continued*)

Table 4.2 Continued

Country/Area	1921 Act	1924 Act	1929 National
	3%-1910	2%-1890	Origins Plan
Total	357,803	164,667	151,714
Great Britain/ Northern Ireland	65,721	34,007	65,721
Irish Free State	"	28,567	17,853
Netherlands	3,607	1,648	3,153
Norway	12,202	6,453	2,177
Sweden	20,042	9,561	3,314
Switzerland	3,752	2,081	1,707
Total NW Europe	197,630	140,999	127,266
Southern/Eastern Europe			
Austria	7,342	785	1,413
Czechoslovakia	14,357	3,073	2,874
Greece	3,063	100	307
Hungary	5,747	472	869
Italy	42,057	3,845	5,802
Poland	30,977	5,982	6,524
Portugal	2,465	503	440
Romania	7,419	603	295
U.S.S.R.	24,405	2,248	2,784
Turkey	2,654	100	226
Yugoslavia	6,426	671	845
Total SE Europe	155,585	20,423	23,235
Minimum per country = 100			

Source: Table by author, based on data in Bernard 1950: 27; and LeMay 1987: 91.

allotted to selected countries under three different versions of the quota system: the 1921 Act, the 1924 Act, and the 1929 National Origins Plan (LeMay 1987: 91).

Finally, Table 4.3 shows the quotas for representative countries as stipulated in President Hoover's Proclamation (Presidential Proclamation 1872, March 22, 1929).

Table 4.3 President Hoover's Proclamation Quotas

Country/Area	Quota	Country/Area	Quota
Afghanistan	100	Japan	100
Albania	100	Latvia	236
Andorra	100	Liberia	100
Arabian Peninsula	100	Lichtenstein	100
Armenia	100	Lithuania	386
Australia	100	Luxemburg	100
Austria	1,413	Monaco	100
Belgium	1,304	Morocco	100
Bhutan	100	Muscat (Oman)	100
Bulgaria	100	Naura	100
Cameroon	100	Nepal	100
China	100	Netherlands	3,153
Czechoslovakia	2,874	New Zealand	100
Danzig	100	Norway	2,377
Denmark	1,181	New Guinea	100
Egypt	100	Palestine	100
Estonia	116	Persia	100
Ethiopia	100	Poland	6,524
Finland	569	Portugal	440
France	3,086	Ruanda and Urundi	100
Germany	25,957	Rumania	295
Great Britain/ Northern Ireland	65,721	Russia/European & Asiatic	2,784
Greece	302	Samoa	100
Hungary	869	San Marino	100
Iceland	100		
India	100		
Iraq	100		
Irish Free State	17,853		
Italy	5,802		

Source: President's Proclamation 1872 of March 22, 1929. Proclamations and Treaties: 1092–1093; LeMay and Barkan 1999: 164–165.

The Great Depression Decade, 1930–1940

The year 1929 not only saw passage of the National Origins Plan that set permanently the quota system, it was the year of the stock market crash that ushered in the Great Depression. This worldwide depression had a greater impact on limiting the level of immigration than did any law ever passed by the Congress. The drop in immigration, already precipitous since the quota acts, was exceptional in the 1930s. While over 4,100,000 entered the United States during the 1920s, immigration fell to slightly more than 0.5 million for the entire decade of the 1930s.

Total immigration was at the lowest level for any decade since 1820.

Periods of depression have always resulted in a slackening off of immigration, since the economic crisis means that the United States will be perceived as offering less opportunity to perspective immigrants even if they can manage to emigrate. When the depression is worldwide, it means the ability and the opportunity to migrate is severely lessened. Periods of economic dislocation—both recessions and depressions in today's terminology—have also been times when the restrictionist movement flowered, instigating new demands for the protection of the native worker against the encroachment of foreign labor. The 1930s were no exception.

During the decade, the major battles over restriction concerned whether to do so by administrative or legislative action, and on the extension of the quotas to the Philippines. The major restriction groups wanted Congress to decrease quotas as set by the 1929 plan by 60 to 90 percent. Opponents of restriction argued that more strict administrative enforcement of the existing laws would be adequate to reduce the flow, which by then was comparatively a trickle.

In 1930, Senator Hugo Black (D-AL) introduced a bill to suspend all immigration except for immediate family members of United States citizens for a period of five years.

While the Senate rejected the Black bill, it was by a fairly close vote, 37–29 (LeMay 1987: 92).

The Department of State reacted to the proposal and related debate in Congress by enforcing administratively a strict interpretation of the "public charge" clause for denying a visa. Within five months, the State Department succeeded in reducing European immigration by 90 percent. Consular officers throughout the decade followed the president's orders to interpret that provision strictly, and the year 1930–1931 saw a drop of 62 percent of quota immigration, and during the decade 1931–1940 those immigrants coming into the United States exceeded repatriated immigrants for a net total of only 68,693 for the entire decade, or an average annual total of only 6,800 (Divine 1957: 78; LeMay 1987: 92). Depression conditions lessened incentives to migrate. The rigid screening process used for granting visas, and the effects of unfavorable economic conditions, depressed quota immigration to levels far below what was allowable under the 1929 plan.

Table 4.4 lists the quota immigration admissions by region of origin for the years 1930–1940. Having successfully passed the National Origins Plan in 1929, restrictionists moved on to plugging what they felt were holes in the immigration barriers. One of the main targets was immigration from the Philippines. The first attempt to do so was a bill introduced in 1928 by Representative Richard Welch (R-CA). It had the staunch support of West Coast labor unions and the AFL. In 1929, when a deadly outbreak of meningitis was traced to a Filipino immigrant, the movement to impose a quota on the Philippines gained momentum (LeMay 1987: 95).

Continuing into the 1930s, the pro-restrictionist movement argued the same mixture of racial and economic fears that had characterized earlier battles. The same organizations were active lobbying the Congress wherein the same members offered their support on the issue. Lobbying for restrictive legislation to impose a quota on the Philippines were the American Coalition, the California Joint Immigration Committee, the AFL, the

Table 4.4 Quota Immigrants Admitted, 1930–1940, by Region

Year	All Countries	NW Europe	SE Europe	Asia	Africa	Pacific
Quotas	153,714	125,853	24,648	1,805	1,200	700
1930	141,497	116,062	24,002	891	273	269
1931	54,118	38,706	14,498	490	206	218
1932	12,983	6,368	6,402	331	72	170
1933	8,220	3,831	4,091	189	20	89
1934	12,483	6,839	6,402	223	33	102
1935	17,483	8,849	5,286	202	41	144
1936	18,675	10,102	8,142	234	40	157
1937	27,762	16,481	10,754	295	64	168
1938	42,494	25,383	16,254	584	74	199
1939	62,402	41,135	20,400	587	78	202
1940	51,997	34,313	16,828	549	99	208

Source: Table by author; data from Table 4.3, LeMay 1987: 93.

National Grange, the American Legion, and the Native Sons of the Golden West (Divine 1957: 69–70; LeMay 1987: 94).

Forces opposing the bill were various Filipino political leaders, particularly Manuel Roxas, the speaker of the Philippine Legislature, who argued eloquently that the right to migrate anywhere in the United States and its territories was a moral right of all residents under the U.S. flag. His position was supported by the U.S. War Department, the U.S. Department of State, Hawaiian sugar planters, and the Pacific American Steamship Association. Senators Harry B. Hawes (D-MO) and George W. Norris (I-NE), both strong advocates of Philippine independence, called the Welch bill "dishonorable" and "amoral." It was defeated in 1930 by a vote of 41 to 23 in the Senate (LeMay 1987: 94).

Southern and western state representatives continued to battle for restriction. In addition to Johnson of Washington and Reed of Pennsylvania, Representatives Thomas Moore (D-TX), Luther B. Johnson (D-TX), and Martin Dies (D-TX) continued to push for limits on immigration. In 1931, they advocated a "reduction of quotas" that was the high point of their legislative efforts during the early years of the Depression era.

Opposition in the Congress to further limits on immigration came largely from representatives from Northeastern states. In the House of Representatives, leading anti-restrictionists, for example, included the New York City delegation of Fiorello LaGuardia (R-NY), John D. O'Conner (D-NY), and Samuel Dickstein (D-NY). In the Senate, they were led by David Walsh (D-MA) and Elmer Thomas (D-OK). In December 1931, Samuel Dickstein, an ardent anti-restrictionist, replaced ardent restrictionist Albert Johnson as chairman of the powerful House Immigration Committee. The anti-restrictionist faction in Congress had the support of the Roosevelt administration, and particularly that of his secretary of labor, Frances Perkins.

In 1932, Representative John W. Moore (D-KY) introduced a new measure to restrict immigration by lowering the quotas and expanding their coverage. It was vigorously opposed by Jewish organizations, such as the Hebrew Sheltering and Immigration Aid Society, which was attempting to increase quotas for those experiencing persecution in Central and Eastern Europe. Lobbying with the Jewish organizations was the Young Women's Christian Association (YWCA), which newly emerged as an anti-restriction organization. Left-wing groups such as the American Communist Party and the Young Communist League joined the fray as well. Also active in the 1930s in the anti-restriction coalition was the National Council for the Protection of the Foreign Born (LeMay 1987: 94).

In 1933, the group lobbying for Philippine independence tried a new ploy, attempting to gain the support of restrictionists in Congress by offering a compromise bill. In essence, the bill provided that if Congress should enact a law fixing a specific date for Philippine independence, the Filipino representatives and their supporters would accept a provision restricting Filipino immigration during the transition period, as long as such restriction was based on economic grounds rather than a racial one. The bill passed in 1934, and President Franklin D. Roosevelt signed it in May. The Philippine Islands were given an annual quota of 50, and the "problem" of Filipino restriction was resolved (Divine 1957: 73–75).

With that issue resolved, the mid-1930s was a time of relative inaction on immigration matters. Representative Dickstein, as chair of the House Immigration Committee, introduced several measures designed to liberalize immigration laws on behalf of Jewish refugees from Germany. His proposals were supported by the lobbying efforts of the American Jewish Congress, the Hebrew Sheltering and Immigration Aid Society, as well as some Catholic and Protestant groups concerned about the refugee issue. In 1933, the League of Nations established a High Commission for Refugees Coming from Germany, headed by a U.S. citizen, James MacDonald. In 1938, the league established a single High Commission on Refugees. Efforts by the league added to the public relations push by forces advocating relaxation of quota restrictions, as by 1938 the Jewish refugee problem was becoming increasingly critical.

Moves to ease restrictions were strongly opposed by John Trevor and the American Coalition, by the American Legion, and by the AFL. Their lobbying efforts were supported in the House by Representatives Thomas A. Jenkins (R-OH) and John Rankin (D-MS). Into the late 1930s, public opinion remained on the side of the restrictionists, and all measures to ease quota limits died in the House (Ibid: 95).

In 1939, another attempt to ease the refugee problem was made, this time by Senator Robert Wagner (D-NY). He introduced a bill to allow for the nonquota entry of 20,000 German refugee *children*. A Nonsectarian Committee for German Refugee Children was organized and it won over the support of organized labor, gaining the endorsement of the American Federation of Labor (AFL) and of John Lewis's Congress of Industrial Organizations (CIO) (the CIO had been a group within the AFL that, led by John Lewis, spun off in 1935 and formed as a national coalition in 1937; the two giant labor union umbrella organizations did not merge again until 1955). Wagner's bill even had the support of some southern proponents, in the persons of Frank Graham, president of the University of North Carolina, and Homer Rainey, president of the University of Texas. Wagner's bill, not surprisingly, was opposed by the American Legion, and the American Coalition. Even this modest proposal to amend the quota system died in Congress.

Somewhat in desperation, the Roosevelt administration acted, applying its own interpretation of rules and procedures for immigration policy making that allowed in some 20,000 children in 1939. In total, some 250,000 refugees entered the United States between 1934 and 1941, but all of them came in under the existing quota laws (Jones 1960: 281).

The issue of how to deal with the refugee problem made evident a major weakness of the quota system—its inflexibility. Full use of the quota system was often prevented by its procedural rules. The 1929 law provided that for quotas more than 100, no more than 10 percent of a yearly quota could be used in a single month. When transportation conditions or refugee-related problems blocked the migration of persons to fill the 10 percent provision, no carryover was allowed. In addition, there was no carryover provided for any unused quotas from one year to another. Red tape involved in acquiring visas during the turbulent 1930s meant that many visas were unused.

The quota laws had their intended impact, as can be seen in Table 4.5, showing the distribution by percentages and by decades for the major regional sources of origin for the decade immediately prior to the quota system, and then for the decade years between 1920 and 1950. Northwestern European immigration, which as we have seen, fell from its more than 70 percent of the total in the 1880s and 1890s to fewer than 20 in the 1910–1920 decade, prior to the shift during the quota system era to nearly 40 percent in the 1930s, whereas Southeastern European immigration fell from more than 70 percent in the 1911–1920 decade to less than 30 percent during the 1930s.

Table 4.5   **Sources of Immigration to the United States, 1910–1950, by Decades and by Percentages from Region**

Decades	All Europe	NW Europe	SE Europe	Canada	Mexico	All Others
1911–1920	76.4	17.4	59.0	12.9	3.8	6.9
1921–1930	60.3	31.2	29.0	22.5	11.2	6.0
1931–1940	66.0	37.4	28.6	20.5	4.2	9.3
1941–1950	44.4	34.9	9.5	23.2	8.7	23.6

Source: Table by author; data from U.S. Bureau of the Census. *Historical Statistics of the United States: Colonial Time to 1970.* Washington, DC: U.S. Government Printing Office, 1975.

The World War II Years

As happened during previous war periods, during World War II, immigration to the United States plunged. Worldwide war impacted immigration far beyond the impact of the quota system. When the Japanese attacked Pearl Harbor on December 7, 1941, they brought on a nightmare experience for Japanese Americans living on the mainland. A total of 112,000 persons of Japanese ancestry, 70,000 of whom were native-born U.S. citizens, were sent to "relocation camps" in the interior because of what was termed "military necessity" (Executive Order 9066, February 10, 1942, and Act of March 22, 1942; LeMay and Barkan 1999: 192–194). The camps were concentration camps where residents lived, particularly in the beginning, in grim conditions. Men and women, grandparents and grandchildren, young children and young adults, were all herded behind 15-foot high, barbed-wire fences guarded by Tommy-gun-armed troops stationed around the perimeter and on spotlight towers. They lived in crude barracks, with stalls of 18 by 21 feet housing families of 6 or 7, partitioned by 7-foot high walls with 4-foot openings affording no real privacy. A barrack building 90 feet by 20 feet housed six families. Residents used outside latrines. They were locked in by 9:00 P.M. and had a 10:00 P.M. lights-out curfew. The camps were governed by a War Relocation Authority and the War Relocation Work Corp (LeMay 2009: 83–85; McClemore 1980: 179).

Enemy aliens from Germany and Italy were treated better than the native-born American citizens of Japanese ancestry. No other ethnic group suffered comparable indignities during World War II. Only racial prejudice accounts for this policy. The chief author of the program, Lt. General John L. DeWitt, commanding general of the Western Defense Command, described the blatantly racist rationale for the plan:

> In the war in which we are now engaged racial affinities are not severed by migration. The *Japanese race is an enemy race* and while many second- and third-generation Japanese born in the United States and possessed of United States citizenship, have become "Americanized," the *racial strains are undiluted* . . . (cited in McClemore 1980: 174. My italics)

General Mark Clark had informed General George Marshall that there was no military necessity for these camps (10 were established housing 114,900 persons in all, LeMay 2009: 83), and although his assessment was concurred in by the director of the FBI, General DeWitt was not dissuaded. Earl Warren, then attorney general of California, and General DeWitt responded to the fact that no acts of sabotage had taken place with the ingenious reasoning that the very absence of sabotage or other evidence of fifth column activity "merely showed how disciplined the resident Japanese were . . . they were merely biding their time to strike a well-planned and devastating blow synchronized with attacks by the armed forces of Japan" (cited in Ringer 1983: 863). And he said elsewhere: "A Jap is a Jap. It makes no difference whether he's an American or not."

Immediately after the Pearl Harbor attack and the declaration of war with Japan, the FBI and naval intelligence officers quickly rounded up everyone who might be considered a threat. Nonetheless, General DeWitt and the congressional delegation from the coast pressed on with the evacuation. Secretary of War Henry Stimson and Attorney General Francis Biddle agreed to go along with the plan, and President Roosevelt issued the executive order 9066, and sought and received congressional approval. It passed overwhelmingly. In the Senate, only Robert Taft (R-OH) spoke against it. By October 1942, more than 110,000 were relocated.

Paradoxically, the territory of Hawaii, in a much more vulnerable position, did not attempt a mass evacuation of its 120,552 Japanese American citizens and the war passed without a proven act of espionage or sabotage by a Japanese American there or on the mainland. Indeed, the army used the term "military necessity" to keep people of Japanese blood on the island, recognizing the shipping situation and labor shortage any evacuation plan would entail (Hosokawa 1969: 457–467).

In 1943, in *Hirobayashi v. United States*, and in 1944 in *Korematsu v. United States*, the Supreme Court upheld the constitutionality of the evacuation program (LeMay and Barkan 1999: 194–200). Its precedent, however, did not last long. In *Endo v. United States, 1944* (323 U.S. 283–310, December 18, 1944; LeMay and Barkan 1999: 201–203), the Supreme Court reversed itself and revoked the West Coast Exclusion order, and by June 1946, all 10 camps were closed.

Wartime hysteria, which so plagued Japanese Americans, led to a slight modification of immigration policy, however, with respect to our wartime alliance with China in the war with Japan that led to repeal of the Chinese Exclusion Act on December 13, 1943 (57 Stat. 600; 8 U.S.C. 212(a); LeMay and Barkan: 196–197), and a small quota was established for China.

Anti-Catholicism arose again during the 1940s and 1950s when the Cold War isolationism and xenophobia increased dramatically. This period saw anti-Catholicism manifested less violently than that of the 1920s, instead being more subtle. The American Council of Christian Churches and the American and Other Protestants United for the Separation of Church and State became the leading proponents of the anti-parochial school movement (LeMay 1985: 109).

In the immediate postwar years, several war-induced problems high-lighted the inflexibilities of the quota system. In 1946, Congress passed the War Brides Act, allowing up to 150,000 wives, fiancées, and some 25,000 children and a few hundred husbands of U.S. citizens serving in the armed forces to be brought in outside the quota limits (Act of December 28, 1945, 59 Stat. 659; 8 U.S.C. 232–236; LeMay and Barkan 1999: 206–207).

The problem of refugees and displaced persons showed the greatest need for some modification of the quota system. By wars end, there were an estimated eight million displaced persons in Austria, Italy, and Germany, over 1 million of whom were in camps. President Harry Truman's first response to the problem was to issue a presidential directive, in 1945, which admitted some 2,500 that year under the quota system and brought in as permanent residents at government expense. Preferences were given to orphans and relatives of U.S. citizens. About half were from Poland and nearly 1,000 were from Italy. Over the next two and one-half years, Truman used the directive to bring in 41,000 persons, some 38,000 of whom were quota immigrants, over 2,000 of whom were nonquota, and more than 1,000 of whom were no-immigrants (students). About 12 percent of displaced persons admitted as quota immigrants had a preference within the quota act as blood relatives of U.S. citizens or of admitted resident aliens (Bennet 1963: 89).

On June 25, 1948, Congress passed the Displaced Persons Act (DPA), which established a preference category and established a Displaced Persons Commission to administer it. Persons beyond a country's quota were allowed to enter by "mortgaging" against future quotas (62 Stat, 1009; LeMay and Barkan 1999: 210–213). President Truman reluctantly signed the DPA, stating he believed it did not go far enough to aid refugees, that it discriminated against Catholics and Jews, and that he felt displaced persons should be admitted as nonquota immigrants. Congress amended the bill in 1950, increasing admissions for Catholics and Jews and ultimately 400,000 refugees entered the United States under the act in a four-year period (Jones 1960: 285; Bennett 1963: 76–77).

President Truman used his proclamation authority to revise a number of immigration quotas for countries for whom the quota Act of 1924 required revisions because of changed boundaries or because some had just established independence. He added the following quota numbers: Greece 310, Italy 5,799, Rumania 291, U.S.S.R 2,798, Israel 100, Jordan 100, Syria 100, and Lebanon 100 (Number 2846, July 27, 1949: LeMay and Barkan 1999: 217).

The growing need for agricultural workers led to enactment of the Agricultural Act of 1949, more commonly known as the "Bracero Program"

(63 Stat. 11051; LeMay and Barkan 1999: 217–18). It formalized by an act of Congress a program begun by Executive Agreement during World War II. It provided for temporary workers (nine months of the year) for farm labor and to work on the railroads, originally begun to fill a labor gap caused by the war. By program's end, about 350,000 workers were coming annually as nonimmigrant "guest-workers."

Also in 1949, Congress amended the Philippine Act of 1946 by extending its benefits to June 1951. In June 1950, Congress made special provisions for 250 special immigrant visas for alien sheepherders for a one-year period, and in August declared Guamanians born after April 11, 1899, to be citizens, thus eliminating any immigration restrictions on them, and passed an act that permitted entry to previously inadmissible alien spouses and minor children of citizen members of the U.S. armed forces (LeMay 1987: 100–101).

Finally, in September 1950, Congress passed the Internal Security Act (64 Stat. 987), which increased the grounds for exclusion and deportation of alleged alien subversives. Reflecting the Cold War tenor of the times, it required Communist organizations and officers to be registered and clarified and augmented the classes of persons considered to be risks to internal security and banned their admission and strengthened the administrative and enforcement work of the Immigration Service as established by the Immigration Act of 1917. It required all resident aliens to annually report their addresses (Ibid: 101–102).

Table 4.6 details the annual immigrant arrivals and departures for the years 1924–1948 and indicates those by several categories of years to highlight the impact of push or pull factors impacting the numbers of arrivals or departures of immigrants aside from the quota system laws.

Table 4.6 Annual Immigrant Arrivals and Departures, United States, 1924–1948

Year	Immigrants Admitted	Emigrant Aliens Departed	Net Immigration
The Prosperity Years			
1924–1925	294,314	92,728	201,586
1925–1926	304,488	76,992	227,496
1925–1927	335,175	73,366	261,809
1927–1928	305,255	77,457	229,798

Year	Immigrants Admitted	Emigrant Aliens Departed	Net Immigration
1928–1929	279,678	69,203	210,475
1929–1930	241,700	50,661	191,039
The Depression Years			
1930–1931	97,139	61,882	35,257
1931–1932	35,576	103,295	−67,719
1932–1933	23,068	80,081	−57,013
1933–1934	29,068	39,771	−10,301
1934–1935	34,956	38,834	−3,878
1935–1936	36,329	35,817	512
The Peak of Refugee Movement Years			
1936–1937	50,244	25,736	23,508
1937–1938	67,895	25,210	42,685
1938–1939	82,998	26,631	56,347
1939–1940	70,756	21,461	49,295
1940–1941	51,776	17,115	34,661
The War Years			
1941–1942	28,781	7,363	21,418
1942–1943	23,725	5,107	18,618
1943–1944	28,551	5,669	22,882
1944–1945	38,119	7,442	30,677
The Postwar Years			
1945–1946	108,721	18,143	90,578
1946–1947	147,292	22,501	124,791
1947–1948	170,570	20,875	149,695

Source: Table by author; data from Bernard 1950: 323; and LeMay 1987: 101.

Hasidic Jewish Migration and Immigration

Hasidic Jews are a subset or sect among Jews and had a different immigration pattern than most American Jews. To put them in context, among self-identified Jews in America, 78 percent are Jewish by religion and

22 percent are Jews of no religion (cultural Jews). Among those professing a denominational identity with religious Jews, 35 percent are Reform Jews, 18 percent are Conservative Jews, 10 percent are Orthodox Jews, 6 percent are "other," and 30 percent claim no denominational affiliation (Pew Research Center). The branches of Judaism are Conservative Judaism, Hasidism, Kabbalah (which are more mystical approaches), Orthodox Judaism, Reform Judaism, and Zionism (Religion Facts).

There are more than 3,700 synagogues in the United States, among them Orthodox synagogues number 1,500, or about 40 percent. Just over 900, or 26 percent, are Reform synagogues. Total Conservative synagogues number just over 800, or about 23 percent. Among the Orthodox are the Hasidic synagogues, numbering 346 Lubavitch/Chabad, and a 4 mixed synagogues of Orthodox Union and Lubavitch, and two Young Israel and Lubavitch (Singer and Grossman 2003: 128–129). Considered "ultra-Orthodox," Hasidic Jews migrated to the United States during World War II. Their movement began in the mid-18th century in what is today Poland, Belorussia, and Ukraine, which at the time had the largest Jewish population of anywhere in the world. Living in Jewish villages (*shtetls*) they were poor and they were forbidden by law to own land. The sect began when Israel ben Eliezer, who was known as Baal Shem Tov, meaning Master of the Good Name, became the first Hasidic Rebbe. He died in 1760 and certain of his followers, who became known as *rebbes*, and the sect spread in Ukraine, Galicia, Belarus, and central Poland, and some groups in Hungary, and eventually some came to the United States during the large Jewish migration in the 1880s.

The institution of the *rebbe* was important to the expansion of the movement as they provided guidance in every sphere of daily life. Each Hasidic group evolved into a dynastic court composed of the *rebbe* and his followers. Some fled to the Holy Land in 1777 and others in Eastern Europe in the 1880s. When the communist party took over Russia, they persecuted Jews more generally and Hasidic Jews in particular. Rabbi Yosef Schneersohn, the sixth Lubaticher rebbe, was imprisoned as a "counterrevolutionary." He was eventually released and allowed to emigrate, migrating first to Latvia, then Poland; and when the Nazis invaded Poland in 1939, he fled to the United States in 1940. He established what became the world headquarters of the Lubavitch Hasidic group, in Crown Heights, Brooklyn. His son-in-law organized three Chabad (Hasidic movement) divisions: publishing, educational outreach, and social services. On the death of Rabbi Josef Schneersohn, in 1950, Rabbi Manchem Schneerson became the seventh Lubatcher rebbe and led the Hasidic group for the next 40 years. They spread to other Hasidic settlements, each centered around a rebbe and his court, soon number-ing 40 courts. They have been characterized as exemplifying "psycho-logical separatism" by maintaining strict cultural separatism despite living within the heart of the majority culture, in a manner similar to the Amish and Mennonites. They have been remarkably successful in their use of psychological separatism and retaining their distinctive subculture despite being economically involved in the majority society (Hoffman 1991; LeMay 2009: 235–237).

Conclusion

The Pet Door phase evidences some of the clearest data to show the dramatic impact of immigration policy making on the flow of immigra-tion to the United States. The forces advocating restriction finally achieved sufficient political influence to succeed in largely framing and determin-ing the perception of the "immigration problem," and to articulate pro-posed legislative solution (policy formulation), and achieve passage of those proposals (policy enactment). Moreover, they achieved a high degree of policy outcomes as well as policy outputs. Their shift from advocating such methods as excluded categories and the literacy test to the use of a quota (a fixed numbers allowed to enter) resulted in their policy goal—limiting deeply the number of immigrants annually.

The Pet Door era shows how policy making changed or shifted as the policy advocates and events oscillated in the weight being given the four elements of immigration policy. During this period, post-World War I isolationism meant there was less concern over the national defense ele-ment. There was no perceived need for population for defense purposes. The depressed economy through much of the era meant less weight was given to the economic element. There was no perceived need for mass labor. The growing industrialization meant more skilled workers were needed, not massive numbers of unskilled workers. The postwar shift to isolationism meant that the element of race was increasingly heavily weighted. A demand for unity, conformity, and homogeneity was per-ceived as requiring racial purity. And that same shift in opinion meant increased weight being placed on the element of national identity or sense of people-hood.

The era saw the same coalition of interest groups arrayed pro- and con-restrictionism, although during the era business interests shifted in a way that enabled enactment of the quota system. These groups, on both sides of the issues, consistently voiced the same arguments, although the con-cept of racism was given greater credence.

The Quota Acts of 1921, 1924, and 1929 had their intended impact. But the very success of those acts soon caused special problems of dealing with refugees, and the human hardships obviously caused by the inflexibility of the quota system. The flow of immigration during the Pet Door phase also demonstrated that both "push" and "pull" factors, beyond immigration law, can and often do have far greater impact than that intended by the immigration laws themselves.

Finally, the growing hysteria and fear of communism associated with the Cold War pointed to the need for a major revision of immigration policy. The result was passage of the Immigration and Naturalization Act of 1952, which ushered in the next era of U.S. immigration policy, the Dutch Door phase, the subject of the next chapter.

References

Bennett, Marion. 1963. *American Immigration Policy: A History.* Washington, DC: Public Affairs Press.

Bernard, William, ed. 1950. *Immigration Policy: A Reappraisal.* New York: Harper.

Burr, Clinton Stoddard. 1922. *America's Race Heritage.* New York: National Historical Society.

Clarke v. Deckenbeck, 274 U.S. 392, 1917.

Divine, Robert. 1957. *American Immigration Policy, 1924–1952.* New Haven, CT: Yale University Press.

Draper, Theodore. 1957. *The Roots of American Communism.* New York: Viking Press.

Fairchild, Henry. 1911. *Greek Immigration.* New Haven, CT: Yale University Press.

Grant, Madison. 1916. *The Passing of the Great Race.* New York: Arno Press.

Higham, John. 1955. *Strangers in the Land: Patterns of American Nativism, 1866–1925.* New Brunswick, NJ: Rutgers University Press.

Hoffman, Edward. 1991. *Despite All Odds: The Story of the Lubavitch.* New York: Simon and Schuster.

Hosokawa, William. 1969. *Nisei: The Quiet Americans.* New York: William and Morrow.

"Immigration Act of 1921 Imposes Quota System, 1921–1924." *Historic U.S. Events.* Detroit: Gale, 2012. *Gale U.S. History in Context.* Web February 5, 2013.

Jones, Maldwyn. 1960. *American Immigration.* Chicago: University of Chicago Press.

LeMay, Michael. 1985. *The Struggle for Influence.* Lanham, MD: University Press of America.

LeMay, Michael. 1987. *From Open Door to Dutch Door.* New York: Praeger Press.

LeMay, Michael. 2009. *The Perennial Struggle,* 3rd edition. Upper Saddle River, NJ: Prentice Hall.

LeMay, Michael, and Elliott Barkan. 1999. *U.S. Immigration and Naturalization Laws and Issues: A Documentary History.* Westport, CT: Greenwood Press.

McClemore, Dale S. 1980. *Racial and Ethnic Relations in America.* Boston: Allyn and Bacon.

Office of the Senate. https://www.senate.gov/history/1878.htm. Accessed April 20, 2015.

Pew Research Center. http://pewforum.org/2013/10/01/jewish-american-beliefs-attitudes-culture-survey. Accessed May 4, 2017.

Religion Facts. www.religionfacts.com/judaism/branches. Accessed 11/21/2016.

Ringer, Benjamin. 1983. *We the People and Others.* New York: Tavistock.

Schrug, Peter. 2010. *Not Fit for Our Society: Nativism and Immigration.* Berkeley: University of California Press.

Select Commission on Immigration and Refugee Policy (SCIRP). 1981. *Staff Report.* Washington, DC: U.S. Government Printing Office.

Singer, David, and Lawrence Grossman, eds. 2003. *American Jewish Yearbook, 2002.* New York: American Jewish Committee.

Taylor, Philip. 1971. *The Distant Magnet: European Emigration to America.* New York: Harper and Row.

Texas Historical Association. https://tshaonline.org/handbook/online/articles/fbo.54. Accessed May 5, 2017.

Zolberg, Aristide. 2008. *A Nation by Design: Immigration Policy in the Fashioning of America.* Cambridge, MA: Russell Sage Foundation at Harvard University Press.

CHAPTER FIVE

The Dutch Door Era, 1950–1985

Introduction: Postwar Immigration Policy

The Displaced Persons Act (DPA) demonstrated vividly the need for a revision in U.S. immigration policy and served as a precursor for later laws that changed even more substantially the direction of policy. While the DPA did not fundamentally alter the basic policy of national origins quotas, it did mark a turning point in that for the first time in the 20th century the U.S. Congress enacted policy that relaxed restrictions on immigration. It signaled the opening of the door a bit, and the beginning of a new phase in immigration policy—the Dutch Door phase. As will be seen in more detail later, the shift in policy nearly doubled the number of immigrants entering the United States during the era. Whereas in the Pet Door phase, 5,670,679 immigrants came during its 30-year span, averaging 189,000 per year, in the Dutch Door period, a total of 12,817,313 entered in its 35-year span, for an annual average of 366,200 immigrants. Not only do the total numbers of immigrants arriving during the era increase substantially, their region of origin also shifts as a result of changing laws governing immigration policy. For the decade 1960–1969, 3,183,749 immigrants came to the United States, an annual average of 318,000. From 1970 to 1979, when the preference system took hold, 4,300,000 immigrants arrived, for an annual average of 430,000. After 1970, the immigration flow shifted from Europe to Latin America and Asia, the direct result of the 1965 Immigration Act, which established the current preference system. As will be seen next, the immigration flow of this era increased religious diversity in America and raised political issues that had to be addressed by the Congress and by the U.S. Supreme Court ruling on the First Amendment's Free Exercise and Establishment Clauses.

The Dutch Door phase overlaps with what several political scientists categorize as the Fifth Political System of political party coalitions, occurring between 1932 and 1980. It was ushered in with the realigning election of Democratic president Franklin D. Roosevelt and was ushered out with the realigning election of Republican president Ronald Reagan (Barone 1990; Bibby 1998; Kleppner 1981; Ladd and Hadley 1978; Skowronek 1997; Sloan 2008). Blue-collar voting preferences and political party affiliations of "white ethnic" voters were instrumental in the development of the Fifth Party System. It was an era dominated by the Democratic Party coalition known as the New Deal Coalition, comprised of the following voting blocs: Catholics, Jews, African Americans, white Southerners, urban machines, white ethnics, progressive intellectuals, and populist farm groups (Chambers and Burnham 1967; Fraser and Gerstle 1990; Kleppner 1981; Milkis 1993; Paulson 2006; Shafer and Badgers 2001; Skowronek 19997; Sloan 2008; Sundquist 1983).

The political party system was essentially liberal Democratic from 1932 through 1968, and mostly Republican at the presidential level since 1968. One expert holds it ended in 1964, when the New Deal Coalition began to break up (with the Solid South's white Southerners increasingly voting Republican for president thereafter) (Paulson 2006). Others hold it continued in weakened form until 1980, with the election of Ronald Reagan and the emergence of the Moral Majority (Fraser and Gerstle 1990; Jenson 1981). Still others argue it continued until the 1990s (Manza and Brooks 1999; Shafer and Badger 2001). Until 1964, Democratic control of Congress was the norm, while since 1968 divided control of Congress was the norm. During the period, Republicans were often split between a conservative wing, led by Ohio senator Robert Taft, and a moderate wing, led by Northeastern Republican leaders such as Governors Nelson Rockefeller (R-NY), George W. Romney (R-MI), William Scranton (R-PA), and Senator Henry Cabot Lodge (R-MA).

The Democrats controlled the White House 32 of the 48 years of the Fifth Party System era; a Republican occupied the White House only 16 of those 48 years. The Democrats also controlled the U.S. Congress in all but four years. The Republicans took control of the House of Representatives in 1946–1948 and 1952–1954. When the New Deal Democratic coalition divided in 1968, it enabled Richard Nixon to take the White House (Fraser and Gerstle 1990; Ladd and Hadley 1978; Ladd 1978; Lawrence 1997).

Throughout the 1960s and 1970s, however, the Democratic Party continued to enjoy the strong support at the national level from major "ethnic/immigrant" groups: About 60 percent of Irish Americans, generally around 70 percent of Italian Americans, about 50 percent of

Greek Americans, 65 to 80 percent among Polish Americans, around 70 percent of Jewish Americans, and 64 to 92 percent of the Mexican American vote, and 53 to 83 percent among all Latinos, and in the low 90 percent among Puerto Rican voters (LeMay 2009: 131–132; 133–135; 142–146; 146–151).

The Dutch Door phase opened with the McCarran-Walter Act of 1952, which reaffirmed the national origins system, but began to modify it, introducing some preferences into the system and allowing for the admission of special refugees and "anti-communist freedom fighters" above and beyond the quota system plan. The changes reflected Cold War and foreign policy considerations during the years of the administration of President Dwight D. Eisenhower. Eisenhower picked California congressman Richard Nixon as his running mate. Their 1952 victory ended a 20 year span of Democrats winning the White House. The Eisenhower-Nixon ticket beat the Adlai Stevenson-John Sparkman Democratic ticket by a comfortable margin: 442 to 89 in the Electoral College vote, and 54.9 percent to 44.4 percent in the popular vote (the American Presidency Project). Foreign policy issues of the Korean War and communism and the Cold War dominated the election. They carried 39 of the then 48 U.S. states.

The height of the Cold War and its focus of Soviet Union versus United States conflict on the world scene impacted domestic policy issues and religious freedom issues. Past immigrants who were adherents of the Russian Orthodox Church got into a legal dispute that became a case which rose to U.S. Supreme Court; *Kedroff v. Saint Nicholas Cathedral* (344 U.S. 94, 1952). The Court was asked to rule on a dispute as to which organizational body of the Russian Orthodox Church had the rights of ownership of their Cathedral in New York City, the Patriarch in Moscow, or the Archbishop of the Orthodox Church in New York City? The Court refused to rule on the case, arguing the Establishment clause and precedent cases, like *Lemon v. Kurtzman* (1971) and its three part test, led the Court to send it back to the jurisdiction of the Supreme Court of the state of New York.

In the 1956 presidential election, it was again Republicans Eisenhower and Nixon running against Democrats Stevenson and his running mate, Senator Estes Kefauver (D-TN). Ike and Nixon won by an even wider margin: 457 Electoral College votes and 57.4 percent of the popular vote to Stevenson/Kefauver's 73 Electoral College votes and 42 percent of the popular vote. This time, the Republican ticket won 41 of the 48 states. It was the last election in which the Democrats still carried the "Solid South." Ike and Nixon won 40 percent of the black vote (the American Presidency Project).

Religious freedom issues arose in the early 1960s, resulting in another landmark Supreme Court decision on the matter, in a 1961 case involving Orthodox Judaism. The dispute hinged on local Sunday Sabbath (also known as Sunday Blue Laws) ordinances. Orthodox Jews and a Kosher meat market sued arguing such laws were unconstitutional infringements on their free exercise rights in the case of *Gallagher v. Crowne Kosher Meat Market of Massachusetts, Inc.* (366 U.S. 627, 1961). In a 6–3 decision, the Court upheld the local laws.

In immigration policy making, the U.S. Congress, by the mid-1960s, with the presidencies of John F. Kennedy and Lyndon B. Johnson, the anti-restrictionists were on the offensive and the restrictionist forces were fighting a holding action. By the end of the era, the need for another substantial revision in immigration policy was rather widely accepted (Chiswick 1982; LeMay 1987: 102–116; SCIRP Report 1981).

The Dutch Door period is characterized by significant changes in the flow of immigration. Total immigration expanded, and nonquota and undocumented immigration rose considerably. The composition of legal immigration shifted markedly during this phase. The substantial increase in immigration from Asian and Western Hemisphere nations (mainly Mexico and other Central and Latin American countries) is apparent, as is the corresponding decline in immigration from Northwestern and other European nations. During the Dutch Door phase, Mexico, Cuba, China, Taiwan, Korea, and the Philippines emerged as the principle sources of legal immigration.

The end of the Pet Door phase saw the development of a general consensus about the need for a comprehensive review of immigration policy. In 1950, a special Senate committee, authorized in 1947 under the chairmanship of Senator William Chapman Revercomb (R-WV), and then continuing under Senator Pat McCarran (D-NV), issued a lengthy report. It was the most comprehensive study of immigration since the Dillingham Commission Report of 1911. Both Senator McCarran and his coauthor, Senator Francis Walter (D-PA), were noted anti-communists. The committee's report served as the basis for the debate and proposed legislation that marked the beginning of the Dutch Door phase—the McCarran-Walter Act of June 27, 1952 (66 Stat. 163; summarized in LeMay and Barkan 1999: 218–225).

The Immigration and Naturalization Act of 1952

The McCarran-Walter Act of 1952 was only a modest revision in the direction of relaxing the restrictions imposed by the national origins quota system. While it basically codified existing legislation, in some cases even making the quota system more rigid, it did grant a token quota to nations in what had been defined as the "Asian Pacific Triangle"—essentially ending the Asiatic Barred Zone of the 1924 law (LeMay 2013, v. 3: 4). While avoiding the more racist arguments that had characterized the original implementation of the quota system, the Senate committee's report, which formed the basis of the proposed act, did reaffirm that immigration policy should favor Northwestern over Southeastern European immigration since, in the committee's words, ". . . the peoples who had made the greatest contribution to the development of this nation were fully justified in determining that the country was no longer a field for further colonization, and henceforth further immigration would not only be restricted but directed to admit immigrants considered to be more readily assimilable because of the similarity of their cultural background to those of the principle components of our population" (U.S. Congress, Senate Committee on the Judiciary 1950, Senate Report 1515: 455).

The anti-restrictionist policy forces in the House of Representatives were led by Representative Emmanuel Celler (D-NY) and in the Senate by Senators Herbert H. Lehman (D-NY) and Hubert Humphrey (D-MN). They argued against continuation of the quota system because of its incorporation of a philosophy of racism not unlike that of Nazi Germany, the espousal of which led to such tragic consequences for the entire world. Major ethnic associations supported the liberalizing efforts of the Lehman-Humphrey forces.

Proponents for continuation of restrictionism argued that the postwar economy could not absorb a large-scale immigration, which would surely follow any substantial easing of restriction limits. They also raised the specter of the Cold War, stressing the dangers of communist subversion and defending the tight security provisions of the McCarran-Walter bill.

The Lehman-Humphrey forces lacked the votes to block passage of the McCarran-Walter Act, or to uphold President Truman's threatened veto. They tried a compromise proposal: pooling unused quotas, which could then be used by countries with small quotas, and increasing the total volume slightly by using census data from 1950 rather than 1920. Congress rejected the compromise proposal and passed the McCarran-Walter Act by voice vote in May 1952 (LeMay 1987: 106).

The law limited the quota of colonies and dependent areas to 100, sharply reducing immigration from the West Indies. While defenders of the bill claimed all colonies were subject to the same restriction, critics noted that black West Indians were the most affected by that change (prior to the enactment, West Indians entered under the large British quota, but as colonists they were limited to 100 per year by the 1952 Act).

A small but ultimately important revision of immigration policy in McCarran-Walter was its inclusion of a preference system within the quotas, based on relatives of U.S. citizens and economic considerations. These provisions foreshadowed the 1965 Act that liberalized immigration policy by replacing the entire quota system with a preference system.

Another modest but liberalizing provision of the McCarran-Walter Act concerned Asian immigration. The act repealed the racial ban on citizenship, thereby winning the support of the Japanese American Citizens League (JACL). While most ethnic organizations had opposed the bill, the JACL supported it, since its enactment would make thousands of elderly Japanese (the Issei) eligible for citizenship (Chapter 2 of the Act; see LeMay and Barkan 1999: 221–223). The repeal of the racial ban was not too controversial. In 1949, the House had passed a similar measure. Congressman Walter H. Judd (R-MN), a former missionary to China, had proposed creating an "Asian-Pacific Triangle," each nation of which would be given an annual quota of 100 for a total triangle quota of 2,000, thereby ending the Asiatic Barred Zone of the 1921 Quota Act. Judd's idea was incorporated into the 1952 Act (Chapter 1, Sec. 202 (b)(2) (3) and (4); LeMay and Barkan 1999: 221).

Even restrictionist agreed with the removal of the racial ban. The Asian Triangle provision, however, did maintain an aspect of racial discrimination within it. While in all other cases the quotas were charged to the country of birth, this provision stipulated that persons of half or more Asian ancestry were to be charged to that Asian quota. Thus, a person born in Colombia of Japanese ancestry would not enter as a Colombian, as though from a Western Hemisphere nation that had no quota, but as part of the much smaller Japanese allotment. The intent of the law was clearly directed at the hundreds of thousands of persons of Asian backgrounds living in Latin America and Canada who would otherwise have been eligible to come in as nonquota immigrants from the Western Hemisphere (Chiswick 1982: 27; LeMay 1987: 107).

The McCarran-Walter Act did not impose a quota for the Western Hemisphere, for which many restrictionists had lobbied, but relied instead on the general categories of exclusion—such as the "public charge" clause—to limit immigration from that region. The act largely ignored the Bracero program and the problems of illegal immigration. It defined nonimmigrants, elaborating on previous law regarding treaty traders, students, temporary workers and the like. It developed the most elaborate provisions concerning the definition of and the process to be used for naturalization (Chapter 2 of the act). In doing so, it strengthened the administrative powers of the attorney general in deciding on borderline or questionable cases (LeMay 1987: 107).

President Truman vetoed the bill, objecting in his veto message to its racially biased quotas. He opposed continuation of the national origins system, holding the quotas were unfair to nationalities from Southeastern Europe. He pointedly noted that it had been increasingly necessary to pass special legislation to admit many of the Southeastern Europeans who were refugees from totalitarian regimes. He objected to the unfair racial provisions of the Asian Triangle quotas, which he viewed as woefully inadequate. He objected to provisions that restricted immigration of aliens who had been convicted of crimes and who had made misrepresentations to obtain visas, suggesting that the standards of justice in some foreign countries were far different from those of the United States, and that the desperation of some to escape repressive regimes meant some fraudulent representation should be forgiven. His veto message objected to the grounds for nonadmission of drug addicts. He objected to the reenactment of provisions regarding the process of denaturalization and deportation of persons suspected of subversive activities, arguing the provision gave too much power to the attorney general (LeMay and Barkan 1999, Document 119: 225–231; *The Papers of the Presidents*, June 25, 1952: 441–447).

Congress overrode Truman's veto and passed the bill 278 to 113 in the House of Representatives, and 57 to 26 in the Senate (LeMay 2013, v. 3: 4; see also Chiswick 1982: 28).

The U.S. Supreme Court reflected some of the fears dominating the Congress that were alluded to in President Truman's veto message. It handed down a decision on March 16, 1953, *Shaughnessy v. United States* (345 U.S. 206; LeMay and Barkan 1999: 231–233) that concerned administrative procedures for dealing with aliens seeking admission who were detained at Ellis Island, while their entry (or reentry, in this case) was being examined. The Court affirmed sweeping powers to deny entry for national security concerns.

Despite or perhaps because of his loss in the veto vote, President Truman established a special commission to study the whole issue of immigration. While the report, titled *Whom Shall We Welcome* (1953), was ignored by Congress, it did lay the groundwork for much of the subsequent revisions to immigration law and policy made in 1965 (LeMay 2006: 148). The report, reflecting President Truman's foreign policy perspective, viewed immigration law as an essential part of the nation's foreign policy, and concluded that the national origins quota system had failed in its avowed purpose as a selection system. The report was highly critical of the then current naturalization processes and procedures, elaborately specified in Section two of the McCarran-Walter Act (LeMay 2013, v. 3: 5). The recommendations of the commission were contained in its report, issued January 1, 1953 (LeMay and Barkan 1999, Document 121: 233–236).

President Truman tried to interject the immigration issue into the 1952 presidential election, as the Senate vote to override his veto had depended on overwhelming Republican support, 32 to 8, plus a few southern Democrats. The issue did not resonate with the electorate, however, and with President Dwight Eisenhower's election, the report and the immigration issue were left to die.

The worldwide refugee situation after World War II, and foreign policy concerns arising out of the Cold War, led Congress to pass the Refugee Relief Act of 1953 (Act of August 7, 1953; 67 Stat. 400; LeMay and Barkan 1999: 237–239). President Eisenhower had called for revisions in the immigration laws to admit escapees from behind the iron curtain. One of the first proposals from his administration to Congress stipulated such, numbering the allowance for them outside the quota system at 120,000 annually for two years. Eisenhower stressed the need to allow them in on both humanitarian grounds and to further U.S. foreign policy vis-à-vis the Cold War.

A House minority report objected to even this modest attempt at liberalizing immigration law since it would "destroy the principle of national origins upon which our immigration system is based" (cited in Chiswick 1982: 30). Representative Francis Walter (D-PA), a prominent member of the House Un-American Activities Committee, 1951–1963, and its chairman between 1954 and 1963, led the House opposition to liberalizing the law, and Senator McCarran, not surprisingly, led the Senate forces to amend the administration's plan, which as seen earlier, passed in August 1953 (see also, Jones 1960: 286). In that act, Congress agreed to admit as special immigrants a group of German ethnic expellees, and Poles, Greeks, Italians, and a few Arabs and Asians. They were required to obtain U.S. citizen sponsors assuring them of jobs and housing, unless they were close relatives. It also involved an elaborate plan to screen them to assure that no subversives would sneak in through the act (LeMay 1987: 108; LeMay 2006: 149).

Debate on the Refugee Act of 1953 typified the conflicts over immigration policy that went on throughout the 1950s. Proposals to amend or radically change the national origins system died in committee. Proposals, however, that were tied to foreign policy and national security, or which stressed humanitarian grounds for special consideration outside the quota system, fared better. However, the actual effects of the "special legislation" served to undercut the origins system as immigrants from Southeastern European countries who came in under these various provisions often ended up doubling or tripling the numbers from that country allowed under the quota system.

Total numbers of immigrants entering the United States were down sufficiently by 1954, that Congress decided to close down the Ellis Island immigration reception station in November 1954 (LeMay 2006: 149; LeMay and Barkan 1999: 241–242; Moreno and LeMay 2013, v. 2: 221).

In 1956, Congress rejected yet another proposal to overhaul the national origins system, but allowed for another "special" act to deal with a particular refugee problem. The failed Hungarian revolution produced a mass exodus of "freedom fighters." President Eisenhower wanted them to be admitted to the United States. Initially, he brought in around 15,000 under the Refugee Relief Act of 1953 (72 Stat. 419; Hungary's annual quota was a mere 869. See LeMay and Barkan 1999: 164). That was still inadequate to the numbers needed to relieve the problem. In early 1957, Eisenhower asked for legislation and some broader changes in the immigration laws. Congress rejected the broad changes but granted the president wider latitude in bringing in the freedom fighters. Congress endorsed his novel use of parole authority, granting permanent residence to those already here by parole authority. A special "parole" status was established enabling more than 30,600 Hungarian refugees to enter that year (Chiswick 1982: 32; Jones 1960: 286; LeMay 1987: 108; LeMay 2013, v. 3: 5). This was the first wide-scale use of the "parole" status. Roughly 12,000 of the 38,000 Hungarian refugees entered under parole status. The remainder was admitted under the regular quotas. Voluntary agencies met the cost of their resettlement, assisting them in finding sponsors, jobs, and housing. In the failed revolt against the Soviet-backed Hungarian communist government, thousands died in the fighting, others were tortured and executed, and some 200,000 forced to flee. The American Hungarian Federation activated a Hungarian relief program for the refugees of the Hungarian revolution, providing $512,560 (or $4.5 million in today's dollars). The federation helped 65,000 refugees (American Hungarian Federation; Chiswick 1982: 32; McClellan 1981: 21).

The religious affiliations of these Hungarian refugees were not explicitly counted, but data from a 1992 study of Hungarian Americans did so, and it probably reflects their affiliations as well: Catholic, 67.8 percent; Reformed Calvinist, 20.9 percent; Evangelical Lutheran, 4.2 percent;

Other (Greek or Byzantine Catholic, Orthodox Christians, Baptists, Adventists), 2.3 percent; and no religious affiliation, 4.8 percent. Many settled in the Greater Pittsburgh area, which soon had dozens of Hungarian churches, although by the 1990s, as that refugee population assimilated or in retirement moved to California or Florida, the churches were closed and the few remaining were struggling to survive.

In 1957, Congress cancelled the mortgage quotas of the DPA, marking a further breakdown in the restrictionist policy of the quota system. While Congress continued to chip away at the system, it became clear that a broader revision was becoming necessary.

Late in the Eisenhower presidency, the Castro revolution in Cuba generated another large wave of refugees from communism seeking entry to the United States. Eisenhower again used parole status to admit them. Ultimately, some 800,000 refugees entered the United States, making it the largest long-term refugee movement in U.S. history (LeMay 2006: 150; Chiswick 1982: 32; McClellan 1981: 22). Most Cuban refugees were Catholic in their religious affiliation, of course, but another affiliation added to America's religious diversity: the Santeria (Way of the Saints). Santeria is an Afro-Caribbean religion based on Yoruba beliefs that blended with some Roman Catholic elements. It is a syncretic religion that grew out of the slave trade in Cuba. Among its religious ceremonial practice is animal sacrifice (usually using chickens). This practice later caused conflict with local ordinances that eventually made it all the way to a 1993 Supreme Court free exercise case in which the Court ruled in favor of the religious practice on First Amendment grounds, *Church of Lukumi Babalu Aye v. City of Hialeah* (508 U.S. 520, 1993) (Religious Tolerance).

President Eisenhower also used parole status for Chinese arriving from Hong Kong. In the national security atmosphere that characterized the Cold War period, Congress obliged the president (LeMay 2006: 150). In all, from the end of World War II until 1980, more than 1.4 million refugees from all over the world immigrated to the Unites States (McClellan 1981: 45). They certainly and significantly added to the religious diversity of the American population during the Dutch Door phase of United States immigration policy.

An important religious free exercise cases rose to the Supreme Court level in 1961: *Gallagher v. Crowne Kosher Market of Massachusetts, Inc.* (366 U.S. 627). In the Gallagher decision, the Court decided by a 6–3 vote, to uphold the local Sabbath closing law as constitutional and turned down the arguments of the appeal of the Orthodox Jewish synagogue and kosher meat business.

Another method to get around the inflexibility of the quota system was the use of the private bill. Under this procedure, an alien sought exception to the quota system through private legislation wherein a member of Congress introduced a bill for his or her relief. The use of this procedure expanded during the 1950s, again serving to undercut the quota system. Table 5.1 shows the number of such bills introduced and those actually allowed to enter under a private bill for the years 1950–1972. While the total numbers were not large, numbering slightly more than 6,000 of more than 52,000 private bills introduced, that it was used as often as that further indicates the inflexibility of the quota system.

A new wave of immigrants, perhaps appropriately called the preference immigrants, was ushered in with the Immigration Act of 1965. The election of John F. Kennedy in 1960 eased the way for a frontal attack on the quota system. While serving as a U.S. senator from Massachusetts, John Kennedy wrote *A Nation of Immigrants* (1958; reissued 2008). In his book, Kennedy advocated increased levels of legal immigration and a major change in the approach used by immigration law. His view on immigration is captured in these words from the Preface to his book: "Every ethnic minority in seeking its own freedom, helped strengthen the American fabric of liberty in American life. Similarly, every aspect of the American

Table 5.1 Private Immigration and Nationality Bills, 1949–1972

Year	Bills Introduced	Enacted
1949–1950	2,811	505
1951–1952	3,669	729
1953–1954	4,797	755
1955–1956	4,474	1,227
1957–1958	4,364	927
1959–1960	3,069	488
1961–1962	3,592	544
1963–1964	3,647	196
1965–1966	5,285	279
1967–1968	7,293	218
1969–1970	6,266	113
1971–1972	2,866	62
TOTAL	52,136	6,043

Source: Table by author, revised and adapted from a table in LeMay 1987: 110.

economy has profited from the contributions of immigrants." The civil rights movement was pushing the nation, its leadership, and national public opinion toward an evaluation of racial bias on which many laws, including immigration law, were based.

In the 1960 presidential election, Kennedy selected his main rival for the nomination, Senator Lyndon Johnson (D-TX), as his running mate. It was an open race. The Republican ticket was Vice President Richard Nixon and Senator Henry Cabot Lodge (R-MA). Kennedy/Johnson prevailed in a narrow win. The Democratic ticket won 303 Electoral College votes and 49.7 percent of the popular vote to the Republican ticket's 219 Electoral College votes and 49.5 percent of the popular vote. It was the first presidential election in which televised debates between the candidates played a crucial role. A dissident faction of southern Democrats, unhappy with the civil rights direction of the national ticket, ran an independent slate of Senator Harry F. Byrd (D-VA) and Senator Strom Thurmond (D-SC). They won only 15 Electoral College votes and less than 1 percent of the popular vote. Kennedy's Catholicism was an issue in the election, as was his age—at 43 he was the youngest person to win the presidency. The 1960 election saw the "Solid South" fracture irreparably for the Democrats. They lost the "white southern" vote that the Republican's seized on by Nixon's "southern strategy" (the American Presidency Project).

In the post-World War II and post-Korean War years, the executive branch and even Congress had chipped away at the quota system, increasingly viewed as too rigid and too ethnically or racially biased to be maintained. The election of President Kennedy and a somewhat more liberal Congress resulted in Congress passing the Migration and Refugee Assistance Act (Act of July 14, 1960, 74 Stat. 504; LeMay and Barkan 1999: 248–249). Acting on the precedent set by the Hungarian freedom fighters, it in part was a response to the Cuban refugee crisis, allowing assistance in the resettlement of Cuban refugees who had been paroled by the attorney general; and in part, the law strengthened the role of the executive branch in the formulation and implementation of immigration policy by granting more authority to the attorney general. Perhaps as important, the law paved the way for the Immigration and Nationality Act of 1965.

On President Kennedy's assassination in 1963, Vice President Lyndon Johnson assumed the office. In the 1964 election, Johnson ran with Senator Hubert Humphrey (D-FL, MN) on the ticket. The Republicans nominated arch-conservative Senator Barry Goldwater (R-AZ) who picked the unknown William E. Miller as his running mate. Miller was an upstate New Yorker and chairman of the Republican Party. Johnson/Humphrey won in a nearly unprecedented landslide. They carried 44 of the 50 states and won 486 electoral votes and 61.1 percent of the popular vote to Goldwater/Miller's six states, only 52 Electoral College votes, and only 38.5 percent of the popular vote. Johnson's campaign stressed foreign policy (the Vietnam War) and his Great Society domestic agenda, which had wide appeal among ethnic voters (the American Presidency Project).

The Immigration and Nationality Act of 1965

Just as the quota approach to immigration and naturalization law reflected the racial ideas and concerns of the Pet Door period, the Immigration and Nationality Act of 1965 (sometimes called the Kennedy Act) reflected the civil rights movement. The success in the first few years of the Kennedy administration in basic economic policy ended the recession that had plagued the United States during much of the Eisenhower administration. The much improved economy worked to undercut much of the traditional opposition to comprehensive immigration reform. The healthy economy meant that even organized labor could support immigration reform. Senator Edward Kennedy (D-MA), the youngest brother of the president, led the effort in the Senate to enact a bill drafted by the administration. The bill was stalled while President Kennedy was alive, but upon his assassination, President Lyndon Johnson resubmitted the bill in January 1965. Officially the bill was sponsored by Representative Emmanuel Celler (D-NY), chairman of the House Judiciary Committee, and in the Senate by Senator Philip Hart (D-MI) and both Senators Robert Kennedy (D-NY) and Edward Kennedy (D-MA), and was cosponsored by 32 senators (LeMay and Barkan 1999: 256). It sought to balance a number of goals: (1) to preserve family unity and reunited separated families; (2) to meet the need for some highly skilled aliens; (3) to ease problems created by emergencies, such as political upheavals, communist aggression, and natural disasters; (4) to assist cross-national exchange programs; (5) to bar from the United States aliens who might present problems with adjustment because of their physical or mental health, or past criminal history, or dependency, or for national security reasons; (6) to standardize administrative procedures; and (7) to establish limits for the Americas. It replaced the national origins quota system with a seven-category preference system. It abolished national origins and emphasized other terms than quota and nonquota immigrants. Prospective immigrants were either non-preference, met one of the preferences, or were not subject to new per country limits because they were immediate relatives of United States citizens or were special immigrants, including persons born in the

Western Hemisphere, former U.S. citizens seeking to resume their citizenship, religious ministers, and former or current employees of the U.S. government abroad. Those seeking admission under the third or sixth employment preferences had to meet stringent labor certification rules. The law, which is more than 20 pages in the U.S. Code of Statutes, is summarized and excerpted in Box 5.1 (see also LeMay and Barkan 1999, Document 32: 257–261 for a bit more detailed excerption). The law was passed and signed into law by President Johnson (Act of October 3, 1965; 79 Stat. 911).

Box 5.1: Summary of Major Provisions of the Immigration and Naturalization Act of 1965 (79 Stat. 911, October 3, 1965)

1. It abolished the national origins quota system after a transition period to June 1968.
2. It abolished the Asian Pacific Triangle provision.
3. It allowed the use of quota numbers unused in the previous year as a pool of additional numbers for each year of the transitional period, for preference applicants chargeable to over-subscribed quotas.
4. It revised previous preference categories (from the 1952 Act) into a new system of preferences strongly favoring (74 percent) relatives of citizens and permanent resident aliens.
5. It required that an alien coming to work in the United States and not entitled to a preference obtain certification from the Secretary of Labor that he or she would not displace nor adversely affect the wages and working conditions of workers in the same field in the United States.
6. It included refugees as one of the preference categories.
7. It set an annual ceiling of 170,000 on immigration of aliens in the preference and nonpreference classifications with a 20,000 limit on any single foreign state.
8. It established an "immediate relative" (previously called "nonquota") status for parents of adult U.S. citizens.
9. It increased the dependent area immigration (previously "subquota") to 1 percent of the 20,000 maximum allowable numbers available to the governing country, that is, from 100 to 200 annually.
10. It set the filing date of the petition to determine the chronological order of preference applicants (a first-come, first-served provision).
11. It required that applicants be considered in the order of their preference class.

12. It created a Select Commission on Western Hemisphere Immigration to study the economic, political, and demographic factors affecting immigration.

13. It set a ceiling of 120,000 on immigration from the Western Hemisphere national after July 1968.

14. It included all independent countries of the Western Hemisphere in "special immigrant" status (previously called "nonquota" system.

15. It established the following seven preference categories:

1. **First preference:** unmarried sons and daughters of U.S. citizens;

2. **Second preference:** spouses and unmarried sons and daughters of permanent resident aliens;

3. **Third preference:** members of the professions and scientists and artists of exceptional ability;

4. **Fourth preference:** married sons and daughters of U.S. citizens;

5. **Fifth preference:** brothers and sisters of U.S. citizens;

6. **Sixth preference:** skilled and unskilled workers in short supply; and

7. **Seventh preference:** refugees

Source: LeMay, Michael. 1994. *Anatomy of a Public Policy: The Reform of Contemporary Immigration Law.* Westport, CT: Praeger Press: 12–13.

In addition to the seven preference categories, the act established a joint presidential/congressional, bipartisan Select Commission of Western Hemisphere Immigration, comprised of 15 members. The president was authorized to appoint the commission's chairman and four other members. The president of the Senate appointed five members from that body, and the Speaker of the House, with the approval of the majority and minority leaders, appointed five members of the House. The commission was charged to study six issues: (1) Prevailing and projected demographic, technological, and economic trends pertaining to the Western Hemisphere; (2) Present and projected unemployment in the United States, by occupations, industries, geographic areas, and other factors in relation to immigration from the Western Hemisphere; (3) The interrelationships between immigration, present and future, and existing and contemplated national and international programs and projects for the Western Hemisphere nations, including programs and projects for economic and social development; (4) The operation of immigration laws in the United States as they pertain to Western Hemisphere nations, including adjustment of status for Cuban refugees; (5) The implications of the foregoing with respect to the security and international relations of Western Hemisphere nations; and (6) Any other issues the commission believed to be germane to its purposes (LeMay and Barkan 1999: 261).

A key compromise was extracted by Senators Everett Dirksen (R-IL) and Samuel Ervin (D-NC) that placed an overall ceiling of 120,000 for the Western Hemisphere, replacing the previously unlimited immigration from the region. It was based on the actual flow of immigration from the region during the few years preceding the act. The Senate approved it by a vote of 76–18; the House by a vote of 320 to 69 (LeMay 1994: 13; see also Harper 1975: 56).

A good sense of the approach and thrust of the new law is apparent in remarks made by President Johnson when signing the act into law at the foot of the Statue of Liberty. They are excerpted in Box 5.2 (see also LeMay 1994: 12–13).

Box 5.2:   President Lyndon Johnson's Statement at the Signing of the 1965 Immigration and Nationality Bill, Liberty Island, New York, October 3, 1965

. . . This bill that we will sign today is not a revolutionary bill. It does not affect the lives of millions. It will not reshape the structure of our daily lives, or really add importantly to either our wealth or our power.

Yet it is still one of the most important acts of this Congress and of this administration. For it does repair a very deep and painful flaw in the fabric of American justice. It corrects a cruel and enduring wrong to the conduct of the American Nation . . .

This bill says simply that from this day forth those wishing to immigrate to America shall be admitted on the basis of their skills and close relationship to those already here.

The fairness of this standard is so self-evident that we may well wonder that it has not always been applied. Yet the fact is that for over four decades the immigration policy of the United States has been distorted by the harsh injustice of the national origins system.

This system violated the basic principle of American democracy—the principle that values and rewards each man of the basis of his merit as a man.

It has been un-American in the highest sense, because it has been untrue to the faith that brought thousands to these shores even before we were a country.

Today, with my signature, this system is abolished.

Asylum for Cuban Refugees

So it is in that spirit that I declare this afternoon to the people of Cuba that those who seek refuge here in America will find it. The dedication of America to our traditions as an asylum for the oppressed is going to be upheld.

I have directed the Department of State and Justice and Health, Education, and Welfare to immediately make all the necessary arrangements to permit those in Cuba who seek freedom to make an orderly entry into the United States of America.

Our first concern will be with those Cubans who have been separated from their children and parents and their husbands and wives and that are now in this country. Our next concern is with those who are imprisoned for political reasons.

And I will send to the Congress tomorrow a request for supplementary funds of $12,600,000 to carry forth the commitment that I am making today. . . .

And today we can all believe that the lamp of this grand old lady is brighter today—and the golden door that she guards gleams more brilliantly in the light of an increased liberty for the people from all the countries of the globe. Thank you very much.

Source: *The Papers of the Presidents, Lyndon B. Johnson, 1965*, vol. II (Washington, DC: Government Printing Office, 1966), 1037–1040.

Despite President Johnson's statement that the law would not affect the lives of millions, it in fact did just that. It resulted in dramatic shifts in the immigration flow. Both the size and its composition of the immigration flow changed during the decade following enactment of the 1965 law. Total immigration increased by 60 percent. Immigration from certain countries registered remarkable shifts. Greek immigration rose by 162 percent; Portuguese by 382 percent; and total Asian immigration rose by more than 3,800 percent, with Korean by 1,200 percent, Pakistan by 1,600 percent, the Philippines by nearly 1,200 percent, Thailand by more than 1,700 percent, and Vietnam by more than 1,900 percent. And in stark contrast, European immigration fell by 38 percent overall; with Austria down by more than 76 percent, Ireland by more than 77 percent, Norway by more than 85 percent, and the United Kingdom falling off by 120 percent (LeMay 2013, v. 3: 6–7).

The third preference category, for professionals, was especially used by Asians: Korean and Philippine health professionals entered in large numbers, and then soon thereafter brought in their families under Preference 2. By the end of the 1970s, more than 70,000 medical doctors alone immigrated, and by the late 1970s there were more Filipino physicians in the United States than there were native-born black doctors (Mamot 1974; Stevens 1978).

The law's seventh category, set aside for refugees, was almost immediately outmoded by events. The law set an annual limit of refugees at 10, 200 (6 percent of the total legal immigration from the Eastern Hemisphere of 170,000), which seemed generous at the time and based on the numbers coming in after World War II and the Korean War. Events in Cuba, Vietnam, Cambodia, Laos, and Haiti, however, soon outstripped the ability to cope with the demand based on the seventh category. From 1960 to 1980, some 800,000 refugees came from Cuba alone. Large numbers fled what amounted to a civil war in El Salvador, and still more the collapse of the economy of Haiti. The fall of the South Vietnamese government in 1975 created another large pool of refugees fleeing communism. From 1975 to 1979, more than 200,000 Vietnamese came to the United States, and the turmoil in Cambodia (now Kampuchea) and Laos added still more (LeMay 2013, v. 3: 7).

In 1966, Congress passed a law adjusting the status of refugees from Cuba (Act of November 2, 1966, 80 Stat. 1161; LeMay and Barkan 1999: 263–264). It adjusted their status to permanent residence, including the spouse and child of any such Cuban refugee.

The definition of refugee in the provision of the 1965 law did not consider refugees from right-wing dictatorships in the Western Hemisphere, such as the government of Francois "Papa Doc" Duvalier in Haiti, which became problematic in the 1970s, when Haitian "boat people" began arriving at America's shores in large numbers.

The 1968 presidential election was an especially contentious one with the Vietnam War and civil rights issues fracturing the Democratic Party and sharply dividing the electorate (Bennett 2013; CQ Weekly Report 1968; Nelson 2014; White 1970). Former vice president Richard Nixon and the Republican governor of Maryland, Spiro Agnew, won 301 Electoral College votes and 43.4 percent of the popular vote. They ran against the Democratic ticket of Vice President Humphrey and his running mate, Senator Edmund Muskie (D-ME), who won the party's nomination after a bitterly fought primary race and national convention.

The Humphrey/Muskie ticket won 191 Electoral College votes and 42.7 percent of the popular vote. Governor George Wallace (D-AL) and retired U.S. Air Force General Curtis E. LeMay (R-CA) ran as independents. Wallace appealed to the white southern segregationist wing of the Democratic Party, and General Curtis LeMay was chosen to give the ticket credentials on foreign policy and anti-communism. Their ticket won 45 Electoral

College votes and 13.5 percent of the popular vote (all in the south). The 1968 election permanently disrupted the New Deal Coalition (Gould 2010; Nelson 2014; White 1970).

An NBC sample poll of precincts in the 1968 election demonstrated the division between the electorate on several demographic characteristics. Nixon won in 63 percent of high-income urban districts to Humphrey's 29 percent (with 5 percent of the districts in the south going to George Wallace). By contrast, in low-income urban precincts, Humphrey won 69 percent to Nixon's 19 percent and Wallace's 12 percent. Among rural precincts (all income levels), Humphrey won only 33 percent to Nixon's 46 percent and Wallace's 21 percent (again, in the south). Black voters in 1968 shifted strongly and permanently to the Democrats. In black precincts, Humphrey won 94 percent to Nixon's 5 percent and Wallace's 1 percent. Among Italian districts, Humphrey won 51 percent, Nixon 39 percent, and Wallace 10 percent. Voters in Slavic precincts went even heavier to the Democrats: Humphrey won 65 percent to Nixon's 24 percent and Wallace's 11 percent. Among Jewish voters, Humphrey received 81 percent to Nixon's 17 percent and Wallace's 2 percent. Union precincts, not surprisingly, went heavily Democratic in 1968: Humphrey with 61 percent to Nixon's 29 percent and Wallace's 10 percent. In the Hispanic south precincts, Humphrey won 92 percent to Nixon's 7 percent and Wallace's 1 percent (CQ 1968: 3218).

In 1972, a landmark decision was handed down by the Supreme Court which ruled on the religious free-exercise rights of the Amish and Mennonite faithful who were in conflict with state laws requiring mandatory education through high school. The Amish and Mennonite objected to the laws maintaining the state laws threatened their religious practices. In *Wisconsin v. Yoder* (406 U.S. 205, 1972) the Court ruled 7–0 for the Amish and Mennonites and overturned the Wisconsin law.

The fall of the South Vietnamese government in 1975 created another huge migration of refugees from the region; one for which the United States felt a moral obligation to assist. Between 1975 and 1979, more than 200,000 Vietnamese refugees came to the United States. When the boat people began to arrive in 1979, the administration committed to allowing 168,000 in 1980. Eventually, some 500,000 refugees from Southeast Asia arrived. Jews fleeing the Soviet Union contributed another 70,000 in the 1970s. Foreign policy exigencies of the Cold War compelled consideration of further changes in immigration law (LeMay 1987: 114–115).

The Vietnam War continued to be a dividing issue in presidential elections that in turn influenced subsequent immigration policy making. In the 1972 election, President Richard Nixon and Vice President Spiro

Agnew won by a landslide over the Democratic ticket of Senator George McGovern (D-MN) and his vice presidential running mate, Sargent Shriver. McGovern had picked Shriver in part as an attempt to unify the party by appealing to the "Kennedy wing." It did not help. Nixon/Agnew won 520 Electoral College votes and 60.7 percent of the popular vote to McGovern/Shriver's 17 Electoral College votes and 37.5 percent of the popular vote. The Republican ticket carried 49 of the 50 states (McGovern won only Massachusetts and the District of Columbia).

In the 1976 presidential election, however, the Democrats bounced back. Vice President Agnew had to resign in a bribery scandal and President Nixon appointed Congressman Gerald Ford (R-MI) to replace him. Then, the Watergate scandal forced Nixon to resign in disgrace. The 1976 race pitted Democrat Jimmy Carter (governor of Georgia) and his running mate, Senator Walter Mondale (DFL-MN) against Republican president Ford and his running mate, Senator Bob Dole (R-KS). Carter/Mondale won with 297 Electoral College votes and 50.1 percent of the popular vote to Ford/Dole's 240 Electoral College votes and 48 percent of the popular vote. The 1976 presidential election was the first since 1848 that a Deep South Democrat won the office, running as a "Washington outsider." The Democratic ticket won 23 states and the District of Columbia and the Ford/Dole ticket won 27 states, but with less population and therefore fewer Electoral College votes and fewer popular votes. In 1976, Carter won 82 percent of the black vote, 75 percent of the Hispanic vote, and only 47 percent of the white vote to Ford's 16 percent of the black vote, 24 percent of the Hispanic vote, and 52 percent of the white vote. In religious affiliation, Protestant voters in 1976 gave Carter 44 percent to Ford's 55 percent; and white Protestants split even more so, with 43 percent for Carter and 57 percent for Ford. Among Catholic voters, however, Carter won 54 percent to Ford's 44 percent. Among Jewish voters, Carter won 64 percent to Ford's 34 percent. Among union voters, Carter won 59 percent to Ford's 39 percent (CBS News/New York Times Exit Polls, November 1976).

In 1980, and again in 1984, the Republican Party reversed their electoral fortunes. In 1980, they ran with governor of California Ronald Reagan and his running mate, George H. W. Bush against President Jimmy Carter and Vice President Walter Mondale. The Iranian hostage crisis and foreign policy issues more generally made President Carter unpopular. The Reagan/Bush ticket won by a landslide: 489 Electoral College votes and 50.7 percent of the popular vote, and carrying 44 of 50 states to the Carter/Mondale ticket's 49 Electoral College votes and 41 percent of the popular vote. John Anderson and Patrick Lucy ran on an Independent

Party ticket that won no Electoral College votes but did manage to win 6.6 percent of the popular vote. Among demographic groups, Carter won 82 percent of the black vote to Reagan's 14 percent, and 54 percent of the Hispanic vote to Reagan's 36 percent. By contrast, white voters went 55 percent for Reagan to only 36 percent for Carter. The religious and union vote again split similarly to that of 1976: Carter lost the Protestant vote to Reagan, 37 to 56 percent, and the white Protestant vote even more so, 31 percent to Reagan's 62 percent. Among Catholics, Reagan did fare better (with an appeal to anti-communism issues) than had Ford in 1976. Reagan won the Catholic vote 51 percent to Carter's 40 percent. In 1980, the Jewish vote split more evenly as well: Carter won 45 percent to Reagan's 39 percent. Showing a strong appeal to the "blue-collar Democrat" vote, Reagan nearly matched Carter in 1980. Carter won 47 percent of the union vote to Reagan's 44 percent (CBS News/New York Times Exit Polls, November 1980).

The Refugee Act of March 17, 1980, created the Office of United States Coordinator, which was charged with monitoring, coordinating, and implementing overall refugee policy variously administered within the Immigration and Naturalization Service (INS), the Department of Justice (DOJ), the Bureau of Refugee Programs in the Department of State (DOS), and the Office of Refugee Resettlement in the Department of Health and Human Service (DHHS). The act's change in the definition of "refugee" increased the number of potentially eligible people from 3 million to 15 million. The question of refugee status is a complex one involving political, social, economic, and legal ramifications. Trends in political turmoil throughout the world led to what was called the global refugee crisis, and since the 1980s, more than 15 million persons have become internationally recognized as refugees, a greater number than in any other period of recorded human history (Ferris 1985: 105; LeMay 2004: 6).

During the 1980s, the population of the industrialized world became almost inured to the waves of refugees coming mostly from Third World nations. But since 1989, the movement has reached levels not seen since the end of World War II, when hundreds of thousands of Europeans began migrating from Eastern Europe to the West: 100,000 people left the former Soviet Union, and 250,000 East Germans, 300,000 Bulgarian Turks, 230,000 Poles, and more than 20,000 Romanians migrated (LeMay 2004: 7). Those refugees reaching the United States once again contributed to the religious affiliation diversity of the American population.

The shift in the nation of origin of massive refugee movements with the sudden outpouring from Eastern Europe heading to the West partially explains why the reduction in tensions between the East and the West did not significantly alleviate the world's refugee problems. This new migration trend changed the world's image of the refugee, from the picture of an emaciated Ethiopian child with a bloated stomach seeking relief from famine in a dusty desert camp or someone fleeing war, civil unrest, or natural disaster to today's image of a person seeking better economic opportunity or political and religious liberty.

In its various provisions, the Refugee Act of 1980 allowed for as many as 70,000 people annually to enter the United States because they had a well-founded fear of persecution. In 1984, for example, 61,750 refugees were admitted (LeMay 2004: 7). They arrived in large numbers from given countries at any given time—that is, they arrived in mass asylum movements. From 1960 to 1985, for example, nearly 800,000 came from Cuba, 340,000 from Vietnam, 110,000 from Laos, nearly 70,000 from the then U.S.S.R., and about 70,000 from Kampuchea (formerly Cambodia), 30,000 from then Yugoslavia, about 25,000 from mainland China and Taiwan, nearly 20,000 each from Romania and Poland, and about 10,000 each from Czechoslovakia, Spain, and Hungary (LeMay 1987: 123). Despite changes in the refugee flows, most of the world's refugees fled their native lands driven simply by the attempt to stay alive—like the four million refugees in Africa and the five million Afghans encamped in Pakistan and Iran.

Receiving nations tend to accept refugee from countries with whom they have had some historic ties. Between 1975 and 1980, for example, the United States took in 677,000 refugees who were then mostly Soviet Jews (two-thirds of all Soviet émigrés came to the United States), Indochinese from countries with whom the United States had a military alliance (i.e., from South East Asian Treaty Organization [SEATO] member states), and people from South or Central America and the Caribbean. That total exceeded by three times that of any other receiving country and was almost as many as all the other receiving nations combined. England and Canada were major receiving nations for refugees from former Commonwealth colonial states, and Germany has traditionally taken refugees from the Middle East (*World Refugee Survey*, cited in Papademetrious and Miller 1984: 264).

As a noted immigration scholar put it: "Massive postwar migrations have posed a fundamental challenge to the nation-states of Europe and North America. They compelled countries to reinterpret their traditions, reshape their institutions, rethink the meaning of citizenship—in short, to reinvent themselves as nation-states" (Brubaker 1989: 1).

The world is becoming increasingly interdependent, and that fact, coupled with an easing of transportation and communication difficulties, made receiving nations of the industrialized world more accessible than ever before. The worldwide population explosion, rising poverty and unemployment in developing nations, with the accompanying political and social turmoil, the resurgence of ethnic and religious tensions, and periodic natural disasters all have acted as powerful push factors driving international migration on an unprecedented scale.

The plight and problems that caused an influx of Haitians who came to the United States as "economic refugees" and who, not incidentally, were black, raised other perplexing issues for United States policy makers. The Vietnamese and other Indochinese refugees were largely political allies about whom many members of Congress felt some moral obligation to assist and to whom the American population was willing to extend help. The black Haitian poor were another matter. The Vietnamese were mostly well-educated, middle-class persons, two-thirds of whom had held white-collar occupations in Vietnam, and 24 percent were from professional, technical, and managerial occupations. Less than 5 percent were farmers and fisherman (Montero 1979: 23). The Vietnamese tended to acculturate more rapidly than any previous group of immigrants from Asia. Haitians, by stark contrast, were treated as illegal immigrants fleeing economic conditions, not political repression. They were not allowed in under refugee status. Arriving in ever-increasing numbers starting in 1972, their legal status was clouded for years as the Department of State grappled with what to do with them. As economic refugees, they were accorded neither aid nor public support such as that given to Cubans, Vietnamese, Hungarians, or Soviet Jews. They were held in detention camps for years, and upon their release, they were not aided in finding jobs or housing or otherwise acculturating to life in America, as were the political refugees (LeMay 2004: 8–9).

Haitian refugees were mostly illiterate, had low-job skills, and had language issues that made them easily exploitable. They often lived in conditions of near-slavery as migrant workers. Public opinion viewed them as special threats to labor markets. Their influx focused attention of the increasing problem of illegal immigration. An estimated three million to six million unauthorized immigrants arrived during the 1970s and 1980s. That issue dominated debate over immigration problems in the early 1980s (LeMay 2007; 2016).

A combination of world economic developments, major political upheavals, and the unanticipated consequences of the 1965 immigration act, all interacted with significant results to the flow of immigration to the United States from the 1970s onward (Muller and Espanshade 1985: 12).

The end of black migration from the South led to increased demand for a new source of low-wage labor in the nation's urban centers. By 1970, moreover, this demand was no longer concentrated in northern industrial cities. Northeast and even Midwest cities stagnated or even declined during the 1970s as the population, and labor demand, shifted to the "Sun Belt" states. As Muller and Espanshade put it:

> The rural and nonmetropolitan sources of low-skilled, low-wage labor to compliment an increasingly educated and skilled metropolitan population had to be replaced if a wage spiral was to be avoided. Changing social and economic conditions affected divorce rates, attitudes toward work, educational progress, and the growth of white-collar employment opportunities in low- and moderate-wage scale and clerical occupations. As a result, the share of all working women over the age of fifteen rose dramatically, from 39 percent in 1965 to 52 percent in the early 1980s; well over 10 million women came into the labor force in a sixteen-year period. (Ibid: 13)

The movement of women into the workforce, however, was still not enough to meet demand. The increase in job opportunities in the American economy, growing overpopulation in sender nations, and increased political and economic instability in Mexico and Central America, lower travel costs, and timely revision in American immigration laws all interwove, changing the very fabric of migration to the United States. The 1970s saw some of the highest levels of immigration (counting both legal and undocumented immigration) since the 1920s. The revisions in the 1965 Act, moreover, "targeted" to a greater degree than previously was the case of immigration to particular occupations where shortages existed— for example, to engineering and the professions. Sending nations began to complain of a "brain drain" in the immigration flow that has been called the "Fourth Wave" (Ibid).

The "Fourth Wave" is comprised of three segments: (1) legal immigrants admitted as permanent residents, (2) refugees, and (3) unauthorized immigrants—both undocumented (about 60 percent of the total) and visa overstayers (about 40 percent of the total). The arrival of this new wave coincided with two major public policy events: (1) the end of the Bracero program, and (2) enactment of the 1965 immigration law. As we have seen, during the quota years a majority of immigration came from Europe; post-1970 the majority of immigrants came from Third World nations—Asian and Latin American. To exemplify by citing one year, 1984, of 544,000 legal immigrants who entered the United States, 10 percent (57,000) were from Mexico, followed by the Philippines (42,000), and Vietnam (37,000). By contrast, British immigration that year was only 14,000, and ranked ninth among sending nations (LeMay 1989: 5).

President Jimmy Carter, through his attorney general, responded to the refugee crisis by using his executive parole power to permit Cubans, Vietnamese, and Southeast Asians (Hmong, Cambodians, Laotians) to enter in numbers far exceeding the refugee category limits. Congress joined in that effort by allocating funds to support the parolees and to adjust their status by enacting the Indochinese Refugee Resettlement Program in 1975. Then, during the final weeks of the congressional session of 1976, Congress enacted a law to amend the Immigration Act of 1965 to deal with the immense backlog of visa requests from Western Hemisphere-sending nations. The 1976 law extended the preference system to Western Hemisphere nations in the hope that it would cut in half the waiting period for immigrants from Mexico, for example (LeMay and Barkan 1999, Document 138: 270–72).

Finally, in 1980, Congress dealt more directly with the refugee crisis. The Refugee Act of 1980 was an effort to systematize refugee policy making. It incorporated the UN definition of a refugee—one who had a well-founded fear of persecution owing to race, religion, nationality, or membership in a social group or political movement—and initially allowed for 50,000 persons annually to enter as refugees. The act empowered the president to notify Congress if he determined that events warranted an increase in the number, and after fiscal year 1982, he would have the responsibility of presenting Congress with a recommended total annual figure. Thus, for example, 72,000 were authorized for 1984 and 67,500 actually arrived and another 11,600 were granted asylum (Act of March 17, 1980, 94 Stat. 102; LeMay and Barkan 1999: 272–275).

In 1981, while the debate over refugee and immigration policy occupied the Congress and much of the public, continued demand from refugee flows outstripped even the numbers allowed by the 1980 Act, and illegal immigration spiked exponentially. Then newly elected president Ronald Reagan appointed a special task force to study those problems and to recommend policy alternatives (LeMay and Barkan 1999: 275–277).

Of even greater importance for future immigration policy making than the Reagan Task Force was the report of the Select Commission on Immigration and Refugee Policy (SCIRP). The commission was appointed and began its work during the final weeks of the Carter administration. The commission was a joint presidential and congressional commission. It began its work in 1979 and issued its final report in 1981. Its recommendations formed the basis of subsequent legislative action that characterized the second half of the 1980s and into the 1990s (the Revolving Door phase). Box 5.3 presents a summary of the major recommendations contained in the commission's final report, which served as a blueprint for immigration policy making throughout the Revolving Door period and have relevance for the comprehensive immigration reform proposals since 2010.

BOX 5.3: EXECUTIVE SUMMARY RECOMMENDATIONS OF THE SELECT COMMISSION ON IMMIGRATION AND REFUGEE POLICY, 1981

The Select Commission recommends that:

1. The United States work with other nations and principal international organizations to collect information and research on migratory flows and treatment of international migration.
2. The United States expand bilateral consultation with other governments, especially Mexico and other regional neighbors regarding migration.
3. Border Patrol funding levels be raised to provide for a substantial increase in the number and training of personnel, replacement of sensor systems and other needed equipment.
4. That regional border enforcement posts be established to coordinate work with the INS, the U.S. Customs Service, the DEA, and the U.S. Coast Guard in the interdiction of both undocumented/illegal migrants and illicit goods, especially narcotics.
5. That high priority be given to the training of INS officers to familiarize them with the rights of aliens and U.S. citizens and to help them deal with persons of other cultural backgrounds.
6. That legislation be passed making it illegal or employers to hire undocumented workers.
7. That a program to legalize illegal/undocumented aliens now in the U.S. be adopted.
8. That eligibility for legalization be determined by interrelated measurements of residence—date of entry and length of continuous residence—and by specified groups of excludability that are appropriate to the legalization program.
9. That voluntary agencies and community organizations be given a significant role in the legalization program.
10. An annual ceiling of 350,000 numerically limited immigrant visas with an additional 100,000 visas available for the first five years to . . . allow backlogs to be cleared.
11. That a substantial number of visas be set aside for reunifying spouses and unmarried sons and daughters and it should be given top priority in the numerically limited family reunifications . . .
12. That country ceilings apply to all numerically limited family reunification preferences . . .

13. That "special" immigrants remain a numerically exempt group but be placed within the independent category.

14. Creating a small, numerically limited subcategory within the independent category to provide for the immigration of certain investors.

15. That specific labor market criteria should be established by the selection of independent immigrants . . .

16. A fixed-percentage limit to the independent immigration from any one country.

17. That U.S. allocation of refugee numbers include both geographic considerations and specific refugee characteristics . . .

18. That state and local governments be involved in planning for initial refugee resettlement and that . . . a federal program of impact aid be established to minimize the financial impact of refugees on local services.

19. That refugee achievement of self-sufficiency and adjustment to living in the U.S. be reaffirmed as the goal of resettlement.

Source: The Select Commission on Immigration and Refugee Policy, *Final Report.* Washington, DC: U.S. Government Printing Office, March 1, 1981, xv–xxxii.

Exponential Rise in Unauthorized Immigration, 1970–1985

As noted earlier, throughout the 1970s and into the early 1980s, unauthorized immigration rose so dramatically that it drew increasing public attention and concern among policy makers. In 1970, the INS apprehended about 0.25 million undocumented aliens attempting to cross the nation's borders, mostly along the 2,000 miles of porous border with Mexico. By 1985, that number approached two million. SCIRP estimated there were between 3.5 and 6 million persons in the United States in unauthorized status (having crossed the border undocumented, or having become illegal by overstaying or otherwise breaking the conditions of their visas). An estimated two-thirds of the undocumented immigrants were Mexicans driven north by dire poverty and unemployment at home, many of whom had come themselves or were family or village compatriots of Bracero workers. They joined the volume of legal immigrants who in the 1970s swelled to nearly 4.5 million, the highest level in legal immigration since the 1910–1920 decade.

Mexican immigrants comprised about 63 percent of Hispanic immigrants, especially the undocumented immigrants, and they tended to come from rural and small-town areas in Mexico. They exhibited a typical "sojourner" attitude, since they resided close to their native areas, and often returned to their place of origin, keeping strong their social and cultural ties. They came from near-feudal societies in Mexico. They considered the U.S.-Mexico border more a nuisance than a barrier (LeMay 2004; 2007).

The growing number of undocumented immigrants coming in the 1970s and early 1980s led to widespread dissatisfaction with the nation's ability to control its borders. During the Iranian crisis, which lasted nearly two years during the Carter administration, the country was shocked when it was revealed that the INS did not even know how many Iranian students were in the United States, let alone how many were living in unauthorized status as visa overstayers. Many Iranians whom the INS was able to identify as being subject to deportation simply failed to attend deportation hearings or to leave when told to do so. The SCIRP report estimated that several hundreds of thousands of Iranians overstayed their visas annually (SCIRP 1981: 8–9).

An exponential rise in illegal alien apprehensions at the borders occurred between 1970 and 2014. Mexicans dominated the number of illegal aliens apprehended throughout most of the period. It is, however, interesting to note that in 2014, non-Mexicans exceeded Mexican border crossers apprehended that year.

The need to "fix" the "illegal immigration problem" dominated immigration policy-making concerns from 1980 to 1985 and influenced the 1984 presidential election.

In 1984, President Reagan and Vice President George H. W. Bush ran against former vice president Walter Mondale and Representative Geraldine Ferraro (D-NY).

Reagan/Bush again won by a landslide: 525 Electoral College votes and 58.8 percent of the popular vote to Mondale/Ferraro's 13 Electoral College votes and 40.6 percent of the popular vote (the American Presidency Project). Illegal immigration and the need to "regain control of the borders" played an important role in the 1984 election.

The most important legislative attempt to resolve the problem, by imposing employer sanctions, was the Immigration Reform and Control Act of 1986 (IRCA), which marked the beginning of the next era of policy making, herein labeled the Revolving Door era, from 1986 to 2001, the focus of the next chapter.

Conclusion

As we have seen, during the Dutch Door phase, more than 12,800,000 legal immigrants entered the United States, averaging more than

360,000 annually. The peak decade of the era was 1970–1979, when the preference system took hold and 4,300,000 entered, for an annual average of 430, 000. The source of those millions of immigrants shifted dramatically from European-sending nations to those coming from Latin America and Asia. Mexico became the leading nation of origin during the era.

Among naturalized citizens a "white ethnic" voting bloc was instrumental in the development of what several political scientists label the Fifth Party System, and what became known as the New Deal Coalition. White ethnic voters enabled the Democratic Party to become the majority party of the era. They were the coalition of interest groups that moved consideration of foreign policy/national security as the most heavily weighted element of policy. They contributed to the stronger weight being given to the economic element as well.

The civil rights movement and civil rights groups were active in the stages of problem formation, policy formulation, and policy adoption. They, too, had a major role in decreasing the weight being given to race as an element in immigration policy. The country moved toward a more progressive view and tolerance for cultural diversity instead of having the national identity element be so heavily weighted with concern for conformity. As the United States emerged as a world superpower and the Cold War became increasingly important during the era, there was less concern for "conformity" and isolationism. The "ethnic bloc" voting patterns influenced foreign policy and linked those concerns with a more "balanced" immigration policy, especially post-Korean war, when the immigration flow shifted from Europe to Asia and Latin America.

The Dutch Door phase began with passage of the McCarran-Walter Act of 1952. It flowered in 1965 with enactment of the preference system that replaced the national origin system of numerical quota limits that was the established immigration policy during the Pet Door phase.

Throughout the Dutch Door period, many immigrant groups entered "at the top," suggesting the metaphor of a Dutch Door. They came over and above the quota system prior to 1965. After 1965, special groups continued to arrive in even greater numbers by using "refugee" related legislation to allow their admission. Concern for their admission and a willingness to support and aid their resettlement imbued aspects of immigration policy making. Vietnamese refugees were notable in how quickly they assimilated. Throughout the period, restrictionist forces, with their amalgamation view of assimilation rather than a cultural pluralist view, were on the defensive while the anti-restrictionist went on the offensive in shaping policy making.

The ending of the Bracero Program in 1964, and passage of the 1965 Act, which established the seven-category preference system, had equally dramatic unanticipated consequences. The 350,000 or so temporary workers who came under the Bracero program continued to come, post-1970, as undocumented immigrants.

From 1970 to 1985, unauthorized immigration rose exponentially. That trend led to widespread dissatisfaction with immigration policy. The system was perceived as broken and in need of a major overhaul to regain control of the borders and to "fix" the "illegal immigration" problem.

The Dutch Door phase is also one in which the executive branch (i.e., the president) increasingly took the initiative and used parole authority, vetoes, proclamations, and executive actions to prod the Congress to act. Concern over the illegal immigration flow marked the final years of the era and set the stage for the imposition of a new policy device—employer sanctions—that marked the beginning of the next phase of immigration policy, the Revolving Door phase, the focus of the next chapter.

References

American Hungarian Federation. www.americanhungarianfederation.org/news_1956.htm. Accessed May 7, 2017.

The American Presidency Project. www.presidency.ucsb.edu.

Barone, Michael. 1990. *Our Country: The Shaping of America from Roosevelt to Reagan*. New York: Free Press.

Bennett, Anthony. 2013. *The Race for the White House from Reagan to Clinton: Reforming Old Systems, Building New Coalitions*. New York: Palgrave Macmillan.

Bibby, John F. 1998. "Party Organizations, 1946–1996." In *Partisan Approaches to Postwar American Politics*. Edited by Byron Shafer, 142–174. New York: Oxford University Press.

British Broadcasting Corporation. www.bbc.co.uk/religion/religions/santeria. Accessed May 7, 2017.

Brubaker, William Roger, ed. 1989. *Immigration and the Politics of Citizenship in Europe and North America*. New York: University Press of America.

CBS News/*New York Times*. Exit Polls, November 9, 1980.

Chambers, William N., and Walter D. Burnham, eds. 1967. *American Party System*. New York: Oxford University Press.

Chiswick, Barry, ed. 1982. *The Gateway: U.S. Immigration Issues and Policies*. Washington, DC: American Enterprise Institute.

Congressional Quarterly Weekly Report. November 1968. "Group Analysis of 1968 Presidential Vote." XXVI(48): 3218.

Converse, Philip E., Warren E. Miller, and Donald E. Stokes. 1964. *The American Voter.* Chicago: University of Chicago Press.

Ferris, Elizabeth G., ed. 1985. *Refugees and World Politics.* Westport, CT: Praeger Press.

Fraser, Steve, and Gary Gerstle, eds. 1990. *The Rise and Fall of the New Deal Order, 1930–1980.* Princeton, NJ: Princeton University Press.

Gould, Lewis L. 2010. *1968: The Election That Changed America.* New York: Ivan R. Dee.

Harper, Elizabeth J. 1975. *Immigration Laws of the United States*, 3rd edition. Indianapolis: Bobbs-Merrill.

Jenson, Richard. 1981. "The Last Party System: Decay of Consensus, 1932–1980." In *The Evolution of the American Electoral System.* Edited by Paul Kleppner et al., 219–225. Westport, CT: Greenwood Press.

Jones, Maldwyn. 1960. *American Immigration.* Chicago: University of Chicago Press.

Kennedy, John F. 1958/2008. *A Nation of Immigrants.* (Re-issued on 50th anniversary). New York: Harper Perennial.

Kleppner, Paul, et al., eds. 1981. *The Evolution of the American Electoral System.* Westport, CT: Greenwood Press.

Ladd, Everett C., Jr. 1978. *Where Have All the Voters Gone? The Fracturing of America's Political Parties.* New York: W. W. Norton.

Ladd, Everett C., Jr. and Charles Hadley. 1978. *Transformations of the American Party System: Political Coalitions from the New Deal to the 1970s.* New York: W. W. Norton.

Lawrence, David G. 1997. *The Collapse of the Democratic Majority.* Boulder, CO: Westview Press.

LeMay, Michael. 1987. *From Open Door to Dutch Door: An Analysis of Immigration Policy from 1820.* Westport, CT: Praeger Press.

LeMay, Michael, ed. 1989. *The Gatekeepers: Comparative Immigration Policy.* Westport, CT: Praeger Press.

LeMay, Michael. 1994. *Anatomy of a Public Policy: The Reform of Contemporary American Immigration Law.* Westport, CT: Praeger Press.

LeMay, Michael. 2004. *U.S. Immigration: A Reference Handbook.* Santa Barbara, CA: ABC-CLIO.

LeMay, Michael. 2006. *Guarding the Gates: Immigration and National Security.* Westport, CT: Praeger Security International.

LeMay, Michael. 2007. *Illegal Immigration: A Reference Handbook.* Santa Barbara, CA: ABC-CLIO.

LeMay, Michael. 2009. *The Perennial Struggle*, 3rd edition. Upper Saddle River, NJ: Prentice Hall.

LeMay, Michael, ed. 2013. *Transforming America: Perspectives on U.S. Immigration. Immigration and Superpower Status: 1945 to Present*, vol. 3. Santa Barbara, CA: ABC-CLIO.

LeMay, Michael, and Elliott Barkan, eds. 1999. *U.S. Immigration and Naturalization Laws and Issues: A Documentary History*. Westport, CT: Greenwood Press.

Mamot, Patricia R. 1974. *Foreign Medical Graduates in America*. Springfield, IL: Charles Thomas.

Manza, Jeff, and Clem Brooks. 1999. *Social Cleavages and Political Change: Voter Alignments and U.S. Party Coalitions*. New York: Oxford University Press.

McClellan, Grant, ed. 1981. *Immigrants, Refugees, and U.S. Policy*. New York: H. W. Wilson.

Milkis, Sidney. 1993. *The President and the Parties: The Transformation of the American Party System since the New Deal*. New York: Oxford University Press.

Montero, David. 1979. *Vietnamese Americans*. Boulder, CO: Westview Press.

Moreno, Barry, and Michael LeMay. 2013. "The Ellis Island Station." In *Transforming America: Perspectives on Immigration*, vol. 2. Edited by LeMay, 197–222. Santa Barbara, CA: ABC-CLIO.

Muller, Thomas, and Thomas Espanshade. 1985. *The Fourth Wave*. Washington, DC: The Urban Institute Press.

Nelson, Michael. 2014. *Resilient America: Reelecting Nixon in 1968, Channeling Dissent, and Dividing Government*. Lawrence: University Press of Kansas.

Papademetrious, Demetrios, and Mark J. Miller, eds. 1984. *The Unavoidable Issue*. Philadelphia: Institute for the Study of Human Issues.

The Papers of the Presidents, Harry S. Truman, 1952, vol. 11. Washington, DC: U.S. Government Printing Office, 1952: 441–447.

The Papers of the Presidents, Lyndon B. Johnson, 1965, vol. II. Washington, DC: U.S. Government Printing Office, 1966: 1037–1040.

Paulson, Arthur. 2006. *Electoral Realignment and the Outlook for American Democracy*. Boston: Northeastern University Press.

Religious Tolerance. www.religioustolerance.org/santeri3.htm. Accessed May 7, 2017.

Select Commission on Immigration and Refugee Policy (SCIRP). 1981. *Final Report*. Washington, DC: U.S. Government Printing Office.

Shafer, Byron, and Anthony J. Badgers. 2001. *Contesting Democracy: Substance and Structure in American Political History, 1775–2000*. New York: Columbia University Press.

Skowronek, Stephen. 1997. *The Politics President's Make*. Cambridge, MA: Harvard University Press.

Sloan, John. 2008. *FDR and Reagan: Transformative Presidents with Clashing Values*. Lawrence: University Press of Kansas.

Stevens, Rosemary. 1978. *The Alien Doctors*. New York: John Wiley and Sons.

Sundquist, James. 1983. *Dynamics of the Party System: Alignment and Realignment of Political Parties in the United States*. Washington, DC: The Brookings Institution Press.

U.S. Congress, Senate Committee on the Judiciary. 1950. *The Immigration and Naturalization Systems of the United States.* 81st Congress, 2nd Session, Senate Report 1515. Washington, DC: U.S. Government Printing Office.

U.S. History. www.ushistory.org/us/60a.asp. Accessed May 7, 2017.

U.S. President's Commission on Immigration and Naturalization. 1953. *Whom Shall We Welcome: Report.* Washington, DC: U.S. Government Printing Office.

White, Theodore. 1970. *The Making of the President—1968.* New York: Atheneum.

CHAPTER SIX

The Revolving Door Era, 1985–2001

Introduction: Religious Trends and Policy—Development of IRCA

Most often, public policy changes in an incremental fashion, with relatively slight modifications being made during a given congressional session or within a few years' time as an amendment to prior policy enactments. Occasionally, as with the Immigration Reform and Control Act (IRCA) of November 6, 1986, public policy is marked by an era-changing shift from the previous state of policy. When such a significant change in policy occurs, it usually comes only after long and difficult maneuvering over the issue. Such was the case with the IRCA, which marked the beginning of a new era in immigration policy making, the Revolving Door phase (LeMay 1994: 29). It is likely this new era would have continued for three to four decades, as had prior periods discussed previously, had it not come to an abrupt end with the terrorist attacks of 9/11 (LeMay 2013, v. 3: 11).

The nature of the "immigration problem," that is, how best to control the borders and cope with the massive migration of undocumented immigrants, had been recognized since the early 1970s. The political conundrum was in formulating a legislative response to the problem that would have sufficient political support from the various factions in Congress to achieve policy adoption.

Legal immigration during the Revolving Door phase's 15-year long span totaled more than 12,600,000 immigrants, with an annual average of 840,000 arrivals. As previously noted, that was immigration on a scale not experienced since the 1910–1920 decade, with its decade-high total of nearly 8.8 million. And, of course, the average annual total of 840,000 legal immigrants does not include the estimated annual influx of 0.5 million unauthorized and therefore uncounted immigrants. It was the exponential rise in undocumented immigrants mostly from Mexico and other Central American countries that drove the political movement to reform immigration law to better cope with the illegal immigration problem (Portes and Rumbaut 1996). The illegal immigration flow across the porous southern U.S.-Mexico border suggests the Revolving Door image for this era.

The changing composition in the flow of immigration, coupled with a troubled U.S. economy suffering from "stagflation" throughout most of the 1970s—a combination of high unemployment and high inflation due in large part to the oil crisis of the decade—led to a growing movement to restrict immigration from the levels legally allowable under the preference system of the 1965 law. The 1965 law also coincided with the rise of affordable air travel. Millions of foreigners discovered that they could fly to the United States for a vacation, or to come as students or with other nonimmigrant visas, and then never leave. An estimated 40 percent of the 10 to 11 million such unauthorized immigrants were visa "overstayers," that is, people who entered with documents but stayed beyond the expiration date of the visas, or people who broke the conditions of their visas (e.g., students who accepted unauthorized employment). Visa overstayers are difficult to find and deport. Federal agents find it much easier to spot a Mexican slipping across the Rio Grande illegally (as an undocumented alien) than to figure out which Irish bartender or nurse, or which Nigerian cabdriver no longer has a valid visa (Gorman 1994: 383; LeMay 2006: 168). The fact that so many of the unauthorized immigrants were Catholics was not explicitly discussed by the opposition forces, but it was likely a contributing factor among some of those forces (Hondagnev-Sotelo 2008; Jenkins 2003; Marquardt and Vasquez 2014).

The 1980 election as president of conservative Republican Ronald Reagan, plus the most severe recession, up to then, since the end of World War II, during the initial years of his administration, heightened public awareness of and concern with the "illegal immigration problem." Public opinion polls spiked from 42 percent of the population (of those surveyed) stating, in 1977, that immigration levels should be decreased to 49 percent stating such in 1986, and 65 percent saying so by 1993 (Gallup Poll).

Politicians described the influx of so many illegal immigrants as "a time bomb," which, if not dealt with, would have dire consequences for

America. They blamed illegal immigration for nearly all that was wrong with the country (Lamm and Imhoff 1985).

The Push to Formulate a Legislative Response

By the mid-1970s, organized labor moved to deal with what they perceived was the threat from illegal immigration. They changed their stance from having supported the Kennedy bill in the mid-1960s, when they were open to less restrictions, back to a position that favored restriction as they had held during the Pet Door phase. Rising unemployment, particularly high in the lower-wage level jobs at the time, induced labor leaders to lobby Representative Peter Rodino (D-NJ). They convinced him that undocumented workers were taking jobs that rightfully belonged to U.S. citizens. Organized labor, led by the American Federation of Labor-Congress of Industrial Organizations (AFL-CIO) and the International Ladies Garment Workers Union (ILGWU), along with the National Association for the Advancement of Colored People (NAACP) (which also viewed illegal immigrants as threatening to the jobs of poor urban blacks), moved Congressman Rodino to propose an employer sanctions amendment to the 1965 law, essentially eliminating the "Texas Proviso" of the 1952 law (LeMay 1994: 29; Perotti 1989: 83–84). The Texas Proviso made it illegal for a person to enter the United States without papers but held employers of such labor immune from prosecution for having hired an undocumented immigrant.

Both the House and the Senate held hearings on the matter. At the time, the Senate Judiciary Subcommittee on Immigration was chaired by Senator James Eastland (D-MS.). Eastland represented the interest of growers (principally the National Council of Agricultural Employers and the American Farm Bureau Federation), who adamantly opposed the employer sanctions proposal. It was growers who had insisted on the Texas Proviso in the 1952 law for the same economic reasons.

In 1974–1975, Senator Edward Kennedy (D-MA) and Representatives Peter Rodino (D-NJ) and Joshua Eilberg (D-PA) developed a different approach, linking the employer sanctions idea with limited legalization and antidiscrimination provisions (LeMay 1994: 31). At the same time, the Ford administration began studying possible solutions to the problem, and the Senate and House Judiciary Committees held hearings on employer sanctions. Rodino and subcommittee chairman Eilberg used an approach that linked employer sanctions to legalization in order to gain the support or minimize the opposition from Hispanic and human rights groups. However, the ploy alerted Hispanic groups to the effects that employer sanctions might have on the Latino community. The proposal died in committee.

In 1975, Senator Eastland, by then chair of the Senate Judiciary Committee and of its Subcommittee on Immigration and Naturalization, took up consideration of immigration reform proposals. Eastland and his staffers made it clear that no immigration reform bill would move forward that did not have a foreign worker's program, making it acceptable to growers by replacing illegal workers with temporary workers by expanding an existing program, the H-2 temporary workers program. Eastland would not release a reform bill from committee. A steadily declining unemployment rate, strong opposition to the bills in both the House and the Senate from employers, ethnic and religious groups, organized labor, combined with Representatives Rodino and Eilberg's failure to move their bill to the House floor, resulted in the bill being killed in committee.

In 1976, the Ford administration established a cabinet-level committee to study immigration policy options, and the Domestic Policy Council recommended to the president support for employer sanctions, limited amnesty, reexamination of the adequacy of the H-2 program, and increased funding for the Immigration and Naturalization Service (INS) and the Department of State. The employer sanctions idea thus gained the support of the administration. That support continued when Ray Marshall, the new secretary of labor of the cabinet of incoming president Jimmy Carter tied his acceptance of the appointment to work on illegal immigration. Marshall was a University of Texas economist long interested in the subject. The administration was split on details of the approach to take on the problem. Secretary Marshall and Attorney General Griffin Bell advocated a limited amnesty and use of a work eligibility card—immediately tagged as a national identity card. INS Commissioner Leonel Castillo and White House aides fought for a liberal amnesty and deplored the detrimental civil rights implications of the work card (Perotti 1989: 94–95).

As we have seen, in 1980, Congress passed the Refugee Act of 1980. While that law addressed many of the refugee issues, it failed to move immigration reform in the direction of employer sanctions, and nothing could pass the Senate because of Senator Eastland's intransigence. Media reports stressed the estimates of an annual flow of illegal immigration approaching 2 million, and an estimated 10 million already in the United States. The media hyped the view that the country was losing control of its borders. A media campaign on the issue helped develop a pervasive

sense of fear that illegal aliens were taking jobs from Americans and causing high unemployment, although many economists attributed the latter
to structural problems, such as increasing mechanization, in the economy. The media raised the danger of a Hispanic separatist movement
developing in the southwest United States akin to the French-speaking
separatist movement in Quebec, Canada. Other Americans feared the
cultural changes from the Hispanic-illegal alien influx and the Asian refugee flow. For example, the rapid and extensive resettlement of Vietnamese
into Monterey Park in California created a "Little Saigon" community. It
prompted bumper stickers reflecting such sentiment that read: "Will the
Last American to Leave Monterey Park Please Bring the Flag?" (LeMay
1994: 34).

The Carter administration responded to these pressures and the failure
of Representative Rodino to move his bill forward by reintroducing Rodino's employer sanctions bill and adding provisions to it and by creating
the Select Commission on Immigration and Refugee Policy (SCIRP),
authorizing it to study the entire issue of immigration.

SCIRP opened in May 1979 during the highly charged political atmosphere of a presidential election and the Mariel boatlift from Cuba and the
liberalization of refugee admissions. The commission issued its final
report in January 1981. It played a critical role for the eventual enactment
of IRCA. Its final report ran more than 450 pages (as was summarized in
Box 5.3) and was supplemented by a staff report in excess of 900 pages.
Its recommendation to "close the back door" to undocumented immigration tied to a somewhat more liberal legal immigration gave political justification to what became the IRCA of 1986 (LeMay 2007: 5–6).

By the fall of 1981, both the House and Senate Judiciary subcommittees had completed their hearings. Their chairpersons, Senator Alan
Simpson (R-WY) and Representative Romano Mazzoli (D-KY) crafted the
SCIRP recommendations into legislative proposals they considered having the essential provisions to serve as incentives for the competing
groups to cooperate. On March 17, 1982, identical Simpson-Mazzoli bills
were introduced into their respective chambers (S-2222 and HR-5872).
Their bills, like the SCIRP recommendations, contained a national identity card, a modified scheme for employer sanctions, and an amnesty provision (Cornelius and Montoya 1983: 318–19; LeMay 1994: 38).

The Simpson-Mazzoli bill followed the SCIRP recommendations for
H-2 expansion and certification, and set up new procedures for asylum
adjudication. The bill specified a U.S. Immigration Board, similar to an
existing Parole Board, which would hear appeals. Its members would be
presidential appointees and were to be independent of the attorney

general. No judicial appeal from these independent tribunals would be permitted. The State Department was excluded from any role in the process.

The adjudication procedures were objected to by both the Reagan administration and by asylum advocate groups. The administration wanted those procedures placed under the attorney general. The Senate Judiciary Committee favored the administration's view of the procedures. By contrast, asylum advocate groups wanted to have a judicial review process placed over a truly independent administrative structure. The House Judiciary Committee adopted the latter approach.

Both chambers held hearings on the respective bills and reported them out in May. The Senate approved the bill after its Judiciary Committee amended it slightly and it passed easily, by a vote of 81 to 19, on August 17, 1982 (*Congressional Record*, August 17, 1982). The bill did not fare so well in the House. Several amendments were made to the bill in committee. Representative Don Edwards (D-CA), at the urging of state and local governments, proposed an amendment assuring 100 percent reimbursement to state and local governments for the costs of legalization. In terms of getting the bill passed on the full House floor, it was what is known as a "killer amendment" (LeMay 1994: 39).

Representatives Mazzoli and Hamilton Fish (R-NY) introduced a clean version of HR-5872 as HR-6514, and with the Senate's passage of S-2222, the House Judiciary Committee took it up in mid-September 1982, and approved the Mazzoli version of the bill.

The Simpson-Mazzoli bills compromised on earlier Reagan administration proposals by excluding a provision for a guest-worker program. Instead, it expanded a version of the H-2 program deemed easier for employers to import temporary workers and incorporating the H-2 program's administrative rules used by the Department of Labor. The Senate version set up a large-scale guest-worker program and rejected one proposed by Senator Kennedy that would have retained H-2 as it was (LeMay 1994: 40). The Senate version greatly restricted the role of the Department of Labor in the certification process. By eliminating this aspect, the Senate version allowed for the INS, an agency less sensitive to domestic labor conditions, to ignore or even to overrule DOL recommendations (Cornelius and Montoya 1983: 133).

Senator Kennedy offered several amendments that would have deleted provisions of greatest concern to Hispanic Americans like easing family reunification, and doing away with H-2 expansion provisions. Groups like the Mexican American Defense League (MALDEF), the Spanish International Network (SIN), and national Spanish-language radio networks lobbied strongly against Simpson-Mazzoli, blasting the bill as the "most blatantly anti-Hispanic bill ever" (LeMay 1994: 40). More than 8,000 letters and mailgrams from outraged Hispanics were delivered to Kennedy's office in less than a week, and the Hispanic groups organized a barrage of telephone calls to Senate offices and to sympathetic Hispanic Caucus members in the House (LeMay 1994: 161–163; see also Crewdson 1983: 323).

Because of overlapping jurisdictions, House Speaker Thomas P. "Tip" O'Neill (D-MA) referred the bill sequentially to four other committees: (1) Education and Labor, (2) Agriculture, (3) Ways and Means, and (4) Energy and Commerce. Each considered the bill, and as a result, the proposal did not reach the Rules Committee until early December, during the "Lame Duck" session of the 97th Congress. After more hearings, the Rules Committee sent it to the floor with an open ruling (meaning any number of amendments could be offered on the floor). By the time it reached the floor of the House in mid-December, more than 300 amendments were filed, indicating clearly the strong opposition that the bill faced in that chamber.

Simpson-Mazzoli, as the bill was then referred to, was vigorously lobbied against by the National Congress of Hispanic American Citizens, by MALDEF, SIN, and the National Council of La Raza. Members of the Hispanic caucus offered more than 100 amendments on the employer sanctions provision alone, and they strongly lobbied Speaker O'Neill. The bill received tepid support, at best, from the Democratic leadership. The speaker worried the bill would increase division in the party caucus among Hispanics, liberals, and moderates. He feared discrimination in the workforce against "dark-skinned" (i.e., Hispanic-looking) workers. He scheduled the bill for floor action only out of courtesy to the Reagan White House and the Republican House leadership (*Congressional Record*, December 18, 1982: H-10319). After three days of emotional, often bitter late-night debates, no action was taken on the bill and it died as the 97th Congress adjourned (*Congressional Record*, December 18, 1982, H-10226; LeMay 1994: 41).

In 1983, with the opening of the 98th Congress, Senator Simpson and Representative Mazzoli renewed their efforts at comprehensive immigration reform by reintroducing versions of their bill identical to those passed in the Senate and by the House Judiciary Committee in 1982. Again, proponents and opponents rallied their respective sides. Agricultural interests, headed by Representative Hamilton Fish (R-NY), developed a proposal for a "transition program" designed to slowly adjust to a foreign "guest-worker" program. Representative Edward Roybal (D-CA), a leader of the Congressional Hispanic Caucus, proposed an alternative bill focusing on tougher enforcement of existing labor and minimum wage laws to clamp down on the hiring aspects of illegal immigration as a substitute for the employer sanctions approach.

By spring of 1983, both the House and the Senate Judiciary subcommittees on immigration had approved their respective versions of the bills. Chairman Rodino, however, once again waited for the senate to complete full action on its version of the bill. In the Senate, the Judiciary Committee reported the bill out to the Senate floor over the objections of Senator Edward Kennedy. Senator Jesse Helms (R-NC) again tried unsuccessfully to delete the amnesty provision. Senator Bradley (D-NJ) likewise failed to get a 100 percent reimbursement provision for state and local governments (Perotti 1989: 159). The Senate passed its version by late April, and Rodino scheduled the House version for the first week in May. The full Senate approved the Simpson version by mid-May.

The Senate version made some important concessions to growers. With the tacit approval of Senators Simpson and Kennedy, Senators DeConcini (D-AZ) and Pete Wilson (R-CA) worked out a three-year transition program for agriculture. Senators Simpson and Kennedy worked out a compromise regarding the opposition among liberals to the asylum adjudication program by establishing a full judicial review of deportation, exclusion, and asylum cases in the Federal Court of Appeals (LeMay 1994: 42).

In the House, the Mazzoli bill again moved sequentially through the four committees. Representatives Mazzoli and Rodino, with the backing of the Reagan administration and of the House Republican leadership, pressed for quick floor action. With the 1984 election season beginning, they felt the timing of the full House consideration of the bill was critical for its passage. Representative Claude Pepper (D-FL) agreed to try but failed to obtain a compromise rule for the floor's debate on the bill.

Various factions used the opportunities afforded by the various committee referrals through which the bill progressed. Representative Tom Kindness (R-OH), a member of the House Judiciary Committee, moved an amendment backed by the U.S. Chamber of Commerce making it voluntary for employers to verify the employment status of their workers. In the Agriculture Committee, Western growers pushed for a separate 300,000 person temporary farm workers program in an amendment moved by Representatives Leon Panetta (D-CA) and Bruce Morrison (D-CT). In the Education and Labor Committee, a coalition of Hispanic, civil liberties, and a coalition of various religious groups (which had long been involved in immigration policy matters, refugee resettlement services, and provided social and medical services to immigrants without regard to their legal status) through an alternative bill sponsored by Representative Edward Roybal, sought to replace employer sanctions with stiffer wage and hour laws and worked on an array of amendments to liberalize the legalization programs and include antidiscrimination provisions (Perotti 1989: 160). The religious-based groups involved in the issue included such Christian groups as the Catholic Church (through the National Conference of Catholic Bishops), the Episcopal Church (Episcopal Relief and Development), the Lutheran Immigration and Refugee Services, the World Council of Churches Refugee Services, the United Methodist Committee on Relief, and Justice for Our Neighbors service.

Speaker O'Neill pulled the bill from the House floor in October, again fearing splits in his party over the measure, convinced once again by Roybal and the Hispanic Caucus of the political repercussions that might ensue if the bill were passed before the upcoming elections. Roybal feared a Reagan veto if the bill passed, in order to curry favor with the Latino vote. The national press (e.g., *NY Times*, *LA Times*, *Christian Science Monitor*, *Washington Post*) unleashed a barrage of criticism of the Speaker for placing short-term political partisanship over the national interest of immigration reform (LeMay 1994: 43).

In April, the House Rules Committee held hearings and reported the Mazzoli bill out with a modified open rule. After seven days of intense debate, the House finally passed the bill by a slim five-vote margin, 216–211. The House's Mazzoli version, after its tortuous progression through many committees, had several amendments to the bill that differed significantly from the senate-passed version of the Simpson bill. These varied on aspects of the legalization program, on an expanded version of a guest-worker program reminiscent of the Bracero program, on an expanded H-2 program, and on strong anti-discrimination provisions moved by Representative Barney Frank (D-MA), which among other things created a special counsel in the Department of Justice. Hispanics had failed to block employer sanctions but had succeeded in gaining an improved legalization program with the help of Rodino and Representative Bill Richardson (D-NM).

> The final vote on the bill in 1984 was like a suspense novel, as its fate teetered back and forth during the final 15 minutes of roll-call. "No" votes outnumbered the "Yes" votes until just a few seconds before the end, when the tally tied at 210 and Congressional arm-twisting on the floor obtained a few more votes that led to its victory. Both Democrats and Republicans were divided in their support (Democrats 138 to 125 and Republicans 91 to 73). (LeMay 1994: 45)

The passage of Simpson-Mazzoli in different versions in the two chambers meant the bills went to a House-Senate Conference Committee, which took place during the heated political context of the presidential electoral race. At the Democratic convention, nominees Walter Mondale and Geraldine Ferraro publically opposed the immigration reform bill. At the Republican convention, the administration's position was less clear. The vice president nominee, in a speech to the National Council of La Raza, said President Reagan would not tolerate a bill that discriminated against Hispanics. Senator Simpson announced that the president, in a telephone conversation, had said that he would sign a conference committee version of the bill if it contained a Senate restriction on reimbursement to the states for legalization costs. Yet later, Attorney General William French Smith raised public objections to the Frank antidiscrimination provisions. The conference committee failed to reach a compromise version, and the 98th Congress adjourned with the conference committee dissolved and the measure once again lost (LeMay 1994: 46).

Although comprehensive immigration reform died in conference committee in 1984, an important base for the future had been laid. The compromise achieved on the Frank antidiscrimination provision became part of that base. Moreover, principle players had become resigned to the fact that some sort of guest-worker program would have to be included. A new player, Representative Charles Schumer (D-NY) began discussions among immigration subcommittee members to bridge the gap between farm labor advocates and growers over a guest-worker provision. After six days of intense "shuttle diplomacy," working closely with Senator Simpson, Representative Mazzoli, and Representative Barney Frank, Schumer announced a compromise on October 5, 1984. His compromise failed by a 15–13 vote in the conference committee.

The 1984 bill died in conference committee in 1984, also over the state and local funding issue, when key negative votes were cast by the California delegation members opposed to the compromise temporary workers program devised by Panetta, Morrison, and Simpson.

In May 1985, Senator Simpson introduced a new version of his bill, this time without the cosponsorship of Representative Mazzoli, who declined to sponsor the measure without the support of the Democratic House leadership and from the black and Hispanic Caucuses, who strenuously opposed it. Simpson's 1985 version had details that changed from the 1984 version, but the centerpiece remained imposition of employer sanctions, including fines up to $10,000 per violation against employers who knowingly hired an illegal alien, and an eventual amnesty program for unauthorized immigrants who had arrived prior to January 1, 1980. His new bill also called for the development of a "tamper-proof" Social Security card. His 1985 version weakened the amnesty program, requiring advanced certification by the president that illegal immigration had been substantially reduced by the Border Patrol enhancement provisions. His bill also placed a $1.8 billion limit of federal reimbursement to states for services extended to those undocumented aliens who were processed through the program.

Senator Kennedy introduced an amendment that granted amnesty at the same time as employer sanctions would take effect, but it failed by a vote of 26 to 65. Senator Pete Wilson (R-CA) offered an amendment that would give growers of perishable crops a large, mobile, temporary workforce of foreign workers to pick fruit and vegetables. It was voted down 48 to 50. Senator Wilson sponsored a new amendment to allow 350,000 guest workers to enter the country annually and its passage, by a narrow margin, signaled that the House bill was going to have to include a guest-worker program as the senate had added its approval to the 1984 Panetta-Morrison program. The only question that remained was precisely what such a program would look like. The bill passed the Senate on September 19, 1985, by a vote of 69 to 30 (LeMay 1994: 47).

In the House, Congressman Rodino introduced a bill cosponsored by Representative Romano Mazzoli in July 1985, that was quite similar to the compromise version that died in the final days of the 1984 conference committee debate. It had the employer sanctions provision and a provision designed to discourage discrimination against Hispanics that established an Office of Special Counsel in the Department of Justice empowered to investigate and prosecute civil rights violators. Like the Senate measure, the Rodino-Mazzoli bill strengthened enforcement of immigration laws and increased funding for the INS and funding and staffing for the Border Patrol.

As in prior years, Hispanic groups and the American Civil Liberties Union opposed both versions of the measure, and working through the Hispanic Caucus and the Black Congressional Caucus, they opposed the employer sanctions provision, arguing it would increase discrimination against all Hispanics, and opposing the guest-worker program arguing that historically such programs had been highly exploitive of workers.

By contrast, the growers insisted on a guest-worker program and opposed both versions of the bills as being too small on the issue. House Judiciary members insisted that amnesty be granted only after a presidential commission had been established and only when employer sanctions were shown to have succeeded in reducing the number of illegal immigrants entering the country. In September 1985, the Senate Judiciary Committee rejected all attempts by the Senate Democrats to make the

Senate version more like the House version. After a conference committee seemed unable to agree upon a compromise, the proposed bill was once again viewed as "a corpse going to the morgue."

Policy Adoption: Passing of IRCA, 1986

When the conference committee failed to achieve a unified, compromise version, a small group of legislators long committed to passage of immigration reform refused to let it die. Some key compromises were worked out enabling passage in October 1986. The September 1986 deadlock was broken by a compromise crafted by several House Judiciary Committee members, led by Representative Charles Schumer. They put the pieces back together again. Schumer met with Rodino and Hamilton Fish (the Ranking Republican). Schumer met with Representatives Howard Berman (C-CA) and Leon Panetta (D-CA), arranging a key compromise on the temporary farm workers provision. Extensive discussion with Representative Dan Lungren (R-CA), the Ranking Republican, and Romano Mazzoli, chairman of the Judiciary Subcommittee on Immigration, Refugees, and International Law, resulted in further fine-tuning of the bill's provisions including numerous points to protect the rights of temporary workers. They then secured Senator Simpson's approval ("Hill Revises Immigration Law," *Washington Post*, October 16, 1986: A-7–8).

After 15 years of dealing with proposals to reform immigration policy, Congress was finally in a better mood and position to act than in any previous year. The Mexican economy had further deteriorated late in 1985 and early 1986, and the peso plunged in value. The INS caught a record number of illegal aliens attempting to cross. Apprehensions at the border spiked by 31 percent during the fiscal year—to a record high of 1.8 million. The growing conservative mood of the country convinced liberal opponents of the measure that continued resistance would likely only lead to even more restrictive legislation in 1987.

A key shift came in the House Roll Call vote on the measure on October 10, 1986, when members of the Hispanic Caucus split their votes on the bill, 5 for the bill to 6 against. That split enabled Black Congressional Caucus members to split their vote as well, 10 for and 8 against (LeMay 1994: Table 3, 53). Representative Schumer's negotiated compromise on the temporary farm workers provision also split opposition to the bill among growers. His compromise provision served the needs of Western fruit and vegetable growers, while allowing for sufficient protection of the workers against exploitation so as to win over enough of the Hispanic, liberal, or union votes in Congress for enactment. He described the new version as slightly "left-of-center," in contrast to the "right-of-center" version killed by House Democrats in 1984, when they had opposed it by a margin of 138 to 125. In October 1986, Democrats supported it 168 to 61. The House passed the new version on October 10, 1986, by a vote of 230 for to 166 against, with 36 not voting (*Congressional Record-House*, Roll Call #457, H9800–01). Democrats more often supported it for its amnesty provision, whereas Republicans very nearly split their vote. Those who favored it did so for its employer sanctions approach.

Again, the two chambers passed different versions and again they went to a conference committee. Six issues remained in significant conflict. They are summarized here.

1. The House version terminated employer penalties automatically after six and one-half years. The Senate version, and the Reagan administration, opposed that provision.

2. The House version contained an amendment, sponsored by Representative Joseph Moakley (D-MA) that granted temporary legal status to Salvadorians and Nicaraguans who were in the United States illegally, while the Senate version, and the White House and the Department of State opposed the Moakley provision.

3. The House version contained the Frank amendment that barred an employer from discriminating in hiring on the basis of citizenship and created a special counsel's office in the Justice Department to investigate such alleged discrimination. This provision was opposed by the Senate and the administration.

4. The two versions differed on the dates for start of the legalization program. The House version set the eligibility date at January 1, 1982; the Senate version set it at January 1, 1980.

5. The two versions differed in how the federal government would reimburse states for costs associated with implementation of the complex amnesty program. The House version provided for 100 percent reimbursement; the Senate version provided for $3 billion over six years after enactment.

6. The House version included a provision sponsored by Representative Howard Berman that provided for free legal services to farm workers entering under the H-2 temporary worker program (LeMay 1994: 54).

The 1986 conference committee agreed on a series of compromises to settle those six issues and were able to report back to their respective chambers a unified bill that was to become the IRCA of 1986 (Act of November 6, 1986, 100 Stat. 3360; Document 144, LeMay and Barkan 1999: 282–288).

House members agreed to the Senate version without an automatic end to employer sanctions. In exchange, Senate members agreed to a three-year annual review of the program by the General Accounting Office (GAO), at which time the program would be terminated by a joint resolution if the GAO had determined the employer sanctions provision had resulted in widespread discrimination. The House members agreed to give up the Moakley provision on Salvadorans and Nicaraguans in return for a pledge by the administration not to deport any Salvadorans to areas stricken by an October earthquake. In addition, Chairman Rodino promised to consider another bill on the subject early in the 100th Congress, and Senator Simpson promised he would not prevent Senate consideration of such a bill if it passed the House. The senate members agreed to accept the Frank amendment and accepted a slightly modified provision on free legal services for H-2 workers, stipulating such service could only apply to job-related problems such as wages, hours, and working conditions.

The state reimbursement issue was resolved by another compromise: it set up a $1 billion per year mandated appropriations for the next four years, with the unspent money in one year being available for the following year. Any unused money at the end of fiscal year 1990 could be carried over through fiscal year 1994 (essentially making it a seven-year program funded at $4 billion). It further provided that the amount of government payments for Social Security supplements and Medicaid be deducted from the $1 billion annual appropriation. Finally, the Senate accepted the House version as to the beginning date for the amnesty program—that of January 1, 1982 (LeMay 1994: 55).

The bill's tangled history helped make these compromises possible in 1986. In part, the immigration problem was viewed as having reached an apparent crisis proportion by the end of 1986. Everyone involved desperately wanted a bill to pass. Previous fights meant there was less need for continued political posturing this time around. There was no longer a looming presidential election to complicate such compromises by legislators representing the interests of the various factions. The conferees did not want to "do this again" (*Congressional Quarterly Weekly Report*, October 18, 1986, 2596). Representative Mazzoli, in urging passage of the bill, stated: "It's not a perfect bill, but it's the least imperfect bill we will ever have before us" (*Washington Post*, October 16, 1986, A 5).

The House passed the measure 238 to 173 on October 15, 1986. The Senate approved it 63 to 24 on October 17, 1986, and President Reagan signed it into law on November 6, 1986. Box 6.1 summarizes the law (a somewhat longer summary is excerpted in LeMay and Barkan 1999: 282–288).

Box 6.1: Summary of the Immigration Reform and Control Act

Employer Sanctions

1. Made it unlawful for anyone to knowingly hire, recruit, or refer for a fee any alien not authorized to work in the United States.

2. Required employers to verify all newly hired people by examining various documents.

3. Permitted the president to implement a more secure verification system upon notice to and approval of Congress.

4. Established civil and criminal penalties for hiring illegal aliens after a six-month education period. During the subsequent 12-month period, a violator would be given a warning citation for the first offense.

5. Established fines after the citation period ranging from not less than $250 for the first offense to not more than $10,000 per illegal alien for the third offense.

6. Authorized criminal penalties of up to six months' imprisonment and/or a $3,000 fine for a "pattern of practice" of knowingly hiring an illegal alien.

7. Required employers, recruiters, and those who refer for employment to keep records, and set civil fines from $100 to $1,000 for failure to do so.

8. Terminated sanctions after three years if the Comptroller General determined that employer sanctions had resulted in discrimination in employment or had unduly burdened employers, and Congress enacted a joint resolution adopting that termination. Expedited procedures for Congress to consider a joint resolution terminating sanctions.

Antidiscrimination Measures

1. Created an Office of Special Counsel in the Department of Justice to investigate and prosecute discrimination from unlawful immigration-related employment practices.

2. Barred employers from discriminating against legal residents simply because they were not full-fledged citizens.

3. Authorized an administrative law judge to order a violator to hire the aggrieved person, to award limited back pay, and to pay a penalty of $1,000 for each individual discriminated against.

4. Terminated the antidiscrimination provisions if the employer sanctions are lifted.

Increased Enforcement and Service

1. Provided a two-year authorization for the INS providing an additional $422 million in FY 1987 and $419 million in FY 1988. It authorized $12 million in FY 1987 and $15 million in FY 1988 for the Executive

Office of Immigration Review to carry out added duties for the INS imposed by the bill.

2. Beefed up penalties for smuggling aliens into the country.
3. Authorized a contingency fund of $35 million for use in immigration emergencies such as the 1980 boatlift from Cuba.

Legalization

1. Provided temporary resident status for aliens who resided continuously in the United States since before January 1, 1982, and who cannot be excluded for reasons specified in the immigration law.
2. Allowed those temporary residents to become permanent residents after 18 months if they can show understanding of English and history and government of the United States or are pursuing a course of instruction to gain such knowledge.
3. Provided permanent resident status for specified Cuban and Haitian refugees who entered the country before January 1, 1982.
4. Appropriated $1 billion in each of four fiscal years after enactment to reimburse states for public assistance, health and education costs resulting from legalizing aliens. Unspent money from one year would carry over to the next year.
5. Reimbursed states for costs of incarceration of certain aliens.

H-2 Workers

1. Revised and expanded the existing temporary workers program.
2. Required the labor secretary to decide on the requests for labor no later than 20 days in advance of an employer's need.
3. Provided an expedited procedure for getting workers if the labor secretary determined that available U.S. workers were found by the employer not to be qualified.

Special Seasonal Agricultural Workers

1. Provided temporary resident status for up to 350,000 aliens who could prove that they lived in the country for at least three years and who could prove they had worked at least 90 days in American agriculture in each of those three years. They could adjust to permanent resident status after an additional year or within three years of enactment, whichever was later.
2. Provided for "replenishment" farm labor to replace those who left agriculture and allowed these new workers to enter the United States as temporary residents. They would have to work at least 90 days in agriculture for three years, after which they could apply for permanent resident status. They would be barred from receiving most public aid.

Miscellaneous

1. Increased the legal immigration ceilings from colonies from 600 to 5,000. This provision is designed to help immigrants from Hong Kong.

2. Authorized the Attorney General and the Secretary of State to establish a three-year pilot program for up to eight countries allowing tourists from these countries to enter the United States without first obtaining a visa.

3. Required the expeditious deportation of convicted illegal aliens and required the government to list facilities available to incarcerate those aliens who were going to be deported.

Reports

1. Required the president to submit several reports to Congress, including three studies on legal immigration, the program for granting visas. Among other reports: one on the factors that cause illegal immigration, two on the legalization program, and two on employer sanctions.

2. Required the administration to submit reports on the H-2 program every two years (LeMay 1994: 55–57).

Split Congressional Voting Blocs

On the final House vote (October 15, 1986) on IRCA, the Hispanic and Black Congressional Caucuses split their votes as they had on the October 10 vote. If one includes "associate members" in the count, the Hispanic Caucus split 20 in favor to 17 against. The Black Congressional Caucus, including associate members, split 15 in favor to 14 against. With respect to political party affiliation, after the Conference Committee compromises, House Democrats split 162 in favor to 80 against, with 11 abstaining. House Republicans split 76 in favor to 93 against, with 10 not voting. In the Senate, the split among Democrats was 34 for passage to 8 against, with 6 not voting. Among Senate Republicans, the vote was 29 in favor to 16 against, with 7 abstaining (LeMay 1994: 58).

Looking at the members of another relevant caucus, the Border Caucus, their members split 9 for the measure to 6 against. Likewise, the leadership in Congress split as well: defining leadership as the Majority and Minority leaders, whips, whips-at-large, and whips-zones, the split was 67 in favor to 26 against. Even state delegations were split on the issue. Six key states (those with the largest number of illegal immigrants residing in them), would be most affected by the legalization program: Arizona, California, Florida, Illinois, New York, and Texas. These states accounted for 90 percent of the legalizing aliens. Those key state delegations split their vote as follows:

1. Arizona (5 votes): 1 for, 3 against, 1 abstaining. 1 Democrat for, 3 Republicans against, 1 Republican not voting.
2. California (45 votes): 31 for, 13 against, 1 abstaining. Democrats totaled 27, with 18 for, 9 against. Republicans had 18 votes, with 13 for, 4 against, 1 not voting.
3. Florida (18 votes): 13 for, 5 against. Democrats had 12 votes, 11 for and 1 against. Republicans had 6 votes, split 2 for to 4 against.
4. Illinois (22 votes): 11 for, 9 against, 2 not voting. Democrats had 13; split 9 in favor to 4 against. Republicans had 9; 2 in favor to 5 against, with 2 not voting.
5. New York (34 votes): 19 for, 13 against, 2 not voting. Democrats split 12 in favor to 5 opposed with 2 not voting. Republicans split their 15 votes, 7 in favor to 8 opposed.
6. Texas (17 votes): 6 voted for the law, 20 opposed it, and 1 did not vote. Democrats split their 17 votes as 6 in favor, 10 opposed, with 1 not voting; Republicans cast all 10 of their votes against IRCA (LeMay 1994: 61).

Two Models of Policy Conflict

Two models can be helpful in understanding the split voting on the IRCA bill.

Often the resolution of conflict in the policy process is viewed and described as *competition*. In this traditional perspective of the policy-making process, the various opposing factions are seen as having conflicting interests. The major actors involved (lobbyists for the opposing groups, their legislative supporters, vested bureaucratic actors, etc.) are seen as acting interdependently, but seeking to maximize their relative gains or minimizing their relative losses. Inter-faction bargaining is competitive in what is essentially a zero-sum game where one faction's gains or losses are directly related to the gains or losses of another competing faction. Policy is described as the result of the competition between the coalition of sides for or against specific policy proposals. Thomas Dye puts it: "Public policy, at any given point, is the equilibrium reached in the group struggle" (1992: 27). This traditional view of group conflict sees policy as equilibrium.

However, one can also view conflict in the policy process as being resolved through cooperation and compromise; that is, by constructive or mutually beneficial resolution rather than by a win-loss solution or simply splitting the differences between opposing factions. Such resolution to conflict may be achieved when two conditions are met enabling the factions to cooperate in public policy making: (1) the factions engaged in the policy debate must be interdependent, that is, where each faction can affect the prospects for policy change; and (2) the factions must be involved in mixed-motive, or non-zero-sum conflict; that is, they must have both complementary and conflicting interests (Quirk 1989: 905–906).

For instance, if the opposing factions in a dispute differ in the importance they attach to the various issues in the dispute, they can achieve joint gains by exchanging concessions accordingly. IRCA exemplifies such a case. The provisions about employer sanctions, amnesty, and seasonal agricultural workers allowed for an exchange among business, labor, and Hispanic ethnic groups, and their respective legislator supporters comprising the factions involved in the immigration policy dispute.

Instead of viewing policy conflict resolution as the equilibrium point achieving a simple balance between opposing groups, one can view policy as the resulting vector of change in the direction of an ongoing policy that is the sum of the contributions or influences of the involved policy factions. Imagine a change in policy at any given time as a billiard ball being struck simultaneously as it rolls along by several other balls. It will move in a direction that is the sum of the forces of impact of all the balls that hit it as it rolls along.

This is a more dynamic view of the policy-making process. Unless acted upon, a policy will continue to follow its path (policy inertia). It will not change its path unless struck, or pressured to change in one direction or another. In the IRCA case, policy change moves in the direction of the sum of all the forces cooperatively or sequentially striking it. The new policy is more restrictionist than prior policy, but it moves less so in that direction (in the model, the vector representing IRCA) than would have been the case had the policy conflict been won by the restrictionist side in a zero-sum competition. The force of the legalization side kept the vector closer to a more open immigration policy than would have been the case had the restrictionist forces won in a zero-sum competition.

The competitive perspective sees policy as involving disputes in which the actors either have no complementary interests or are unwilling or unable to act upon them. They follow a strategy that Quirk labels "conflictual strategy." Each side in the dispute seeks distributive gains or avoids distributive loss through defeat of the opposing side. Each faction uses competitive tactics, such as making high demands, withholding

information about its positions, manipulating other negotiator's perceptions of their preferences, and so on. The final outcome of such a policy
process is often a stalemate, a win-loss situation, or a compromise along
only one dimension. In the latter case, one faction is able to impose its
policy preferences on the other side.

When several factions are involved, some win and some lose on the
issue. This type of policy conflict is exemplified by such policy concerns
as the abortion debate, or the debate over the Equal Rights Amendment.
The very nature of the issue, or the inability of the competing groups to
see any common ground, leads them to forego negotiations and compromise and inspires them to adopt and pursue a confrontational approach.
Resolution of such conflict, if achieved at all, typically comes about by
forging a minimum winning coalition, or a competitive coalition, and
taking a vote in the hopes of having a majority (Perotti 1989: 394–395).

The alternative policy view, as suggested by Quirk, is one that more
accurately depicts what happened in the IRCA case. It entails cooperation. This occurs in public policy disputes when the sides have complementary interests and adopt a strategy seeking joint gains or the avoidance
of joint losses. They employ tactics that involve increasing joint gains.
Involved parties exchange information about their respective interests.
Mediators use integrative methods to find common grounds. As long as
the other faction reciprocates, involved factions moderate their own
demands and consider significant concessions (Quirk 1989: 395).

The final outcome of this process, if the actors are able to stay at the
negotiating table long enough to achieve one, is one of a set of integrative
solutions. They are resolved through face-to-face deliberations and discussion that attempt to forge a consensus. The solution achieved means
more than a win-loss one arrived at by a majority winner-take-all principle, although there are distributive aspects to any solution. Resolving
conflict through cooperation means developing acceptable proposals that
improve the situation for both or all major factions than can be achieved
by continued competition and no compromise. Thus, resolution is more
than simply molding a winning coalition necessitated by the legislative
decision-making process. Rather, it is a coalition of factions wherein all
the factions perceive they have won a little yet lost less in a dispute. Such
was the case in reaching enactment of IRCA—the policy adoption stage of
the policy-making process.

The IRCA case is among the types of cases that one might call—in
Quirk's words—negotiable disputes. The basic conditions for cooperation
existed in this dispute. There were complementary interests, although
initially they were not readily apparent to the involved factions. Clearly,

the factions were interdependent. Early on in the dispute it became clear that labor's desire for employer sanctions had significant implications for growers, and of course, the growers' need for a cheap and flexible force had significant implications for organized labor unions. As the conflict developed, other interdependent factions emerged. The need of Hispanic and black minority groups for protection against discrimination had a significant impact on the restrictionists' desire to limit the number of aliens in the United States. The underlying conditions to the dispute meant there was a possibility that immigration reform could be resolved cooperatively.

During the 1970s, the various factions all used competitive tactics. They began moving toward cooperation in the very late 1970s and early 1980s, with the work of the Select Commission on Immigration and Refugee Policy (SCIRP). As they moved tentatively toward negotiation, each involved group saw some opportunity for joint gain. The adding of the legalization program, an increase in the H-2 program, and antidiscrimination measures were included as tentative steps toward a comprehensive agreement on immigration reform. Once the various factions decided to negotiate rather than compete, they bickered only over the details of an agreement. Key actors served as mediators who acted as the crucial force maintaining a cooperative posture among the involved groups: Senators Simpson, Kennedy, and Wilson; Representatives Berman, Fish, Frank, Lungren, Mazzoli, Moakley, Morrison, Panetta, Rodino, Schumer, and Torres. They forged three key integrative agreements: (1) compensation, in the amnesty and antidiscrimination provisions; (2) logrolling, in various temporary worker provisions; and (3) bridging, in the Seasonal Agricultural Workers (SAWs) provisions. The SCIRP recommendations exemplified a trade-off—a loosening of legal immigration for a tightening of the law to cope with illegal immigration. Restrictionists got employer sanctions and liberals were offered greater opportunities for legal immigration and the legalization of unauthorized immigrants already in country. A farm worker legalization program replaced an earlier proposal for a guest-worker program (a key compromise negotiated by Representative Schumer).

IRCA illustrates that when a public policy dispute exhibits the preconditions essential for cooperation—interdependence and mixed-motive conflict—then many solutions are possible to use as trade-offs to resolve the underlying interests of the involved factions. In IRCA, what became three of the main provisions of the act had not been anticipated prior to their being discussed and developed with SCIRP and congressional staff in the mid- to late 1970s: the legalization program, the antidiscrimination provision, and the seasonal agricultural workers provision. Major segments of each of the involved factions—labor, business, the growers, black, and Hispanic groups—made the deliberate choice to negotiate.

The availability of moderate actors marginalized the more rigid actors who refused to recognize new interests or positions. The staffs of the immigration subcommittees of both chambers, and staff members of the moderate legislators in both chambers, soon came to view the intransigent legislators as no longer being key players.

Among the lobbying interest groups moderates willing to negotiate emerged, splitting the business faction. Lobbyists for large businesses, such as NAM and the Business Roundtable accepted the compromise agreements. Smaller businesses, represented by lobbyists for the National Federation of Independent Business and the U.S. Chamber of Commerce, remained opposed to the final bill (LeMay 1994: 70). Among restrictionist groups, some moderates emerged as well, splitting that faction. The Federation for American Immigration Reform (FAIR) split from nativist groups and from restrictionist legislators like Representatives William McCollum (R-FL) and Carlos Moorhead (R-CA). The restrictionist faction's most significant concession was accepting the SAW program after only minor changes. FAIR continued its support of IRCA's enactment because its executive director, Roger Conner, felt the need to remain consistent (Perotti 1989: 413; LeMay 1994: 156–159).

Legislative Strategies and Intent

Discerning the legislative intent of the policy makers is helpful to analyzing policy because it focuses on the interrelationship among the stages of problem definition, agenda setting, policy formulation, policy adoption, implementation, and evaluation as policy results in impacts (anticipated and unanticipated) on the political environment.

By enacting IRCA, Congress modified existing immigration policy by expanding the targets of immigration policy. It did so by including illegal immigrants and by creating conditions that would make it more problematic for undocumented immigrants to remain, and for those still in sending nations to be less likely to come. That was the legislators' *primary* purpose (U.S. Commission on Immigration Reform 1994). It sought to do so through a variety of intermediate targets: individual employers, the INS, local educational and social service agencies, and community-based organizations. Its provisions aimed at getting them to respond to the law in ways that would encourage the individual alien, the ultimate policy target, to behave in ways consistent with the law's basic assumptions.

IRCA relied on various policy instruments: strong mandates regulating employers' hiring practices; inducements like the amnesty program designed to encourage undocumented aliens in country to change their status; and financial grants to states and localities who serve that population.

IRCA was a large program, covering all U.S. employers. It processed more than three million legalizing aliens in its regular and SAW legalization programs. Its state and local assistance grants (SLIAG) exceeded those allocated for the first few years of federal welfare programs.

Finally, IRCA was time-bound and contingent legislation. Its legalization programs were set up as a one-time grant of amnesty, all phases of which were to be completed by September 1990. SLIAGs were allocated for a fixed four-year period. Employer sanctions provisions were contingent, to be automatically terminated after three years by a joint congressional resolution if the GAO found they had caused a widespread pattern of discrimination. In short, IRCA was a large-scale and complex law that could be nominally ended after only a relatively short implementation phase.

Congressional supporters of IRCA made certain assumptions. They assumed undocumented immigrants were coming primarily for economic reasons—they were being "pulled" by the draw of the U.S. economy, rather than being "pushed" by conditions in the sending nations (such as a virtual civil war in El Salvador, or fear of the violence of the drug cartel in Nicaragua). They sought to ensure that U.S. laws were consistent with each other. The mediator most responsible for this view was Senator Alan Simpson. His concern for legal formalism led him to focus on the internal inconsistency of having American law making it illegal to come as an undocumented immigrant, but not illegal for employers to hire them. Other legislators saw IRCA as a sort of "jobs bill." They assumed IRCA would protect the employment of citizens and legal resident aliens from illegal ones. Other supporters assumed that current enforcement procedures aimed largely at apprehending and deporting undocumented border crossers were ineffective and that significant improvement required increases in enforcement personnel and unwanted intrusions into local communities. Finally, as with most immigration law, a nativist sentiment shaped the manner in which policy makers defined the problem they were addressing. Their multifaceted perception of the "immigration problem" led policy makers to the strategies that relied on employer sanctions and legalization. Sanctions weakened the pull of the labor market. Legalization was a humanitarian provision and a strategy to reduce the enforcement burden on the INS. By legalizing millions of undocumented immigrants already here, the INS could focus on interdicting the flow of new illegal aliens. The capture of unauthorized aliens already here was viewed as more difficult and costly a task than apprehension at the border, and posed more infringement of civil rights and civil liberties of American citizens (LeMay 1994: 72–75).

In crafting IRCA, legislators made several important assumptions. They assumed a causal chain—from INS enforcement to individual employers to the undocumented immigrants. They assumed the INS, despite its history, was capable of implementing the complex liberal legalization program with the involvement of Qualified Designated Entities (QDEs) (nongovernmental organizations, many religious-based organizations that had an ongoing, long-term, organizational commitment to serve the immigrant community). They assumed it would not be greatly costly to administer. They assumed compliance would be widespread, largely voluntary and that the compliance costs to employers would be minimal (LeMay 1994: 73–79).

Policy Implementation: Problems with IRCA

The long and rocky road to enactment of IRCA was followed by an equally bumpy effort to implement the complex and often contradictory law. The very compromises enabling passage of the bill sowed the seeds for difficulties in implementation. Employer sanctions did not seem to work well in demagnetizing the draw of the U.S. economy. The law allowed for 14 different documents accepted as valid proof of a person's eligibility to work. That fueled a phony documents industry enabling illegal aliens to continue coming and employers to continue hiring them without fear of legal penalty for "knowingly hiring" undocumented workers. Border crossings declined for only a brief period.

Implementing the amnesty program also had mixed results. Slightly more than three million unauthorized immigrants were legalized through the program. But the INS had to do a 180 degree change in its prevailing philosophy and tradition—never an easy task for any agency of government. Undocumented immigrants distrusted the agency and even those fully meeting the criteria came forward only after the extensive involvement of nongovernmental organizations (called qualified designated entities [QDEs] in the law). The record of approval of applicants varied extensively across the country and by type of category of applicant. IRCA entailed essentially three legalization programs: the regular one referred to as Legalizing Authorized Workers (LAWs), through which 1, 759,705 were legalized; a Seasonal Agricultural Workers program (SAWs), through which 1,272,143 were legalized; and the Cuban/Haitian Adjustment program (LeMay 2004: 17; 1994: 83–85, 93–94). The INS found higher rates of the use of fraudulent documents in the SAW program by its own SAW Fraud Task Force in early 1989 (Baker 1990: 141–145; LeMay 1994: 96). However, the INS had difficulty proving the fraud to the satisfaction of the courts. A federal district court issued a sweeping injunction requiring the INS to readjudicate all applications where improper procedures were used (*Haitian Refugee Center, Inc. et al. v. Nelson et al.* 1988). That injunction led to a review of approximately 21,000 SAW applications (Baker 1990: 141; Kurzban 1989: 25). Some of the agency's problems with discovering fraud were related to the sheer size of the task. In each region of the INS field offices, investigative agents were assigned hundreds of thousands of cases. By 1989, the INS had placed 390,000 SAW applications on hold because of suspected fraud, and arrested 750 people for selling phony labor documents. Packets of such documents were selling for up to $2,000 in central Texas, and $1,500 to $3,000 in California (LeMay 1994: 96).

IRCA allowed for a 50 percent increase in Border Patrol staff but actual increases fell short of that because of difficulties in recruiting and in expanding training staff and facilities. Moreover, as the Border Patrol staff increased, so did its duties. The interdiction of drugs became a prime focus after enactment of the 1986 Omnibus Anti-Drug law, shifting their emphasis from alien apprehension and smuggling to work with the Drug Enforcement Agency (DEA) on what was called "Operation Alliance." And Border Patrol staff had increased duty as guards at refugee camps and to identify, prosecute, and deport alien criminals, many of whom were serving time in state prisons and local jails (Bean, Vernez, and Keely 1989: 44; LeMay 1994: 85–87).

Another implementation problem was the possibility that IRCA increased discrimination against those persons being hired or retained who looked and sounded like foreigners, particularly of Latino heritage. A study by the Department of Labor found few instances of the outright displacement of native workers. Three important GAO studies called for in the IRCA law were conducted. The first two did not find an extensive increase in discrimination, but its third report did find there was widespread discrimination that was a direct result of IRCA (GAO 1990: 3). That report found about 9 percent of employers (430,000) began hiring only persons born in the United States and not hiring persons with temporary work eligibility documents. Further evidence of discrimination was found by the Office of Special Counsel in the Department of Justice and by such nongovernmental groups as MALDEF and the ACLU, and by a 1988 study by the New York State Assembly Task Force on New Americans (LeMay 2004: 18; see also LeMay 1994: 82–100). Despite these findings of widespread discrimination, Congress did not even consider a joint resolution ending IRCA as was provided for in the law.

Legislative Policy Making Post-IRCA

In 1990, recognizing many of the problems evident in the implementation of IRCA, and seeing that undocumented immigration, as measured by apprehensions of attempted border crossers at the southwestern border, increased back to pre-IRCA levels, Congress moved to enact reforms of legal immigration law and to clarify certain provisions in IRCA, setting new ceilings for a worldwide level of immigration, especially as related to the reunification of immediate family members, by redefining the preference system with respect to family reunification and to employment, and by introducing a new category called "diversity immigrants," first introduced in IRCA as a temporary measure.

Its major authors were Senators Kennedy, Simpson, and Paul Simon (D-IL), and in the House, Representative Bruce Morrison (D-CT). The Immigration Act of November 29, 1990 (IMMACT), increased total immigration under a flexible "cap" of 675,000 beginning in 1995, revised grounds for exclusion and deportation, revised the H-1B temporary workers program, broadened the definition of "aggravated felony," authorized an increase of 1,000 agents of the Border Patrol, and established a Commission of Legal Immigration Reform, and provided for a temporary stay of deportation for certain aliens on the grounds of family unity and temporary protected status. It passed the House by a vote of 264 to 118, and the Senate by 89 to 8, with 3 not voting (104 Stat. 4981; LeMay and Barkan 1999, Document 145: 288–295; and for a thorough discussion of the act, LeMay 2004: 18–21).

California had the highest number of LAWs and SAWs applicants approved for legalization, 1,622,517 (nearly 54 percent of the total number nationwide) (LeMay 1994: 84). California, Florida, and Texas, which received the largest numbers of both legal and illegal immigrants during the 1990s, sued the federal government in their respective federal district courts for the estimated billions of dollars they were forced to bear for costs related to illegal immigrants and their children. Fed up with what it saw as the federal government's failure to control the border, in 1994 California attempted legislatively to reduce the draw of its economy and services and to send a message to the U.S. Congress, by passing an anti-immigration measure known as Proposition 187, the "Save Our State" initiative (LeMay and Barkan 1999, Document 146: 296–299). It made it a felony to produce or sell fraudulent documents, gave California law enforcement personnel wide authority to enforce immigration laws for the INS, including stopping persons any officer suspected of being an illegal immigrant, excluded illegal aliens from a host of public services including health services and public schools, and excluded them from postsecondary schools. Its final provision, a "severability" clause, anticipated a federal court challenge as to its constitutionality.

It was, in fact, immediately challenged in *LULAC et al. v. Wilson et al.* (November 20, 1995, 905 F. Supp. 755, C.D. Cal.; summarized in LeMay and Barkan 1999: 100–101). Most of its provisions were declared unconstitutional, but Proposition 187 succeeded in its goal to "send a message to Congress."

The highly popular voter approval of the "Save Our State" initiative (more than 60 percent) coupled with Governor Pete Wilson's (R-CA) easy margin of victory in his election bid did not go unnoticed by Congress (LeMay 2004: 22–23). Congress moved to enact national legislation to essentially enforce those provisions of Proposition 187 ruled unconstitutional as state infringements of the national government's sole authority to enact immigration law or where state actions were preempted by federal law. In 1996, Congress passed and President William Clinton signed into law two measures that essentially enacted the provisions of Proposition 187. First, Congress passed a welfare reform act, which contained several immigrant-related provisions covering both legal and illegal immigrants that were similar to those in the Save Our State initiative. It was known as the Personal Responsibility and Work Opportunity Act of August 22, 1996 (1996 *Congressional Quarterly Almanac*, v. 52, Washington, DC: Congressional Quarterly, 1997: 6–18; summarized in LeMay and Barkan 1999: 301–304; LeMay 2004: 24–26; and LeMay 2013, v. 3: 8–9).

Congress then passed an Omnibus Spending bill containing an immigration law within it: the Illegal Immigration Reform and Immigrant Responsibility Act of September 30, 1996 (LeMay 2004: 24–26; LeMay and Barkan 1999, Document 149: 304–310). Like Proposition 187, it had provisions on document fraud and alien smuggling, authorized an increase in Border Patrol agents that doubled their number from 5,000 to 10,000, authorized funding of 900 additional INS agents to investigate and prosecute alien smuggling cases, authorized a three-tiered border fence, and border-crossing cards. It gave the DOJ increased wire-tap authority for immigrant smuggling or document fraud, ordered the attorney general to develop within two years an entry-exit system, allowed for pre-inspection stations at 10 foreign airports staffed by INS personnel, and allowed the INS to enter into agreements with state and local governments for help in investigating, arresting, detaining, and transporting illegal immigrants, and allowed courts to seize assets of immigration law violators. It streamlined deportation proceedings, called for the attorney general to create an employment verification program in three years, including a machine-readable document pilot program, banned public benefits like food stamps, and made it unlawful for unauthorized immigrants to use means-tested benefits and to falsely apply for benefits, and required the Social Security administration to develop a prototype tamper-proof identity card (LeMay 2004: 26–27).

The 1996 welfare reform act and its provisions targeting legal resident aliens provoked a strong reaction among many ethnic groups and others that surfaced once the anti-immigrant fervor eased and the U.S. economy improved, as it did during the final term of the Clinton presidency. In 1997, 1998, and 1999, several legislative actions were taken to ease the 1996 law. The Balanced Budget Act of 1997 restarted Supplemental Security income for the disabled as well as Medicaid benefits for 420,000 legal resident aliens. The Agricultural Research Act of 1998 once again provided for food stamps for 225,000 legal immigrant children, senior citizens, and persons with disabilities. The FY 2000 budget included provisions restoring medical benefits to legal resident aliens with disabilities, made food stamps available to legal immigrants who reached the age of 65 and otherwise qualified for the food stamp program, and provided health coverage for legal immigrant children who entered the United States after August 22, 1996, and gave the states the option of providing Medicaid coverage for prenatal care to legal immigrant women who arrived after August 22, 1996 (Janofsky 1999: 1, 19).

Conclusion

The IRCA of 1986 ushered in a new era of immigration policy making—what was termed here as the Revolving Door phase, 1985–2001. The period saw record levels of immigrants coming to the United States—more than 12, 600,000 legal immigrants and an estimated annual influx of a half-million unauthorized immigrants for the 15-year span of the policy phase. The illegal immigration flow across the porous U.S.-Mexico border suggested the Revolving Door image for characterizing the period.

During the 1970s, the composition of immigrants entering the United States shifted in their regions of origin from Europe to Mexico and Central America, Latin America, and Asia. That change in the source of immigration fueled a renewed xenophobic concern that the immigration policy system was broken and in need of a major overhaul.

The conservative political movement led by President Ronald Reagan set in place the conditions for that major overhaul in immigration policy making. A substantial and politically influential coalition of interest groups, political party, and legislators advocating their more restrictionist perspective were able, by the early 1980s, to redefine what became perceived of as "the immigration problem." They organized a coalition that was able to place comprehensive immigration reform on the agenda of the national government in hopes of breaking the legislative stalemate on the issue that prevailed throughout the last half-decade of the 1970s.

The Reagan administration established a Task Force on Immigration Reform. Even more important, Congress established, in 1979, the Select Commission on Immigration and Refugee Policy (SCIRP). The final report of SCIRP proved to be especially influential in the policy formulation phase of immigration policy making and set the stage for the negotiation and compromises that culminated in the immigration reform proposals in both chambers of the Congress known after their principal sponsors as the Simpson-Mazzoli bills.

It took five years of rather torturous maneuvering in Congress to finally achieve a negotiated balance in the provisions of the reform proposals to finally attain policy enactment of IRCA in 1986. Key legislators, congressional committees and their staffs, and informal caucuses played critical roles as mediators in the struggle to craft a comprehensive reform measure capable of enactment. The most notable committees in that effort were the immigration subcommittees of the House and Senate Judiciary Committees, and several conference committees. Important caucuses were the black, Hispanic, and Border caucuses. Key legislators serving as mediators crafting a consensus were Senators Simpson, Kennedy, and Wilson. Key representatives were Mazzoli, Rodino, Fish, Panetta, Morrison, Schumer, Frank, Richardson, Berman, Lungren, Moakley, and Torres.

The most important lobbying organizations which initially battled and eventually cooperated to achieve critical compromises were MALDEF, SIN, LULAC, La Raza, western growers, NAM, Business Roundtable, and "ideological" interest groups like the Federation for Immigration Reform and the ACLU.

IRCA balanced three major elements contained in its numerous provisions: an employer sanctions program, a legalization program with three types (LAWs, SAWs, and the Cuban Haitian Adjustment program), and a guest-worker program plus an expansion of the H-2 temporary worker program.

However, the very compromises necessary to achieve policy adoption sowed the seeds for subsequent difficulties and problems in policy implementation. Employer sanctions failed to demagnetize the draw of the U.S. economy. The legalization programs had mixed results—achieving legalization of more than three million unauthorized immigrants but marred by extensive fraud and causing a degree of discrimination in the workforce, and more long-term, Republican resistance against any future legalization as "amnesty."

Dissatisfaction with the policy outcomes of IRCA led to further legislative actions on immigration policy making in the 1990s. The most important of those laws were the Immigration Act of 1990 (IMMACT), the Welfare Reform Act of 1996, and the immigration-related provisions of the Omnibus Spending bill of 1996.

It is probable that the era would have continued on for the first and possibly even the second decade of the 21st century, with continued tinkering with laws reforming illegal immigration policy as well as legal immigration reform had not the era come to an abrupt end with the terrorist attacks on 9/11. Those attacks on the Twin Towers in New York City, the Pentagon in Washington, D.C., and an attempted attack on Capitol Hill that ended in a farm field in Pennsylvania changed in one day the entire mood, the very psyche, of America and ushered in a new era of immigration policy making, the Storm Door phase, the subject of Chapter 7.

References

Baker, Susan G. 1990. *The Cautious Welcome: The Legalization Program of the Immigration Reform and Control Act.* Santa Monica, CA: The Rand Corporation and the Urban Institute Press.

Bean, Frank, Georges Vernez, and Charles B. Keely. 1989. *Opening and Closing the Doors.* Santa Monica, CA, and Washington, DC: The Rand Corporation and the Urban Institute.

Congressional Quarterly Almanac. 1997, v. 52, Washington, DC: Congressional Quarterly.

Congressional Quarterly Weekly Reports, October 18, 1986. 2595–2598; 2621–2613.

Congressional Record, August 17, 1982. H-10226.

Congressional Record, December 18, 1982. H-10319-H-10336.

Congressional Record-House, Roll Call Vote #457, H-9800-01.

Cornelius, W. A., and Ricardo A. Montoya. 1983. *America's New Immigration Law: Origins. Rationales and Potential Consequences.* San Diego: Center for U.S./Mexican Studies, University of California.

Crewdson, John. 1983. *The Tarnished Door.* New York: Times Books.

Dye, Thomas. 1992. *Understanding Public Policy.* Upper Saddle River, NJ: Prentice Hall.

Gallup Poll. 2004. *The Gallop Poll: Public Opinion 2003.* Denver: Scholarly Resources, Inc.

General Accounting Office. 1990. *Immigration Reform: Employer Sanctions and the Question of Discrimination: Report to Congress.* GAO/GGD-90-62. Washington, DC: U.S. Government Printing Office.

Gorman, Stobhan. 1994. *Historical Dictionary of Refugees and Disaster Relief.* Lanham, MD: Scarecrow Press/Rowman and Littlefield.

Haitian Refugee Center, Inc. et al. v. Nelson et al. August 22, 1988. 88-1066-Civ-Atkins 1988, SD Fla.

"Hill Passes Compromise Immigration Bill." October 16, 1986. *The Washington Post,* A 5.

"Hill Revises Immigration Law." October 16, 1986. *The Washington Post,* A 1, 7–8.

Hondagnev-Sotelo, Pierrette. 2008. *God's Heart Has No Borders: How Religious Activists Are Working for Immigrant Rights.* Berkeley: University of California Press.

Janofsky, Michael. January 25, 1999. "Legal Immigrants Would Regain Aid in Clinton Plan." *New York Times,* 1, 19.

Jenkins, Philip. 2003. *The New Anti-Catholicism: The Last Acceptable Prejudice.* New York: Oxford University Press.

Kurzban, Ira. 1989. "Amnesty: Can We Learn a Simple and More Generous Approach?" In *In Defense of the Alien,* vol. II. Edited by Lydio Tomasi, 19–26. New York: Center for Migration Studies.

Lamm, R. D., and G. Imhoff. 1985. *The Immigration Time Bomb.* New York: Truman Talley Books.

LeMay, Michael. 1994. *Anatomy of a Public Policy: The Reform of Contemporary American Immigration Law.* Westport, CT: Praeger Press.

LeMay, Michael. 2004. *U.S. Immigration: A Reference Handbook.* Santa Barbara, CA: ABC-CLIO.

LeMay, Michael. 2006. *Guarding the Gates: Immigration and National Security.* Westport, CT: Praeger Security International.

LeMay, Michael. 2007. *Illegal Immigration: A Reference Handbook,* 1st edition. Santa Barbara, CA: ABC-CLIO.

LeMay, Michael, ed. 2013. *Transforming America: Perspectives on U.S. Immigration, v. 3, 1945 to Present.* Santa Barbara, CA: ABC-CLIO.

LeMay, Michael, and Elliott Barkan. 1999. *U.S. Immigration and Naturalization Laws and Issues: A Documentary History.* Westport, CT: Greenwood Press.

LULAC et al. v. Wilson et al. November 20, 1995. 905 F. Supp. 755, C.D. Cal.

Marquardt, Marie T. T., and Manuel A. Vasquez. 2014. "To Persevere in Our Struggle: Religion Among Unauthorized Latino Immigrants in the United States." In *Hidden Lives and Human Rights in the United States: Economics,*

Politics, and Morality, vol. 3. Edited by Lois Ann Lorentzen, 303–323. Westport, CT: Praeger Press.

Migration Policy Institute. http://www.migrationpolicy.org/article/asian-immigrants-united-states. Accessed May 8, 2017.

Perotti, Rosanna. 1989. *Resolving Policy Conflict: Congress and Immigration Reform.* PhD Dissertation, University of Pennsylvania.

Portes, Alejandro, and Reuben G. Rumbaut. 1996. *Immigrant America: A Portrait.* Berkeley: University of California Press.

Quirk, Paul. 1989. "The Cooperative Resolution of Policy Conflict." *American Political Science Review* 83(3): 905–921.

Sawyer, Mary R. 2003. *The Church on the Margins: Living Christian Communities.* London: A & C Black Publishing.

"Simpson: The 'Anglo' Behind the Immigration Bill." October 19, 1986. *The Washington Post*, A 8–9.

Smith, Jane. 1999. *Islam in America.* New York: Columbia University Press.

Teaching Tolerance. http://www.tolerance.org/publication/american-muslims-united-states. Accessed May 8, 2017.

U.S. Commission on Immigration Reform. 1994. *U.S. Immigration Policy: Restoring Credibility.* Washington, DC: U.S. Government Printing Office.

CHAPTER SEVEN

The Storm Door Era, 2001–2018

Introduction: Religious Trends and the Making of Fortress America

The attacks of 9/11 on the New York City World Trade Center Twin Towers and on the Pentagon in Washington, D.C., led Congress and the president to take actions by issuing executive orders and by passing several laws that are very nearly unprecedented in the speed of their introduction and passage, and in the sweeping nature of the powers they grant to the government, and, finally, in the extent of change they involved for immigration policy making and implementation. In part, the disarray at the Immigration and Naturalization Service (INS), made apparent by the attacks and their aftermath, sped up the process. Immediately after the attacks, U.S. attorney general John Ashcroft ordered strict enforcement of a rule requiring foreign visitors to file change of address forms that the national government had supposedly been using to keep track of visitors. However, the INS reported that an estimated four million visitors were in the country with expired visas and whose exact whereabouts were simply unknown. That shocking admission was soon topped when it was revealed that the INS sent a letter to the Florida flight school approving student visas for two of the 9/11 terrorists six months after the attacks in which the two had participated, and who had been flight-trained at the school. An overall management assessment in the 2002 Federal Performance Report gave the INS a D rating. Border Patrol agents were leaving the INS faster than they could be replaced. INS investigators were assessed as being undertrained, overworked, and overstressed. The agency's information management system was assessed as abysmal. It was readily clear that drastic restructuring was needed; and it was quickly called for in Congress (LeMay 2013, v. 3: 10).

In less than a month after the attacks, President George W. Bush issued executive order 13328, of October 8, 2001, that established the Office of Homeland Security (OHS) and the Homeland Security Council within the Executive Office of the President (Relyea 2003: 613). Congress followed suite with bills to establish a Department of Homeland Security (DHS) as a cabinet-level department, such as the bill (S-1534) sponsored by Senator Joseph Lieberman (I-CT). Lieberman and Representative Mac Thornberry (R-TX) later introduced a more elaborate version, in early May 2002 (S 2452 and H.R. 4660). While at first opposing the idea of creating a new cabinet-level department, President Bush reacted to political pressure to do more than what an executive order could accomplish. He secretly had a team from his administration begin drafting a response and alternative to the Lieberman-Thornberry bills. The administration's team was comprised of Mitchell Daniels, Jr., director of the Office of Management and Budget (OMB), Tom Ridge, appointed to the OHS, Andrew Card, Jr., the White House chief of staff, and Alberto Gonzales, the White House counsel. They began drafting the president's departmental plan on April 23. It was introduced as HR 5005, on June 24, 2002 (LeMay 2006: 204; Relyea 2003: 617).

More than any other actions, two laws passed in response to the 9/11 attacks most effectively characterize the current era of immigration policy making as the Storm Door era and symbolizing Fortress America: the USA Patriot Act and the law establishing the DHS (Clarke 2004; Crotty 2003; LeMay 2006: 204).

Both laws impacted the processing of immigration but not the numbers arriving, except for a slight dip in 2003 and 2004. From 2001 to 2013, 13,571,356 legal immigrants arrived, with an annual average of 1,131,000.

The USA Patriot Act

Within six weeks of the 9/11 terrorist attacks, a jittery Congress was essentially exiled from their Capitol Hill offices by an anthrax contamination incident. For nearly three weeks, from the initial outbreak on October 4, 2002, Congress and the public were unable to obtain clear information about the anthrax attack from the Center for Diseases Control and Prevention (CDC). Anthrax is a serious infectious disease caused by rod-shaped bacteria known as *Bacillus anthracis*. Although rare, people get sick with anthrax by contact with infected animals or contaminated animal products. It can be weaponized (aerosolized) and used for bioterrorism when its spore state (in powdered form) is used to contaminate through inhalation. It causes hemorrhagic bleeding in the mid-chest, progressing to a body-wide infection and high mortality rate (Center for Disease Control).

The incident demonstrated how vulnerable the country was to this new threat (Flynn 2004). Fear of the anthrax threat, however, exceeded actual damage in 2001.

> The fall of 2001 anthrax outbreak was a far cry from the apocalyptic scenarios envisioned in the movies and government simulations. A mere twenty-one persons caught the disease, and only five died. Nonetheless, this handful of individuals changed America's world view forever because they were far from the only casualties of the still untracked attacks, also severely stricken were the already shaky economy, the U.S. postal system, and, perhaps most telling of all, the public's confidence that "it can't happen here." (Yount 2004: 9)

Congress, confronted with dire warnings of more terrorist attacks to come if action were not taken, responded to President Bush's demands for a new arsenal of antiterrorism policies that had direct impact on immigration policy making. Despite vigorous objections from civil liberties organizations, like the American Civil Liberties Union, Congress overwhelmingly approved the USA Patriot Act (PL 107–56, HR 3162). The law's title is an acronym for the Uniting and Strengthening America by Providing Appropriate Tools Required to Intercept and Obstruct Terrorism Act (LeMay 2004: 27). In the House, it passed by a vote of 356 to 66, and in the Senate by a vote of 98 to 1 (LeMay 2006: 205; see also Birkland 2004; Crotty 2003; Demmer 2002; Flynn 2004).

The bill was hastily drafted, complex, and far-reaching. It spans 342 pages in the U.S. Code, yet it was passed with virtually no public hearings or debate, and it was accompanied by neither a conference nor a committee report, and apparently unread by many members of Congress. On October 26, 2001, the bill was signed into law by a triumphant President George W. Bush (Torr 2004: 43–44). Box 7.1 provides excerpts of the act.

BOX 7.1: EXCERPTS FROM THE USA PATRIOT ACT OF 2001 (HR 3162)

Sec. 102. Sense of Congress Condemning Discrimination against Arab and Muslim Americans.

(a) Findings, Congress makes the following findings:
  (1) Arab Americans, Muslim Americans, and Americans from South Asia play a vital role . . . and are entitled to nothing less than the full rights of every American.

(2) The acts of violence . . . taken against [them] since September 11, 2001 . . . should be condemned by all Americans who value freedom.

(b) Sense of Congress. It is the sense of Congress that—

    (1) The civil rights and civil liberties of all Americans, including Arab Americans, Muslim Americans, and Americans from South Asia, must be protected, and every effort made to preserve their safety.

    (2) Any acts of violence or discrimination against any American be condemned.

    (3) The Nation is called upon to recognize the patriotism of fellow citizens of all ethnic, racial, and religious backgrounds.

Title IV—Protecting the Border goes on to the following sections,
Subtitle A—Protecting the Northern Border
Sec. 401—Ensures adequate personnel on the northern border.
Sec. 403—Grants access by the Department of State and the INS to certain identifying records of visa applicants and applicants for admission to the United States.
Sec. 405—Establishes an integrated automated fingerprint identification system for ports of entry and overseas consular posts.
Subtitle B—Enhanced Immigration Provisions
Sec. 411—Defines terrorism
Sec. 412—Mandates detention of suspected terrorists; suspends habeas corpus under certain conditions; and limits judicial review.
Sec. 413—Ensures multilateral cooperation against terrorists.
Sec. 414—Provides for increased integrity and security of visas.
Sec. 415—Mandates participation of the Office of Homeland Security on the Entry-Exit Task Force.
Sec. 416—Establishes a foreign student monitoring program.
Sec. 417—Calls for machine-readable passports.
Subtitle C—Preservation of Immigration Benefits for Victims of Terrorism
Sec. 421—Grants special immigration status to victims of the 9/11 attacks.
Sec. 423—Grants humanitarian relief for certain surviving spouses and children.
Sec. 427—Denies such benefits to terrorists or family members of terrorists.
Title X—Miscellaneous
Sec. 1006—Provides for the inadmissibility of aliens engaged in money laundering.

Source: Box excerpts by author. Electronic Privacy Information Center (EPIC) Website. http://www.epic.org/privacy/terrorism/hr3162.html. Accessed April 20, 2003.

The new law granted powers to the attorney general and the Department of Justice (DOJ) that restricted the civil liberties of U.S. citizens, broadened the terrorism-related definitions in the 1965 Immigration and Naturalization Act, expanded grounds of inadmissibility to include aliens who publicly endorse terrorist activity, and gave the government broad powers to monitor students and resident aliens and to detain and expedite the deportation of noncitizens even merely suspected of links to terrorist organizations—that is, of those whom the attorney general certifies as threats to national security on whatever grounds. It legalized guilt by association. Critics also maintain that the act legalized racial profiling of Middle Easterners (Etzioni and Marsch 2003; LeMay 2004: 27; Platt and O'Leary 2004).

Proponents of the new law argued it was needed to catch terrorists, especially those acting as "lone wolfs," and to deter further attacks. Its advocates called for coercive interrogation techniques (called "enhanced interrogation") by the administration, although critics argued it was no less than torture of the sort specifically prohibited by the Geneva Convention, to which the United States was a signatory. Vice President Dick Cheney argued suspected terrorists should be treated as enemy combatants, and as such were not subject to the Geneva Convention protocols.

Advocates stated flatly that its sweeping powers were necessary to penetrate al Qaeda cells. The new powers granted to the DOJ include expanded surveillance, use of informants, revisions to search and seizure, use of wiretaps, arrests and interrogations, and detentions of suspected terrorists. These new powers were all uninhibited by the prior web of laws, judicial precedents, and administrative rules that the law's advocates argued had hamstrung law enforcement officials in dealing with the new terrorist threat. The USA Patriot Act removed many restrictions on law enforcement officials' ability to gather intelligence through physical searches, wiretaps, electronic surveillance, and increased access to criminal records (Torr 2004: 29; see also Clarke 2004; Flynn 2004).

Critics of the USA Patriot Act argued that it was too sweeping and too dangerous an intrusion on civil liberty protections and was a threat to constitutional checks and balances, to open government, and to the rule of law that made it a greater threat than that posed by terrorists (Demmer 2002). As one such critic noted: "Not since the World War II internment of Japanese Americans have we locked up so many for so long with so little explanation" (Nancy Chang, cited in Torr 2004: 16). Still other critics maintained that the act evaded the Fourth Amendment by letting agents conduct sneak-and-peak searches or covert searches of a person's home or office that are conducted without notice to the person (LeMay 2013, v. 3: 11; Torr 2004: 49). The mass arrests conducted secretly and without judicial oversight outraged civil libertarians on the right and the left of the political spectrum. To such critics, the USA Patriot Act was a threat to patriotic dissent, liberty, and equality (LeMay 2006: 206; Platt and O'Leary 2004: 7). One such critic, David Cole, the legal affairs correspondent of *Nation* put it in the following words:

> It appears the greatest threat to our freedoms is posed not by the terrorists themselves but by our own government's response . . . Administration supporters argue the magnitude of the new threat requires a new paradigm. But so far we have seen only a repetition of the old paradigm—broad incursions on liberties, largely targeted at unpopular noncitizens and minorities in the name of fighting a war. What is new is that this war has no end in sight, and only a vaguely defined enemy, so its incursions are likely to be permanent. (cited in Torr 2004: 12)

And another such critic states:

> But we should remember the words of German Pastor Martin Niemoller said after spending seven years in [the Nazi death camp at] Dachau. "In Germany, they came first for the communists, and I didn't speak up because I wasn't a communist." He went on to lament his failure to speak up for Jews, trade unionists, and others, and concluded . . . "Then they came for me, and by that time there was no one left to speak up." (cited in Torr 2004: 67)

And in point of fact, the non-terrorists most affected by the act were immigrants, mostly Muslims, despite the language of Section 102 of the act. In several months' time after the 9/11 attacks, an estimated 1,200 Muslim immigrants were swept up by police and immigration officials across the nation, many held for months without access to a lawyer or even having charges brought against them before an immigration judge. While a few of those thus rounded up were deported, and few were charged with any crime, most were subsequently released as totally innocent persons, victims of the post-attack hysteria. Their treatment was similar to that against so-called radicals in the summer of 1919 during the "Red Scare" and the infamous Palmer Raids. In essence, the law made any aliens deportable for wholly innocent association with suspected terrorist organizations so broadly defined that potentially every organization that had been involved in a civil war or a crime of violence, from a pro-life group that once threatened workers at an abortion clinic to the African National Congress to the Irish Republican Army or to the Northern

Alliance in Afghanistan (United States' allies there). All would fit under the law's definition. An estimated 2,000 persons were detained under the act. None of those detained had been involved in the 9/11 attacks, and most were cleared by the FBI of any involvement in terrorism (Etzioni and Marsch 2003: 37–38; LeMay 2006: 207; LeMay 2013, v. 3: 11–12).

Soon after its passage, the DOJ announced it had broken up terrorists cells in Portland, Oregon, Detroit, Michigan, and Buffalo, New York. The DOJ charged 17 individuals with terrorism-related activities. It also targeted terrorist financing.

Scholars of terrorism have more specifically defined it, such as the following:

> Terrorism is defined as the deliberate creation and exploitation of fear through violence or the threat of violence in the pursuit of political change. . . . Terrorism is specifically designed to have far-reaching psychological effects beyond the immediate victim(s) or object of terrorist attack. It is meant to instill fear within, and thereby intimidate, a wider "target audience" that might include a rival ethnic group or religious group, an entire country, a national government or political party, or public opinion in general. Terrorism is designed to create power where there is none or to consolidate power where there is little. Through the publicity generated by their violence, terrorists seek to obtain leverage, influence, and power they otherwise lack to effect political change on either a local or an international scale . . . Timothy McVeigh . . . when asked by his defense lawyer why he could not have aired his grievances without killing anyone, said: "that would have not gotten the point across. We need a body count to make our point." (Cooper 2004: 31)

International terrorists find the very technological development of the United States provides them with soft targets that are exploitable for the agenda of terror. Technological changes make it easier to kill and have locked societies into a cycle of attack and counterattack that render impossible the normal trajectory of political and economic development. As Thomas Dixon puts it:

> True, the terrorists used simple box cutters to hijack the planes, but the box cutter was no more than the "keys" that allowed the terrorists to convert a high tech means of transport into a high-tech weapon of mass destruction. Once the hijackers had used those keys to access and turn on their weapons, they were able to deliver a kiloton of explosive power to the World Trade Center with deadly accuracy . . . Complex terrorism operates like jujitsu—it redirects the energies of our intricate society against us. (Dixon 2002: 55)

Dissolving the INS, Creating the DHS

Approximately one year after passing the USA Patriot Act, Congress acted once again with remarkable alacrity in passing a massive and complex law. The Bush administration backed a bill to establish a new DHS, introduced into Congress and passed quickly in the House. The Senate debated its version of the bill through early November 2002. On November 19, 2002, Congress passed the Homeland Security Act (HR 5005) establishing the DHS. The Senate passed the House version by a 90–9 vote. The House agreed to a slightly amended Senate version on November 22, and sent it to the president for his signature (Relyea 2003: 622). When President Bush signed the measure on November 25, 2002, the DHS was established. In one sweeping law (it runs more than 400 pages), the Congress abolished the Immigration and Naturalization Service, restructuring its jurisdiction and functions into a new behemoth department composed of 22 agencies subsumed into it. Many of its provisions dramatically changed the way in which immigration policy was implemented. It constituted the most extensive reorganization of the federal bureaucracy since the creation of the Department of Defense after World War II (LeMay 2013, v. 3: 12). It merged 22 agencies with more than 190,000 employees, comprising the third largest department in the federal executive branch (after the Department of Defense and the Department of Veteran Affairs). With the merger into the new department, the INS ceased to exist, closing an often controversial history of more than 100 years. It created within the new department two bureaus: the Directorate of Border and Transportation Security, and a Bureau of Citizenship and Immigration Services. Highlights of the immigration-related provisions of the law are provided in Box 7.2.

Box 7.2:   Summary of the Immigration-Related Provisions of the Homeland Security Act of 2002 (HR-5005)

Title IV—Border and Transportation Security

Subtitle A—General Provisions
Sec. 401—Creates the Under Secretary for Border and Transportation Security.
Sec. 402—Responsibilities—Transfers functions of the INS to the DHS.
The Secretary, acting through the Under Secretary for Border and Transportation Security shall be responsible for the following:

(1) Preventing the entry of terrorists and the instruments of terror into the U.S.

(2) Securing the borders, territorial waters, ports, terminals, waterways, air, land and sea transportation systems of the United States, including managing and coordinating those functions transferred to the Department at ports of entry.

(3) Carrying out the immigration enforcement functions vested by statute in, or performed by, the Commissioner of Immigration and Naturalization (or any officer, employee, or component of the Immigration and Naturalization Service) immediately before the date on which the transfer of functions specified under section 441 takes effect [March 1, 2003].

(4) Establishing and administering rules, in accordance with section 428, governing the granting of visas or other forms of permissions, including parole, to enter the United States to individuals who are not a citizen or an alien lawfully admitted for permanent residence in the United States.

(5) Establishing national immigration enforcement policies.

Subtitle B—Immigration and Nationality Functions
Chapter 1—Immigration Enforcement
Sec. 411. Details the transfer of functions of the Border Patrol, INS, to the Under Secretary for Border and Transportation Security in the DHS.
Sec. 412. Establishes a Bureau of Border Security headed by a Director.
Sec. 415. Calls for a report to Congress on improving enforcement functions.
Chapter 2—Citizenship and Immigration Services
Sec. 421. Establishes a Bureau of Citizenship and Immigration Services headed by a Director.
Sec. 422. Establishes a Citizenship and Immigration Services Ombudsment office.
Sec. 425. Establishes an Office of Immigration Statistics within the Bureau of Justice Statistics.
Sec. 426. Concerns the application of internet-based technologies.
Chapter 3—General Provisions
Sec. 41. Abolishes the INS as of March 1, 2003.
Sec. 45. Requires reports and implementation plans to Congress.
Sec. 46. Details immigration functions.

Source: Summary by author.

When the 36,000 men and women of the INS were absorbed into the new department, they left the only entity within it that was abolished. The aftermath of the attacks of 9/11 provided the "coup de grace" to the INS, a finale to the long-standing efforts within the Congress to eradicate an agency hampered by notorious mismanagement and a string of failures including backlogs in the millions of citizenship and naturalization applications, more millions of lost paperwork, a backlog of change-of-address forms in the millions, failure to keep track of an estimated four million foreigners in the country with expired visas, and the outrageous approval of student visas, six months after the attacks, for two of the 9/11 hijackers (September 11 Commission Report: 80–82).

In part, the failure of the INS to adequately control the nation's borders was seen as a major factor in the attacks, and in some measure the agency was blamed for them. Even though none of the hijackers had gained entry by illegally crossing the border, it was widely recognized in Congress that the terrorists very well could have done so. Prior cases of terrorists crossing the U.S.-Canada border were recalled. In 1996, a Palestinian emigrant, Ghazi Ibrahim Abu Maizar, was caught crossing illegally in a bomb plot aimed at New York City. In 1999, Ahmed Ressan, a weapons expert and member of al Qaeda, was caught smuggling explosives across the U.S.-Canada border intent on using them in Los Angeles during the millennium festivities (Krauss and Pacheco 2004: 173–174). The INS and its border patrol were viewed as unable to control the border. Prior to 9/11, there were fewer than 400 border patrolmen guarding the 4,000 mile U.S.-Canada border, stretching from Washington to Maine. That meant there was only about one patrolman for every ten miles of often rugged terrain with many obstacles limiting the Border Patrol's methods of travel for enforcement purposes (Ibid: 175).

Groupthink and Other Problems in the Rush to Create DHS

When the policy adoption stage of policy making is rushed, as it was with the decision to dissolve the INS and establish the DHS, a pattern of decision-making behavior called *groupthink* is exhibited. When a large, complex organization is created by merger, simply managing policy, yet alone innovation, is related to and dependent upon the organization's ability to comprehend and decide how potential future technologies and organizational impacts could be affected. Innovation requires *insightful* ways of achieving breakthroughs. It requires those insightful ideas be considered and synthesized into its organizational procedures and practices. Innovation requires strategic foresight (LeMay 2006: 216; Mitchell 2003: 16).

The act to create the DHS shows evidence of several aspects of group-think (Chen et al. 1996; Janis 1982; Kowert 2002; Reich 2004; Sneider 2004). Congress perceived the post-9/11 situation to be an emergency, and emergencies can cry out for drastic and expensive changes in public policy that later, on reflection, seem ill-conceived (Roots 2003: 503). According to Irving Janis, under conditions of stressful decision making, groups can become excessively concerned with concurrence seeking that leads to groupthink and subsequent policy fiascoes. He defined group-think as:

> a mode of thinking that people engage in when they are deeply involved in a cohesive in-group, when the members striving for unanimity override their motivation to realistically appraise alternative courses of action . . . Groupthink refers to a deterioration of mental efficiency, reality testing, and moral judgment that result from in-group pressure. (Janis 1982: 9)

The very nature of policy making is decisions made by groups rather than individuals deciding alone. Organizational decision making is inherently a social process (Chen et al. 1996: 581).

There are several aspects of apparent groupthink behavior in the decision to create the DHS. For such an extensive reorganization of the federal bureaucracy, the law passed in a very short time—just over two years after the 9/11 attacks. It sped through nearly a dozen committees. President Bush issued the executive order establishing the Office of Homeland Security and appointed former Pennsylvania governor Tom Ridge as its director in less than a month after 9/11. By October 26, 2001, President Bush signed the USA Patriot Act into law. By June 2002, he abandoned his initial resistance to elevating Homeland Security to a cabinet-level department, and after the 2002 election, Bush got his department and Tom Ridge became its first Secretary of Homeland Security (Walcott and Hult 2003: 151).

In addition to its speed, there was unusual congressional unanimity in voting, especially considering the massive and complex nature of a nearly 500-page bill and the reshuffling of many agencies with the accompanying "turf" considerations. As mentioned, in the Senate the vote was 90–9; in the House 299–121. Among Republicans, the vote was 212 in favor to only 6 opposed. In the months leading up to the vote there was little or no debate, and what debate there was centered on the unionization and civil service protections of employees of the new department. Initially, some committees wanted to leave the Coast Guard, the Federal Emergency Management Agency (FEMA), and half of the INS out of the new department. The House Republican leadership undid most of those objections (LeMay 2006: 218; O'Beirne 2002).

The DHS exhibited a reduced emphasis on immigration and citizenship matters in personnel, services, and budget (LeMay 2013, v. 3: 12). The massive new department faced several obstacles to effective management: (1) its mission complexity, (2) the incompatibility in their political cultures of the many agencies involved in the merger; (3) task obfuscation, and (4) symbolic versus real performance results (Krauss 2003: 51–58; Light 2002).

In budgeting for the new department, the very agencies coming from the INS most responsible for border control and the agencies most in need of attention and improvement in their management ended up with the least improvement in discretionary budget funding. The Immigration and Customs Enforcement (ICE) received the lowest percentage of total discretionary funding in the department for fiscal years 2003 and 2004, and the second lowest in fiscal years 2002 and 2005 (LeMay 2006: 222–223).

Soon after its establishment, the DHS launched the National Security Entry-Exit Registration System (NSEERS), as called for by the 2002 law. NSEERS was comprised of three components: point-of-entry registration, special registration, and exit/departure controls. Its purpose was to prevent future 9/11-like terrorist attacks. The special registration component established a national registry for temporary foreign visitors (i.e., nonimmigrant aliens) coming from 25 designated countries (which the attorney general listed as supporters and exporters of international terrorism), and others who met a combination of intelligence-based criteria that identified them as potential risks (LeMay 2007: 24).

NSEERS addressed a variety of security-related deficiencies in immigration policy and implementation procedures. In 2003, all commercial passenger carriers (air or sea) were required to submit detailed passenger lists electronically before an aircraft or vessel arrived in or departed from the United States. In December 2003, the DHS suspended one of NSEERS provisions, however, concerning the need for aliens residing in the United States to register every year. It did so because the government had millions of such forms backlogged and stored, unprocessed, in warehouses in Kansas, and ICE simply could not keep up with the paperwork. NSEERS required foreign nationals from Iran, Iraq, Libya, Syria, and the Sudan to go through special registration at ports of entry, and to report to immigration officials before departing the country. Foreign nationals from other countries were registered as well if Customs and Border Protection officers (a new bureau within DHS) warranted it necessary based on initial questioning upon arrival in the United States. By January 2005, individuals from more than 160 countries were registered in the NSEERS program. The system contains detailed information on each nonimmigrant relating their background and the purpose of their visit to the United States, as well as departure confirmation when they leave (Information Plus 2006: 75; LeMay 2007: 25).

In April 2002, the DOJ issued a report on visa overstays substantiating the fact that between 40 and 50 percent of unauthorized immigrants were not persons who had crossed the borders without papers but rather were persons who entered with proper documents as temporary visitors who then failed to depart when required to do so. According to the report, nonimmigrant overstayers were growing by at least 125,000 per year (DOJ 2002).

U.S. Immigration and Customs Enforcement (ICE) is the bureau responsible for collecting documents from incoming travelers, but airline and shipping lines are responsible for collecting departure forms and for sending such forms to ICE. Departure forms may have gone unrecorded, however, because they were not collected, or were collected by the airlines and shipping lines but were not sent to ICE, or the forms were sent to ICE but were incorrectly recorded. Such problems make difficult an accurate assessment of visa overstays. A 2004 General Accounting Office (GAO) report stated the DHS estimated number of visa overstays in the United States to be 2.3 million as of the year 2000. However, the GAO observed that this figure did not account for an unknown number of short- and long-term overstays from Mexico and Canada, inasmuch as citizens of Canada admitted for up to six months and Mexican citizens with border-crossing cards entering at the southwestern border for a stay of less than 72 hours are exempt from the visa admissions procedures. The GAO faulted the tracking system that identified those who entered the country on visas but did not accurately track when, or if, those persons actually left the United States (GAO 2004).

Of course, it must be acknowledged that keeping track of the volume of persons coming to the United States annually is no small task. In 2001, the INS reported nearly 33 million arrivals at U.S. ports of entry (air and sea). That number did not include Mexican and Canadian business or pleasure visitors. Of the 33 million, an estimated 79 percent departed before their authorized stay had expired. While there is no departure records for nearly 15 percent of all persons who arrived by land and sea, departure records were missing for 71 percent of those who had so arrived (Information Plus 2006: 76). In the post-9/11 investigations, the GAO, in a report in May 2004, noted that of the six hijackers, who actually flew the planes involved in the attacks, two were overstayers and one had violated a student visa by not attending school. In response to the post-9/11 investigation findings, the DHS began an ongoing, multiagency effort called Operation Tarmac. It was designed to identify unauthorized foreign nationals working in places vulnerable to terrorism, such as the security areas of airports (Commission Report-9/11; Flynn 2004; GAO 2004; Information Plus 2006).

FEMA established an Integrated Emergency Management System for Threat Analysis and Assessment to coordinate information about terrorist threats. It combined six programs from agencies such as the FBI and the Department of Energy. It was responsible for the much-derided color-coded scheme of warnings about threats, produced daily homeland security briefings for the president based on analysis from the Terrorist Threat Integration Center, the nominally independent center housed in the CIA as a joint venture of the FBI, CIA, and DHS. It is largely staffed by the CIA, however, and top DHS officials are not always kept in the loop (Lehrer 2004: 72; LeMay 2006: 221–222).

The GAO report, *Overstay Tracking*, found that as of April 2004, a total of 195 airports had been investigated and nearly 6,000 businesses had been audited. In checks on employment eligibility forms (known as I-9 forms), of some 385,000 workers around the nation, the DHS found nearly 5,000 unauthorized workers. Of more than 600 unauthorized workers arrested, 30 percent were overstays. Perhaps not surprising, but certainly ironic, one of the busiest ports of entry for such unauthorized workers was Houston's Bush International Airport. Ten unauthorized workers were from countries identified as "of special interest" under the NSEERS program, and five of those were overstays (GAO 2004; LeMay 2007: 26).

Of particular concern, the GAO noted that many unauthorized workers had access to supposedly secured areas and were employed by the airports themselves, by airlines, or by support service companies in jobs such as aircraft maintenance, airline cabin service attendant, airplane fueler, baggage handler, and predeparture screener. One such unauthorized worker was employed in the airport badging office. These individuals had used fraudulent Social Security numbers and identity documents to obtain airport jobs and security badges. Operation Tarmac found unauthorized workers at numerous infrastructure sites, such as nuclear power plants, sensitive national landmarks, military installations, and the Alaska pipeline, at the 2002 Olympics in Salt Lake City, and at the Super Bowl game. Seventy-nine unauthorized workers were arrested at the 2003 Super Bowl in San Diego, according to the GAO report. Of those, eight were overstays, and twelve came from countries included in the NSEERS "special registration" category (GAO 2004: 78; LeMay 2007: 26).

Further Actions to Build Fortress America

Congress included further immigration-related provisions in the Intelligence Reform and Terrorism Prevention Act of 2004, which created a Director of National Intelligence (DNI) (aka the intelligence czar), and a National Counterterrorism Center (NCTC) (PL-108–458). As was the case with the law to establish the DHS, President Bush initially resisted the idea of creating an intelligence czar or substantially restructuring U.S. intelligence operations. Pressure from the September 11 Commission, coupled with the public being aroused by joint hearings held by the House and Senate intelligence committees on the "intelligence failure" that contributed to the attacks, however, moved the president to accept the need for reform legislation. The new law enacted H.R. 5150 and S. 2845, introduced in late September 2004. The Congress passed the bill in early October 2004 and it was signed into law by President Bush on December 17, 2004. Its leading Senate sponsors were Senator Susan Collins (R-ME) and Senator Joseph Lieberman (I-CT). In the House, it was sponsored by Representatives Pete Hoekstra (R-MI) and Representative Jane Harman (D-CA) (LeMay 2006: 231).

The law created a DNI to oversee 15 government agencies involved in intelligence, and a NCTC, among its many sections. The law gives the DNI authority to ensure adequate exchange of information, a condition obviously lacking pre-9/11. President Bush quickly appointed John Negroponte, the U.S. ambassador to Iraq, as the first DNI.

It included an array of antiterrorism provisions and added 2,000 additional Border Patrol agents each year for five years, improved baggage screening procedures, new standards of information that must be contained in driver's licenses, and making it easier to track suspected terrorists not tied to known terrorist groups (what quickly became known as a "lone-wolf").

Its intent was to get the intelligence community to think about intelligence more strategically than operationally. Its creation of the NCTC was seen as a model for the way the government might organize itself to think more strategically about a variety of problems. It extended the model, for example, to concerns about weapons of mass destruction by establishing a National Counter-Proliferation Center, and it gives the DNI authority to establish other such centers focusing on new threats as the need arises (bioterrorism, chemical, etc.). While it gives the DNI a role in the budget process, it does not endow the office with clear and absolute budget authority as recommended by the September 11 Commission (LeMay 2006: 231).

Critics of the Intelligence Reform and Terrorism Prevention Act expressed skepticism of its "czar" approach (Roberts 2005: 78). Another criticism centers on intelligence collection. The act addresses analysis and integration of intelligence through the NCTC, but it fails to make a similar structural change in the collection process. The law simply directs the DNI to establish objectives, priorities, and requirements for the timely collection, processing, analysis, and dissemination of national intelligence.

Finally, it grants the government broader surveillance authority over any noncitizen suspected of being a threat, including the so-called lone-wolf terrorist inspired by but not associated with groups like al Qaeda, ISIS, and al Qaeda affiliates (Ibid). The immigration-related provisions of the law are presented in Box 7.3.

BOX 7.3: IMMIGRATION-RELATED PROVISIONS OF THE INTELLIGENCE REFORM ACT OF 2006

1. It requires the Secretary of Health and Human Services (HHS) to promulgate standards for birth certificates in consultation with the DHS and the Commissioner of Social Security.

2. Standards for birth certificates must include a requirement for proof and verification of identity as a condition for issuance of a birth certificate.

3. Requires HHS to coordinate with SSA to award grants to states to assist them in computerizing their birth and death records; developing the capability to match birth and death records within and among the states, and noting the fact of death on birth certificates of deceased persons.

4. Beginning in 2008, prohibits federal agencies from accepting, for any official purpose, a driver's license or identification card newly issued by a state to any person unless the driver's license or personal identification card conforms to such minimum standards as set forth by the 2004 law.

5. Such standards would include, among other things, a requirement for documentation of proof of identity of an application for such a license/

card and a standard for the verifiability of documents to obtain such license/card.

6. Requires the SSA to issue regulations to restrict the issuance of multiple replacement cards not later than 180 days after enactment of the law.

7. Requires the SSA to verify records provided by an applicant for an original Social Security card, other than for purposes of enumeration at birth, within one year of enactment.

8. Requires the SSA to add death, fraud, and work authorization indicators to the Social Security number verification system within 18 months of enactment.

9. Requires SSA, in consultation with DHS, to form an interagency task force for the purpose of further improving the Social Security cards and numbers. Not later than one year after enactment, the task force will establish social security requirements, including standards for safeguarding cards from counterfeiting, tampering, alteration, and theft; for verifying documents submitted for the issuance of replacement cards, and actions to increase enforcement against the fraudulent use or issuance of Social Security numbers and cards.

10. Authorizes, for each fiscal year 2005–2009, appropriations to the Commissioner of Social Security of such sums as are necessary to carry out the requirements of the law.

Source: Box by author, from Box 6.7 in LeMay 2006: 234.

On May 11, 2005, President Bush signed into law the Real ID Act (P.L.-109–13; 119 Stat. 302). It was enacted by a vote of 368 to 58 in the House and 100 to 0 in the Senate. It modified national law to better ensure the authentication and issuance procedures for state driver's licenses, identification cards, and several related issues pertaining to application for asylum and deportation for terrorism activity, and included provisions waiving laws that would interfere with the construction of physical barriers (a fence) at the borders. All 50 states requested extensions for the May 11, 2008, compliance deadline, and by October 2009, 25 states approved bills to not participate in the program. Critics opposed the Real ID act as unnecessary intrusion of the civil rights and a constitutional violation of the Tenth Amendment. The act remains highly controversial, and several bills have been introduced since 2008 to amend it or repeal it (LeMay 2013, v. 3: 13).

In March 2006, Congress enacted a law renewing, with very minor amendments aimed at some civil liberty concerns, the USA Patriot Act, a law referred to as Patriot Act II. Changing regulations making it easier for the DHS to remove aliens contributed to a substantial increase in the number of aliens expelled, or who voluntarily departed since 2002. While there were a total of 101,205 removals from 1961 to 1970, and 1,334,528 voluntary departures, from 1971 to 1980 those increased to 240,217 formal removals and 7,246,812 voluntary departures; and from 1981 to 2000 those numbers increased to 939,749 formal removals and 13,587,684 voluntary departures (Ibid.; Annual Report, BCIS, at https://www.dhs.gov/immigration-statistics/special-reports/legal-immigration).

On October 26, 2006, President Bush signed the Secure Fence Act (P.L. 1 109–367). The bill passed the House by a vote of 238 to 138, and the Senate by a vote of 90–18, on mostly partisan voting, with Republicans supporting the bill and Democrats opposing it. The act approved $1.2 billion to construct a 700-mile bollard type security fence along the Mexican-U.S. border. Critics contend it will take $4.8 billion more to actually build the fence along the 2,000-mile border with Mexico. They also argued it would strain U.S.-Mexico relations, disrupt the environment and wildlife, increase the danger of immigrants trying to cross, and be ineffectual in stopping illegal immigration. By 2009, 613 miles of fencing and vehicle barriers were constructed from California to Texas, and in 2010, a bill to require the DHS to build another 35.3 miles was introduced (LeMay 2013, v. 3: 13).

In 2008, the newly elected president Barack Obama's administration began a surge in the use of expedited removals to deport unauthorized immigrants under the Trafficking Victims Protection Reauthorization Act (TVPRA). The Victims of Trafficking and Violence Protection Act (P.L. 106–386), the Trafficking Victims Protection Reauthorization Act of 2003 (H.R. 2620), the Trafficking Victims Protection Reauthorization Act of 2005 (H.R. 972), and the Trafficking Victims Protection Reauthorization Act of 2008 (H.R. 7311) provide the tools to combat trafficking in persons both worldwide and domestically. These acts authorized the establishment of G/TIP and the President's Interagency Task Force to Monitor and Combat Trafficking in Persons to assist in the coordination of anti-trafficking efforts (U.S. Laws on Trafficking in Persons).

In 2009, President Obama used his executive action authority to mitigate certain provisions of the 1996 Illegal Immigration Reform and Immigrant Responsibility Act (IIRIRA), the law enacted during President Clinton's administration, which had some 60 provisions to "crack down" on illegal immigrants but applied some of its provisions to lawful permanent resident (LPR) aliens as well.

In 2009, the state of Arizona passed a highly controversial law mandating that state and local police demand anyone suspected of being illegal to show documents to prove their legal status. As anticipated, in 2010, in *Arizona v. U.S.* (132 S. Ct. 2492), the Supreme Court ruled the Arizona law unconstitutional, basically for the same legal rationale it held Proposition 187 unconstitutional.

Democrats in Congress introduced a number of measures to establish a path to citizenship for unauthorized immigrants that they referred to as "earned legalization."

Progressives in Congress have been proposing a bill annually since 2001 for enactment of what became known as the Dream Act (Development, Relief, and Education of Alien Minors). The most recent bill was reintroduced into the Senate on May 11, 2011, by then Senate Majority Leader Harry Reid (D-NV). Progressives have introduced bills to adjust to temporary, conditional legal status to what became known as the "Dreamers." These were unauthorized immigrants brought to the United States as children. All such legalization measures were castigated by the Republicans in Congress as "amnesty," and were blocked and died in Congress. Perhaps somewhat ironically, the "fiscally conservative Republicans" oppose the bills despite a Congressional Budget Office estimate that the act would reduce deficits by $1.4 billion over the 2011–2020 period, and increase government revenues by a projected $2.3 billion over 10 years. A UCLA study estimates that if enacted the Dream Act would generate between $1.4 and $3.6 trillion in taxable income over a 40-year period (LeMay 2013, v. 3: 16).

Table 7.1 shows the trends in removals of unauthorized immigrants from 2001 to 2013, rising over those years from slightly more than 387,000 in 2011 to more than 438,000 in 2013.

Another development that challenged immigration policy making was a trend in the arrival of alien children from Central America who came to

Table 7.1   Trends in Removals, 2011–2013

Year	2011(%)	2012(%)	2013(%)
Expedited	122,236 (31.6)	163,308 (39.0)	193,032 (44.0)
Reinstatements	124,784 (32.2)	146,044 (34.9)	170,247 (38.8)
All Others	140,114 (36.2)	109,045 (26.1)	75,142 (17.1)
TOTAL	387,134 (100)	418,397 (100)	438,421 (100)

Source: DHS, Yearbook of Immigration Statistics, 2013. http://www.dhs.gov/sites/default/files/publications/ois_enforcement_ar_2013.pdf.

Table 7.2   Unaccompanied Alien Children Encountered, by Fiscal Year, Country-of-Origin, 2009–2014

Country	2009	2010	2011	2012	2013	2014
El Salvador	1,221	1,910	1,394	3,314	5,990	16,404
Guatemala	1,115	1,517	1,565	3,835	8,068	17,057
Honduras	968	1,017	974	2,997	6,747	18,244
Mexico	16,114	13,724	11,768	13,974	17,240	15,634
TOTAL	19,418	18,168	15,701	24,120	38,045	67,339

Source: Table by author; data from https://www.cbp.gov/newsroom/stats/southwest-border-unaccompanied-alien-children/fy-2014. Accessed March 10, 2015.

the United States unaccompanied by adults. These rose from more than 19,000 in 2009 to more than 67,000 in 2014. That trend is detailed in Table 7.2.

Frustrated by the stalemate in Congress and its inability to do anything about the problems, in 2012 President Obama took executive action granting temporary, conditional legal status to the Dreamer children. The Deferred Action for Childhood Arrivals (DACA) and the Deferred Action for Parents of Americans and Lawful Permanent Residents (DAPA) were executive actions projected to affect 4.4 million persons. In 2013, with the surge of arrivals of children unaccompanied by adults, President Obama granted "Temporary Protected Status" to about 5,000 such children for whom it was deemed too unsafe to return to their country of origin.

On February 17, 2015, Andrew Hanen, the U.S. district judge for southern Texas, placed an injunction of the Obama administration's implementation of DAPA or expanded DACA, ordering the DHS to cease accepting applications until a court issues an order that allows the initiatives to go forward. Deferred action is an administrative relief from deportation that has been around for a long time. The president's executive action authorizes the DHS to allow certain non-U.S. citizens to remain in the United States temporarily, granted on a case-by-case basis.

DACA applicants, the "Dreamer Children," must have come before their 16th birthday, lived in the United States continuously since January 1, 2010, be present in the United States on June 15, 2012, and every day since, have graduated or obtained a GED certificate, or be in school on the date the person submits an application, and pay an application fee of $465, which consists of a $380 fee for employment authorization, and an $85 fee for fingerprints.

Persons eligible for the DAPA program include: a parent of a U.S. citizen or lawful permanent resident; have continuously lived in the United States since January 1, 2010, have been present in the United States on November 20, 2014, not have a lawful immigration status as of November 20, 2014—meaning one entered the country undocumented, or if lawfully entered, must have stayed beyond the expiration of the temporary visa, and must not have been convicted of certain criminal offenses, including felonies and some misdemeanors (National Immigration Law Center).

On February 18, 2015, President Obama granted an expansion of DACA by executive action. The expanded DACA had no age cap, changed the years lived in the United States to since January 1, 2010, granted three year DACA work grants (rather than two years), allowed application for DACA and for Advanced Parole status at the same time, and continued the guidelines of DACA previously noted, and that the individual posed no threat to national security or public safety (United We Dream).

Legislative Proposals Introduced and Pending Since 2013

The two major political parties have been essentially deadlocked in taking legislative action since President Obama's reelection in 2012. Republicans insist on introducing bills that are piecemeal rather than comprehensive approaches, that is, they are only "strengthening border control" proposals. Republicans are adamant in opposing any proposal they deem as "amnesty." The Democrats keep proposing (as they have nearly every year since 2001) Dreamer bills. They insist on a comprehensive immigration reform approach. They respond that "earned legalization" is not amnesty, and oppose any measure proposed by Republicans that does not include some sort of earned legalization provision and a pathway to citizenship for the 10 million or so unauthorized immigrants currently residing in the United States.

The closest Congress came to enacting a comprehensive immigration reform bill was in 2013 when the Senate passed S.744, a measure that had some bipartisan support. It was blocked in the House of Representatives. The official title of S.744 is the Border Security and Economic Opportunity Act of 2013. It was a comprehensive approach measure crafted by a bipartisan group of senators who became known as the "Gang of 8": Chuck Schumer (D-NY), Dick Durbin (D-IL), Robert Menendez (D-NJ), and Michael Bennett (D-CO); Lindsay Graham (R-SC), Marco Rubio (R-FL), John McCain (R-AZ), and Jeff Flake (R-AZ). The Senate Judiciary voted the bill out of committee and to the floor by a vote of 13–3 on

June 11, 2013. On the senate floor, the bill passed on June 27, by a vote of 68–32. All 54 Democrats voted for the bill, along with 14 Republicans. The 14 Republicans who voted for cloture for S.744 were the following: Jeff Chiese (NJ), Susan Collins (ME), Bob Corker (TN), Jeff Flake (AZ), Lindsay Graham (SC), Lamar Alexander (TN), Kelly Ayotte (NH), Marco Rubio (FL), Orin Hatch (Utah), Dean Heller (NV), Johen Hoeven (ND), Mark Kirk (IL), John McCain (AZ), and Lisa Murkowski (Alaska).

The major provisions of S.744 are a 13-year path-to-citizenship, a fine and the legalizing immigrant must pay back taxes owed, stronger border control provisions, a computerized oversight system regarding temporary visas to find and deport visa overstayers, and an expanded guest-worker program.

The House of Representatives had its version of a comprehensive immigration reform bill introduced in 2013 as well. As was the case in the Senate, the House bill was crafted and advocated in the House Judiciary Committee by the House "Gang of 8" members: Representative Xavier Becera (D-TX), John Carter (R-TX), Mario Diaz Belart (R-FL), Luis Gutierrez (D-IL), Sam Johnson (R-TX), Raul Labrado (R-ID), Zoe Lofgren (D-CA), and John Yarmouth (D-KY). They were unable to get the bill out of committee and to the House floor, and then Speaker John Boehner (R-OH) announced he would not bring any such bill to a floor vote, so the measure died in committee.

The major provisions of the House bill for comprehensive immigration reform had a few differences with the Senate-passed version. The House bill contained a 15-year path to citizenship, and unauthorized immigrants approved for the program would be given a work authorization card for 10 years. It strengthened border control with provisions even tougher than the Senate version. It expanded the border fence and increased funding for electronic surveillance. Its program for computerized oversight of visas to control overstayers has a timetable of implementation even faster than that passed by the Senate. The House version has a less expansive guest-worker program than the Senate-passed version.

Also in 2013, Senator David Vitter (R-LA) and Representative Steve King (R-IA) introduced a bill to end birthright citizenship to persons born in the United States of parents who are in illegal status. Many legal scholars contend it would be ruled unconstitutional short of a constitutional amendment approach.

Senator John Cornyn (R-TX) and Representative Henry Cuellar (D-TX) introduced a bill, the Humane Act, to amend section 235 of the Trafficking Victims Protection Reauthorization Act (TVPRA) of 2013

(H.R. 898, 113th Congress, 2013–2014, https://www.congress.gov/bill/113th-congress/house-bill/898. Accessed December 27, 2016). It would have eased the deportation of women who were victims of human trafficking.

In 2014, Representative Matt Salmon (R-AZ) introduced the Expedited Family Reunification Act of 2014. It allowed all Unaccompanied by Adult Children (UAC) to be treated equally under the TVPRA, removing any distinction between contiguous and noncontiguous nations of origin (i.e., Mexico versus the other Central American nations), allowing for all UAC to be processed as Mexican children are now processed, and be subject to immediate voluntary return.

Senators Jeff Flake and John McCain introduced the CREST Act, which requires mandatory detention, use of asylum judges (and authorizes the addition of 100 temporary immigration judges), and increases the number of refugee visas to 5,000 each for El Salvador, Honduras, and Guatemala. Similarly, in 2014, in the House, Representative John Carter (R-TX) introduced the Protection of Children Act—which treats all UAC equally under TVPRA.

Representative Bob Goodlatte (R-VA) and Jason Chaffetz (R-UT) introduced the Asylum Reform and Border Protection Act placing all UAC under expanded expedited removal. Senator Mike Johanns (R-NE) introduced the UAC State Notification Act, and Representative Steve King (R-IA) introduced a resolution calling on states along the southern border to deploy national guard troops to secure the border. Senator Ted Cruz (R-TX) introduced a bill to stop the DACA program.

In 2015, House Republicans on the Homeland Security Committee introduced the "Secure Our Borders First Act." On March 3, 2015, after maneuvering to block funding the DHS for several months unless a provision to defund President Obama's executive actions on immigration were included, the House passed a "clean" bill to fund the DHS, approving a Senate-passed version, by a vote of 257 to 167, with all Democrats and some Republicans voting for the "clean" DHS funding bill.

President Trump and the Attack on Muslims and Sanctuary Cities

The 2016 elections proved to be a surprising, and sweeping, election victory for the Republicans. Although the polls preceding the election projected a win of more than 300 ECV and a 2–3 percent margin in the popular vote to Democrat Hillary Clinton, in fact she lost the ECV to Republican Donald Trump, who won just over 300 ECVs, as detailed in Table 7.3. Trump's "outsider" image carried the election, despite—or

Table 7.3   Highlights of the 2016 Elections

Electoral College Vote: Clinton/Keane, 232; Trump/Pence, 306

Popular Vote: Clinton/Keane, 65,788,583, 48.3%; Trump/Pence, 62,955,363, 46.2%

Some Key State Races:

Arizona: Clinton/Keane, 45.4%; Trump/Pence, 49.5%

Colorado: Clinton/Keane, 47.3%; Trump/Pence, 44.4%

Florida: Clinton/Keane, 47.8%; Trump/Pence, 49.1%

Georgia: Clinton/Keane, 46.5%; Trump/Pence, 51.3%

Iowa: Clinton/Keane, 42.2%; Trump/Pence, 51.8%

Michigan: Clinton/Keane, 47.3%; Trump/Pence, 47.6%

Nevada: Clinton/Keane, 47.6%; Trump/Pence, 45.5%

North Carolina: Clinton/Keane, 46.7%; Trump/Pence, 50.5%

Ohio: Clinton/Keane, 43.5%; Trump/Pence, 52.1%

Pennsylvania: Clinton/Keane, 47.6%; Trump/Pence, 48.5%

Utah: Clinton/Keane, 27.8%; Trump/Pence, 45.9%

Virginia: Clinton/Keane, 49.9%; Trump/Pence, 45.0%

Wisconsin: Clinton/Keane, 47.0%; Trump/Pence, 47.8%

Gender: Male, Clinton/Keane, 41%; Trump/Pence, 52%

Female, Clinton/Keane, 54%; Trump/Pence, 41%

Age: 18–29, Clinton/Keane, 55%; Trump/Pence, 36%

30–44, Clinton/Keane, 51%; Trump/Pence, 41%

45–64, Clinton/Keane, 44%; Trump/Pence, 52%

65+, Clinton/Keane, 45%; Trump/Pence, 52%

Senate Seats: Democrats, 48; Republicans, 52

House Seats: Democrats, 194; Republicans, 241

Gubernatorial Wins: Democrats: WA, MT, OR, WV, DE, NC

Republicans: VT, NH, ND, IN, UT, MO

State Houses and Legislatures: Republicans hold a majority control of 67 chambers; and total control (governor and both houses of the state legislature) in 24 states.

Source: Table by author; data from www.cnn.com/election/results. Accessed December 27, 2016.)

perhaps in part because of—his unconventional campaign style and strategy. His openly anti-immigrant rhetoric, his proposals to totally ban Muslim immigrants, to "build a border wall and make Mexico pay for it," and his populist-nationalist policy positions which amounted to a somewhat hostile takeover of the Republican Party for the party establishment, and a 180 degree pivot from the policies of President Obama, appealed to enough voters in the key swing states that Trump won office despite losing the popular vote by nearly three million votes.

President Trump's cabinet selections are in line with the "Fortress America" approach to immigration policy, and his nationalist-populist campaign rhetoric. He selected retired general John Kelly to lead the DHS, and billionaire businessman (Exxon Corporation) Rex Tillerson as secretary of state. Indeed, his cabinet picks are an array of millionaires, billionaires, fellow outsiders with little or no government experience, and a few politicians who oppose the very agencies they were tapped to lead, like former governor of Texas Rick Perry for the Department of Energy, Representative Tom Price, one of the most outspoken critics of the Affordable Care Act, to lead Health and Human Services, staunch charter school and school voucher advocate, Betsy DeVos, to head the Department of Education, Dr. Ben Carson to lead the Department of Housing and Urban Development, and Andy Puzder to lead the Department of Labor.

As the new president, Donald Trump, in his first week in office, issued executive orders to rescind the executive actions of President Obama, DACA and DAPA, to fund the building of a wall along the border with Mexico, although not to make Mexico pay for it (that will fall to American taxpayers). He ordered to cut all federal funds going to U.S. cities that maintain "sanctuary city" status. He issued a six-month ban on all refugees from Syria, and rescinded all visas for immigrants from Syria, Iraq, Iran, Libya, Somalia, Sudan, and Yemen. On signing the ban, he charged the Department of State to develop new, aggressive vetting measures. He renewed his pledge to create a "deportation force" to immediately begin deporting unauthorized immigrants, starting with "criminal illegal aliens." For dramatic political symbolic effect, President Trump signed the executive orders at the DHS.

Conclusion

The decade 2001–2010 saw the greatest number of arrivals of legal immigrants in American history, 10,487,131, for an annual average of 1,480,000. Despite the crackdowns and increased restrictions discussed in this chapter, illegal immigration, complex refugee issues, and the continued pressure for high levels of legal immigration to the United States make immigration policy making more complex and less predictable. The total Hispanic population in the United States has continued to surge, as has illegal immigration. The current high levels of both legal and illegal immigration, which have been rising exponentially since 1985, are resulting in a demographic shift that is remarkable. In 1900, when the population of the United States was about 76 million, there were slightly more than one-half million Hispanics. The Census Bureau estimates that by 2050, 25 percent of the projected population of 438 million will be of Hispanic descent, a shift fueled by immigration from Mexico, Central America, and Latin America, and by their high birth rates compared to that of the general population. The Census Bureau estimates that 82 percent of the increase in population between 2010 and 2050 will be from immigration. The Hispanic population will rise to 47 percent of the total U.S. population by 2050. Asian population is projected to triple by 2050.

The economic impact of immigration—whether on balance immigrants are a cost or a benefit—continues to be controversial, with very different assessments depending upon how costs and benefits are measured. Proponents for comprehensive immigration reform advocate a large-scale temporary worker program, increased funding and staffing of ICE and the DHS, coupled with increased expedited removal and better technology to track and control immigrants and visitors.

As with their economic impact, the social impact of immigrants is also highly controversial and debated. Nearly every new wave of immigrants has aroused fears that they could not or should not be assimilated, and that they were adversely affecting American society and culture. That remains the case today. After 9/11, suspicions about immigrants of Middle Eastern origin, especially of Muslims, rose dramatically. Mexican immigrants are also perceived as incorporating more slowly and acquire English fluency more slowly than do non-Mexican immigrants. Moreover, the politics of immigration policy-making reform is complicated by the increasing spread of immigrants to more urban areas within 30 states. The shift in the nations of origin since 2000 is having profound effects on a host of related public policy areas (Barone 2013; Daniels 2005; Motomura 2006; Navarro 2005; Zuniga and Hernandez-Leon 2005).

There is great political controversy about the health-care and welfare impacts of continued high levels of immigration, especially of undocumented immigration.

Federal sanctions against employers who hire illegal immigrants (undocumented or visa overstayers) are at best poorly enforced. Expectations among persons in Mexico and Central America that asylum or some sort of amnesty will be granted results in some 150,000 to 200,000 undocumented Mexicans arriving annually. Tighter border controls since 9/11 seem to have done little to stall the flow of undocumented immigrants, particularly those from Central America, who are more driven by push factors.

The terrorist attacks of 9/11 ushered in a new era in immigration policy making—the Storm Door era. The unprecedented speed with which the INS was dissolved and the USA Patriot Act and the act creating the DHS were passed resulted in unanticipated consequences for policy implementation.

A pattern of groupthink behavior in the policy adoption stage, coupled with the very massiveness of the new department comprised by its merging of 22 agencies, resulted in obvious and significant management problems.

The dissolving of the INS and establishment of the DHS interweaves issues of immigration and national security policy making. Immigration control measures continue to remain on the agenda of Congress. Political stalemate and partisan gridlock, however, have stymied efforts for enacting comprehensive immigration reform. Republican efforts at piecemeal reform, stressing only the border control approach, are blocked by Democrats insistent on a comprehensive reform approach and some sort of earned legalization and a path to citizenship for the 10 million or so estimated population of unauthorized immigrants living in the United States. Democratic efforts to enact reform are stymied by Republican insistence that no amnesty program be enacted. The Republican Party sweep of the national government offices in the 2016 election will likely end the gridlock and result in enactment of the "hardening of the border" approach to immigration policy.

High levels of concern—sometimes to the point of hysteria—over international terrorism and terrorist cells coming to the United States smuggled in among the undocumented flow have propelled efforts to enact a Fortress America approach to immigration policy making.

Frustrated with the inability of Congress to enact comprehensive immigration reform of an immigration system so obviously broken and out of control, President Obama used his executive action authority over immigration implementation to change immigration policy at the margins. His actions pitted the executive branch against the legislative branch and quickly involved federal court action on the issue. Federal courts have also held unconstitutional several state actions driven by frustration with the perceived failure of the federal government to control the border in states most impacted by the illegal immigration problem. Federalism in immigration policy making is evidencing a dynamism and variety of state actions both pro- and con-immigrants and immigrant rights (Suro 2015).

President Trump, during his first year in office, initiated what can be characterized as a 270 degree change in policy from that of the Obama administration. Despite his often stated criticism of President Obama for using executive action during the 2016 presidential campaign, President Trump did so exclusively through executive orders and his presidential appointment powers and executive ability to change administrative procedures of the DOJ and of the DHS.

On January 21, 2017, President Trump's nominee for Secretary of Homeland Security, John F. Kelly, was sworn into office. Kelly was a retired Marine Corp General. Since he was retired less than one year, the U.S. Senate gave him a special waiver to serve in the cabinet and confirmed him on January 20, 2017, as the fifth Secretary of Homeland Security (https://www.dhs.gov/secretary. Accessed July 10, 2017).

On January 25, 2017, President Trump issued an executive order to build a wall on the U.S.-Mexico border. The action also ordered the immediate detainment and deportation of illegal immigrants and requires state and federal authorities to tally how much foreign aid they are sending to Mexico, and orders the U.S. Customs and Border Protection agency to hire 5,000 additional border patrol agents. Despite his often made campaign promise that Mexico would be made to pay for the wall, the executive order has only U.S. taxpayers footing the bill to fund construction of the wall. Since construction of a border wall of hundreds to more than 1,000 miles would need congressional allocation of massive (billions) of dollars to fund the wall, the executive order is for a "pilot" wall program, funded by shifting a few million dollars in the existing budget (White House. Accessed July 15, 2017).

On January 25, President Trump signed another executive order, titled "Enhancing the Public Safety in the Interior of the United States," cutting funding for "sanctuary cities" (https://www.whitehouse.gov/presidential-actions/executive-order-enhancing-public-safety-interior-united-states. Accessed July 15, 2017). The city of San Francisco immediately filed a suit in federal court claiming the order is unconstitutional.

On January 27, President Trump issued the first immigration "travel ban" that targeted seven Muslim-majority nations (Iran, Iraq, Libya, Somalia, Sudan, Syria, and Yemen). The ban blocked entry to the United States of Syrian refugees and temporarily suspended entry to other refugees and citizens from those nations for admission to the United States for 90 days. The ban was justified as necessary in order to provide the administration with sufficient time to develop new "extreme vetting" of immigrants from those seven countries (White House. Accessed July 15, 2017).

On January 31, President Trump fired acting attorney general Sally Yates for refusing to defend in federal court his immigration travel ban order. AAG Yates had argued that the ban was unconstitutional and refused to implement the ban. On February 3, U.S. district judge James Robart of the 9th Circuit Court of Appeals in Seattle, Washington, an appointee of President George W. Bush, ruled that the ban was unconstitutional and halted enforcement of the ban by the Trump administration. The travel ban barred hundreds of refugees seeking entrance into the United States (Brunner, Lee, and Gutman, February 3, 2017).

That judicial ruling prompted President Trump to issue a second immigration travel ban by executive order on March 6, 2017. The second order banned immigrants from six Muslim countries (dropping Iraq from the list) and suspended all refugees for 120 days. The revised order cut the number of refugees that would be accepted in 2017 by more than half—from 110,000 to 50,000. Refugees from Syria were no longer banned indefinitely. The new ban revised the language that favored religious minorities, which President Trump had stated would apply to persecuted Christians from the Middle East.

On March 15, U.S. district judge Derrick Watson, of Hawaii, put an emergency hold on the ban. Hours later, in a separate judicial case, U.S. District Court Judge Theodore Chuang, of Maryland, issued a nationwide preliminary injunction prohibiting the revised travel ban from taking effect. The ban stipulated guidance for agencies to implement the new travel ban. With the judicial ruling placing an injunction on the ban, President Trump and AG Sessions vowed to appeal the decision to the U.S. Supreme Court ("Trump Travel Ban"; Kendall and Meckler 2017).

In May, President Trump's DHS established an office called the Victims of Immigration Crime Enforcement (VOICE). In June, the administration (particularly the DOJ) struggled with language to legally define what exactly constitutes a "sanctuary city" that would thereby be denied federal funds.

On June 21, 2017, the Supreme Court partially upheld Trump's second executive travel ban and announced it would hold full oral arguments on the ban in the fall session, 2017. However, the ruling exempted from the ban persons with previously approved visas. It further exempted persons with a "bona fide" connection (e.g., "close family member") to a U.S. citizen or permanent resident alien (i.e., a green-card holder) (JD Supra).

Immediately after the Supreme Court ruling, the Trump administration issued guidelines as to what constituted "close family ties," which excluded grandmothers and other extended family relatives. In July, a Hawaii judge ruled that grandparents could not be excluded. On July 15, 2017, U.S. district judge Derrick Watson stated: "Common sense, for instance, dictates that close family members may be defined to include grandparents. Indeed, grandparents are the epitome of close family members." State Department counselor officials had earlier revised their first guidelines that had excluded fiancés, now allowing them to obtain visas. Attorney General Jeff Sessions stated that the Justice Department would reluctantly return again to the Supreme Court and filed a "notice of appeal" (*Washington Post*).

The near future of immigration policy making in the Storm Door era portends federal court action to resolve conflicts between the national and state levels of government, and between the executive and legislative branches. No comprehensive immigration reform at the national level will be politically possible given the 2016 election results, with the Republicans retaining control of both chambers of Congress. Moreover, President Donald Trump's proposed ban on refugees and immigrants from six mostly Muslim nations, increased deportations, the executive orders to fund building a wall on the southern border, and similar "border control" provisions and approaches echo the rhetoric and policy positions of the highly restrictive "Pet Door era," as discussed in Chapter 4.

While there is ample evidence that the "border control approach" alone will not substantially change the push pressures sending annually hundreds of thousands of Mexican and Central Americans, as well as many Asians, to the borders to attempt entry, legal or illegal, it is clear that the demographic shifts resulting from immigration, both legal and unauthorized, will have profound impact on the culture, economy, and politics for decades to come. Those trends will undoubtedly further impact the national electoral fortunes of the Democratic and Republican Parties.

References

Barone, Michael. 2013. *Shaping Our Nation: How Surges in Migration Transformed America and Its Politics.* New York: Crown Forum.

Birkland, Thomas. March 2004. "The World Changed Today: Agenda-Setting and Policy Change in the Wake of 9/11 Terrorist Attacks." *The Review of Policy Research* 21(2): 179–201.

Brunner, Jim, Jessica Lee, and David Gutman. "Judge in Seattle Halts Trump's Immigration Order Nationwide; White House Vows Fight." *The Seattle Times.* February 3, 2017. https://www.seattletimes.com/seattle-news/politics/federal-judge-in-seattle-halts-trumps-immigration-order.

Center for Disease Control. https://www.cdc.gov/anthrax/index.html. Accessed December 28, 2016.

Chen, Zenglo, Robert Lawson, Lawrence Gordon, and Barbara McIntosh. Fall 1996. "Groupthink: Deciding with the Leader and the Devil." *The Psychological Record* 46(4): 581–591.

Clarke, Richard. 2004. *Against All Enemies: Inside America's War on Terror.* New York: The Free Press.

Commission Report-9/11. n.d. *Final Report of the National Commission on Terrorist Attacks on the United States.* New York: W. W. Norton.

Cooper, Barry. 2004. *New Political Religion, or an Analysis of Modern Terrorism.* Columbia: University of Missouri Press.

Crotty, William. August 2003. "Presidential Policymaking in Crisis Situations: 9/11 and Its Aftermath." *Policy Studies Journal* 31(3): 451–465.

Daniels, Roger. 2005. *Guarding the Golden Doors.* New York: Hill and Wang.

Demmer, Valerie. January–February 2002. "Civil Liberties and Homeland Security." *The Humanist* 62(1): 7–10.

Department of Homeland Security. 2002. "HR 5005: To Establish the Department of Homeland Security, and for Other Purposes." www.gpo.gov/fdsys/pkg/BILLS-107hr5005rh/content-detail.html.

Department of Homeland Security. 2013. *Characteristics of H-1B Specialty Occupation Workers: 2012 Annual Report.* Washington, DC: Department of Homeland Security.

Department of Justice. 2002. *Follow-Up Report on INS Efforts to Improve the Control of Nonimmigrant Overstays, Report No. 1–2002–006.* Washington, DC: U.S. Government Printing Office.

Dixon, Thomas. January–Februry 2002. "The Rise of Complex Terrorism." *Foreign Policy* 81(1): 53–58.

Electronic Privacy Information Center. http://www.epic.org/privacy/terrorism/hr3162.html.

Etzioni, Amitai, and Jason H. Marsch, eds. 2003. *Rights v. Public Safety after 9/11: America in the Age of Terrorism.* Lanham, MD: Rowman and Littlefield.

Flynn, Stephen. 2004. *American the Vulnerable: How Our Government Is Failing to Protect Us from Terrorism.* New York: Harper Collins.

General Accounting Office. 2004. *Overstay Tracking: A Key Component of Homeland Security and a Layered Defense. GAO-04–82.* Washington, DC: U.S. Government Printing Office.

Information Plus. 2006. *Immigration and Illegal Aliens: Blessing or Burden?* Farmington Hills, MI: Thompson/Gale.

Janis, Irving. 1982. *Groupthink*, 2nd edition. Boston: Houghton-Mifflin.

JD Supra. https://www.jdsupra.com/legalnews/muslim-country-travel-ban-upheld-in-part-70428/.

Kendall, Brent, and Laura Meckler. "Trump Appeals Latest Travel-Ban Ruling." *The Wall Street Journal.* 2017. https://www.wsj.com/articles/trump-appeals-latest-travel-ban-ruling-1500072777?mod-ex_picks&ex_naySource=ex_picks&.

Kowert, Paul. 2002. *Groupthink as Deadlock: When Do Leaders Learn from Their Advisors?* Albany: SUNY Press.

Krauss, Elishia. 2003. "Building a Bigger Bureaucracy: What the Department of Homeland Security Won't Do." *The Public Manager* 32(1): 57–59.

Krauss, Erich, and Alex Pacheco. 2004. *On the Line: Inside the U.S. Border Patrol.* New York: Citadel Press.

Lehrer, Eli. Summer 2004. "The Homeland Security Bureaucracy." *Public Interest* 1156: 71–86.

LeMay, Michael. 2004. *U.S. Immigration: A Reference Handbook.* Santa Barbara, CA: ABC-CLIO.

LeMay, Michael. 2006. *Guarding the Gates: Immigration and National Security.* Westport, CT: Praeger Security International.

LeMay, Michael. 2007. *Illegal Immigration: A Reference Handbook*, 1st edition. Santa Barbara, CA: ABC-CLIO.

LeMay, Michael, ed. 2013. *Transforming America: Perspectives on U.S. Immigration*, vol. 3. Santa Barbara, CA: ABC-CLIO.

Light, Paul C. 2002. *Homeland Security Will Be Hard to Manage.* Washington, DC: Brookings Institute's Center for Public Service.

Mitchell, Kenneth. Spring 2003. "The Other Homeland Security Threat: Bureaucratic Haggling." *The Public Manager* 32(7): 15–19.

Motomura, Hiroshi. 2006. *Americans in Waiting: The Lost Story of Immigration and Citizenship in the United States.* New York: Oxford University Press.

National Immigration Law Center. www.nilc.org/issues/daca.

Navarro, Armando. 2005. *Mexican Political Experience in Occupied Aztlan.* Lanham, MD: Altamura Press.

O'Beirne, Kate. August 25, 2002. "Bureaucratic Nightmare on the Way?" *National Review*, Opinion Page, in *The Press Enterprise.* San Bernardino, CA: D-1.

Platt, Tony, and Cecilia O'Leary. 2004. "Patriot Acts." *Social Justice* 30(1): 5–22.

Reich, Robert B. August 2004. "A Failure of Intelligence." *The American Prospect* 15(8): 72–73.

Relyea, Harold. 2003. "Organizing for Homeland Security." *Presidential Studies Quarterly* 33(3): 602–625.

Roberts, Marta. February 2005. "20–20 Spy Sight." *Security Management* 59(2): 76–80.

Roots, Roger. Spring 2003. "Terrorized into Absurdity: The Creation of the Transportation Security Administration." *Independent Review* 7(4): 503–518.

Secretary of Homeland Security. https://www.dhs.gov/secretary/.

Sneider, Daniel. September 10, 2004. "The Groupthink Failure: A Centralized Bureaucracy Won't Improve Intelligence." *Knight Ridder/Tribune News Service*, 4246.

Suro, Roberto. 2015. "California Dreaming: The New Dynamism in Immigration Federalism and Opportunities for Inclusion on a Variegated Landscape." *Journal on Migration and Humane Society* 3(1): 1–25.

Torr, James D., ed. 2004. *Homeland Security.* San Diego: Greenhaven Press.

"Trump Travel Ban Blocked Nationwide by Federal Judges in Hawaii, Maryland." National Public Radio. https://www.npr.org/sections/thetwoway/2017/03/15/520171478/trump-travel-ban-blocked-nationwide-by-federal-judges-in-hawaii-and-maryland.

United States Citizenship and Immigration Services. Legal Immigration and Adjustment of Status Report fy2017, Q 4. https://www.dhs.gov/immigration-statistics/special-reports/legal-immigration.

United We Dream. "Breaking: USCIS Just Released Official Details on DACA Expansion! What's New?" https://www.unitedwedream.org/2018/01/uscis-begins-to-accept-daca-renewal-applications-again-what-you-should-know/.

U.S. Customs and Border Protection. https://www.cbp.gov/newsroom/stats/south west-border-unaccompanied-alien-children/fy2014.

U.S. Laws on Trafficking in Persons. http://www.state.gov/j/tip/laws/.

Walcott, Charles E., and Karen Hult. 2003. "The Bush Staff and Cabinet System." *Perspectives on Political Science* 32(3): 150–156.

Washington Post. https://www.washingtonpost.com/world/national-security/judge-rejects-hawaii-bid-to-exempt-grandparents-from-trumps-travel-ban/2017/07/06/8e3a3252-625d-11e7-8adc-fea80e32bf47_story.html.

White House. https://www.whitehouse.gov/presidential-actions/executive-order-pro tecting-nation-foreign-terrorist-entry-united-states/.

White House. https://www.whitehouse.gov/presidential-actions/executive-order-enhancing-public-safety-interior-united-states.

White House. www.whitehouse.gov/presidential-actions/executive-order-border-security-immigration-enforcement-improvements/.

Yount, Lisa, ed. 2004. *Fighting Bioterrorism*. San Diego: Greenhaven Press.

Zuniga, Victor, and Ruben Hernandez-Leon, eds. 2005. *New Destinations: Mexican Immigration in the United States*. New York: Russell Sage.

Bibliography

Ackerman, Alissa, and Rick Furman, eds. *The Criminalization of Immigration: Contexts and Consequences*. Durham, NC: Carolina Academic Press, 2013.

Adamic, Louis. *A Nation of Nations*. New York: Harper Brothers, 1945.

Ahlstrom, Sydney. *A Religious History of the American People*. New Haven, CT: Yale University Press, 1972.

Alexander, Thomas. "Persistent Whiggery in the Confederate South, 1860–1877," *Journal of Southern History* 27, no. 3 (1961): 305–329.

Alienkoff, T. Alexander, and Douglas Klusmeyer, eds. *From Migrants to Citizens: Membership in a Changing World*. Washington, DC: Brookings Institute, 2000.

Allport, Alan, and John Ferguson, eds. *Immigration Policy*, 2nd edition. New York: Chelsea House, 2009.

American Experience. https://www.britannica.com/topic/Know-Nothing-party.

American Experience. www.pbs.org/wgbh/americanexperience/features/timeline/tcrr-timeline.

American Hungarian Federation. www.americanhungarianfederation.org/news_1956_htm.

The American Presidency Project. www.presidency.ucsb.edu.

The American Presidency Project. www.presidency.ucsb/showelection.php?Year.

Americans for Religious Liberty. http://www.arlinc.org/about/history.html.

Anbinder, Tyler. *Nation and Slavery: The Northern Know-Nothing and the Politics of the 1850s*. New York: Oxford University Press, 1992.

Anderson, James. *Public Policymaking*. New York: Holt, Rinehart and Winston, 1979.

Anderson, Stuart. *Immigration*. Westport, CT: Praeger Press, 2010.

Andrews, Anthony. *First Cities*. Washington, DC: Smithsonian Books, 1995.

Archdeacon, Thomas. *Becoming American: An Ethnic History*. New York: Free Press, 1983.

Arnold, Kathleen, ed. *Anti-Immigration in the U.S.: A Historical Encyclopedia*. Westport, CT: Greenwood Press, 2011.

Babcock, Kendrick. *The Scandinavian Element in the United States.* Urbana: University of Illinois Press, 1914.

Bailey, Thomas. *Voices of America.* New York: Free Press, 1976.

Baker, Susan G. *The Cautious Welcome: The Legalization Program of the Immigration Reform and Control Act.* Santa Monica, CA: The Rand Corporation and the Urban Institute, 1990.

Bakken, Gordon, and Alexandra Kindell. *Encyclopedia of Immigration and Migration in the American West.* Los Angeles: Sage Publications, 2006.

Baltzell, E. Digby. 1996. *Puritan Boston and Quaker Philadelphia.* New Brunswick, NJ: Transaction Books.

Barone, Michael. *Shaping Our Nation: How Surges in Migration Transformed America and Its Politics.* New York: Crown Forum, 2013.

Bayor, Ronald. *Neighbors in Conflict.* Baltimore: The Johns Hopkins University Press, 1978.

Beals, Carleton. *Brass Knuckle Crusade.* New York: Hastings House, 1960.

Bean, Frank, George Vernez, and Charles B. Keely. *Opening and Closing the Doors.* Santa Monica, CA, and Washington, DC: The Rand Corporation and the Urban Institute, 1989.

Bennett, Anthony. 2013. *The Race for the White House from Reagan to Clinton: Reforming Old Systems, Building New Coalitions.* New York: Palgrave Macmillan.

Bennett, David. *The Party of Fear: From Nativist Movement to the New Right in American History.* New York: Random House, 1988.

Bennett, Marion. *American Immigration Policy: A History.* Washington, DC: Public Affairs Press, 1963.

Bernard, William, ed. *American Immigration Policy: A Reappraisal.* New York: Harper, 1950.

Bernstein, Richard. *Fragile Glory: A Portrait of France and the French.* New York: Knopf, 1990.

Bibby, John. "Party Organizations, 1946–1996," in *Partisan Approaches to Postwar American Politics.* Edited by Byron Shafer, 142–174. New York: Oxford University Press, 1998.

Billington, Ray. *The Origins of Nativism in the United States, 1800–1844.* New York: Arno Press, 1974.

Billington, Ray. *The Protestant Crusade, 1800–1860.* New York: Macmillan, 1938.

Birkland, Thomas. "The World Changed Today: Agenda-Setting and Policy Changes in the Wake of 9/11 Terrorist Attacks," *The Review of Policy Research* 20, no. 2 (March 21, 2004): 179–201.

Bonomi, Patricia U. 1986. *Under the Cope of Heaven: Religion, Society, and Politics in Colonial America.* New York: Oxford University Press.

Boyton, Linda L. *The Plain People: An Ethnography of the Holdeman Mennonites.* Salem, WI: Sheffield, 1986.

Bressaux, Carl. *The "Foreign French": Nineteenth Century French Immigration to Louisiana.* Lafayette Center for Louisiana Studies, University of Southwestern Louisiana Press, 1990.

Brewer, Stuart. *Borders and Bridges*. Westport, CT: Praeger Press, 2006.

Brinks, Herbert. *Dutch Immigrant Voices, 1850–1930*. Ithaca, NY: Cornell University, 1995.

British Broadcasting Corporation. www.bbc.co.uk/religion/religions/santeria.

Brotherton, David, and Philip Kretsedemas, eds. *Keeping Out the Others: A Critical Introduction*. New York: Columbia University Press, 2008.

Brown, Thomas. *Irish-American Nationalism*. New York: J.P. Lippincott, 1966.

Brubaker, William Roger, ed. *Immigration and the Politics of Citizenship in Europe and North America*. New York: University Press of America, 1989.

Brunet-Jailly, Emmanuel, ed. *Border Disputes: A Global Encyclopedia*. Westport, CT: Greenwood Press, 2015.

Bryne-Hessick, Carisa, and Gabriel Chin, eds. *Strange Neighbors: The Role of States in Immigration Policy*. New York: New York University Press, 2014.

Bugelski, B. R. "Assimilation through Intermarriage," *Social Forces* 40 (1961): 148–153.

Bureau of the Census. *2000 Profile of Social Characteristics*. Washington, DC. Available at: http://www.census.gov/.

Burgess, Thomas. *Greeks in America*. Boston: Sherman, French & Company, 1913.

Burr, Clinton Stoddard. *America's Race Heritage*. New York: National Historical Society, 1922.

Butler, Jon. *Religion in Colonial America*. New York: Oxford University Press, 2006.

Byrd, James P. *Sacred Scriptures, Sacred Wars: The Bible and the American Revolution*. New York: Oxford University Press, 2013.

Byrne-Hessick, Carissa, and Gabriel J. Chin, eds. *Strange Neighbors: The Role of the States in Immigration Policy*. New York: New York University Press, 2014.

Calavita, Kitty. *Inside the State: The Bracero Program, Immigration and the INS*. New York: Routledge Press, 1992.

CBS News/New York Time, Exit Polls, November 9, 1980.

Central Pacific Railroad Photographic History Museum. http://www.cprr.org/Museum/.

Chambers, William N., and Walter D. Burnham, eds. *American Party System*. New York: Oxford University Press, 1967.

Chen, Zenglo, Robert Lawson, Lawrence Gordon, and Barbara McIntoch. "Groupthink: Deciding with the Leader and the Devil," *The Psychological Record* 46, no. 4 (Fall 1996): 581–591.

Chiswick, Barry R., ed. *The Gateway: U.S. Immigration and Politics*. Washington, DC: American Enterprise Institute, 1982.

Chomsky, Aviva. *Undocumented: How Immigration Became Illegal*. Boston: Beacon Press, 2014.

Cieslik, Thomas, et al. *Immigration: A Documentary and Reference Guide*. Westport, CT: Greenwood Press, 2008.

Civil War. German. http://www.civilwarhome.com/german/htm.

Civil War. Irish. http://www.civilwarhome.com/irishbri.htm.

Clarke, Richard. *Against All Enemies: Inside America's War on Terror.* New York: Free Press, 2004.

Clarke v. Deckenbeck, 274 S.S. 392, 1917.

Cohen, Steve, Beth Humphries, and Ed Mynott, eds. *From Immigration Controls to Welfare Controls.* New York: Routledge, 2001.

Commission Report-9/11. *Final Report of the National Commission on Terrorist Attacks on the United States.* New York: W. W. Norton, n.d.

Congressional Medal of Honor Society. http://www.cmohs.org/recipients-archive .php.

Congressional Quarterly Almanac, vol. 52. Washington, DC: Congressional Quarterly, 1997.

Congressional Quarterly Weekly Reports, 2595–2598; 2613–2621, October 18, 1986.

Congressional Quarterly Weekly Reports. "Group Analysis of 1968 Presidential Vote" XXVI, no. 48 (November 1968): 3218.

Congressional Record, House. Roll Call Vote #457, H-9800-01.

Congressional Record, House. August 17, 1982, H-10226.

Congressional Record, House. December 18, 1982, H-10319-H-10336.

Converse, Philip E., Warren Miller, Donald E. Stokes. *The American Voter.* Chicago: University of Chicago Press, 1964.

Cooper, Barry. *New Political Religion, or an Analysis of Modern Terrorism.* Columbia: University of Missouri Press, 2004.

Cornelius, W. A., and Ricardo A. Montoya. *America's New Immigration Law: Origins, Rationales and Potential Consequences.* San Diego: Center for U.S./ Mexican Studies, University of California, 1983.

Craig, Richard. *The Bracero Program: Interest Groups and Foreign Policy.* Austin: University of Texas Press, 1971.

Crane, Keith, et al. *The Effects of Employer Sanctions on the Flow of Undocumented Immigrants to the United States.* Santa Monica, CA: The Rand Corporation Press, and the Urban Institute Press, 1990.

Crewdson, John. *The Tarnished Door.* New York: Times Books, 1983.

Crotty, William. "Presidential Policymaking in Crisis Situations: 9/11 and Its Aftermath," *Policy Studies Journal* 31, no 3 (August 2003): 451–465.

Daniels, Roger. *Coming to America: A History of Immigration and Ethnicity in American Life.* New York: Harper, 1990.

Daniels, Roger. *Guarding the Golden Doors.* New York: Hill and Wang, 2005.

Davis, Jerome. *The Russian Immigrant.* New York: Arno Press, 1976.

DeJong, Gerald. *The Dutch in America, 1609–1974.* Boston: Twayne, 1975.

Demmer, Valerie. "Civil Liberties and Homeland Security," *The Humanist* 62, no. 1 (January-February 2002): 7–10.

Department of Homeland Security. *Characteristics of H-1B Specialty Occupation Workers: 2012 Annual Report.* Washington, DC: Department of Homeland Security, 2013.

Department of Homeland Security. "HR 5005: To Establish the Department of Homeland Security, and for Other Purposes." Available at: www.gpo.gov/fdsys/pkg/BILLS-107hr5005rh/content-detail.html.

Department of Justice. *Follow-Up Report on INS Efforts to Improve the Control of Nonimmigrant Overstays, Report No. 1-2002-006.* Washington, DC: U.S. Government Printing Office, 2002.

DeSipio, Louis, and Rodolfo de la Garza. *U.S. Immigration in the 21st Century: Making Americans, Remaking America.* Boulder: Westview Press, 2015.

DHS, Yearbook of Immigration Statistics, 2013. http://www.dhs.gov/sites/default/files/publications/ois_enforcement_ar_2013.pdf.

Dinnerstein, Leonard, and David Reimers. *Ethnic Americans.* New York: Harper and Row, 1975.

Dinnerstein, Leonard, and Frederick Jaher. *Uncertain Americans.* New York: Oxford University Press, 1977.

Divine, Robert A. *American Immigration Policy, 1924–1952.* New Haven, CT: Yale University Press, 1957.

Dixon, Thomas, "The Rise of Complex Terrorism," *Foreign Policy* 81, no. 1 (January-February 2002): 53–58.

Draper, Theodore. *The Roots of American Communism.* New York: Viking Press, 1957.

Draper, Theodore. *American Communism and Soviet Russia.* New York: Viking Press, 1960.

Dreisbach, Daniel. *Thomas Jefferson and the Wall of Separation of Church and State.* New York: New York University Press, 2002.

Duroselle, Jean-Baptiste. *France in the United States: From Beginnings to Present.* Chicago: University of Chicago Press, 1976.

Dye, Thomas. *Understanding Public Policy.* Upper Saddle River, NJ: Prentice Hall, 1992.

Ekberg, Carl. *French Roots in the Illinois County: The Mississippi Frontier in Colonial Time.* Urbana: University of Illinois Press, 1998.

Electronic Privacy Information Center. http://www.epic.org/privacy/terrorism/hr3162.html.

Encyclopedia Britannica. https://www.britannica.com/topic/Know-Nothing-party.

Etzioni, Amitai, and Jason H. Marsch, eds. *Rights vs. Public Safety after 9/11: America in the Age of Terrorism.* Lanham, MD: Rowman and Littlefield, 2003.

Expansion! What's New?" http://www.unitedwedream.org/blog/breaking-daca-expansion-application-accepted-starting-february-18th/.

Fairchild, Henry. *Greek Immigration.* New Haven, CT: Yale University Press, 1911.

Fantel, Hans. *William Penn: Apostle of Dissent.* New York: William Morrow, 1974.

Federal Writers Project. *The Italians of New York.* New York: Arno Press, 1969.

Ferris, Elizabeth G., ed. *Refugees and World Politics.* Westport, CT: Praeger Press, 1985.

Fitzpatrick, Joseph. "The Importance of Community in the Process of Immigration Assimilation," *International Migration Review* 1, no. 1 (January 1966): 6–16.

Flynn, Stephen. *America the Vulnerable: How Our Government Is Failing to Protect Us from Terrorism.* New York: Harper Collins, 2004.

Foner, Nancy. *In a New Land: A Comparative View of Immigration.* New York: New York University Press, 2005.

Fraser, Steve, and Gary Gerstle, eds. *The Rise and Fall of the New Deal Order, 1930–1980.* Princeton, NJ: Princeton University Press, 1990.

French, Laurence A. *Running the Border Gauntlet.* Westport, CT: Praeger Press, 2010.

Friis, Erick, ed. *The Scandinavian Presence in North America.* New York: Harper and Row, 1976.

Fox, Stephen. *Transatlantic.* New York: Perennial/Harper Collins, 2003.

Fuchs, Lawrence. *American Ethnic Politics.* New York: Harper, 1968.

Gallup Poll. 2004. *The Gallop Poll: Public Opinion 2003.* Denver: Scholarly Resources, Inc.

Gans, Judith, et al. *Debates on Immigration.* Los Angeles: Sage Publications, 2012.

Gaustad, Edwin S. *Liberty of Conscience: Roger Williams in America.* Valley Forge, PA: Judson Press, 1999.

General Accounting Office. *Immigration Control: A Role for the Social Security Card,* GAO-HRD-88-4. Report by the General Accounting Office. Washington, DC: U.S. Government Printing Office, 1988.

General Accounting Office. *Immigration Reform: Employer Sanctions and the Question of Discrimination: Report to Congress.* GAO/GGD-90-62. Washington, DC: U.S. Government Printing Office, 1990.

General Accounting Office. *Overstay Tracking: A Key Component of Homeland Security and a Layered Defense.* GAO-04–82. Washington, DC: U.S. Government Printing Office, 2004.

Glazer, Nathan, and Daniel Moynihan. *Beyond the Melting Pot.* Cambridge, MA: Harvard University Press, 1963.

Glazer, Nathan, and Daniel Moynihan. *Ethnicity: Theory and Experience.* Cambridge, MA: Harvard University Press, 1975.

Golash-Boza, Tanya Maria. *Immigration Nation: Raids, Detentions and Deportations in Post-9/11 America.* Fort Collins, CO: Paradigm Books, 2012.

Gomez, Laure. *Manifest Destinies.* New York: New York University Press, 2007.

Gonzales, Alfonso. *Reform without Justice: Latino Migrant Politics and the Homeland Security State.* New York: Oxford University Press, 2013.

Goodfriend, Joyce. *Before the Melting Pot: Society and Culture in Colonial New York City, 1664–1730.* Princeton, NJ: Princeton University Press, 1992.

Gorman, Stobhan. *Historical Dictionary of Refugees and Disaster Relief.* Lanham, MD: Scarecrow Press, 1994.

Gould, Lewis L. *1968: The Election That Changed America.* New York: Ivan Dee, 2010.

Grant, Madison. *The Passing of the Great Race.* New York: Arno Press, 1916.

Greely, Andrew M. *Ethnicity in the United States.* New York: John Wiley, 1974.

Green, Steven K. 2010. *The Second Disestablishment: Church and State in Nineteenth Century America*. New York: Oxford University Press.

Greenstein, Fred. *The American Party System and the American People*. Upper Saddle River, NJ: Prentice Hall, 1970.

Hampshire, David. *U.S. Immigration Handbook*. Bath, UK: Survival Books, 2010.

Handlin, Oscar. *The Americans*. Boston: Little, Brown, 1963.

Handlin, Oscar. *Boston's Immigrants*. Cambridge, MA: Harvard University Press, 1979.

Handlin, Oscar. *Immigration as a Factor in American History*. Upper Saddle River, NJ: Prentice Hall, 1959.

Handlin, Oscar. *The Uprooted*. Boston: Little, Brown, 1973.

Hansen, Marcus. *The Atlantic Migration, 1607–1860*. New York: Harper Torch, 1961.

Harper, Elizabeth J. *Immigration Laws of the United States*, 3rd edition. Indianapolis: Bobbs-Merrill, 1975.

Hartman, E.G. *The Movement to Americanize the Immigrant*. New York: AMS, 1967.

Haugen, David. *Immigration*. Boston: Greenhaven/Cengage, 2009.

Hayes, Patrick. *The Making of Modern Immigration: An Encyclopedia of People and Ideas*. Santa Barbara, CA: ABC-CLIO, 2012.

Heimert, Alan. *Religion and the American Mind: From the Great Awakening to the Revolution*. Cambridge, MA: Cambridge University Press, 1966.

Hening, William Walton, ed. *Statutes at Large of Virginia*, vol. 12: 84–86, VaGenWeb, 1823. www.vagenweb.org/hening/vol01-00.htm.

Hernandez, Kelly. *Migra! A History of the U.S. Border Patrol*. Berkeley: University of California Press, 2010.

Higham, John, ed. *Ethnic Leadership in America*. Baltimore: The Johns Hopkins University Press, 1978.

Higham, John. *Strangers in the Land: Patterns of American Nativism, 1866–1925*. New Brunswick, NJ: Rutgers University Press, 1955.

"Hill Passes Compromise Immigration Bill," *The Washington Post*, October 16, 1986: A 5.

"Hill Revises Immigration Law," *The Washington Post*, October 16, 1986: A 1, 7–8.

Hoerder, Dirk, ed. *American Labor and Immigration History, 1877–1920*. Urbana: University of Illinois Press, 1982.

Hoffman, Edward. *Despite All Odds: The Story of the Lubavitch*. New York: Simon and Schuster, 1991.

Hofstadter, Richard, and Michael Wallace. *American Violence*. New York: Knopf, 1971.

Holmes, David R. *The Faith of the Founding Fathers*. New York: Oxford University Press, 2006.

Holt, Michael. *Political Parties and American Political Development: From the Age of Jackson to the Age of Lincoln*. New York: Barnes and Noble, 1992.

Hosokawa, William. *Nisei: The Quiet Americans*. New York: William and Morrow, 1969.

Houde, Jean Louis (translated by Hubert Houle). *French Migration to North America, 1600–1900*. Chicago: Editions Houde, 1994.

Howe, Daniel. *The American Whigs: An Anthology*. New York: John Wiley, 1973.

Howe, Irving. *World of Our Fathers*. New York: Simon and Schuster, 1976.

"Immigration Act of 1921 Imposes a Quota System, 1921–1924," *Historic Events*. Detroit: Gale, 2012. *Gale U.S. History in Context*, Web February 5, 2013.

Immigration and Naturalization Service. *Population Trends and Public Policy*. Washington, DC: U.S. Government Printing Office, 1979.

Immigration to the United States. www.immigrationtounitedstates.org/immigrant-groups.

Industrial Workers of the World. http://www.iww.org/.

Information Plus. *Immigration and Illegal Aliens: Blessing or Burden?* Farmington Hills, MI: Thompson/Gale, 2006.

Ingraham, Patricia. "Toward a More Systematic Consideration of Policy Design," *Policy Studies Journal* 15, no. 4 (1987): 610–628.

Iorrizzo, Luciano, and Salvatore Mondello. *The Italian Americans*. New York: Twayne, 1971.

Italian American One Voice Coalition. http://www.iaovc.org/.

Janikowsky, Oscar. *The American Jews: A Reappraisal*. Philadelphia: Jewish Publications Society of America, 1964.

Janis, Irving. *Groupthink*, 2nd edition. Boston: Houghton Mifflin, 1982.

Janofsky, Michael. "Legal Immigrants Would Regain Aid in Clinton Plan," *New York Times*, January 25, 1999: 1, 19.

Jenson, Richard. "The Last Party System: Decay of Consensus, 1932–1980," in *The Evolution of the American Electoral System*. Edited by Paul Kleppner et al., 219–225. Westport, CT: Greenwood Press, 1981.

Jones, Maldwyn. *American Immigration*. Chicago: University of Chicago Press, 1960.

Keller, Morton. *America's Three Regimes: A New Political History*. Oxford: Oxford University Press, 2016.

Kenefick, John. *Union Pacific and the Building of the West*. New York: Newcomen Society, 1985.

Kennedy, John F. *A Nation of Immigrants*. New York: Harper Perennial, 2008 (Re-Issued on 50th Anniversary).

Kettner, James H. *The Development of American Citizenship, 1608–1970*. Chapel Hill: University of North Carolina Press, 1978.

Kitano, Harry. *Japanese Americans: The Evolution of a Subculture*. Upper Saddle River, NJ: Prentice Hall, 1976.

Kivisto, Peter, and Thomas Faist. *Beyond a Border: Causes and Consequences of Contemporary Immigration*. Los Angeles: Sage Publications, 2010.

Kleppner, Paul, et al., eds. *The Evolution of the American Electoral System*. Westport, CT: Greenwood Press, 1981.

Kohn, George C., ed. *Encyclopedia of Plague and Pestilence*. New York: Facts of File, 1995.

Kornelly, Sharon. "A Holy Experiment: Religion and Immigration to the New World," in *Transforming America: Perspectives on U.S. Immigration*, vol. 1. Edited by Michael LeMay, 189–214. Westport, CT: Praeger Press, 2013.

Kowert, Paul. *Groupthink as Deadlock: When Do Leaders Learn from Their Advisors?* Albany: State University of New York Press, 2002.

Krauss, Elisha. "Building a Bigger Bureaucracy: What the Department of Homeland Security Won't Do," *The Public Manager* 32, no. 1 (2003): 57–59.

Krauss, Erick, and Alex Pacheco. *On the Line: Inside the Border Patrol*. New York: Citadel Press, 2004.

Kraut, Alan. *Silent Travelers: Germs, Genes, and the "Immigration Menace."* Baltimore: The Johns Hopkins University Press, 1994.

Kritz, Mary. *U.S. Immigration and Refugee Policy: Global and Domestic Issues*. Lexington, KY: Lexington Books, 1983.

Kurzban, Ira. "Amnesty: Can We Learn a Simple and More Generous Approach?," in *In Defense of the Alien*, vol. II. Edited by Lydio Tomasi, 19–26. New York: Center for Migration Studies, 1989.

Ladd, Everett C., Jr. *Where Have All the Voters Gone? The Fracturing of America's Political Parties*. New York: W. W. Norton, 1978.

Ladd, Everett C., Jr., and Charles Hadley. *Transformations of the American Party System: Political Coalitions from the New Deal to the 1970s*. New York: W. W. Norton, 1978.

Lambert, Frank. *The Founding Fathers and the Place of Religion in America*. Princeton, NJ: Princeton University Press, 2003.

Lamm, R. D., and G. Imhoff. *The Immigration Time Bomb*. New York: Truman Talley Books, 1985.

Latham, Earl. *The Group Basis of Politics*. New York: Octagon Books, 1965.

Lawrence, David G. *The Collapse of the Democratic Majority*. Boulder, CO: Westview Press, 1997.

Lee, Jonathan, Fumitake Matsuoka, Edmond Yee, and Ronald Nakasone, eds. *Asian American Religious Cultures*, 2 vols. Santa Barbara, CA: ABC-CLIO, 2015.

Lehrer, Eli. "The Homeland Security Bureaucracy," *Public Interest* 1156 (Summer 2004): 71–86.

Leip, David. *David Leip's Atlas of U.S. Presidential Elections, 1789–2012*, 2012. www.uselectionatlas.org; www.ushistory.org/us/56a.asp.

LeMay, Michael. *The American Political Party System: A Reference Handbook*. Santa Barbara, CA: ABC-CLIO, 2017.

LeMay, Michael. *Anatomy of a Public Policy: The Reform of Contemporary Immigration Law*. Westport, CT: Praeger Press, 1994.

LeMay, Michael. "Assessing Assimilation: Cultural and Political Integration of Immigrants and Their Descendants," in *In Defense of the Alien, 2001*. Edited by Lydio Tomasi, 163–176. New York: Center for Migration Studies, 2001.

LeMay, Michael. *Doctors at the Borders: Immigration and the Rise of Public Health.* Westport, CT: Praeger Press, 2015.

LeMay, Michael. *From Open Door to Dutch Door.* Westport, CT: Praeger Press, 1987.

LeMay, Michael, ed. *The Gatekeepers: Comparative Immigration Policy.* Westport, CT: Praeger Press, 1989.

LeMay, Michael. *Global Pandemic Threats: A Reference Handbook.* Santa Barbara, CA: ABC-CLIO, 2016.

LeMay, Michael. *Guarding the Gates: Immigration and National Security.* Westport, CT: Praeger Security International, 2006.

LeMay, Michael. *Illegal Immigration: A Reference Handbook*, 1st edition. Santa Barbara, CA: ABC-CLIO, 2007.

LeMay, Michael. *Illegal Immigration: A Reference Handbook*, 2nd edition. Santa Barbara, CA: ABC-CLIO, 2015.

LeMay, Michael. *The Perennial Struggle*, 3rd edition. Upper Saddle River, NJ: Prentice Hall, 2009.

LeMay, Michael. *Religious Freedom in America: A Reference Handbook.* Santa Barbara, CA: ABC-CLIO, 2017.

LeMay, Michael. *The Struggle for Influence.* Lanham, MD: University Press of America, 1985.

LeMay, Michael, ed. *Transforming America: Perspectives on Immigration*, 3 vols. Santa Barbara, CA: ABC-CLIO, 2013.

LeMay, Michael. *U.S. Immigration: A Reference Handbook.* Santa Barbara, CA: ABC-CLIO, 2004.

LeMay, Michael, and Elliott Barkan, eds. *U.S. Immigration and Naturalization Laws and Issues: A Documentary History.* Westport, CT: Greenwood Press, 1999.

Leventman, Seymour. *The Ghetto and Beyond.* New York: Random House, 1969.

Levine, Edward. *The Irish and the Irish Politician.* Notre Dame: University of Notre Dame Press, 2006.

Levy, Leonard W. *The Establishment Clause and the First Amendment.* Chapel Hill: University of North Carolina Press, 1994.

Levy, Mark, and Michael Kramer. *The Ethnic Factor.* New York: Simon and Schuster, 1972.

Lieberson, Stanley. *A Piece of the Pie: Black and White Immigrants since 1880.* Berkeley: University of California Press, 1980.

Light, Paul C. *Homeland Security Will Be Hard to Manage.* Washington, DC: Brookings Institute, Center for Public Service, 2002.

Litt, Edgar. *Ethnic Politics in America.* Glenview, IL: Scott, Foresman, 1970.

Lopata, Helena. *Polish Americans.* Upper Saddle River, NJ: Prentice Hall, 1976.

Louky, James, et al. *Immigration in America Today: An Encyclopedia.* Westport, CT: Praeger Press, 2006.

Lynch, Timothy. "Immigration and Shipping Lines, 1865–1945," in *Transforming America: Perspectives on U.S. Immigration*, vol. 2. Edited by Micheal LeMay, 73–89. Santa Barbara, CA: ABC-CLIO: 2013.

Maguire, John F. *The Irish in America.* New York: Arno Press, 1969.

Malek, Alia. *Patriot Acts: Narratives of Post-9/11 Injustice.* San Francisco: McSweeney's Publishing, 2011.

Mamot, Patricia R. *Foreign Medical Graduates in America.* Springfield, IL: Charles Thomas, 1974.

Manning, Bayless. "The Congress, the Executive, and Intermestic Affairs: Three Proposals," *Foreign Affairs* (January 1977). Available at: www.foreignaffairs.com/authors/bayless-manning.

Manza, Jeff, and Clem Brooks. *Social Cleavages and Political Change: Voter Alignments and U.S. Party Coalitions.* New York: Oxford University Press, 1999.

Massey, Douglas, Rafael Alarcon, Jorge Durand, and Humberto Gonzalez. *Return to Aztlan: The Social Process of Immigration from Western Mexico.* Berkeley: University of California Press, 1987.

McClain, Charles. *In Search of Equity: The Chinese Struggle against Discrimination in Nineteenth Century America.* Berkeley: University of California Press, 1994.

McClellen, Grant, ed. *Immigrants, Refugees, and U.S. Policy.* New York: H.W. Wilson, 1981.

McClemore, Dale. *Racial and Ethnic Relations in America.* Boston: Allyn and Bacon, 1980.

McGreevey, John T. *Catholicism and American Freedom: A History.* New York: W.W. Norton, 2003.

McLaughlin, James. "The Common and Uncommon Schooling of Immigrants to the United States, 1787–1865," in *Transforming America: Perspectives on Immigration*, vol. 1. Edited by Michael LeMay, 97–119. Santa Barbara, CA: ABC-CLIO, 2013.

Meier, Matt S., and Margo Gutierrez. *Encyclopedia of Mexican-American Civil Rights Movement.* Westport, CT: Greenwood Press, 2000.

Melton, Tracy. *Hanging Henry Gambrill: The Violent Career of Baltimore's Plug Uglies, 1851–1860.* Baltimore: Maryland Historical Society, 2005.

Merino, Noel. *Illegal Immigration.* Boston: Greenhaven/Cengage, 2012.

Milkis, Sidney. *The President and Parties: The Transformation of the American Party System since the New Deal.* New York: Oxford University Press, 1993.

Miller, Debra. *Immigration.* Boston: Greenhaven/Cengage, 2014.

Miller, Kerby. *Emigrants in Exile: Irish and the Irish Exodus to North America.* New York: Oxford University Press, 1985.

Miller, R.M., and T.D. Marzik, eds. *Immigrants and Religion in Urban America.* Philadelphia: Temple University Press, 1977.

Miller, William Lee. 1986. *The First Liberty: Religion and the American Republic.* Washington, DC: Georgetown University Press.

Mitchell, Kenneth. "The Other Homeland Security Threat: Bureaucratic Haggling," *The Public Manager* 32, no. 7 (Spring 2003): 15–19.

Montero, David. *Vietnamese Americans.* Boulder, CO: Westview Press, 1979.

Moreno, Barry, and Michael LeMay. "The Ellis Island Station," in *Transforming America: Perspectives on Immigration.* Edited by Michael LeMay, 197–223. Santa Barbara, CA: ABC-CLIO: 2013.

Moskos, Charles. *Greek Americans: Struggle and Success.* Upper Saddle River, NJ: Prentice Hall, 1980.

Motomura, Hiroshi. *Americans in Waiting: The Lost Story of Immigration and Citizenship in the United States.* New York: Oxford University Press, 2006.

Motomura, Hiroshi. *Immigration Outside the Law.* New York: Oxford University Press, 2014.

Mulkern, John. *The Know-Nothing Party in Massachusetts.* Boston: University of Massachusetts Press, 1997.

Mullan, Fitzhugh. *Plagues and Politics: The Story of the United States Public Health Service.* New York: Basic Books, 1989.

Muller, Thomas, and Thomas Espanshade. *The Fourth Wave.* Washington, DC: The Urban Institute Press, 1985.

National Immigration Law Center. www.nilc.org/issues/daca.

Navarro, Armando. *Mexican Political Experience in Occupied Aztlan.* Lanham, MD: Altamura Press, 2005.

Nelli, Humbert. *Italians in Chicago: 1830–1930.* New York: Oxford University Press, 1970.

Nelson, Michael. *Resilient America: Reelecting Nixon in 1968, Channeling Dissent, and Dividing Government.* Lawrence: University Press of Kansas, 2014.

Nevins, Allan. *Ordeal in the Union: A House Dividing.* New York: Charles Scribner and Sons, 1947.

Ngai, Mae. *Impossible Subjects: Illegal Aliens and the Making of Modern America.* Princeton, NJ: Princeton University Press, 2014.

Ngai, Mae. *Major Problems in American Immigration History: Documents and Essays.* Boston: Wadsworth/Cengage, 2011.

Nolt, Steven M. *A History of the Amish.* Intercourse, PA: Good Books, 1992.

Nuovo, Victor. 2002. *John Locke: Writings on Religion.* New York: Oxford University Press.

O'Bierne, Kate. "Bureaucratic Nightmare on the Way?" *National Review,* Opinion Page, in *The Press Enterprise,* D 1. San Bernardino, CA: August 25, 2002.

O'Connor, Thomas. *The German Americans.* Boston: Little, Brown, 1968.

Office of the Historian. http://www.history.state.gov/milestones/1801-1829/louisiana-purchase.

Office of the Senate. https://www.senate.gov/history/1878.htm.

O'Grady, Joseph. *How the Irish Became American.* New York: Twayne, 1973.

Orreniris, Pia. *Beyond the Gold Door: U.S. Immigration in a New Era of Globalization.* Washington, DC: American Enterprise Institute Press, 2010.

Orthodox Church in America. http://www.oca.org.

Overdyke, W. Darrell. *The Know Nothing Party in the South.* Gloucester, MA: Peter Smith, 1968.

Overmyer-Valesquez, Mark, ed. *Beyond the Border: The History of Mexican-U.S. Migration.* New York: Oxford University Press, 2012.

Papademetrious, Demetrios, and Mark J. Miller, eds. *The Unavoidable Issue.* Philadelphia: Institute for the Study of Human Issues, 1984.

Papers of the President, Harry S. Truman, 1952, vol. 11, 441–447. Washington, DC: U.S. Government Printing Office, 1952.

Papers of the Presidents, Lyndon B. Johnson, 1965, vol. II, 1037–1040. Washington, DC: U.S. Government Printing Office, 1966.

Parrillo, Vincent. *Diversity in America.* Thousand Oaks, CA: Pine Forge Press, 1996.

Parrillo, Vincent. *Strangers to These Shores.* Boston: Houghton Mifflin, 1980.

Paulson, Arthur. *Electoral Realignment and the Outlook for American Democracy.* Boston: Northeastern University Press, 2006.

Payan, Tony. *The Three U.S.-Mexico Border Wars: Drugs, Immigration, and Homeland Security.* Westport, CT: Praeger Press, 2006.

Perea, Juan. *Immigrants Out! The New Nativism and the Anti-Immigrant Impulse in the United States.* New York: New York University Press, 1997.

Perotti, Rosana. *Resolving Policy Conflict: Congress and Immigration Reform.* PhD Dissertation, University of Pennsylvania, 1989.

Peterson, Merrill D., and Robert C. Vaughn, eds. *The Virginia Statute for Religious Freedom: Its Evolution and Consequences in American History.* Cambridge, MA: Cambridge University Press, 1988.

Peterson, William. *Japanese Americans: Oppression and Success.* New York: Random House, 1971.

Pew Research Center. www.pewforum.org/2013/10/11/jewish-american-beliefs-attitudes-culture-survey.

Pew Research Center. http://www.pewhispanic.org/2014/11/18/unauthorizedimmigrant-totals-rise-in-7-states-fall-in-14/.

Pitkin, Thomas. *Keepers of the Gate.* New York: New York University Press, 1975.

Platt, Tony, and Cecelia O'Leary. "Patriot Acts," *Social Science* 30, no. 1 (Spring 2003): 5–22.

Portes, Alejandro, and Reuben G. Rumbaut. *Immigrant America: A Portrait.* Berkeley: University of California Press, 1996.

Portman, Rob, and Cheryl Bauer. *Wisdom's Paradise: The Forgotten Shakers of Union Village.* Wilmington, OH: Orange Frazer Press, 2004.

Powell, John. *Encyclopedia of North American Immigration.* New York: Facts on File, 2005.

Quirk, Paul. "The Cooperative Resolution of Policy Conflict," *American Political Science Review* 83, no. 3 (1989): 905–921.

Ravitch, Diane. *The Great School Wars: New York City, 1805–1973.* New York: Basic Books, 1974.

Reich, Robert B. "A Failure of Intelligence," *The American Prospect* 15, no. 8 (August 2004): 72–73.

Reimers, David. *Natives and Strangers,* 2nd edition. New York: Oxford University Press, 1990.

Religion Facts. www.religionfacts.com/judaism/branches. Accessed 11/21/2016.

Religious Tolerance. www.religioustolerance.org/santeri3.htm.

Relyea, Harold. "Organizing for Homeland Security," *Presidential Studies Quarterly* 33, no. 3 (2003): 602–625.

Ringer, Benjamin. *We the People and Others.* New York: Tavistock, 1983.

Ripley, William. *The Races of Europe.* New York: Lowell Institute, Columbia University Press, 1899.

Rippley, Levern T. *The German Americans.* Chicago: Claretian Press, 1973.

Rischin, Moses, ed. *Immigration and the American Tradition.* Indianapolis: Bobbs-Merrill, 1976.

Robbins, Albert. *Coming to America: Immigrants from Northern Europe.* New York: Delacorte Press, 1981.

Roberts, Marta. "20–20 Spy Sight," *Security Management* 59, no. 2 (February 2005): 76–80.

Roots, Roger. "Terrorized into Absurdity: The Creation of the Transportation Security Administration," *Independent Review* 7, no. 4 (Spring 2003): 503–518.

Rosenblum, Gerard. *Immigrant Workers: Their Impact on American Labor Radicalism.* New York: Basic Books, 1973.

Rosengarten, Joseph. *The German Soldier in the Wars of the United States.* Philadelphia: J. B. Lippencott, 1980.

Roucek, Joseph S., and Bernard Eisenber, eds. *America's Ethnic Politics.* Westport, CT: Greenwood Press, 1982.

Safire, William. *Safire's Political Dictionary.* New York: Oxford University Press, 2008.

Salomone, Rosemary. *True Americans.* Cambridge, MA: Harvard University Press, 2010.

Sarnito, Christian. *Becoming American under Fire.* Ithaca, NY: Cornell University Press, 2009.

Schafer, Joseph. "Who Elected Lincoln?," in *American Ethnic Politics.* Edited by Lawrence Fuchs, 32–49. New York: Harper, 1968.

Schrug, Peter. *Not Fit for Our Society: Nativism and Immigration.* Berkeley: University of California Press, 2010.

Select Commission on Immigration and Refugee Policy (SCIRP). *Final Report.* Washington, DC: U.S. Government Printing Office, 1981.

Select Commission on Immigration and Refugee Policy. *Staff Report.* Washington, DC: U.S. Government Printing Office, 1981.

Shafer, Byron, and Anthony J. Badgers. *Contesting Democracy: Substance and Structure in American Political History, 1775–2000.* New York: Columbia University Press, 2001.

Silbey, Joel H. *The American Political Nation, 1838–1893.* Stanford, CA: Stanford University Press, 1991.

Singer, David, and Lawrence Grossman, eds. 2003. *American Jewish Yearbook, 2002.* New York: American Jewish Committee.

Skowronek, Stephen. *The Politics President's Make: Leadership from John Adams to Bill Clinton,* 2nd edition. Cambridge, MA: Belknap Press of Harvard University, 1997.

Skowronek, Stephen. *Presidential Leadership in Political Time*, 2nd edition. Lawrence: University Press of Kansas, 2011.

Sloan, John. *FDR and Reagan: Transformative Presidents with Clashing Values*. Lawrence: University Press of Kansas, 2008.

Smith, Theodore. *Parties and Slavery*. New York: Negro University Press, 1969.

Sneider, Daniel. "The Groupthink Failure: A Centralized Bureaucracy Won't Improve Intelligence," *Knight Ridder/Tribune News Service*, September 10, 2004: 4726.

Snodgrass, Michael. "The Bracero Program, 1942–1964," in *Beyond the Borders: The History of Mexican-U.S. Migration*. Edited Mark Overmyer-Valisquez, 79–102. New York: Oxford University Press, 2011.

Soloutos, Theodore. *The Greeks in the United States*. Cambridge, MA: Harvard University Press, 1964.

Sowell, Thomas, ed. *Essays and Data on American Ethnic Groups*. Washington, DC: Urban Institute Press, 1978.

Sowell, Thomas. *Ethnic America: A History*. New York: Basic Books, 1981.

Steen, Ivan. *Urbanizing America: The Development of Cities in the United States from the First European Settlements to 1920*. Malabar, FL: Krieger, 2006.

Stephenson, George M. *The Religious Aspect of Swedish Immigration*. New York: Arno Press, 1969.

Stevens, Rosemary. *The Alien Doctors*. New York: John Wiley and Sons, 1978.

Strobel, Christopher. *Daily Life of the New Americans: Immigration since 1965*. Westport, CT: Praeger Press, 2010.

Sundquist, James. *Dynamics of the Party System: Alignment and Realignment of Political Parties in the United States*. Washington, DC: The Brookings Institution Press, 1983.

Suro, Roberto. "California Dreaming: The New Dynamism in Immigration Federalism and Opportunities for Inclusion on a Variegated Landscape," *Journal on Migration and Human Society* 3, no. 1 (2015): 1–25.

Swierenga, Robert. *The Dutch in America: Immigration Settlement and Cultural Change*. New Brunswick, NJ: Rutgers University Press, 1985.

Taylor, Philip. *The Distant Magnet: European Emigration to America*. New York: Harper and Row, 1971.

Texas Historical Association. http://tshaonline.org/handbook/articles/fbo.54.

Thernstrom, Stephen. *Harvard Encyclopedia of American Ethnic Groups*. Cambridge, MA: Harvard University Press, 1980.

Thomas, William, and Florian Znanicki. "The Polish American Community," in *Uncertain Americans*. Edited by Leonard Dinnerstein and Frederick Jaher, 232–249. New York: Oxford University Press, 1977.

Thompson, William. *Native American Issues*. Santa Barbara, CA: ABC-CLIO, 1996.

Torr, James D., ed. *Homeland Security*. San Diego: Greenhaven Press, 2004.

Truckee-Donner Historical Society. www.truckeehistory.org/history-and-research .html.

270 to Win. www.270towin.com/1972_election/.

Ulrich, Laurel Thatcher. *A Midwife's Tale*. New York: Vintage Books, 1991.

United Mine Workers of America. http://www.umwa.org/.

United States Citizenship and Immigration Services. Legal Immigration and Adjustment of Status Report fy2017, Q 4. https://www.dhs.gov/immigration-statistics/special-reports/legal-immigration.

United We Dream. "USCIS Begins to Accept DACA Renewal Applications Again. What You Should Know." www.unitedwedream.org/2018/01/uscis-begins-to-accept-daca-renewal-applications-again-what-you-should-know/.

U.S. Bureau of the Census. *Historical Statistics of the United States: Colonial Times to 1970.* Washington, DC: U.S. Government Printing Office, 1975.

U.S. Census Bureau. http://www.census.gov/acs/www/.

U.S. Commission on Immigration Reform. *U.S. Immigration Policy: Restoring Credibility.* Washington, DC: U.S. Government Printing Office, 1994.

U.S. Congress, Senate Committee on the Judiciary. *The Immigration and Naturalization Systems of the United States, 1950.* 81st Congress, 2nd Session, Senate Report 1515. Washington, DC: U.S. Government Printing Office, 1950.

U.S. Customs and Border Protection. https://www.cbp.gov/newsroom/stats/southwest-border-unaccompanied-alien-children/fy-2014.

U.S. Department of Commerce. *Statistical Abstract of the United States, 2002.* Washington, DC: U.S. Government Printing Office, 2003.

U.S. History. www.ushistory.org/us/60a.asp.

U.S. Laws on Trafficking in Persons. http://www.state.gov/j/tip/laws/.

U.S. President's Commission on Immigration and Naturalization. *Whom Shall We Welcome? Report.* Washington, DC: U.S. Government Printing Office, 1953.

U.S. Supreme Court. 1952. *Kedroff v. St. Nicholas Cathedral.* caselaw.findlaw.com/us-supreme-court/344/94.html.

Van Hinte, Jacob. *Netherlanders in America: A Study of Emigration and Settlement in Nineteenth and Twentieth Centuries of the United States of America.* Grand Rapids, MI: Baker Book House, 1985.

Vecoli, Rudolph, and Joy Lintelman. *A Century of American Immigration, 1884–1984.* Minneapolis: University of Minnesota Continuing Education and Extension, 1984.

Vile, John R. *Encyclopedia of Constitutional Amendments, Proposed Amendments, and Amending Issues, 1789–2015,* 4th edition, 2 vols. Santa Barbara: ABC-CLIO, 2015.

Voss-Hubbard, Mark. *Beyond Party: Cultures of Antipartisanship in Northern Politics Before the Civil War.* Baltimore: Johns Hopkins University Press, 2002.

Walcott, Charles E., and Karen Hult. "The Bush Staff and Cabinet System," *Perspectives on Political Science* 32, no. 3 (2003): 150–156.

Walters, Kerry S. *The American Deists: Voices of Reason and Dissent in the Early Republic.* Lawrence: University Press of Kansas, 1992.

Ward, David. *Cities and Immigrants: A Geography of Change in 19th Century America.* New York: Oxford University Press, 1971.

Warner, Judith, ed. *Battleground Immigration.* Westport, CT: Praeger Press, 2008.

Warner, Judith. *U.S. Border Security: A Reference Handbook.* Santa Barbara, CA: ABC-CLIO, 2010.

Waters, Mary C., Reed Ueda, and Helen B. Marrow, eds. *The New Americans: A Guide to Immigration since 1965.* New York: Russell Sage, 2007.

Wenger, John. *The Mennonites in Indiana and Michigan.* Scottsdale, PA: Herald Press, 1961.

White, M. J., F. D. Bean, and T. J. Espanshade. *The U.S. Immigration Reform Act and Undocumented Migration to the U.S.* Washington, DC: The Urban Institute Press, 1989.

White, Theodore. *The Making of the President—1968.* New York: Atheneum, 1970.

Wilentz, Sean. *The Politicians and the Egalitarians: The Hidden History of American Politics.* New York: W. W. Norton, 2016.

Wilentz, Sean. *The Rise of American Democracy: Jefferson to Lincoln.* New York: W. W. Norton, 2005.

Wily, Irwin. *Billy Yank: The Common Soldier of the Union.* Baton Rouge: Louisiana State University Press, 1979.

Witte, John, Jr. *No Establishment of Religion: America's Original Contribution to Religious Liberty.* New York: Oxford University Press, 2012.

Wittke, Carl. *We Who Built America.* Akron, OH: Case Western Reserve University Press, 1967.

Wong Wing v. United States, 163 U.S. 228, 1986.

World Culture Encyclopedia. http://www.everyculture.com.

World Culture Encyclopedia. http://www.everyculture.com/multi/Ha-La/Hungarian-Americans.html.

Yount, Lisa, ed. *Fighting Bioterrorism.* San Diego: Greenhaven Press, 2004.

Zolberg, Aristide. *A Nation by Design: Immigration Policy in the Fashioning of America.* Cambridge, MA: Russell Sage Foundation at Harvard University Press, 2008.

Zuniga, Victor, and Ruben Hernandez-Leon, eds. *New Destinations: Mexican Immigration in the United States.* New York: Russell Sage, 2005.

Index

Acculturation, 108. *See also*
  Assimilation
Act of March 26, 1790, 16, 28
Act of January 29, 1795, 16, 48, 67
Act of June 25, 1798, 16, 48, 67
Act of March 2, 1819, 16, 23, 50–51
Act of May 20, 1862, 28
Act of May 6, 1882, 18
Act of August 3, 1882, 18–19, 29, 114
Act of February 26, 1885, 29, 114
Act of February 23, 1887, 19, 31
Act of September 13, 1888, 29, 115
Act of March 3, 1891, 29, 115, 116
Act of March 3, 1903, 30
Act of February 20, 1907, 19, 30
Act of June 25, 1910, 121
Act of February 5, 1917, 19–20, 31,
  129, 160
Act of May 9, 1918, 31
Act of May 19, 1921, 6, 20, 31,
  130–39, 172
Act of September 22, 1922, 31
Act of May 26, 1924, 6, 21, 31, 130,
  139–45
Act of March 2, 1929, 6, 32, 145–50
Act of June 27, 1952, 22, 33
Act of September 22, 1959, 23, 33,
  164, 170
Act of October 3, 1965, 23, 33, 177,
  191

Act of November 6, 1986, 25
Act of November 29, 1996, 26, 36
Act of October 24, 2001, 26, 38,
  234
Act of November 19, 2002, 26, 38,
  234, 240
Act of December 17, 2004, 27, 247
Act of March 8, 2006, 27, 40, 249
Adams, John, 48, 67–68
Adams, John Quincy, 71, 74
Adjustment to immigrant status,
  Cuban, 184
AFL-CIO, 202. *See also* American
  Federation of Labor
African National Congress, 238
Agnew, Spiro, 184–86
Alien and Sedition Acts, 16, 67, 68
Alien Contract Labor Law (Foran Act),
  114
Allport, Gordon, 97
Al Qaeda, 237, 242
Amalgamated Clothing Workers
  Union, 109. *See also* International
  Ladies Garment Workers Union
Amalgamation theory, 135, 141, 195
American Civil Liberties Union
  (ACLU), 211, 225–26, 229, 235
American Coalition, 147, 153, 155–56
American Communist Labor Party,
  108

American Communist Party, 108, 154. *See also* American Communist Labor Party

American Community Survey Program, 1

American Council of Christian Churches, 158

American Economic Association, 116

American Farm Bureau Federation, 203

American Federation of Labor, 22, 59–60, 121–22, 131, 135, 137, 139, 147, 153–56

American Hellenic Educations Progressive Association (AHEPA), 104

American Hungarian Federation, 175

American Immigration Control Act, 1986. *See* Immigration Reform and Control Act (IRCA)

Americanization Movement/ 100 Percent campaign, 30, 130–31

American Jewish Committee, 22

American Legion, 22, 122, 134, 137, 139, 147, 155

American Miners Association, 59

American Party, 6, 56, 58, 70, 73, 75, 77–78, 86

American Protective Association, 97, 114, 116

American Revolutionary War, 10, 66

Americans and Others United for the Separation of Church and State, 158

American Socialist Party, 120

Amish, 185

Amnesty, 35, 213, 223, 251. *See also* Earned legalization

Anabaptists, 9, 11–12, 59. *See also* Simons, Menno

Anchor babies, 2

Ancient Order of Hibernians, 119

Anglican Church of England, 8–9, 10–11, 54, 66, 69

Anthrax (*Bacillus anthracis*), 234

Anthrax, Attack of 2001, 234

Anti-black, 131, 234–35

Anti-Bolshevik/Communist, 26, 108

Anti-Catholic, 6, 17, 24–25, 58, 61, 70, 77, 85, 97, 100, 114, 131, 158

Anti-Chinese, 17–18, 83–84, 85, 111–13

Anti-foreign reaction, 17, 83

Anti-German, 20, 69–70

Anti-Greek, 104

Anti-immigrant sentiment, 16, 76–77, 83, 84–86, 100

Anti-Japanese, 14

Anti-Jewish (Semitism), 59, 70, 110, 131

Anti-miscegenation laws, 115

Anti-National Origins Clause League, 137, 147

Anti-Restrictionist League, 147, 154; forces in Congress, 171

Apprehensions, 194

Arizona v. United States, 40, 251

Arthur, Chester A., 113

Ashcroft, John, 233

Asian Exclusion League, 119–20

Asian immigrants, 6, 167, 170, 195, 204

Asian Pacific Triangle, 171–73

Asiatic Barred Zone, defined, 122, 171–72

Assimilation, 64, 66–68, 108, 195

Asylum: defined, 7, 258; in Refugee Act of 1980, 34

Bacillus anthracis, 234

Balanced Budget Act of 1997, 228

Balkan War, 103

Baltimore, 79–81, 101, 108

Baptists, 9–10, 48–49

Bell, Griffin, 204

Bill of Rights, 49–50

Bioterrorism, 234–35

Birth of a Nation, 131

Black, Hugo, 152
Black Caucus, 210–12, 217, 221
B'nai B'rith, Anti-Defamation League, 110
Boards of Special Inquiry, 118
Boat lift, 34
Boat people (Cuban, Haitian, Vietnamese), 34, 184–85
Boehner, John, 254
Bolshevist Revolution/Bolshevism, 20, 31, 105, 122
Bonaparte, Napoleon, 50
Border and Transportation Security, Directorate of, 38
Border caucus, 217
Border control, 253–54, 262
Border fence, 27. *See also* Secure Fence Act
Border patrol, 21, 27, 32, 146, 225–27, 242, 247
Border Security and Economic Opportunity Act of 2013 (S.744), 253–54
Box, John Calvin, 146, 148–49
Bracero program, 24–25, 32–33, 159–60, 172, 196, 209
Bradley, Bill, 208
Brain drain, 190
British Isles, 3, 6, 15, 52
Buddhists, 117. *See also* Shintoists
Buford (Soviet Ark), 108
Bureau of Border Transportation Security, 27
Bureau of Citizenship and Immigration Services, 27
Bureau of Immigration, 116, 118, 121
Bureau of the Census, 1, 258
Burke, Martin, 114. *See also* Knights of Labor
Burlingame, Anson, 81–82
Burlingame Treaty, 111
Burton, Theodore, 143
Bush, George Herbert Walker, 186–87

Bush, George Walker, 234–36, 240, 243, 247, 250, 261
Bush Administration, 234
Business Roundtable, 222, 229

Cable Act of 1922, 31
Cajuns, 68
California, 9, 81
Calvanists, 11, 13, 52, 69
Calvert, Cecelius, Lord Baltimore, 9
Cambodia (Kampuchea), 184, 188
Card, Andrew, 234
Carter, Jimmy, 34, 186–87, 191, 204
Carter administration, 34, 194, 204–5
Castillo, Leonel, 204
Castle Garden Reception Station, 28, 113, 115
Castro Revolution, 176
Catholicism, 130
Catholics, sentiment against, 6, 57, 202
Celler, Emanuel, 171, 179
Center for Disease Control (CDC), 234
Central America, 190; immigrants from, 1–2, 6, 25, 190, 258; refugees, 35, 190
Chabad, 162. *See also* Hasidic Judaism
Chae Chan Ping v. United States, 29, 115
Chain migration, defined, 21
Cheney, Dick, 237
Chicago, 96, 98, 100, 101, 104–5, 107, 115
Chinese Exclusion Act of 1882, 18, 113; and amendments to, 30, 115; and Burlingame Treaty, 111; and repeal of, 21, 158
Chinese immigrants, 112–13; and the Door Ajar Era, 58

Church of Lukumi Babalu Aye v. City of Hileah, 1993, 176
Church of Sweden, 63
Church of the Brethren, 12. *See also* Dunkers
Citizens Committee for Displaced Persons, 22
Civil rights movement, 23, 195
Civil War, 12, 52, 55–56, 58–59, 60–64, 85–86, 93, 97–99
Cleveland, Grover, 19
Clinton, William Jefferson, 227–29
Close family ties, 261–62
Coast Guard, 243
Cold War, 7, 23, 160, 169, 171, 174, 195
Colt, LaBaron, 143
Commission on Immigration Reform, 226
Committee for German Refugee Children, 155
Conference Committee of House/ Senate, Joint, 210, 213
Congregationals, 9, 13
Congress, 15–16, 20, 22–24, 47, 112–13, 118, 129, 131, 154, 167–68, 170, 178, 212, 226–27, 233, 235, 247, 251
Congressional Budget Office, 251
Congressional Medal of Honor, 55, 59
Congress of Industrial Organizations, 155. *See also* Lewis, John
Constitution, 48
Contract Labor Law of 1857, 19, 29
Coolidge, Calvin, 140, 143–44
Coolie labor, 117
Copeland, Royal, 147
Cornyn, John, 254
Council of the Union of American Hebrew Congregations, 119
Cuban refugees, 33, 176, 178, 184; Cuban-Haitian Adjustment Act, 33, 229

Customs and Border Protection, 244–45, 260
Czar Alexander II, 95. *See also* Russia, pogroms

DACA and DAPA, 252–53; rescinded, 257
Danish Brotherhood of America, 138
Danish National Church, 63
Daughters of the American Revolution, 139
DeCrevecoer, J. Hector St. John, 69
Deism, 49
De jure segregation, 23
Democratic Party, 56–57, 101, 106, 131, 168–69, 178, 195, 209, 213, 217, 259, 262
Department of Commerce and Labor, 30
Department of Defense, 26, 240
Department of Health and Human Services, 37, 187
Department of Homeland Security, 26–27, 38, 234; Act of, 234, 244, 258–59
Department of Justice, 26, 187, 209, 211, 227, 237, 239, 245
Department of Labor, 37, 206, 225
Department of State, 152–54, 187, 189
Detainee camps, 189
DeWitt, John, 157
Dickstein, Samuel, 154–55
Dillingham, William, 19, 131, 138
Dillingham Commission, 19–21, 30, 121, 170
Director of National Intelligence, 27, 247–48
Dirkson, Everett, 182
Disease epidemics, 59, 95, 99, 123
Displaced Persons Act of 1948, 22, 159, 167
Diversity immigrants, defined, 35, 226

Divine, Robert
Dole, Bob, 186
Door Ajar Era, 14, 18–20, 86,
  93–123
Dream Act, 38, 251
Drug Enforcement Agency, 225
Dunkers, 11–12, 52, 54
Dutch, 64–66
Dutch Door Era, 14, 22–24, 164,
  167–96
Dutch Reformed Church, 10, 12,
  65–66, 77
Duvalier, "Papa Doc," 184. *See also*
  Haitian boat people
Dye, Thomas, 218

Earned legalization, 216
Eastern European Jews, 109–11;
  Orthodox, Reformed, Conservative,
  Hasidic, 110
Eastern Europeans, 6, 94, 96–97, 103,
  117, 187
Eastern Hemisphere, 22, 33
Eastern Orthodox Church, 6. *See also*
  Greek Orthodox Church; Russian
  Orthodox Church
Eastland, James, 203–4
Edwards, Don, 206
Eileberg, Joshua, 203
Eisenhower, Dwight D., 23, 33, 169,
  174, 176
Ellis Island, 30, 95, 101–2, 108, 116,
  118–19, 120, 122, 134; closure of,
  175
El Salvador, 223; refugees from, 34,
  214
Embarkation, ports of, 101
Emergency Quota Act of 1921, 138,
  140
Emigration, 107, 117
Employee verification, 228
Employer sanctions, 213–14, 215,
  223–24
Endo v. United States, 1944, 158

Enhanced interrogation, 237. *See also*
  Cheney, Dick
Episcopal Church, 47, 69, 209
Equal protection of the law, defined
Ervin, Sam, 182
Espanshade, Thomas
Espionage Act of 1917, 108. *See also*
  Palmer Raids; Red Scare
Established religions, 7
Ethnic theories, 135; ethnic bloc, 95
Eugenics, defined, 147
Europeans, 5; colonial powers of, 5,
  61, 95, 187
Excluded categories, defined, 19
Exclusion, defined, 19
Executive Orders, 30, 252–53; 9066,
  1942 (Japanese Evacuation), 32,
  158
Ex parte Mitsuye Endo, 32
Expedited removal, 37, 255

Fairchild, Henry Pratt, 135
Federal Emergency Management
  Agency (FEMA), 243–46
Federalist Party, 16, 48, 54, 57, 67, 71
Federation for American Immigration
  Reform (FAIR), 222, 229
Ferraro, Geraldine, 194
Fifth Political Party System, 168, 195
Filipinos, 122, 153
Fillmore, Millard, 71, 77, 122, 153.
  See also American Party; Know-
  Nothing Party
First Amendment, 8, 47, 49–50, 167;
  clauses of, 8, 167
Fish, Hamilton, Jr., 80, 206, 212
Flake, Jeff, 255. *See also* Gang of
  Eight
Foran Act (Alien Contract Labor Law),
  114
Forced assimilation, 30
Ford, Gerald, 186, 204
Ford, Henry, 20
Foreign-born population, 1–3

Foreign Miner's Tax, 84, 112

Fortress America, 26, 233, 247–50, 259

Forty-Eighters, 55

Founding Fathers, 49–50, 71

Fourteenth Amendment, 28, 47

Fourth Wave, 190

Frank, Barney, 209–10, 213–14

Franklin, Benjamin, 49

Freedom Fighters. *See* Hungarian immigrants

French-Canadians, 68; immigrants, 66–68

French Revolution, 67. *See also* Alien and Sedition Acts

Gallagher v. Crowne Kosher Meat Market of Massachusetts, Inc., 170, 176

Gang of Eight: House, 254; Senate, 253–54

Garibaldi Guard, 99

Geary Act (1892), 116

General Accounting Office (GAO), 214, 225, 245–46

Gentleman's Agreement, Executive Order 589, 1907, 30, 120, 142–43

George II, King of England, 10

German-American Citizens League, 138

German immigrants, 16–17, 52–57, 59; belt, 55; German-American Alliance, 119

Gold rush, 17, 98

Goldwater, Barry, 178–79

Gonzales, Alberto, 234

Goodlatte, Bob, 255

Grant, Madison, 121, 135–36, 139

Great Awakening, 10, 17; Second Great Awakening, 74

Great Depression, 21, 32, 152–56

Great Society, 179. *See also* Johnson, Lyndon

Greek immigrants, 6, 103–5, 169

Greek Orthodox Church, 6, 18, 94, 97, 104

Greely, Horace, 82

Greenback Party, 63

Green card, 261

Groupthink, 242; defined, 242; symptoms of, 243

Guest-worker programs, 206, 211

Gulick, Dr. Sidney, 137. *See also* Quota system

Haiti, 184

Haitian boat people, 34, 184, 185

Haitian Refugee Center, Inc. et al. v. Nelson, et al. (1988), 225

Haitian refugees, 33, 189, 225

Harding, Warren G., 21, 131, 138

Harrison, William, 71, 116

Hart, Philip, 179

Hasidic Jewish immigration, 161–63

Hasidic Judaism, 161–63

Haymarket Riot (1886), 115

Hebrew Sheltering and Immigration Aid Society, 119, 154–55

Helms, Jesse, 203

Henderson v. Mayor of New York (1875), 113

High Commission on Refugees (League of Nations), 155

Hirabayashi v. United States, 32, 158

Hispanic Americans, 193, 204, 206, 258

Hispanic Caucus, 207–12, 217, 221

Homeland Security, Office of, 234. *See also* Ridge, Tom

Homeland Security Act, 26, 240; excerpts of, 240–41

Homestead Act of 1862, 28, 56, 63

Hong Kong, 176

Hoover, Herbert, 21

Hoover proclamation on quotas, 21, 32, 150–51

House Judiciary Committee, 205–8, 212, 229

House Un-American Activities Committee, 174

H-2 program, 206, 209, 213–14, 216–17, 221, 229

Huddle, Donald, 36

Huguenots, 10, 66

Humphrey, Hubert, 171

Hungarian immigrants (Freedom Fighters), 23, 33, 175, 178

Hungarian refugees, religious affiliations of, 175–76

Hungarian Revolution, 175

Hutchinson, Anne, 9. *See also* Pietists

ICE. *See* Immigration and Customs Enforcement

Illegal alien, defined, 193

Illegal immigrants, 193

Illegal immigration, 172, 193–94, 196

Illegal Immigration Reform and Immigrant Responsibility Act (IIRIRA), 26, 36–37, 227, 250; and Border Patrol, 250; and detention/deportation provisions of, 250

IMMACT. *See* Immigration Act of 1990

Immigrants Protective League, 121

Immigration, 3; factors affecting flows of, 183

Immigration Act of 1882, 18

Immigration Act of 1907, 19

Immigration Act of 1917, 19–20

Immigration Act of 1921, 6, 20, 31, 130–39, 172. *See also* Emergency Quota Act of 1921

Immigration Act of 1924, 6, 21, 31, 130, 139–45. *See also* Johnson-Reed Quota Act

Immigration Act of 1929, 6, 32, 145–50. *See also* Hoover proclamation on quotas

Immigration Act of 1990 (IMMACT), 226, 230

Immigration Act of 1996, 26, 36

Immigration and Customs Enforcement (ICE), 27, 244–45, 258. *See also* Department of Homeland Security

Immigration and Nationality Act of 1952, 22, 34, 145–50, 164. *See also* McCarran-Walter Act

Immigration and Naturalization Act of 1965, 23, 33, 177, 179–84, 191, 237; amendment to, 1976, 34; excerpts of, 180–83; H-1 Category of, 35, 37; preferences of, 177

Immigration and Naturalization Service (INS), 38, 187, 193, 212, 215–16, 224–25, 227–28, 233, 242; and Border Patrol, 21, 27, 32; dissolving of, 240–41, 259

Immigration policy, 1, 7, 15, 23, 26, 79, 93, 96–97, 134, 167, 171; phases of, 13–28, 222–23; and policy making, 13, 28

Immigration process, 23

Immigration Reform and Control Act (IRCA), 14, 25, 35, 194, 201, 212–17; amnesty program of, 25; Employer Sanctions provisions of, 25; and excerpts of, 216–17; enactment of, 213; and guest-worker program of, 217

Immigration Restriction League, 116, 118–19, 121, 137, 139

Implementation of policy, 224–26; problems with IRCA, 224–26

Incorporation (of immigrants and their children), 56, 60–61, 64, 69

Indochinese Refugee Resettlement Program, 34

Indochinese refugees, 34

Industrialization, 5, 47, 95–96

Industrial Revolution, 3

Industrial Workers of the World, 107. *See also* Red Scare

In re Rodriquez, 30
INS. *See* Immigration and
    Naturalization Service
INS v. Aguirre-Aguirre, 37
INS v. Cardoza-Fonseca, 35
INS v. Chadha et al., 35
Intelligence Reform and Terrorism
    Prevention Act, 27, 247–48;
    excerpts of, 248–49
Internal Security Act of 1950, 160
International Ladies Garment
    Workers Union, 202
Irish Brigade, "Fighting Irish," 59
Irish-Catholic Benevolent Union
    (ICBU), 79–80
Irish famine, 4–5
Irish immigrants, 16, 57–60; and
    Irish-Americans, 168–69
Irish Republican Army, 238
Isolationism, 132, 135
Italian immigrants, 98–103, 168–69;
    and Italian-American Mutual Aid
    Societies, 100; and Italian-
    American politics, 98, 101

Jackson, Andrew, 54, 65
Jacksonian-Democrats, 54, 65, 71, 74
Janis, Irving, 243. *See also*
    Groupthink
Japanese-American Citizens League,
    172
Japanese and Korean Exclusion
    League, 119–20
Japanese immigrants, 117–18,
    142–43; and Gentlemen's
    Agreement of 1907, 120
Japanese internment/relocation,
    157–58
Jean v. Nelson, 35
Jefferson, Thomas, 10, 13, 49–50
Jeffersonian Democrats, 16, 48, 67
Jewish immigrants, 11, 52, 96–97,
    111, 162

Job discrimination, 58
Johnson, Albert, 131, 138–39, 146,
    154
Johnson, Hiram, 131, 148
Johnson, Lyndon, 24, 170, 178–80;
    and remarks on signing 1965 Act,
    182–84
Johnson-Reed Quota Act, 31, 139,
    144; excerpts of, 144–45. *See also*
    Immigration Act of 1924
Jordan Commission on Immigration
    Reform, 37
Judaism, 130, 162; and branches of,
    162–63

Kampuchea (Cambodia), 184, 188
Kansas-Nebraska Act of 1850, 74–75,
    78
Kearney, Dennis, 113. *See also*
    Workingmen's Party
Kedroff v. Saint Nicholas Cathedral
    (1952), 169
Kefauver, Estes, 169
Kelly, John F., 260. *See also*
    Department of Homeland
    Security
Kennedy, Edward, 179, 203, 206, 208,
    211, 226
Kennedy, John F., 23, 33, 106, 170,
    177; assassination of, 178
Kennedy, Robert, 179
Killer amendment, 206
Knights of Labor, 59–60, 114, 116–17
Know-Nothing Party, 6, 17, 56, 58,
    69–70, 75–76, 81–82, 84, 112; and
    movement of, 58, 76, 79–80, 84;
    and platform of, 84–85
Korean immigrants, 184
Korean War, 169, 184
Korematsu v. United States, 32, 158
Ku Klux Klan, 20, 58, 70, 85, 101,
    104, 110, 131–32, 137, 140, 144
Kvale, Ole, 147

Labor force, 3
LaGuardia, Fiorello, 101
Lamm, Richard, 222. *See also*
    Federation for American
    Immigration Reform
La Raza, 229
Latin American immigrants, 24, 167,
    195
League of Latin American Citizens
    (LULAC), 36, 227, 229
League of Nations, 132, 155
Lee, Ann, 10–11
Legal immigrants, 5
Legal Immigration and Family Equity
    Act, 2000, 26
Legalization, 216, 230. *See also*
    Amnesty; Earned legalization
Legalizing Authorized Workers
    (LAWs), 224–25, 229
Legislative intent, 222–24
Legislative policy making, 226–30
Lehman, Herbert H., 171
LeMay, Curtis E., 184–85
Lemon v. Kurtzman (1971), 169
Lewis, John, 155
Lieberman, Joseph, 234, 247
Lincoln, Abraham, 71; as a Whig,
    71
Literacy bills, 19–20, 129
Literacy test, 19, 31, 119, 121, 129.
    See also Immigration Act of 1917
Little Italy, 99
Little Saigon, 204
Lobbying groups, 222
Lodge, Henry Cabot Jr., 168, 178
Lodge, Henry Cabot Sr., 116, 118,
    131, 143
Logrolling, 221
Lone-wolf terrorist, 237
LULAC. *See* League of Latin American
    Citizens
LULAC et al. v. Pete Wilson et al., 36,
    227

Lungren, Dan, 212
Lutherans, 11–12, 52; German, 77;
    Norwegian, 63; Pietist, 63

Madison, James, 49
MALDEF. *See* Mexican American
    Legal Defense Fund
Marshall, F. Ray
Marshall, Ray, 204
Maryland, 9
Massachusetts, colony of, 9
Mass migration, 201–2
Matthews v. Diaz, 34
Mazzoli, Romano, 35, 205–6, 210,
    212
McCain, John, 255
McCarran, Pat, 170
McCarran-Walter Act, 22–23, 169–74,
    195. *See also* Immigration and
    Nationality Act of 1952
McGovern, George, 186
McGuire, Peter, 59–60. *See also*
    AFL-CIO
Melting pot, 67, 134
Mennonites, 9, 11–12, 185. *See also*
    Simons, Menno
Methodists, 10, 48–49, 64
Mexican American Legal Defense
    Fund (MALDEF), 206–7, 225–26,
    229
Mexican immigrants, 6, 148–49, 190,
    202, 258; and illegal entry, 190, 202
Mexico, 6, 190, 202; migrants and
    economy of, 190
Middle East, 23
Migration and Refugee Assistance Act
    of 1960, 178
Miller, William, 178
Milwaukee, 55
Moakley, Joseph, 213–14
Molly McGuires, 114–15
Models of public policy process,
    218–19; competitive, 218–19;

cooperative, 218–20; Equilibrium, 218–19. *See also* Dye, Thomas; Quirk, Paul
Mondale, Walter, 186, 194
Mongrelization, 7, 142
Monroe, James, 50
Moral Majority, 168
Moravian Brethren, 10–11, 12, 54
Morrison, Bruce, 226
Mortgaging, defined, 22, 159, 176
Muller, Thomas, 190. *See also* Espanshade, Thomas; Fourth Wave
Muskie, Edmund, 184–85
Muslims, 238; and travel ban of, 257–58, 260, 262

National Association for the Advancement of Colored People (NAACP), 202
National Association of Manufacturers, 20, 135, 138–40, 222, 229
National Conference of Catholic Bishops, 209
National Congress of Hispanic American Citizens, 207
National Council for the Protection of the Foreign-Born, 154
National Council of Agricultural Employers, 203
National Council of La Raza, 207
National Counterterrorism Center, 27, 39, 247
National Grange, 122, 137, 154
National Liberal Immigration League, 119
National Origins Quota Act, 117, 150, 170. *See also* Immigration Act of 1921; Immigration Act of 1924; Johnson-Reed Quota Act
National Origins quota system, 14, 20–21, 117; abolished, 179

National Security Entry-Exit Registration System (NSEERS), 244–45, 247
A Nation of Immigrants, 1958, 177. *See also* Kennedy, John F.
Native American Citizenship Act of 1919, 31
Native American Party, 71, 79
Native Americans, 15
Native-born, 3
Nativism, 18, 69, 79
Nativist sentiment, 18, 78–79
Naturalization, 47–48; defined, 47; laws on, 48; rates of assimilation, 96
Negroponte, John, 247. *See also* Director of National Intelligence
New Deal Coalition, 168, 185, 195
New Immigrants, 6; wave of, 6, 18, 96–98
The New Republic, 134
New World, 7
New York City, 96, 99, 105, 107, 109; and Ellis Island, 95; and World Trade Center, 233
New York Times, 136, 146
NGOs. *See* Nongovernmental organizations
Nicaraguan refugees, 214, 223
9/11 Commission, 230, 247–48, 259
Nine-Eleven event, 201, 233
Nishimura Ekui v. United States (1892), 116
Nixon, Richard, 169, 178, 184–86
Non-Christian sects, 18
Nongovernmental organizations (NGOs), 25, 212–17, 223, 224, 251
Nonimmigrant, defined, 202
Nonquota immigrant, defined, 33
Nordic race superiority theory, 135, 140
North America, 5, 7
North American colonies, 8; and population of, 15

North American Free Trade Agreement (NAFTA), 36
Northern Alliance in Afghanistan, 238–39
Northwestern Europeans, 3, 6, 17, 20–21, 31, 47, 93, 97, 130, 138, 140, 170

Obama, Barack, 40, 250, 252–53, 257, 259
Office of Homeland Security, 234. *See also* Department of Homeland Security; Ridge, Tom
Office of Management and Budget, 234
Office of Special Counsel, DOJ, 215, 225
"Old" immigrants, wave of, 5–6, 18, 51–53
Old Order Amish, 11–12, 54
Old Order Mennonites, 11–12, 54
Old World, 3, 7, 9
Omnibus spending bill, 26. 36–37. *See also* Illegal Immigration Reform and Immigrant Responsibility Act (IIRIRA)
"One Hundred Percenters," 20, 108, 134
O'Neill, Tip, 207, 209
Open-Door Era, 13–18, 21, 47–86, 93–94
Order of American Mechanics, 114
Order of Caucasians, 85, 112–13
Order of the Star Spangled Banner, 56, 75–76, 81. *See also* Know-Nothing Party
Ordnung (understandings), 11–12. *See also* Old Order Amish; Old Order Mennonites
Orthodox Jewish synagogues, 176
Orthodoxy, 130
Overstayers, 202, 246; defined, 202
Ozawa v. United States (1922), 132, 136

Pacific Triangle, 171–73; defined, 171
Padrone system, 103
Padroni system, 99
Page law, 111
Palmer Raids, 108, 122, 238. *See also* Red Scare
Pan-Americanism, 149
Panetta, Leon, 208, 210, 212
Panic (aka, Depression), 18, 115
Parole status, 24, 33; system of, 175–76
The Passing of the Great Race in America, 121, 135. *See also* Grant, Madison
Patriotic Order of the Sons of America, 137
Pearl Harbor attack, 157–58
Penn, William, 11
Pennsylvania Dutch, 12
People-hood, 13, 135
Pepper, Claude, 208
Percentage quota system, 137
Permanent quota system, 146–47, 149
Personal Responsibility and Work Opportunity Act of 1996, 25, 36, 227
Pet-Door Era, 13, 20–22, 129–64, 170, 203
PEW Hispanic Center
Philadelphia, 11, 49, 75, 78–79, 96, 101, 109
Philippine Act of 1946, 160
Philippines, 152–53, 155. *See also* Filipinos
Picture brides, 30
Pietists, 9–10, 12–13, 53–54
Pinckney Treaty of 1795, 50
Plug-Uglies, 70, 80, 85
Pogroms, 94–95, 110
Polish immigrants, 105–6, 169; Mutual Aid Societies of, 106
Polish National Alliance, 106

Polish National Catholic Church, 106
Polish Roman Catholic Union, 105
Polonia, 106
Potato famine, 54, 57; blight, 49
Powderly, Thomas, 119. *See also*
    Knights of Labor
Preference system, 172; defined, 179;
    established, 179–82; professionals,
    category of, 183–84
Presbyterians, 9, 11, 49, 69, 77
President Donald J. Trump, 27
President Franklin Roosevelt, 32,
    155
President George Washington, 14–15
President John Adams, 48–49,
    67–68
President John Quincy Adams,
    71, 74
President Millard Fillmore, 71, 77
President Warren G. Harding, 21,
    131, 138
President Woodrow Wilson, 106, 122,
    129, 138
Private immigration bills, 177
Progressive Party, Era of, 134
Proposition 187, 36, 226–27;
    severability clause of, 227
Protestant Reformation, 8
Protestants, 6. *See also* White-
    Anglo-Saxon-Protestants (WASPs)
Protocol, 38
Public charge clause, 172
Public policy, 60; defined, 60, 218–19
Pull factors, defined, 3–4, 54, 94,
    95–96, 100, 103, 108, 111–12, 164
Puritans, 8, 10
Push factors, defined, 3, 94, 95,
    99–100, 103, 108, 111–12, 169,
    189, 258

Quakers, 10, 49, 56, 63
Qualified designated entities (QDEs),
    224–25. *See also* Immigration
    Reform and Control Act (IRCA)

Quirk, Paul, 218–20
Quota Act of 1921, 20, 130–39;
    excerpts of, 132–33, 172
Quota Act of 1924, 6, 21, 31, 130,
    139–45. *See also* Johnson-Reed
    Quota Act
Quota Act of 1929, 145–51
Quota immigrants, defined, 32
Quotas assigned (1929)
Quota system, 23, 129–30;
    inflexibility of, 177

Reagan, Ronald, 34, 168, 186–87,
    191; Task Force of, 191–92,
    194–95, 214, 229
Reagan administration, 34
REAL ID Act, 27, 38, 249
Realigning election, 168
Rebbe, 162–63. *See also* Hasidic
    Judaism
Red Scare, 31, 122, 129, 134, 238
Reed, David, 140, 143, 146, 148,
    154
Refugee Act of 1980, 24, 34, 187–88;
    numbers admitted under, 188, 191,
    204
Refugee-parolee, defined, 24, 38
Refugee Relief Act of 1953, 22–23,
    174–75
Refugees, defined, 24, 187; 1965 Act
    provisions for, 184; U.S. legislation
    on, 24, 33. *See also* Asylum
Registration law, 32
Reign of Terror, 67. *See also* French
    Revolution
Religious affiliations, 41
Religious Freedom, 3; movement for,
    8
Religious persecution, 3
Relocation camps, 157–58
Republican Party, 55–56; founding of,
    56–57, 62–63, 73, 101, 131,
    168–69, 175, 209, 213, 217, 253,
    257, 259, 262

Restrictionism, 7
Restrictionist laws, 111–15, 116–22
Restrictive policy, 18–19, 111–22,
  129–30, 152, 171
Revolutionary War, 54
Revolving Door Era, 14, 24–26, 194,
  196, 201–30
Rhode Island, 9
Ridge, Tom, 234, 243. *See also*
  Department of Homeland
  Security
Riis, Jacob, 121
Risorgimento, 99
Rockefeller, Nelson, 168
Rodino, Peter, 202–3, 208, 210–12,
  214
Rodino-Mazzoli bill, 211
Roman Catholics, 9, 11, 25, 50,
  69–70, 176
Romney, George, 168
Roosevelt, Franklin D., 32, 155–56,
  168
Roosevelt, Theodore, 30, 119–20
Roybal, Edward, 207–9. *See also*
  Hispanic Caucus
Rules Committee, 207–9
Russia, pogroms, 95
Russian immigrants, 106–8
Russian Jews, 107; mutual aid
  societies, 107
Russian Orthodox Church, 18, 94, 97,
  104–7, 169
Russian Revolution, 107–8

Sabath, Adolph, 144
Sabbath (Sunday/Blue) laws, 170;
  closing laws, 176
Salvadorans. *See* El Salvador
Sanctuary cities, 42, 259–60
San Francisco, 112
Santeria, 176
Saturday Evening Post, 134, 136
Save Our State Initiative, 36, 226–27.
  See also Proposition 187

Scandinavian immigrants, 60–64;
  defined, 61
Schneersohn, Yosef, 162–63. *See also*
  Hasidic Judaism; Rebbe
Schumer, Charles, 210, 212–13
Schurz, Carl, 55
Schwenkfelders, 9–12. *See also*
  Pietists
Scotch-Irish immigrants, 68–69
Scott Act (1888), 29, 115
Seasonal Agricultural Workers
  (SAWs), 216, 221–23, 225–26, 229.
  See also Immigration Reform and
  Control Act (IRCA)
Secret Order of the Star Spangled
  Banner, 17, 58. *See also* Know-
  Nothing Party
Secure Fence Act, 250
Secure Our Borders First bill, 41,
  255
Select Commission on Immigration
  and Refugee Policy (SCIRP), 34,
  191–93, 204–5, 221, 229
Senate Judiciary Committee, 204–6,
  208, 211–12, 229, 253
Separation of church and state, 8
Sessions, Jeff, 261–62
Shakers, 10, 49. Shaking Quakers
Shaughnessy v. United States, 173
Shintoists, 117
Shriver, Sargent, 186
Simons, Menno, 11
Simpson, Alan, 35, 205–6, 210, 214,
  226
Simpson-Mazzoli bill, 35, 205–8, 210,
  229
Sinophobia, 113
Slavic peoples, 1–5
Smith, William French, 210
Sojourners, defined, 105, 193
Solid South, 169, 178
Sons of Norway, 138
Sons of the American Revolution,
  137

South, Central, Eastern Europeans
  (S/C/E), 6, 17–18, 20–21, 31, 93, 97,
  103, 109, 130, 140, 156, 173, 175
South America, 2
Southeast Asia, 184–85; SEATO, 188
Southern strategy, 178
South Vietnam, 184–85
Soviet Ark (*Buford*), 108
Soviet immigrants/refugees, 188
Soviet Union, 7, 185
Spanish American War, 95
Spanish International Network (SIN),
  206–7, 229
Special agricultural workers (SAWs).
  See Immigration Reform and
  Control Act (IRCA)
Stagflation, defined, 202
State and local assistance grants
  (SLIAG), 223
Statue of Liberty, 18, 114, 134
Stevenson, Adlai, 169
Stoddard, Lothrop, 139. *See also*
  Immigration Restriction League
Storm Door Era, 14, 26–27, 230,
  233–62
Sun Belt states, 190
Superintendent of Immigration, 116
Supreme Court, 16, 47, 113, 115, 170

Taft, Robert, 158, 168
Taft, William Howard, 121–22
Tammany Hall, 60
Task Force on Immigration and
  Refugee Policy (1981), 229
Taylor, Zachary, 71. *See also* Whig
  Party
Teamsters, 113
Temperance League movement, 97
Temporary worker program, 206, 211.
  See also Guest-worker programs
Terrorism, defined, 239; terrorist
  cells, 239
Texas Proviso, 202
Third World, 187

Thornberry, Mac, 234
Trafficking, 38, 41, 254
Trafficking Victims Reauthorization
  Act of 2008 (TVPRA), 40–41, 250,
  254
Treasury Department, 113, 116, 119
Treaty of Guadalupe Hidalgo, 28, 30
Trevor, John, 139–41, 147, 155
Truckee Raid of 1876, 85, 112
Truman, Harry S., 22–23, 159;
  Commission on Immigration,
  22–23; veto of Immigration and
  Naturalization bill of 1952,
  173–74
Trump, Donald J., 27, 42, 255–56,
  259–60, 262

Unaccompanied Alien Children,
  251–52
Unauthorized immigration, 25,
  193–94, 251
Undocumented aliens, 24–25,
  193–94, 201–2
Unitarians, 13
United Mine Workers, 3
United Nations Protocols on the
  Status of Refugees, 33
United Society of Believers in Christ's
  Second Appearance, 11
United States Constitution, 15
United States Marine Hospital
  Service, 95
United States Public Health Service,
  95
United States v. Bhagat Singh Thind, 31
Urbanization, 95–96
USA Patriot Act II of 2006, 27,
  249–50
USA Patriot Act of 2001, 26, 234;
  excerpts of, 235–36, 238, 243,
  259
U.S. Chamber of Commerce, 138–39,
  147, 208, 222
U.S. Department of Labor, 31

U.S. Department of State, 31
U.S. Supreme Court, 118, 132, 136, 167, 173, 185, 251, 261–62

Van Buren, Martin, 65. *See also* Jacksonian-Democrats
Vasa Order of America, 138
Victims of Immigration Crime Enforcement (VOICE) program, 42, 261
Vietnamese immigrants, 184; and refugees, 184, 189, 195
Vietnam War, 184–86
Vikings, 60
Virginia Statute of Religious Freedom, 10, 49
Visas, 144, 191, 245; applications and processing of, 144; defined, 144; overstayers, 245–46
Voting blocs, 217–18

Wagner, Robert, 155
Wallace, George, 184–85
War Brides Act of 1946, 22, 159
War Department, 154
War Relocation Authority, 157
Warren, Earl, 157–58
Washington, George, 14–15
Watson, Derrick, 261–62
Waves of immigration, 5–7, 93–96
Webb-Henry bill, 120
Welch, Richard, 153–54
Welsh, 68–69
Wesley, John, 10
Western Alliance, 7

Western Hemisphere, 6, 22–23, 33–34, 147–48, 170, 172, 180–82, 184, 191
Whig Party, 71, 73–74, 77–78
White-Anglo-Saxon-Protestants (WASPs), 69–70, 74, 86, 94, 97, 104, 112, 123, 130
White-ethnic, 195
Whitefield, George, 10, 13
White-Slave Traffic Act, 30, 121
Whom Shall We Welcome, 173. *See also* Truman, Harry
William III, King of England, 9
Williams, Roger, 9
Wilson, Pete, 208, 211, 227
Wilson, Woodrow, 106, 122, 129, 138
Wisconsin, 185
Wisconsin v. Yoder (1972), 185
Wong Kim Ark v. United States, 30
Wop, 101; dago defined, 101
Workingmen's Party, 85, 112–13
World War I, 12, 19–20, 30–31, 94–95, 99, 104, 106, 117–18, 121–22, 130, 135, 163
World War II, 21, 23, 130, 157–61, 174, 176, 184, 237, 240

Xenophobia, 17, 20, 48, 67; defined, 70, 69–70, 129, 153, 229

Yates, Sally, 250–61
Yellow Peril, 112, 119, 141
Yick Wo v. Hopkins, 29
Young Women's Christian Association, 154

Zero-sum model, 219–20

About the Author

Michael LeMay, PhD, is professor emeritus from California State University-San Bernardino, where he served as director of the National Security Studies program, an interdisciplinary master's degree program, and as chair of the Department of Political Science and assistant dean for student affairs of the College of Social and Behavioral Sciences. He has frequently written and presented papers at professional conferences on the topic of immigration. He has also written numerous journal articles, book chapters, published essays, and book reviews. He has published in *The International Migration Review, In Defense of the Alien, Journal of American Ethnic History, Southeastern Political Science Review, Teaching Political Science*, and the *National Civic Review*. He is author of more than a dozen academic volumes dealing with immigration history and policy. His prior books on the subject are *Illegal Immigration: A Reference Handbook*, 2nd edition (2015, ABC-CLIO); *Doctors at the Borders: Immigration and the Rise of Public Health* (2015, Praeger), series editor and contributing author of the three-volume series, *Transforming America: Perspectives on Immigration* (2013, ABC-CLIO); *Illegal Immigration: A Reference Handbook*, 1st edition (2007, ABC-CLIO); *Guarding the Gates: Immigration and National Security* (2006, Praeger Security International); *U.S. Immigration: A Reference Handbook* (2004, ABC-CLIO); *U.S. Immigration and Naturalization Laws and Issues: A Documentary History*, edited with Elliott Barkan (1999, Greenwood); *Anatomy of a Public Policy: The Reform of Contemporary Immigration Law* (1994, Praeger); *The Gatekeepers: Comparative Immigration Policy* (1989, Praeger); *From Open Door to Dutch Door: An Analysis of U.S. Immigration Policy Since 1820* (1987, Praeger); and *The Struggle for Influence* (1985). Professor LeMay has written two textbooks that have considerable material related to these topics: *Public Administration: Clashing Values in the Administration of Public Policy*, 2nd edition (2006); and *The Perennial Struggle: Race, Ethnicity and Minority Group Relations in the United States*, 3rd edition (2009). He frequently lectures on topics related to immigration history and policy. He loves to travel and has lectured around the world and visited more than 100 cities in 40 countries. He has two works in progress: *Winning Office and Making a Nation: Immigration and the American Political Party System* (under review, coauthored with Scot Zentner), and *Reforming Immigration: A Reference Handbook*.